JONATHAN EDWARDS'S WRITINGS

JONATHAN EDWARDS'S *Writings*

Text, Context, Interpretation

EDITED BY

STEPHEN J. STEIN

Indiana University Press

BLOOMINGTON AND INDIANAPOLIS

The paper used in this publication meets the minimum requirements of American National Standard for Information Sciences—Permanence of Paper for Printed Library Materials, ANSI Z39.48-1984.

MANUFACTURED IN THE UNITED STATES OF AMERICA

Library of Congress Cataloging-in-Publication Data

Jonathan Edwards's writings : text, context, interpretation / edited by Stephen J. Stein.
p. cm.
Selected papers from a June 1994 conference at Indiana University. Bloomington, Ind.
Includes index.
ISBN 0-253-33082-3 (cloth : alk. paper)
1. Edwards, Jonathan, 1703–1758—Congresses. I. Stein, Stephen J., date.
BX7260.E3J67 1996
230'.58'092—dc20 95-49862

1 2 3 4 5 01 00 99 98 97 96

CONTENTS

ACKNOWLEDGMENTS / vii

INTRODUCTION BY STEPHEN J. STEIN / ix

Part I

TEXT: INTEGRATING UNPUBLISHED MANUSCRIPTS AND PUBLIC TEXTS

1. Brides of Christ and Signs of Grace: Edwards's Sermon Series on the Parable of the Wise and Foolish Virgins AVA CHAMBERLAIN 3

2. Misrepresentations Corrected: Jonathan Edwards and the Regulation of Religious Discourse CHRISTOPHER GRASSO 19

3. The Deist Connection: Jonathan Edwards and Islam GERALD R. MCDERMOTT 39

4. The Other Unfinished "Great Work": Jonathan Edwards, Messianic Prophecy, and "The Harmony of the Old and New Testament" KENNETH P. MINKEMA 52

Part II

CONTEXT: INTERPRETING TEXTS AND IDENTIFYING INFLUENCES

5. "The Death of the Prophet Lamented": The Legacy of Solomon Stoddard PAUL R. LUCAS 69

6. The Godly Will's Discerning: Shepard, Edwards, and the Identification of True Godliness WILLIAM K. B. STOEVER 85

7. Did Berkeley Influence Edwards? Their Common Critique of the Moral Sense Theory RICHARD A. S. HALL 100

8. Perception and Love in *Religious Affections* WAYNE PROUDFOOT 122

Part III
INTERPRETATION: IDENTIFYING AND CLAIMING THE EDWARDSIAN TRADITION

9. Nathaniel William Taylor and the Edwardsian Tradition: A Reassessment
DOUGLAS A. SWEENEY 139

10. Oberlin Perfectionism and Its Edwardsian Origins, 1835–1870
ALLEN C. GUELZO 159

11. "Reason for a Hope": Evangelical Women Making Sense of Late Edwardsian Calvinism GENEVIEVE MCCOY 175

12. Edwards A. Park and the Creation of the New England Theology, 1840–1870 JOSEPH CONFORTI 193

CONTRIBUTORS / 209

INDEX / 211

ACKNOWLEDGMENTS

Several organizations and individuals played a significant part in making possible this volume and the conference at which earlier versions of these chapters were a part of the program. Major funding for the conference came from support given by the Pew Charitable Trusts to the Yale Edition of *The Works of Jonathan Edwards*, Harry S. Stout, General Editor. Additional funding was obtained from several offices at Indiana University, Bloomington, including those of the Chancellor of the Bloomington campus, the Dean of Research and the Graduate School, the Dean of the College of Arts and Sciences, and the Department of Religious Studies. Respondents to the earlier versions of these essays at the conference also need to be acknowledged for their collective role in this volume, as do E. Brooks Holifield and T. Dwight Bozeman, who read and critiqued revised versions of these essays. Special thanks to Jenny Harrell, who handled many of the practical details involved in all of these stages.

INTRODUCTION

STEPHEN J. STEIN

Only a few years separate us from the tercentennial of Jonathan Edwards's birth in 1703. Before that anniversary, however, the world will mark the coming of a new millennium, a moment which promises to overshadow all other celebrations. In all likelihood festivities surrounding the year 2000–2001 will exhaust our collective capacity to commemorate most other historic moments with more than a passing glance. And yet, if present evidence is any indication of future prospects, the odds are rather good that 2003 will not pass without substantial attention being paid by some to Jonathan Edwards, who is, arguably, America's most significant religious thinker.

Were Edwards alive today and moving with us toward the close of the century, there is reason to believe that he would be fully engaged with watching the waning years of this millennium, probably urging his parishioners and his readers to be ready for an impending event of great significance. As a young man, in the fall of 1723, Edwards speculated that the year 2000 is the moment at which "Satan's kingdom in the world" will be "totally overthrown" and "receive its finishing stroke." He expected that the "sabbath of rest," or the millennial age, would be inaugurated at that time.[1] More than twenty years later, he was less confident about his forecast, suggesting that it might take a miracle for the progress of the gospel in the world to be sufficient to meet that deadline.[2] Either way, for certain his own birth date would have faded in significance for him when compared with the potential events anticipated at the turn of the millennium.

Historians, fortunately, are not required to be accurate predictors of the future, and so my speculations about future directions in the study of Jonathan Edwards are exactly that—speculations. And yet there are substantial grounds for offering such a judgment. The study of Jonathan Edwards—his life, thought, and influence—remains a growth industry today. No more striking evidence of this fact exists than the recent publication of a new updated bibliography of works focusing on Edwards.[3] An astonishing amount of scholarly attention is being lavished on him today. And there appears to be no end to this stream of publications.

Another kind of evidence of the continuing interest in Edwards is the frequency of major conferences focusing on him and his work.[4] In June 1994, for instance, more than one hundred scholars from across the country assembled at Indiana University, Bloomington, to participate in a meeting focusing on the writings of Jonathan Edwards. What distinguished this gathering from others dealing with Edwards was the presence on the program of four identifiable generations of scholars who have participated in the renaissance of interest in Edwards over the last half-century. The lineage in this field extends from the patriarch of Edwards studies, Thomas A. Schafer, through a generation identified with established scholars, such as Roland Delattre and Wilson H. Kimnach, and another generation of younger scholars, such as Gerald R. McDermott and Kenneth P. Minkema, to graduate students working on the completion of dissertations.[5] Among those present at the Bloomington conference was an especially significant number of younger scholars who have not yet achieved widespread recognition in the field. The range and quality of the scholarship being produced by these latter individuals gives cause for predicting that the wave of interest in Edwards may not have crested yet. We should, in fact, expect the rising tide of research to continue through 2003 and beyond.

The essays that comprise this volume have been selected from among the papers delivered at the June 1994 conference. They tend to share a number of characteristics making them accessible to a wide audience interested in Edwards. In an age when academics are increasingly preoccupied with theoretical, deconstructive, and postmodern agendas, scholarship in the field of Edwards studies, with a few notable exceptions, has remained strikingly traditional in outlook.[6] That may prove both an advantage and a disadvantage. On the positive side, it results in research publications that are relatively free of jargon, not driven by scholarly fads, and readable by a general audience. On the negative side, this traditional caste may hinder conversation with others more venturesome, conversation from which both parties might profit.

The single most striking quality shared by the essayists in this volume is the seriousness with which they take written texts. The texts generated by Edwards occupy center stage here. They are the principal object of consideration. They are the medium of communication between Edwards and these scholars. They appear to be the reason why these scholars are engaged in their research. Edwards's texts constitute a working canon for those in the field. (Admittedly, it is an expanding canon, as portions of his voluminous manuscript materials are only now being put into print.)[7] In this respect the hermeneutic operating in this field resembles that found in other areas of classical studies. Many of the questions asked of the Edwards corpus derive from his concerns rather than from a contemporary theoretical agenda. Those working on Edwards today are joining a long line of individuals for whom his writings have been significant—first his family and students, then his contemporaries and successors as well as his detractors and critics, subsequently students of American thought and culture, including those who value ideas for their own sake and others who see them reflecting eternal truths, and finally, historians who may follow one or another or all of these lines of development.[8]

It appears that a wide variety of motives operates among those interested in Edwards today. In other words, the reason why so many scholars will attend conferences on Edwards and write so many essays and books about him is not singular but multiple. Some scholars are preoccupied with Edwards's eighteenth-century world; he serves for them as a window into that century. Others address perennial philosophical or theological questions by means of engagement with his answers to those questions. Still others are most concerned about Edwards's influence on subsequent generations of American thinkers. And then there are the admirers—those who are convinced that he was religiously correct in his formulations of Christian thought and practices or those who simply stand in awe of his intellectual efforts. Only a handful of contemporary scholars have been openly critical of Edwards—a somewhat surprising fact.[9] The June 1994 conference mirrored all of these concerns through its engagement with Edwards as historian, theologian, philosopher, moralist, pastor, preacher, and person. Each of the three clusters of essays that follow offers something different to the ongoing conversation about the writings of Edwards and contributes something distinctive to the larger field of Edwards studies.

Part I of this volume showcases some of the most promising of the younger scholars, all of whom are occupied to one extent or another with the study of Edwards's unpublished manuscripts. Their scholarship is groundbreaking in several respects. They are adding to our knowledge of Edwards's unpublished texts and attempting to integrate these new materials into the established canon of his published writings. Their use of private notebooks and manuscript sermons provides an occasion to check the adequacy of existing scholarly judgments. In every case, the chapters in this section expand our knowledge of his work and force us to rethink the established ways of presenting his ideas.

The opening chapter by Ava Chamberlain introduces a major unpublished manuscript sermon series on Matthew 25:1–12 preached by Edwards in 1737–38, years that fell between the early religious revival in Northampton and the later widespread outbreak of awakenings at the beginning of the 1740s. His exposition of the parable of the wise and foolish virgins became the occasion for reflection on the Christian's relationship with

Christ as well as on the proper relationship among members of the Northampton community. Chamberlain shows the ways in which Edwards capitalizes on the marriage metaphor in the text. She relates his interpretation of this text to the social circumstances in Northampton at the time. She also demonstrates that his contrast between true saints and hypocrites in this sermon series anticipates the lines of his most extensive public statement concerning signs of grace in the *Treatise concerning Religious Affections* (1746). In doing so, Chamberlain sheds new light on the evolution of his ideas regarding the nature of true religion—admittedly, one of his most celebrated and central theological concerns.

Christopher Grasso (chapter 2) also utilizes unpublished manuscript sermons by Edwards in his analysis of the rhetorical dimensions of the communion controversy in Northampton, the episode that led to Edwards's dismissal from the pulpit in that town. Through careful examination of the language of the conflict, Grasso alerts us to the fact that more was at stake than simply points of ecclesiastical doctrine. At issue also was the definition of a covenanted people. Grasso shows how Edwards used the pulpit beginning already early in his years in Northampton to articulate a position at variance with his grandfather and colleague, Solomon Stoddard, as he sought to reduce the gap between professed and real spirituality in his congregation. Edwards's position contrasted sharply with the judgments of his contemporaries, as Grasso makes clear in the essay. In the controversy with his congregation in the late 1740s, Edwards consistently worked to strengthen the role of the minister over against the laity, which also contributed to his dismissal. Finally, Grasso sets out to reconcile Edwards's position in the communion controversy with his later support for the use of covenantal terminology during the Seven Years War against the French in the 1750s, a change which has implications for understanding his role and that of the Puritans in civil religion as well as his place in the larger tradition of New England theology.

Gerald R. McDermott's essay (chapter 3) on Edwards's hostility to Islam brings an entirely new topic into public focus. Drawing on unpublished entries from the "Theological Miscellanies" and from scriptural notebooks, he places Edwards's negative judgments about Muslims into context, showing both their derivative nature and their place in his overall eschatological framework. Although Edwards reflects a certain ambivalence about Islam when compared with other religious positions outside Reformed Christianity, McDermott argues persuasively that his polemic is driven by more than simply interreligious animosity or even negative eschatological functions. McDermott links Edwards's anti-Muslim views with a more pressing concern that occupied the cleric during the last decade of his life, namely, his defense of scriptural revelation against the sufficiency of reason and against the notion that one is able to arrive at true knowledge of God and divine realities by natural means. The Deists were mounting these challenges to orthodox Christianity at the time. The linking of these two polemical targets helps us understand the intensity of Edwards's judgments. McDermott's search for some redeeming quality in the judgments about Islam reflects a late twentieth-century ecumenical mindset.

In chapter 4 Kenneth P. Minkema shows how Edwards's attack on the Deists and his defense of the unity and authority of biblical revelation became a dominant preoccupation during the last years of his life. Taking his lead from the famous 1757 letter to the trustees of the College of New Jersey in which Edwards sketched the intellectual projects on which he was working, Minkema provides a detailed description of the undertaking identified as "The Harmony of the Old and New Testament." He describes its overall design and the specific private notebooks that were part of it, the majority of which still remain in manuscript. Prophecy and its fulfillment, typology, and harmonization of the testaments—these three elements were central to Edwards's defense of the authority of the Bible against Enlightenment thinkers who were attacking traditional notions of its authorship, historical reliability, and christocentric character. Minkema's essay makes the case for the significance of the exegetical side of Edwards's thought, which has received far less attention from scholars than either his philosophical or his theological writings.

Part II represents another kind of endeavor as more established scholars in the field turn their attention to the relationship between Edwards's writings and those of other major religious and philosophical figures. These researchers are asking questions of influence and comparison. By indirection they are also arguing for the stature and significance of Edwards in the general world of Western thought and ideas. And they are attempting to position him within larger religious and philosophical traditions.

Paul R. Lucas's essay (chapter 5) explores the ideas of a man who is acknowledged to have been a critical influence on Edwards: his grandfather and senior colleague for a short time at Northampton, Solomon Stoddard. Lucas argues that the physical environment of Northampton was one factor contributing to the local tradition of an "Instituted church" of the visible saints, a view reinforced by the practice of "open communion." Stoddard's advocacy of this presbyterian view and of a corollary, the idea of a national covenant, was also informed by his reading of seventeenth-century English authors, including William Prynne, John Knox, and Samuel Rutherford. These authors led Stoddard to a vision of state-led moral reformation—a view that Edwards ultimately rejected, even though, according to Lucas, he shared other aspects of Stoddard's pastoral program. (Here Lucas's essay joins cause with Grasso's in Part I.) On that ground Lucas declares that Stoddard as well as Edwards anticipated later nineteenth-century religious and cultural patterns that flourished in the new American republic.

In the second essay in part II William K. B. Stoever (chapter 6) provides a detailed analysis of the use that Edwards made of Thomas Shepard's *Parable of the Ten Virgins Unfolded* (1660). Shepard, a Puritan theologian in early New England, came to prominence in the years of the Antinomian controversy in Massachusetts. Through close textual study Stoever shows how Shepard's description of the signs of true godliness, as distinct from pretenses of the same, was applied by Edwards, first in his sermons on the wise and foolish virgins, as discussed by Chamberlain in chapter 1, then in his sermon series of 1738 published posthumously as *Charity and Its Fruits,* and finally and most deliberately in the *Treatise concerning Religious Affections.* The pastoral situations faced by Shepard and Edwards had important similarities, as each dealt with the task of distinguishing the signs of true godliness from claims of sanctification resting on extraordinary testimonies or special experiences. Stoever agrees with Chamberlain that ultimately these theological and pastoral distinctions had immense implications for Edwards's parishioners. In fact, these implications may have been devastating, in Stoever's judgment. Who could possibly rise to the standards that Edwards established for true godliness?

Richard A. S. Hall's essay (chapter 7) joins a longstanding debate among historians of philosophy, asking whether the English philosopher George Berkeley exerted any direct influence on Edwards. The usual way of engaging this question is to focus on their respective commitments to philosophical idealism. But taking his lead from a recent volume by Edwin S. Gaustad,[10] Hall argues that the place to look for Berkeley's influence is in Edwards's posthumous publication, *The Nature of True Virtue* (1765). This document, he maintains, invites close comparison with Berkeley's *Alciphron, or the Minute Philosopher* (1732). Hall sets both of these works into their proper contexts, then proceeds to examine in detail their thematic continuities. Both are polemical attacks on the weaknesses of the moral sense theory of ethics. Both were directed against the rising influence of Enlightenment thought and its challenges to Christianity. Hall closes his essay with a series of judgments that show the usefulness of this comparative exercise for the understanding of both thinkers.

In the last essay in part II Wayne Proudfoot (chapter 8) brings his analytical skills to bear on the text of the *Treatise concerning Religious Affections* with an eye toward underscoring the sophistication of its argument concerning religious experience. To effect this result, he utilizes William James's *Varieties of Religious Experience* (1902) as a comparative foil. Proudfoot is careful to note the radically different situations and intentions of Edwards and James. Edwards's commitments as a Christian theologian contrast sharply with James's assumptions as a modern psychologist and philosopher. The heart of this essay is Proudfoot's examination of Edwards's judgments concerning the "perceptual and moral components of religious experience." Edwards sets out to distinguish true religion, or "holy love," from counterfeit or spurious love, using the language of understanding and will, belief and desire. Proudfoot shows how this objective leads to Edwards's theory of signs, which still does not provide absolute certainty for distinguishing genuine religious affections from those driven by self-love, not even in the case of the final sign—practice or behavior—which is the most useful of all. This view of religious experience, Proudfoot asserts, also has a bearing on Edwards's position in the communion controversy. By contrast, Proudfoot finds James's efforts at examining the perceptual and moral dimensions of religious experience less sophisticated and more limited because his approach is less able to deal with the self-reflexive aspects of religious experience. Proudfoot closes by recommending Edwards as a model for the contemporary study of religious experience.

Part III reflects an issue attracting increasing attention in the field of Edwards studies, the debate concerning the nature and constituency of the Edwardsian tradition. Who were the authentic successors of Edwards? Much of the scholarship has focused on the generations immediately following Edwards in the eighteenth century, but now there is new concern with his nineteenth-century heirs. The competition for Edwards's mantle in the nineteenth century is proof of his stature in the religious culture of the United States. The contemporary debate concerning his successors is not simply an abstract discussion among disinterested parties; it appears to be informed in subtle but real ways by current religious concerns.

The opening essay in part III comes from the hand of the youngest contributor to this collection, Douglas Sweeney, at the time of the Bloomington conference a graduate student at Vanderbilt University. Sweeney (chapter 9) sets out on an explicitly revisionist course, challenging the now-standard characterization of Nathaniel William Taylor's relationship to the Edwardsian tradition. Taylor served as a professor of theology at Yale Divinity School for more than thirty-five years in the period before the Civil War. Sweeney argues that Taylor's own claim to be doing theology after the manner of Edwards must be taken at face value—a claim that has been set aside by the scholarly tradition informed by the work of Joseph Haroutunian.[11] Sweeney makes his case by arguing that the narrow doctrinal definition of the Edwardsian tradition needs to be scrapped in favor of a definition of Edwardsianism as a multifaceted "theological culture." He attempts to show the range of institutions reflecting this culture whereby immense influence was exerted throughout New England, what Sweeney calls "an Edwardsian enculturation of Calvinist New England." When viewed from this perspective, according to Sweeney, Taylor cannot be denied the Edwardsian label, even though admittedly he was engaged in modifications of the heritage, most notably in his "rearticulation" of the doctrine of original sin. In sum, Sweeney sees Taylor as a major avenue of Edwardsian influence on culture in the United States.

Allen C. Guelzo (chapter 10) joins the revisionist attack on the received characterizations of the Edwardsian tradition, but from a different standpoint than Sweeney. He sets out to bring the most prominent revivalist of the first half of the nineteenth century, Oberlin's Charles Grandison Finney, into the Edwardsian fold. It is commonplace in the literature of religion in the United States to contrast the Calvinism of Edwards with the Arminianism of Finney, and no theological opinion held by Finney is seen as more conclusive proof of the difference than the doctrine of moral perfection—the perceived opposite of Edwards's judgment concerning human depravity. Guelzo builds his case in part on the self-claims of Oberlin theologians, who began with Edwards's distinction between natural ability and moral inability. By accenting the former, both Oberlin theologians and earlier New Divinity men were able to retain the principle of accountability and responsibility; and that, Guelzo declares, is a step toward perfectionism. But arriving at perfection was a very different thing. Guelzo shows what happens to this Edwardsian perfectionism at Oberlin. Some advocates moved off into Methodism, raising a larger question about its potential influence on the Holiness movement; Oberlin perfectionism itself died with Finney.

Genevieve McCoy (chapter 11) provides a very different take on Edwardsianism by her examination of the religious ideals driving evangelical Protestant women during the Second Great Awakening, women who were caught up indirectly in the theological debates that occupied the tradition. Drawing on Congregational and Presbyterian publications, McCoy argues that engagement with the Edwardsian tradition produced at best mixed results for these women, results in considerable tension with the prevailing scholarly opinion concerning the outcome of the feminization of religion in the United States in the nineteenth century.[12] It was in benevolent organizations that these women exercised religious influence—maternal associations, missionary societies, prayer groups. The works by Edwards directed to them underscored the importance of piety, self-sacrifice, and a sense of unworthiness. These were the virtuous traits to which evangelical women aspired under the influence of Edwardsian Calvinism.

The final essay is Joseph Conforti's account (chapter 12) of the work of Edwards Amasa Park, whom he identifies as "the last major Edwardsian Consistent Calvinist" and the one who by his historical studies of the tradition gave rise to a historical reality that still is the object of intense scholarly discussion and debate, as evidenced by part III of this collection. Park used his position as a professor at Andover Seminary for forty-five years to both protect and interpret Edwardsianism. According to Conforti, Park created the "Edwardsian narrative of New England theological history," a tradition that included neither Nathaniel William Taylor nor Charles Grandison Finney. Again in this essay Edwards's distinction between natural ability and moral inability comes to the fore as Conforti sketches Park's position on the "exercise-taste" controversy concerning the human will. One other result of Park's studies was his championing of Nathanael Emmons as the principal figure in the nineteenth-century Edwardsian tradition.

A few closing observations are in order concerning this collection of essays. The division into clusters identified with text, context, and interpretation is patently artificial. In all three clusters interpretation is the critical concern of the essayists. The authors employ different approaches to achieve this end, but in no case are they content simply to describe—whether it be new light from an unpublished manuscript, from juxtaposition with another thinker in a different time or place, or from the tracing of ideas through subsequent generations. In all cases the desire is to make sense of Edwards's writings.

Several points of intersection emerge from these essays. What is most striking is the continuing scholarly focus on Edwards's efforts to determine what constitutes authentic religion. Inevitably this conversation returns to two of his publications, the *Treatise concerning Religious Affections* and *The Nature of True Virtue.* Perhaps these two writings, more than any others, represent the quintessential Edwards. The issues he addressed in them continue to be relevant to a world that is very different from eighteenth-century New England. The challenge of distinguishing authentic from inauthentic religion remains at the heart of the religious enterprise and at the center of the effort by those who stand outside this enterprise as critics. It is as timely a concern today as it was in 1746 or 1836.

Perhaps all of our judgments about Edwards's writings should remain somewhat tentative given the fact that so much that he wrote has not yet been published. The essays in part I confirm that there is still much to be learned about Edwards, in terms not only of filling in the story of his evolving ideas as evident especially in unpublished sermons and private notebooks but also of projecting the substance of his future writing if he had lived longer in view of the manuscript evidence from his later years. In others words, we need to remind ourselves that by the time of the three hundredth anniversary of his birth we will know more about Edwards's writings than we do today.

One area that will in all likelihood receive more attention is Edwards's planned response to the challenges of the Enlightenment. The "Catalogue" of his reading makes it clear how closely he was monitoring the literature emerging from the circles of the new critics of religion.[13] Entries in his primary notebooks—theological, philosophical, and exegetical—also document his major investment in coming to terms with issues being raised by the Deists and others. One result of this attention will be a far more nuanced understanding of Edwards's relationship to the Enlightenment than that proposed many years ago by Perry Miller in his intellectual biography of Edwards.[14]

Part II suggests that other comparative studies might profitably be carried out in the future. Stoever's work on Shepard and Hall's on Berkeley invite imitation with a host of other authors whom Edwards read, including a number of those cited in the essays in part I, such as Thomas Manton, John Tillotson, Robert Millar, William Warburton, Thomas Sherlock, Arthur Bedford—to name but a few. In no case should we expect an individual author to end up providing a golden key to Edwards's system of thought. Rather it is more likely that we will discover how heavily dependent Edwards was for many of his ideas on the sources that he read. Or to put the matter another way, one effect of comparative studies is likely to be the reduction of the aura of genius surrounding Edwards and the more realistic presentation of him as a product of his times.

The search for the successors of Edwards, as evidenced in part III, is attracting a great deal of attention from diverse parties. Much of the effort of late has focused on the nineteenth century, but there is no reason to believe that the search will stop with that century. On the contrary, the twentieth century seems an equally appropriate period for such research. Various parties in the United States today, representing a wide spectrum of religious perspectives, look with great favor on Edwards. Some of these groups see themselves as the intellectual heirs of the Neo-Orthodox movement; others align themselves with one or another wing of contemporary evangelicalism. All seem eager to maximize access to the writings of Edwards. Witness the continuing sales of unreliable nineteenth-century editions of his works at the same time that Yale University Press is publishing a modern critical edition.[15] The world of Edwards studies is filled with competing proprietary claims. More than one party desires the Edwardsian mantle.

For all of these reasons the scholarly study of the writings of Jonathan Edwards represents one of the most unusual and successful chapters in contemporary intellectual history in the United States, and it seems likely to continue so in the future.

NOTES

1. *The Works of Jonathan Edwards, 5, Apocalyptic Writings,* ed. Stephen J. Stein (New Haven, 1977), 129–30.

2. Ibid., 411.

3. See M. X. Lesser, *Jonathan Edwards: An Annotated Bibliography, 1979–1993* (Westport, Conn., 1994). This volume updates Lesser's earlier bibliography, *Jonathan Edwards: A Reference Guide* (Boston, 1981).

4. In 1984 a conference entitled "Jonathan Edwards and the American Experience" was held at Wheaton College, and in 1990 a "National Conference on Edwards and Franklin" was held at Yale University. The former resulted in *Jonathan Edwards and the American Experience,* ed. Nathan O. Hatch and Harry S. Stout (New York, 1988), and the latter led to *Benjamin Franklin, Jonathan Edwards, and the Representation of American Culture,* ed. Barbara B. Oberg and Harry S. Stout (New York, 1993).

5. See *The Works of Jonathan Edwards, 13, The "Miscellanies," a-500,* ed. Thomas A. Schafer (New Haven, 1994); Roland Andre Delattre, *Beauty and Sensibility in the Thought of Jonathan Edwards: An Essay in Aesthetics and Theological Ethics* (New Haven, 1968); *The Works of Jonathan Edwards, 10, Sermons and Discourses 1720–1723,* ed. Wilson H. Kimnach (New Haven, 1992); Gerald R. McDermott, *One Holy and Happy Society: The Public Theology of Jonathan Edwards* (University Park, Penn., 1992); and John E. Smith, Harry S. Stout, and Kenneth P. Minkema, eds., *A Jonathan Edwards Reader* (New Haven, 1995).

6. An exception to this pattern is R. C. De Prospo, *Theism in the Discourse of Jonathan Edwards* (Newark, 1985). See also Stephen H. Daniel, *The Philosophy of Jonathan Edwards: A Study in Divine Semiotics* (Bloomington, Ind., 1994). Both of these potentially provocative works have much to offer scholars working in more conventional ways.

7. The Yale Edition of *The Works of Jonathan Edwards* (New Haven, 1957–) is publishing previously unpublished manuscripts by Edwards. See, for example, vols. *5, 6, 10, 11,* and *13*. Future volumes will include more sermons and notebooks as well as correspondence and personal writings.

8. A comprehensive list of Edwards's manuscripts is in the Beinecke Rare Book and Manuscript Library at Yale University. For a useful account of the general interest in Edwards and his writings, see the introduction to Lesser, *Jonathan Edwards: A Reference Guide,* pp. xv–lix.

9. Two examples of critical studies by prominent historians are Alfred Owen Aldridge, *Jonathan Edwards* (New York, 1964), and Peter Gay, *A Loss of Mastery: Puritan Historians in Colonial America* (Berkeley, 1966), pp. 88–117.

10. Edwin S. Gaustad, *George Berkeley in America* (New Haven, 1979).

11. See Joseph G. Haroutunian, *Piety versus Moralism: The Passing of the New England Theology* (New York, 1932).

12. See Ann Douglas, *The Feminization of American Culture* (New York, 1977).

13. Edwards's "Catalogue" (MS, Beinecke Library, Yale University) is his lifelong bibliographical register of books that came to his attention or that he actually read. It is dramatic evidence of the range of Edwards's intellectual interests.

14. Perry Miller, *Jonathan Edwards* (New York, 1949).

15. For example, the Banner of Truth Trust continues to print the 1834 edition of *The Works of Jonathan Edwards* (2 vols.) edited by Edward Hickman.

Part I

TEXT

INTEGRATING UNPUBLISHED MANUSCRIPTS AND PUBLIC TEXTS

ONE

Brides of Christ and Signs of Grace

EDWARDS'S SERMON SERIES ON THE PARABLE OF THE WISE AND FOOLISH VIRGINS

AVA CHAMBERLAIN

In the winter of 1737–38, Jonathan Edwards preached a nineteen-unit sermon series on Matt. 25:1–12, the parable of the wise and foolish virgins.[1] He began the series in November, and, although the manuscript does not indicate the date of its final preaching occasion, he must have finished it by the end of March,[2] for between April and October 1738 he delivered the twenty-one-unit sermon series known as *Charity and its Fruits.* Only five months after finishing the *Charity* sermons, in March 1739, he began the thirty-unit series, *A History of the Work of Redemption.* Edwards's interpretation of the parable of the wise and foolish virgins was, therefore, the first of three extended sermon series that he preached between the ending of the Connecticut Valley revival in 1735 and the beginning of the colonywide revivals in 1740. Prior to this time, Edwards had not attempted to sustain the examination of a particular sermon text beyond six or seven separate preaching occasions. Although he wrote several small sermon series in the years following the *Redemption* series, there is no evidence that he ever attempted anything even remotely as ambitious as these three.[3] Edwards had from the early years of his ministry taken sermon composition as an occasion to explore matters of faith and doctrine, but in no other period did this exploration acquire such great breadth and depth. After 1740, the treatise gradually came to supplant the sermon as the principal locus of theological inquiry.[4]

Puritan theologians frequently used the sermon series as a vehicle for theological inquiry. The parable of the wise and foolish virgins was a particularly popular subject for a series precisely because its complex narrative presented an opportunity to consider a wide variety of issues that were of interest to Puritan theologians. Among the many analyses of the parable, we know from *Religious Affections* that Edwards had carefully studied Thomas Shepard's *The Parable of the Ten Virgins,* which had been published posthumously in 1659.[5] He must also have been familiar with Thomas Manton's exposition of the text, because he admired Manton's writings and apparently had access to one or more collections of his works.[6] Both of these ministers used the division of the company of virgins into wise and foolish, prepared and unprepared, to explore such issues as the distinction between saints and hypocrites, the signs of grace, and the nature of justifying faith, counterfeit faith and faith of assurance. These themes also dominated Edwards's treatment of the parable, and the fact that his interpretation generally agreed with that of his predecessors indicates that they exerted some influence.

In this essay I will argue that Edwards had both a pastoral and a speculative purpose in choosing to write his first sermon series on the parable of the wise and foolish virgins. In his role as pastor, Edwards delivered this series as a response to a variety of social and religious problems occurring in Northampton in the winter of 1737–38. There is evidence that in the late 1730s changing economic conditions in the town had caused instability within the family structure. Because the parable concerned attendance at a wedding, it allowed Edwards to discuss the domestic order proper for the Puritan household. Also at this time, Northampton was suffering from religious declension; according to Edwards, backsliders were numerous. Recent work of Amanda Porterfield illustrates how Edwards used the parable's marriage metaphor to promote the life of faith among members of his congregation. But it was specifically the division within the parable between wise and foolish virgins that made it a particularly appropriate means to address what Edwards considered to be the primary cause of Northampton's declension, hypocrisy.

Second, this sermon series was part of a speculative project concerning the signs of grace and the means of assurance that Edwards had been pursuing in his sermon composition for many years. Although this inquiry would culminate in 1746 in his composition of *Religious Affections,* the virgins series was Edwards's most extensive analysis of these issues prior to his publication of that treatise. The series and the treatise share many common features, in terms of both structure and content. Significant for an understanding of Edwards's intellectual development is the fact that he expressed in the sermon series the same complex of views that would later define his argument in the *Affections.* The resemblance between these two texts demonstrates, I will argue, that the traditional interpretation, which views *Religious Affections* as a product of Edwards's participation in the debate over revivalism that inflamed the colonies in the early 1740s, is inadequate. Certainly the Awakening shaped Edwards's argument in the *Affections,* but before George Whitefield even arrived in New England, Edwards had adopted the views that would establish his position as a moderate New Light in the upcoming years.

THE PASTORAL PROJECT

Amanda Porterfield, in *Female Piety in Puritan New England,* identifies a homiletical theme common in colonial New England that helps to explain why Edwards's decision to deliver a sermon series on the parable of the wise and foolish virgins to his Northampton congregation in the late 1730s was a particularly shrewd pastoral move.[7] Porterfield argues that although Christian theologians had traditionally depicted the church as the bride of Christ and used marriage metaphors to represent the life of faith, the "Puritans redefined the implications of this tradition by interpreting it in the context of domestic life."[8] Puritans accepted the dominant Reformation view that marriage, not celibacy, was the appropriate social context in which to pursue a religious vocation. As a consequence, in their frequent sermonizing on the nature of marriage, ministers delivered a twofold message. They used the metaphor of the marriage bond to describe the nature of the believer's union with Christ through faith, but at the same time they intended to convey to their congregations a social and moral message on the proper domestic relations within the Puritan household. These two aims had more than a simple metaphorical connection. Not only did instability within the family structure cause social disruption; it also was linked to religious declension.[9] Puritan ministers, therefore, promoted the harmonious cohabitation of husbands and wives both as a means to maintain order in society and as a means of grace.

The model of the marital relation ministers used to depict the life of faith was, according to Porterfield, "simultaneously hierarchical and affectionate."[10] The proper posture of the Puritan saint was analogous to that of the faithful wife who lovingly and willingly submitted to the authority of her husband. Accordingly, lack of faith was represented by the image of the adulterous wife who betrayed her marriage vows by her self-interested pursuit of other lovers. Although within the covenant of grace this posture of obedient submission applied equally to both men and women, the conflation of this covenant with the marriage covenant indirectly implied that only the subordination of the wife to the husband was necessary for domestic stability. It also gave to the saint's union with Christ through faith an erotic dimension that "lent a primitive kind of sexual excitement to desires for grace."[11] Pastors intended by this erotic depiction of grace to increase their congregations' longings for salvation while confining sexual relations within the community to well-ordered family units.

Edwards begins his sermon series on the wise and foolish virgins with a three-unit excursus on the nature of marriage that reflects the precise pattern of discourse identified by Porterfield.[12] These three units comprise one sermonic sequence of text, doctrine, and application, and together they function as an introduction to the whole series. Edwards takes as his text the first verse of Matt. 25 and draws from it the doctrine, "The church is espoused to the Lord Jesus Christ." Just as Porterfield suggests, in his exposition of this doctrine Edwards describes the union between Christ and his church in terms drawn almost exclusively from the social conventions regulating espousal and marriage in eighteenth-century New England. According to Edwards, Christ alone is most excellent and truly beautiful. In comparison with him, all other lovers "are base and vile in their nature." These rivals have a "seeming beauty and loveliness," but it is "a mask that they put on . . . a shadow without substance." Christ also is infinitely rich. "He is the great possessor of heaven and earth," states Edwards, "and if you will yield to his suit and your soul becomes his spouse, his riches shall be yours." He has "wherewithal to feed you" and will "feast you and satisfy your soul." He has "wherewithal to clothe you"; if you marry him, he will adorn you in "glorious robes." His rivals, on the other hand, will leave you "in rags and nakedness as you are."[13]

In keeping with the understanding of the marriage bond developed by New England Puritans, Edwards characterizes the relation between Christ and the church as one not simply of willing subjection but of mutual companionship. Christ perfectly and eternally loves his spouse. The church in return "loves Christ above all, sets him on the throne of her affections" and "gives up herself to be his and his only, and that forever or as long as they both live." Their union is one of "mutual communion, cohabitation and enjoyment as friends and companions." Between them is a "mutual great love" of both "benevolence" and "complacence"; however, it is not a relation of equality. "The husband is companion of his wife, but yet has authority over her." Christ condescends to accept "a little feeble poor insect to be his bride," and she responds by depending on him "for guidance, protection and provision." Furthermore, the church's affectionate subjection to Christ has the intimate and erotic dimension described by Porterfield. "The king shall bring [the church] into his chamber," writes Edwards, paraphrasing the Song of Solomon, "to behold his glory and to enjoy his love forever and to enjoy the most free and intimate converse with [him]." Christ's spouse is not "barren," but "fruitful in good works," which she "bring[s] forth through the seed of divine grace." She "travails in birth with souls and is the instrument of propagating the church." Christ, therefore, is an attractive, wealthy, loving, wise, strong, and fertile suitor. Edwards warns his congregation, as if he were a parent admonishing a reluctant daughter, that to "reject so honorable a match . . . will end in everlasting disgrace and contempt."[14]

In this introductory discourse, Edwards was encouraging his congregation to emulate his idealized portrait of the marriage bond in their own lives, both as Christians and as family members. During the late 1730s Northampton evidently needed to hear this twofold message. In this period the town was experiencing the social dislocation that accompanied the gradual transition to a market economy. According to Patricia Tracy, this economic uncertainty manifested itself in an increased marriage age for young adult men.[15] The reluctance of the young people to marry threatened social stability both by prolonging the dependence of children upon their parents and by depriving the community of new household units. Moreover, in November 1737, the very month in which Edwards preached the introduction to his series on the wise and foolish virgins, there was additional cause in Northampton for contention between and within families: a committee was convened to determine the seating arrangements for the new meetinghouse that had been constructed in the town during the previous year.[16] In the old meetinghouse age had taken precedence over wealth, and men and women were seated opposite one another on rows of benches; nevertheless, the seating committee decided to rank church members in the new meetinghouse primarily according to wealth.[17] It also replaced the old benches with family pew boxes, an arrangement that affirmed the integral role of the family in the life of the church while creating conflict by emphasizing the hierarchical relation among the families.

Furthermore, in the years following the 1734–35 Connecticut Valley revival, Edwards believed that his congregation was experiencing a period of religious declension. "Are we asleep or awake?" he asks in the application to sermon 5. "It has been a time wherein religion has been flourishing," but now "the town in general" is in "a backslidden state, and it is now a time of the great decay of religion in comparison of what has been heretofore."[18] For Edwards, Northampton itself was the company of virgins that had eagerly gone forth together, with lamps blazing, to meet the bridegroom, but that had also together fallen asleep while waiting for the bridegroom to arrive. The marriage metaphor that dominates Edwards's introduction to his series on the wise and foolish virgins addressed this decline in piety because, in its portrayal of Christ as an infinitely attractive marriage partner, it encouraged unbelievers to join with Christ through faith. Furthermore, insofar as the metaphor promoted well-ordered families, it reinforced that social structure Puritans considered to be the nursery of piety.

Despite these features, as an awakening strategy the marriage metaphor also had its limitations. First, Edwards never considered domestic order and social harmony to be ends in themselves. He supported a wife's submissive obedience to her husband only if it did not compromise her eternal salvation.[19] And according to Tracy, Edwards was fully capable of jeopardizing domestic stability in the interests of piety. She argues that during the Connecticut Valley revival he influenced the conversion of many Northampton adolescents by replacing what he perceived to be the ineffective religious instruction of their parents with his own direct authority.[20] Second, the metaphor failed to respond directly to the principal cause of Northampton's declension. In 1737, Northampton did not need to be convinced that Christ was an infinitely attractive marriage partner. Having recently displayed a religiosity unprecedented in New England history, most members of Edwards's congregation already believed themselves to be espoused to Christ through faith. They needed, according to Edwards, to be taught the signs of hypocrisy. The marriage metaphor did not lend itself to this task; however, the juxtaposition of wise and foolish virgins within the parable was an ideal vehicle for exploring the differences between true and counterfeit Christians. Therefore, following the introductory discourse, Edwards's attention in the remaining eleven sermons of the series shifts from the bridegroom to the company of virgins. Because he continues to refer to Christ as the "bridegroom," the marriage metaphor remains in the background throughout the series, but he sets aside its twofold message in favor of a single sustained examination of the means to distinguish a truly gracious assurance of salvation from that which is false and self-deceptive.

Following the traditional interpretation of the parable, Edwards takes the company of virgins to represent the whole of the visible church in the world. Because its membership includes all those persons who "have the profession and outward appearance of Christians," the visible church contains "not only true Christians, but many that are not Christians in deed but only in appearance." The division between wise and foolish virgins, therefore, corresponds to that between saints and hypocrites in the visible church. This division forms the focus of Edwards's analysis of the parable. The eschatological perspective of the narrative is important, for it lends urgency to the virgins' need to awake and prepare for the coming of the bridegroom. It is, however, the distinct methods of their preparation that most interest Edwards, because they suggest to him a means of differentiating insufficient from sufficient evidences of grace. To begin, Edwards draws from the general observation that "the visible church of Christ is made up of true and false Christians" the proposition that these "two sorts of Christians do in many things agree and yet in many other things do greatly differ." This proposition, in turn, determines the broad structure of Edwards's argument in the sermon series.[21]

In the first main section of the series, which comprises sermons 3–8, Edwards considers the things wherein true and false Christians agree. Within the parable, one feature shared by the wise and foolish virgins is that they both have lamps. These lamps represent the many religious beliefs and actions that hypocrites have in common with saints. Edwards includes within this category all the external and observable phenomena used to judge that a person is a visible saint, such as a profession of faith, diverse religious affections and experiences, and compliance with the moral law. These characteristics create the appearance of godliness, but because both gracious and natural persons may manifest this appearance, they have no real evidential value. The church is constrained to judge by these phenomena; as a result it inevitably contains both saints and hypocrites. Personal assurance, however, must be subject to a higher standard. Edwards states, "before we conclude ourselves to be godly, [let us] see to it that we have . . . some thing or other that is beyond all that wherein true Christians and false agree. . . . Let us seek those things that are distinguishing, and see to it that we have 'em before we conclude ourselves to be in a good estate."[22]

Another feature shared by the wise and foolish virgins is that they both "slumber and sleep" while waiting for the bridegroom to arrive. Whereas the first shared feature depends upon the hypocrite's ability to manifest an appearance of godliness, this slumbering and sleeping represents a commonality that is created because of "the infirmities and failings of true Christians." Hypocrites resemble saints because they are capable of a wide variety of religious beliefs and actions; saints resemble hypocrites because "there is abundance of corruption in the hearts of [true Christians], as well as others." The sin that lingers in the godly after conversion causes them to fall into "very stupid and senseless frames," to "walk in evil ways," and frequently to appear as godless persons. Edwards concludes from this that although people find in themselves "such kinds of sin and corruption that they never imagined were in the hearts of the godly," it does not necessarily signify an unconverted state. Comparing saints and hypocrites and identifying the characteristics common to both are the method Edwards employs in this sermon series, not only to eliminate many aspects of the Christian life as certain signs of grace but also to deny that sinful acts and the lack of religious experience are necessary signs of hypocrisy. Professing Christians, however, need not rest in this ambiguity, for by means of a similar method Edwards also identifies those "clear evidences" that allow the saint properly to prepare for the bridegroom's arrival.[23]

In the second main section of the series Edwards again compares saints and hypocrites; however, he considers in these final four sermons the things not "wherein they agree" but "wherein they differ." Within the parable, both wise and foolish virgins have lamps and both fall asleep when the bridegroom tarries; the principal difference between them is that the wise alone include a supply of oil in their preparations to meet the bridegroom. Therefore, in addition to the similarities, there are specific differences between true and false Christians that can be identified as the distinguishing evidences of grace. There is, according to Edwards, one "great and most essential difference between true and false Christians wherein they always differ": true saints have "a spiritual and abiding principle in their hearts that may be said to be a new nature in the soul consisting in the Christian spirit that they are of." Hypocrites, who are guided in their beliefs and actions wholly by natural causes, cannot have this principle because, by definition, it is "a principle that is not from nature but is wrought in the heart wholly by the spirit of that which is supernatural or above nature." Consequently, it establishes not merely a quantitative but a qualitative difference between saints and hypocrites. "It don't consist in that," states Edwards, "that false Christians have but little oil in their vessels and true Christians have a great deal. But in that, that true Christians have oil and false Christians have none." Hence Edwards exhorts his congregation to get this oil, because "no profession of religion, no morality, no religious affections, no illuminations will avail anything without it."[24]

Whether or not a professing Christian has this spiritual principle cannot be determined by direct observation. Like the oil that is hidden inside the wise virgins' vessels, that which distinguishes saints from hypocrites is an internal principle. Although gracious persons feel within themselves "a divine sense of things renewed in a degree time after time," Edwards is not willing to establish personal assurance solely on the basis of a sporadic feeling; concerning "things internal," he argues, there is "room for many cavils and disputes." However, the spiritual principle has external effects that are "plain and visible and can't be denied." According to Edwards, the spiritual principle "don't remain [in the heart] inactive and motionless"; it lives there "as an inward, ardent, powerful principle of operation" and "action." As a consequence, the behavior of true saints differs from that of hypocrites, especially in times of trial. In the parable, the foolish virgins do not withstand the trial of waiting for the arrival of the bridegroom. Because they have no oil, their lamps go out while they are sleeping, and they are not prepared for the midnight cry. Similarly, Edwards maintains, "the external religion of false Christians [is] wont to fail in times of trial." Without a spiritual principle acting in their hearts, hypocrites do not persevere. Over time they "by degrees grow into a distaste and dislike of religion." They "leave off the laborious parts of religion" and come "secretly to live in ways of known sin." True Christians, on the other hand, may backslide. As the wise virgins fall asleep along with the foolish, they may have difficulty maintaining a lively faith in times of trial. Their lamps may grow dim, but they will not go out. "Their religion," states Edwards, "can't be said to fail as the religion of hypocrites is wont to do at such times, because their declining ben't of that nature as to carry in them a practical casting off God and religion."[25]

By this analysis of the sufficient and insufficient evidences of grace Edwards's aim was to impress upon his congregation that the most reliable and truly scriptural means of judging the sincerity of a profession was by the professor's ability to withstand trials of faith. Many in Northampton had undergone dramatic religious experiences during the recent revival, but according to their pastor such experiences were an inadequate foundation for assurance. Edwards preached the virgin series to rouse slumbering members of his church and convince them adequately to prepare for the midnight cry. However, a consideration of Edwards's speculative aim in the series will show that he was complicit in their slumber. Edwards himself did not recognize the centrality of perseverance until it was demonstrated to him by the backsliding of his congregation.

THE SPECULATIVE PROJECT

In the preface to *Religious Affections* Edwards wrote that identifying the distinguishing marks of a true saint was "a subject on which my mind has been peculiarly intent, ever since I first entered on the study of divinity."[26] This process of inquiry is often conceived as beginning when Edwards entered the debate over revivalism in 1740 and culminating in his publication of *Religious Affections* in 1746. According to this interpretation, Edwards first staked out the position he would defend in *Distinguishing Marks* (1741), and, as the New Lights developed a radical wing and Charles Chauncy's criticisms became more strident, he followed this treatise with the publication of *Some Thoughts concerning the Revival* (1742). Brooding over the issues even after the revival had ended, he published *Religious Affections* as his final and most sophisticated defense of experimental religion.[27] Edwards's sermon series on the wise and foolish virgins questions this interpretation, for *Religious Affections* bears a stronger resemblance to this series than to either of the other revival treatises. The two texts are identical in structure; following their respective introductions, both are divided into, first, a section that considers the insufficient evidences or uncertain signs of grace and, second, a section that considers the distinguishing evidences or certain signs. *Distinguishing Marks* shares this structure, but its resemblance to *Religious Affections* does not extend beyond structure to content. Edwards designed the uncertain and certain signs in *Distinguishing Marks* primarily to demonstrate that the revival as a historical event was the work of the Holy Spirit. *Religious Affections* and the virgins series, on the other hand, are both concerned with personal religious experience, and the resemblance in their contents reflects this commonality of purpose.[28]

Edwards's participation in the debate over revivalism did decisively influence his composition of *Religious Affections;* however, the virgins series allows us to identify more precisely those aspects of the argument in *Re-*

ligious Affections that Edwards advocated prior to 1740 and to distinguish them from those that were a direct product of the Awakening debate. For example, in both texts Edwards included among the uncertain signs of grace such things as having high religious affections, complying with the moral law, making an acceptable conversion narrative, and maintaining a confident assurance of salvation. The uncertain signs in *Religious Affections* were an uncompromising attack against New Light enthusiasm, but the fact that Edwards articulated a similar position in the virgins series suggests that the extreme behavior of the radical revivalists did not cause him to deny the epistemological significance of the affections but only reinforced a preexisting conviction. Edwards also in *Religious Affections* identified the "new sense of the heart" as the distinguishing mark of the saint and carefully described the operation of this principle to avoid any possible antinomian interpretations, but this resembles the position he adopted earlier in the virgins series.[29] Finally, it is at times asserted that Edwards's emphasis upon Christian practice in *Religious Affections* was a corrective to New Light antinomianism and a concession to Old Light moralism. The twelfth sign functioned for Edwards in both of these ways but, judging from the virgins series, Edwards advocated a similar view as early as 1737.[30]

Edwards's sermon series on the wise and foolish virgins does not, therefore, contain ideas unarticulated in his published writings; but it does contribute to our understanding of Edwards's intellectual development. The fact that each of the major components of the argument in *Religious Affections* was expressed in the series in a similar way and for similar reasons signifies that *Religious Affections* was the final expression of a process of inquiry that began and took shape prior to the wave of revivals that engulfed New England in the early 1740s. Edwards's participation in the debate over revivalism no doubt accelerated this inquiry and shaped its final outcome. His publication of *Distinguishing Marks* and *Some Thoughts* was integral to the intellectual formation that preceded the composition of *Religious Affections.* However, it appears that the evolution of the ideas articulated in *Religious Affections* can be traced more directly and at greater length in Edwards's unpublished sermon corpus than in his published treatises.[31]

As early as 1729 Edwards preached a sermon on Matt. 15:26 having the doctrine, "there is a great difference between converted and unconverted men." In this brief, two-unit discourse, Edwards considers only the distinguishing marks of a true saint; these he identifies primarily as the saint's "understanding of spiritual things," "conviction of the reality of spiritual things," and "love to God." Although he states that "'tis a very common thing for men . . . to imagine that they are converted when they are not converted," Edwards displays no awareness that such self-deception is caused by a person's using uncertain signs of grace as the foundation for assurance. In the sermon's first application, he does list several characteristics of the Christian life the absence of which may be taken as a sign of hypocrisy. Among these characteristics he includes "being fruitful in a holy life" and withstanding trials of faith, but these ideas receive no real development, nor are they integral to the sermon's thesis.[32]

Soon after the Connecticut Valley revival, in August 1735 or 1736, Edwards preached a seven-unit sermon on 2 Cor. 13:5.[33] Drawing from this text the doctrine, "Persons ought not to rest ignorant and unresolved about their own state, whether they be real Christians or no," Edwards proceeds to discuss, first, "what are needless grounds of doubting of a good estate" and, second, "what are just grounds." The first section corresponds to a determination of the uncertain signs insofar as Edwards lists phenomena that do not jeopardize a preexisting conviction of grace. In the second section, however, he considers not the certain signs of grace, but the certain signs of *hypocrisy.* Failure to withstand trials of faith is only one of seventeen such signs cited by Edwards; however, in his concluding discussion of the "best method" to resolve spiritual doubt, Edwards balances self-examination with action. Professing Christians should engage in frequent, strict, and prayerful self-examination, but if doubts persist despite such scrutiny, increased introspection will be unhelpful, if not positively harmful. Don't "continue looking over what you have met with," states Edwards, "don't spend your time from day to day in melancholy and discouraging apprehensions about yourself." Finally, the only reliable means of resolving doubt is "earnestly seeking God and his grace and your own salvation in the diligent use of all the means of grace."[34]

In tracing the development of Edwards's views concerning the signs of grace, next in chronological order is his series on the wise and foolish virgins. This series should then be followed by *Distinguishing Marks,*[35] but there are within Edwards's unpublished sermon corpus some perhaps more direct links between the virgins series and *Religious Affections.* One example is a short series that Edwards delivered in January 1743 on Matt. 7:15, which has the doctrine "that though there may be a very great likeness between true Christians and false professors, yet there is also a vast unlikeness."[36] Edwards develops this doctrine along familiar lines, identifying the "holy principle of [a] new nature" as the distinguishing mark of the saint and maintaining that "the experiences Christians have by their enduring trials [of faith] give the highest ground of hope." However, the revival context permeates the discourse. The text itself, "Beware of false prophets which come to you in sheep's clothing, but inwardly are ravening wolves," is an unveiled reference to enthusiastical itinerants such as James Davenport. And it is the revival context that perhaps accounts for one striking difference between this sermon and its predecessors. Although Edwards clearly recognizes in the virgins series that saints and hypocrites have a deceptively similar outward appearance, an exploration of the nature and limits of this resemblance is the dominant theme of his series on Matt. 7:15. In this series, hypocrites do not simply manifest an appearance deceptively similar to that of true saints; hypocrites have a nearly inexhaustible capacity to counterfeit every aspect of the Christian life. Because of the influences of the devil, the operations of common grace, and impressions on the imagination, there "is a counterfeit of every qualification of a saint."[37] Therefore, although Edwards continues to maintain that professing Christians should engage in frequent self-examination, the ability to withstand repeated trials of faith becomes the primary vehicle of self-knowledge.[38]

In the ten years preceding his composition of the virgins series, Edwards had consistently maintained that the only truly distinguishing mark of a saint was the knowledge of divine excellency that the new spiritual principle imparted to the saint in the conversion moment. But he was unresolved about the most reliable method to discern the presence of this principle. The foregoing survey of the sermon literature suggests that two trends mark the development of Edwards's views on this issue: first, an increasing appreciation of the power of both human nature and the devil to counterfeit the effects of grace, and second, a gradual shift away from self-examination and toward persevering Christian practice as the most reliable means of assurance.[39] These two trends are not unrelated; the more nearly hypocrites resemble saints in their outward appearances, the less effective are the signs of grace distinguishing between them. As a consequence, self-examination decreases and Christian practice increases proportionately in importance.

During the 1734–35 revival, Edwards had had confidence in self-examination and had relied upon identifying signs of grace to distinguish between true and false conversions. He had known that hypocrites could easily be mistaken for saints and that withstanding trials of grace was a valuable means of assurance. However, his awareness of the complexity of the resemblance and the centrality of perseverance increased as he watched his congregation backslide in the years following the revival. Edwards's sermon series on the wise and foolish virgins was a decisive moment in the evolution of these views, because in this series he articulated his position on the signs of grace in its mature form for the first time. He clearly identified not an introspective search for the signs of grace but the ability to withstand trials of faith as the appropriate means of assurance.

Edwards stated in 1741, "I once did not imagine that the heart of man had been so unsearchable as I find it is. I am less charitable, and less uncharitable than once I was. I find more things in wicked men that may counterfeit, and make a fair shew of piety, and more ways that the remaining corruption of the godly may make them appear like carnal men, formalists and dead hypocrites, than once I knew of."[40] This statement confirms that over time Edwards became increasingly convinced of the deceptive similarity between saints and hypocrites. The virgins series suggests that this moment of realization occurred in the period between the awakenings and was primarily based on the behavior not of the radical New Lights but of his own Northampton congregation. Edwards's second experience with mass revivalism allowed him to articulate his convictions with greater depth and sophistication. His increased awareness of the manifold expressions of counterfeit faith produced in *Religious Affections* an analysis of the signs of grace and the means of assurance more subtle and insightful than that found in the virgins series. But between his composition of the virgins series and *Religious Affections* Edwards did not alter, but merely refined, his views.

Edwards's sermon series on the wise and foolish virgins, therefore, reflected two homiletical traditions common in New England Puritanism. His pastoral project fell within the tradition identified by Amanda Porterfield that conflated the marriage covenant with the covenant of grace in order both to reinforce the social structure and to promote the life of faith. His speculative project was continuous with Puritan literature of spiritual direction, which discussed such issues as how to unmask the self-deception of the hypocrite, how to identify the signs of grace, and what were the most reliable means of assurance. Thomas Shepard was master of both these traditions. Although his *Parable of the Ten Virgins* was one of the chief representatives of the latter tradition in seventeenth-century colonial Puritan literature, in this and other of his writings Shepard also reflected the former.[41] Edwards's treatment of the parable similarly merged these two traditions in what was perhaps a self-conscious appropriation of the master's form. In *Religious Affections* he eliminated the marriage metaphor and abandoned the narrative framework he had used in the series to distinguish uncertain from certain signs of grace; nevertheless, this treatise is the final product of the same course of inquiry that led Edwards to write his first extended sermon series on the parable of the wise and foolish virgins.

NOTES

1. This series has never been published. Unless otherwise indicated, all manuscripts discussed in this essay are housed in the Beinecke Rare Book and Manuscript Library, Yale University. Untitled manuscript sermons are cited by initial biblical text.

2. The first booklet (containing sermon 1, units 1–3) is dated November 1737; the second (sermon 2, unit 4) is dated December 1737; the third (sermon 3, unit 5) is dated January 1738; the fourth (sermons 4–7, units 6–9) is dated 1737–38; the fifth (sermon 8, units 10–11) is dated February 1738. The remaining five booklets (sermons 9–12, units 12–19) are not dated.

3. Jonathan Edwards (hereafter, JE) preached short sermon series on the parable of the sower (Matt. 13:3–8) in 1740, the parable of the rich young man (Mark 10:17–27) in 1743, and the dragnet (Matt. 13:47–50) in 1746.

4. John F. Wilson argues that in *A History of the Work of Redemption* JE "turned" the sermon form "inside out" (*The Works of Jonathan Edwards, 9, A History of the Work of*

Redemption, ed. John F. Wilson [New Haven, 1989], p. 40). After this accomplishment, JE may have judged it appropriate to move on to another form of expression. Furthermore, his polemical activities during the debate over revivalism required the more public and systematic form of the treatise.

5. John E. Smith states that in *Religious Affections* "Edwards quoted more from Shepard than from any other writer, depending chiefly upon *The Parable of the Ten Virgins.*" *The Works of Jonathan Edwards, 2, Religious Affections,* ed. John E. Smith (New Haven, 1959), p. 54.

6. In his "Catalogue" JE refers to "Dr. Manton's Sermons," "Twenty select sermons by Dr. Manton," and "Manton's sermons in various books." A number of Manton's sermons, including his series on Matt. 25:1–13, were collected posthumously in five volumes (London, 1678–1701). Of the many other treatments of the parable by Puritan divines, it is likely that JE had access to Benjamin Colman, *Practical Discourses upon the Parable of the Ten Virgins* (London, 1707); John Tillotson, *The Parable of the Ten Virgins* (London, 1694); and Henry Stebbing, *Parable of the Ten Virgins. Being the Substance of Two Practical Discourses* (London, 1769). It is also likely that in preparation of the series JE consulted one of Matthew Poole's commentaries on the scripture, either the *Synopsis criticorum* (5 vols., London, 1669–76) or the *Annotations upon the Holy Bible* (2 vols., London, 1683–85).

7. Amanda Porterfield, *Female Piety in Puritan New England: The Emergence of Religious Humanism* (New York, 1992). See also Margaret W. Masson, "The Typology of the Female as a Model for the Regenerate: Puritan Preaching, 1690–1730," *Signs* 2 (Winter 1976), pp. 304–15.

8. Porterfield, p. 3.

9. Porterfield, pp. 11–12.

10. Porterfield, p. 20. This characterization implies that the relation between husband and wife, although hierarchical, was not for New England Puritans analogous to the hierarchical relations between parent and child or master and slave. For an insightful discussion of the Puritan contribution to the transition from wife-as-subordinate to wife-as-companion, see Carol F. Karlsen, *The Devil in the Shape of a Woman: Witchcraft in Colonial New England* (New York, 1987), pp. 160–81.

11. Porterfield, p. 15.

12. Porterfield derives her thesis primarily from a study of seventeenth-century New England divines. In the afterword to her book she briefly considers JE and concludes that he in many ways fits the proposed model. See pp. 155–56.

13. Series on Matt. 25:1–12, booklet 1, leaves 3, 24, 25, 26.

14. Series on Matt. 25:1–12, booklet 1, leaves 7, 14, 10, 6, 11, 16, 11, 10, 13, 26–27.

15. Patricia J. Tracy, *Jonathan Edwards, Pastor: Religion and Society in Eighteenth-Century Northampton* (New York, 1979), pp. 101–2.

16. Tracy, p. 125; Ola E. Winslow, *Jonathan Edwards, 1703–1758* (New York, 1961), p. 161.

17. Tracy, p. 126.

18. Series on Matt. 25:1–12, booklet 4, leaf 16.

19. For example, in February 1743 JE was called to Westfield, Massachusetts, to participate in an ecclesiastical council concerning the case of Bathsheba Kingsley. Hains Kingsley, Bathsheba's husband, had requested the council because his wife's religious activities had caused her to neglect her duties in managing their household. The council's decision, in JE's hand, admonished Bathsheba for exhorting, censoriousness, and enthusiasm and instructed her "to keep chiefly at home" and take proper care of her family. However, it also directed Hains to give her "reasonable liberty" to attend religious meetings, not only in Westfield but also in surrounding towns, and to engage in "Christian conversation" at her neighbors' homes. The council's decision is housed in the Congregational Library, London.

20. Tracy, p. 110–12.

21. Series on Matt. 25:1–12, booklet 2, leaf 2.

22. Series on Matt. 25:1–12, booklet 3, leaf 12.

23. Series on Matt. 25:1–12, booklet 4, leaves 1, 6, 8, 10.

24. Series on Matt. 25:1–12, booklet 6, leaves 1, 24, 2, 6, 2; booklet 7, leaf 11.

25. Series on Matt. 25:1–12, booklet 7, leaf 4; booklet 8, leaf 12; booklet 6, leaves 8, 9; booklet 8, leaves 2, 6, 7, 9.

26. *Works, 2,* p. 84.

27. See, for example, Perry Miller's characterization of this sequence of publications in *Jonathan Edwards* (New York, 1949), p. 178.

28. In his preface to *Religious Affections,* JE remarks that "my design is somewhat diverse from the design of what I have formerly published." As he explains, in *Distinguishing Marks* his aim was "to show the distinguishing marks of a work of the Spirit of God, including both his common, and saving operations." In *Religious Affections,* on the other hand, he limits himself to a consideration of the signs of saving grace. This difference, of course, is decisive: only the signs of *saving* grace can help to distinguish between counterfeit and true conversions. *Works, 2,* p. 89.

29. Even the language JE uses in the virgins series to define the meaning of "spiritual," when the term is used in reference to the new spiritual principle, bears a marked resemblance to the parallel discussion in *Religious Affections.* See *Works, 2,* pp. 198–205. That Edwards developed in the 1730s the substance of his position on the new spiritual sense is confirmed not only by the publication in 1734 of "Divine and Supernatural Light" but also by a miscellanies entry (no. 782) entitled "Sense of the Heart" that dates from 1739. When Perry Miller published this entry in the *Harvard Theological Review,* he conjectured that JE wrote it around 1745 ("Jonathan Edwards on the Sense of the Heart," *Harvard Theological Review,* 41 [April, 1948], p. 124). Thomas A. Shafer's dating of the "Miscellanies" contradicts this estimate.

30. That this position predates the Awakening can be confirmed by the fact that Edwards wrote in 1739 a miscellanies entry (no. 790) entitled "Signs of Godliness" that so closely resembles the twelfth sign as to be considered a draft.

31. JE kept a manuscript notebook entitled "Signs of Godliness," but its entries consist primarily of scripture citations.

32. Sermon on Matt. 15:26, leaves 2, 3, 7, 8.

33. JE wrote the preaching date on the sermon, but because the first leaf has a frayed right margin, the last numeral of the year is missing. According to Thomas A. Schafer, the watermarks indicate a preaching date of August 1735, with August 1736 the only likely alternative.

34. Sermon on 2 Cor. 13:5, leaves 2, 8, 63, 70–71.

35. As the original title page notes, *Distinguishing Marks* was first preached as a sermonic discourse at the Yale commencement in September 1741. It was published "with great enlargements" in Boston soon thereafter. Because the original manuscript of the discourse on 1 John 4:1 is not extant, there is no way of judging its relation to the published treatise. See *The Works of Jonathan Edwards, 4, The Distinguishing Marks of the Work of a Spirit of God,* ed. C. C. Goen (New Haven, 1972), p. 214.

36. Trask Library, Andover Newton Theological School, Newton Centre, Massachusetts.

37. Sermon on Matt. 7:15, leaves 1, 6, 47, 1.

38. This series on Matt. 7:15 is written in outline form, but even so it has many textual similarities to *Religious Affections.* Most strikingly, it includes a discussion of the "twofold defect" that prevents saints from directly perceiving the operation of grace in their hearts, which is repeated, with only a little amplification, in *Religious Affections.* (See *Works, 2,* pp. 194–95.) Sereno Dwight states that *Religious Affections* "was a series of sermons, which [Edwards] preached from his own desk . . . probably, in the years 1742, and 1743" (*The Life of President Edwards* [New York, 1830], p. 223). The manuscripts of this series are apparently not extant. However, it is tempting to speculate that the series on Matt. 7:15 was the series

that formed the foundation of *Religious Affections,* not only because it was preached in January 1743 but also because of the resemblance of the series to the published treatise. However, *Religious Affections's* text (1 Pet. 1:8) and doctrine do not agree with that of the series.

39. Edwards's growing preoccupation with Christian practice in the years following the Connecticut Valley revival is confirmed by the fact that in the "Miscellanies" after 1736 there is a rapid proliferation of entries having the subject heading "Perseverance." Prior to 1731, Edwards wrote only five entries under this heading; between 1731 and 1736 he wrote none.

40. *Works, 4,* p. 285.

41. See Porterfield's discussion of Shepard, pp. 55–66 and passim.

TWO

Misrepresentations Corrected

JONATHAN EDWARDS AND THE REGULATION OF RELIGIOUS DISCOURSE

CHRISTOPHER GRASSO

"The great thing which I have scrupled," Jonathan Edwards declared in the preface to his *Farewell Sermon* (1751), was that when people came to be admitted to communion, they publicly assented only to "a Form of Words . . . without pretending thereby to mean any such Thing as a hearty Consent to the Terms of the Gospel Covenant."[1] By common custom and established principle, a public profession of faith in Northampton had come to rest on a "diverse use" of words and signs. "People have in effect agreed among themselves," he complained in *An Humble Inquiry,* that persons who use the words need not intend their proper meaning, "and others need not understand them so."[2] Professing Christianity and "owning" the church covenant had become empty formalities for many young couples who wanted to have their babies baptized. He also argued that when families in Northampton and inhabitants of New England called themselves "Christians," they merely flattered themselves with a name while growing fat off the land and resting content with the hollow forms of faith. Edwards asserted his authority as preacher of the Word and teacher of words to bring practice and profession closer to the gospel truth. He tried to discipline his congregation by policing the meanings of words, sacramental symbols, and other signs within Northampton.

The communion controversy in Northampton and Edwards's subsequent dismissal is a familiar story in the annals of American religious history; the tale of the great theologian's being rejected by his own flock belongs, according to Perry Miller, "to the symbolism of America."[3] Miller told the story as the triumph of the merchant ethic over Christian virtue. Other scholars, looking more closely at Northampton than at the archetypal forces of American mythology, have tried to reveal the personal, social, and political tensions woven through the town's debate over church polity and practice.[4] Less attention has been given to the published arguments the controversy generated. But the rhetoric of the communion controversy reveals the ways that communal cohesiveness and corporate identity were rooted in public religious discourse; it shows questions arising about how public language was meaningful and who had the authority to regulate those meanings.

Edwards attempted to regulate public religious discourse—to control the meaning of signs *in* a community and to redefine the language *of* Christian community. First, he insisted that the minister, not the parishioners, set the terms of debate. Second, he sought to clear away the ambiguity and confusion arising from a diverse use of signs, some of which can be found in his own earlier preaching. Third, Edwards's definition of "visible sainthood" involved spelling out not just *what* this term should mean but also *how* terms in religious discourse should signify meaning. His disagreements with his cousin Solomon Williams and the Separatist position articulated by Ebenezer Frothingham reveal how each writer's position was based upon different epistemologies and different conceptions of signification.[5] Williams, writing from Lebanon, Connecticut, for the Stoddardean opposition, attacked Edwards's scriptural argument for restricted communion and his epistemological explanation of Christian profession. Frothingham, a Middletown Separatist, embraced Edwards's stricter view of the church as a gathered communion of saints, but found his arguments mystifying and contradictory.

Fourth and finally, Edwards wanted to restrict the rhetorical uses of flattering titles like "God's Covenant People" for all nominally Christian New Englanders, even when such language could be doctrinally justified. This is related to a rhetorical strategy that sought to accent the difference between nature and grace, and is connected to the question of Edwards and the national covenant. Clerical rhetoric during the Seven Years War (including Edwards's own) once again exploited the systematic equivocations at the heart of New England's system of interlocking covenants.

More than a sacramental controversy, therefore, the dispute Edwards set in motion made New Englanders question what it meant to call themselves "God's People." The issue involves broader questions of rhetorical emphasis as much as the narrower points of ecclesiastical doctrine, and understanding that rhetoric is essential to finding Edwards's place between his Puritan predecessors and the New Divinity theologians who followed him. The language of corporate identity changed in Edwards's preaching, as it would change throughout mid-eighteenth-century New England.[6] Arguments articulated during and after the communion controversy help reveal what Edwards perpetuated and what he discarded in the image of New England as "God's New Israel," as well as what he contributed to the myth of America as a "Redeemer Nation."

THE LANGUAGE OF THE CHURCH

Edwards would grant people the liberty of conscience. But he knew that a collection of individuals following the dictates of their private judgments did not make a community. He believed that the church's public rituals should not be a marketplace for people to come and choose what they needed or wanted, but a communal expression of a single commonly understood idea. Yet the value of religious words and signs in New England seemed to depreciate as fast as the public bills of credit.

Edwards did not want to change what people said, but what they meant. He would be content with a simple statement, similar to those already used by candidates for church membership:

> I hope, I do truly find a Heart to give myself wholly to God, according to the Tenor of that Covenant of Grace which was seal'd in my Baptism, and to walk in a way of that Obedience to all the Commandments of God, which the Covenant of Grace requires, as long as I shall live.[7]

But what did these words mean? In Northampton, Edwards complained, they meant some indeterminate degree of "a common faith and moral sincerity short of true Godliness." A candidate, awakened but unconverted, could utter these words to express that she wanted to obey God's commandments and that she hoped someday to have a "heart"—that is, a predominant inclination—to give herself wholly to the Lord. The candidate *should* be professing, Edwards argued, that she believes she *presently* finds such a heart within herself, and hopes she is right. In Edwards's scheme, people with merely awakened consciences but not true religious affections need not apply; their so-called desire to obey God did not flow from their heart's love to God, but merely from their natural fear of hell.

The Northampton brethren interpreted Edwards's break from local church practices as a bid for ministerial power over the congregation, and they were right. But it was not, as some murmured, that he wanted to set himself up as the exclusive judge of other people's religious experiences, for he continued to maintain that even the most experienced eye could be deceived in such matters. Nor did he claim the sole right to measure a candidate's behavior against his profession, for when a minister did so, he acted publicly and only as an officer of the whole church. But Edwards did insist "that it belonged to me as a Pastor, before a Profession was accepted, to have

Full Liberty to instruct the Candidate in the Meaning of the Terms of it, and in the Nature of the Things proposed to be professed."[8]

When he first brought his case before his congregation in a 1750 sermon on Ezekiel 44:9, Edwards made his arguments by establishing what basic terms like *professing* Christianity, *owning* the covenant, and *visible* sainthood should mean.[9] His 1750 demand for "a higher sense" of these terms was part of an effort to stem the erosion of meaning that had continued under his own ministry as scriptural words and phrases had been applied like rhetorical tags to a variety of circumstances. He was not just renouncing the doctrine of his grandfather and predecessor Solomon Stoddard, who had allowed striving sinners to come to the Lord's Table in the hope that they might be converted there. He was also renouncing the rhetorical imprecision of his own earlier preaching, which had moved among the "various senses" in which the covenant was offered and owned, and had acknowledged the different "degrees" of Christian profession.[10]

He had explained in 1737 that we can recognize a covenant people as such because they have access to the scriptures, they visibly take hold of the covenant in their profession, and they receive special mercies and judgments in God's providence.[11] But all covenanted nations were not equally favored. Edwards's fast and thanksgiving sermons, from a very early effort in the late 1720s to some of his laments during the French wars through the 1740s, describe how the English nation had been raised up above all other covenanted peoples to enjoy the peculiar blessings of religious liberty. God had distinguished "the Land" (New England) even above the rest of the nation; while England was overrun with deists and skeptics, New England had trained Protestant preachers and built churches in every village. New England, Edwards wrote, more closely paralleled God's covenant people Israel as "perhaps no People now on the face of the Earth."[12]

Every community where the Word was preached and acknowledged could call itself a "covenant people" or a "professing society." But Edwards explained that God distinguished a community as a covenant people not just by revealing the gospel light to them but by, in greater or lesser degrees, pouring out his Spirit among them and blessing their religious efforts.[13] Similarly, the community's profession in response to God's offer and blessings had varying degrees. A people made "a higher profession" when they acknowledged a greater degree of God's presence or mercies, or "when there is a far Greater Number among them that do make a Profession of special Experiences & of Extraordinary Light."[14]

A year after Northampton's 1735 revival, Edwards delivered a remarkable sermon that raised the town above all New England "as a city set on a hill."[15] He was not just a preacher tailoring a time-worn simile to his own locale. The religious excitement and "surprising conversions" in Northampton manifested an outpouring of the Spirit that had up to that point surpassed any local revival in living memory. The eyes of New England were therefore upon Northampton; but also "in new york . . . the Jerseys . . . upon Long Island . . . the Highlands on Hudson's River" and even in London eyes were turning toward God's People in Northampton.[16] The town now had to honor its high profession with godly practice, for the stakes had been raised.

But the "high profession" refers here to those reports of religious experiences being spread abroad, most notably by Edwards himself, first in a letter that Boston's Benjamin Colman summarized for his London correspondents, then in the famous *Faithful Narrative.*[17] In 1737, Edwards urged that the townspeople's profession become more formal and explicit in a reaffirmation of their obligations under the covenant of grace.[18] As the town's new church was raised, he called for a "Joint Resolution" made by the civil magistrate and the ministers of the Gospel, "the Leading men amongst a People and those that are Led by them," the rich and the poor, the old and the young.[19] Like the High Priest Jehoiada in Second Chronicles, Edwards called his people to bind themselves to God and to one another under God's covenant. He urged them to make their identity as God's People manifest in clear words and plain practices in their business and public affairs.[20]

At the height of the Awakening in March 1742, Edwards again called on the people of Northampton to commit themselves to be God's People. This time it was no mere public resolution; he asked every person in the congregation over fourteen years old to stand up, solemnly "own" the covenant, and vow to seek and serve God. Each congregant was to swear adherence to a sixteen-paragraph summary of proper Christian behavior, committing all to Christ and promising to treat neighbors in a spirit of meekness and charity.[21] This was a solemn oath to God, Edwards reminded his people a year later; it was an "extraordinary explicit vow" that was greater than an "ordinary implicit" one in that it called upon God to confirm the truth of what was said.[22] "Take heed," Edwards warned, "words are gone out of your mouths and you can not go back."[23] He told backsliders in 1747 that "their own former voice" would witness against them on Judgment Day, "so they will be sentenced out of their own mouths."[24]

In 1745 and again in 1747, Edwards explained that the 1742 covenant was more explicit but "not essentially different" from what parents dedicated their children to in baptism.[25] It was a fuller expression of what people implicitly acknowledged by attending church on the sabbath, and what their actions signified and renewed at the Lord's Table. By 1749, Edwards was arguing that any "implicit" professions such as joining public prayers and keeping the sabbath *only* take on meaning *if* they are rooted in "a declarative explicit covenanting" that all baptized true believers must make upon reaching adulthood. Eating and drinking at the Lord's Supper are only "speaking Signs" that symbolically reiterate a meaning that must already be fixed by the communicant's words.[26] Solomon Williams argued that Edwards's call for a personal explicit profession as a requirement for admission had no scriptural basis and no precedent in ecclesiastical history.[27] Edwards answered that actions, by themselves, were not properly a profession at all.[28] "[T]he Reason of Mankind teaches them the Need of joining *Words* & *Actions* together in publick Manifestations of the Mind, in Cases of Importance: *Speech* being the great and peculiar Talent, which God has given to Mankind, as the special Means and Instrument of the Manifestation of their Minds one to another."[29]

Edwards's use of the term *profession,* therefore, had narrowed, its meaning refined from a vague or implicit acknowledgment of God's gospel offer to the explicit, personal oath of the individual Christian. *What* Edwards expected people to profess (and not just *how* they professed) underwent a similar redefinition. What did it mean to visibly "own" the covenant? Edwards's early position resembled his cousin Solomon's. The candidate must signify his belief that the doctrines of the Gospel are true, submit himself to the terms of Christ's covenant, and endeavor to obey all the moral rules of the Gospel. No one with this belief and resolve can know for sure that he is not regenerated, and the church must give him the benefit of the doubt.[30]

Edwards's "new scruples" about the Stoddardean Lord's Supper and full membership in the visible church began appearing in his private notebooks as early as 1728.[31] His first corollary to a 1736 treatment of the covenant of grace was that "the revelation and offer of the gospel is not properly called a covenant till it is consented to," and as in the *Humble Inquiry* thirteen years later, he compared this consent to a woman's acceptance of an offer of marriage.[32] But we need to look beyond the gloss that Edwards's private writings give to his pulpit utterances, for if some sermon passages seem to tighten the requirements for owning the covenant, others leave room for a broader Stoddardean interpretation.

In his 1737 fast sermon on 2 Chronicles 23:16, for example, Edwards told his congregation what was stipulated on their part in being God's People. It is not just "an acknowledgment of the mouth," a professing of Christ in name only, for owning the covenant while having "an inward prevailing opposition" to God's rule is no real *consent* to it at all.[33] Only converts could so renounce the world and embrace Christ as a spouse. But this is the same sermon in which Edwards also speaks more broadly of the people's consent to the covenant as a public resolution, of at least visibly "taking hold" of the covenant, of "each one contribut[ing] what in him lies towards it that we may be the Lords People."[34] Could not the unconverted, therefore, in some sense own the covenant as well?

For loyal Stoddardean Solomon Williams, the answer was yes. The unregenerate could own the covenant and be counted among God's People because to do so meant to consent *to the terms* of Christ's offer.[35] They need not profess saving faith, since the term *belief* in the New Testament can signify "no more than the Assent of the Understanding" or "a Conviction of the Judgment and Conscience, that Jesus was the Messiah, or that the Gospel was true."[36] The unconverted "do enter into Covenant with God, and with all the Earnestness and Sincerity of soul they possibly can, do engage to keep Covenant."[37] They submit to the rules and ordinances of Christ, and vow to obey him to the utmost of their natural and legal—but not gracious—powers.

In his 1750 pulpit defense of his new position, Edwards made a clean break from both Stoddardeanism and the ambiguities of his own earlier preaching. "I cant understand that there is any such notion of owning the Covenant any where in the Christian world but in this Corner of it here in New England," he announced.[38] He then looked behind Stoddard to the Synod of 1662 and the New England forefathers for an earlier custom. "But now the Great part of the Country has forgotten the meaning of their forefathers and have gradually brought in a notion of owning the Covenant of Grace without pretending to profess a compliance."[39] Owning the covenant means not only acknowledging its terms but complying with them, he argued. Christ offers salvation for saving faith; the unconverted who offer only the promise of outward obedience are in no sense parties to the covenant.[40]

But Solomon Williams answered that this notion of covenanting confuses entering a covenant with fulfilling one, and destroys the whole concept of visible sainthood. Williams, Edwards, and even Separatist Ebenezer Frothingham agreed that only visible saints should be allowed to own the covenant and sit at the Lord's Table—but the three completely disagreed about what the term *visible sainthood* meant. Their definitions reveal the very different epistemologies that helped shape their visions of the church.

For Williams, visible saints are Christians according to all that is visible: profession of the gospel truth and good behavior. Arguing from Stoddard's skepticism about the ability of men to distinguish the truly gracious from the morally sincere, Williams described visible sainthood as a larger category that included real saints. Not all who are visible saints on earth will turn out to be real saints on Judgment Day, but until then the church has no business trying to search hearts and separate sheep from goats. At the other extreme, Frothingham maintained that a true Christian could *certainly* discern the presence of sanctifying grace in someone else. The Holy Spirit makes manifest, or visible, the godliness of saints to each other: "the Beams or Rays of Divine Light shining into the soul" enlighten the understanding and guide a Christian's judgment of his neighbor.[41]

Edwards tried to take the middle ground between Stoddardean uncertainty and Separatist certainty. For him, visibility was neither a category distinct from the real nor a supernatural manifestation of the real, but a *sign* that referred to the real the way a properly used word refers to the essence of the thing signified. He contended that there must be a stronger relation between the visible and the real—between what man sees and what God sees—than Stoddardeanism recognized. For both Edwards and the Separatists, the reality at the heart of public worship was the "peculiar love" Christians had for one another.[42] This affection "must have some Apprehension of the Understanding, some Judgment of the Mind, for its Foundations."[43] Perhaps Williams's lukewarm "benefit of the doubt" could be extended to all moral people who called themselves Christians, but for Edwards the "mind must first Judge some Amiableness in the Object" before affections are bestowed. Edwards wanted something to tip the scales of uncertainty in a positive direction, some sign that gave the church probable grounds for judging a candidate a real saint before calling him a visible saint.[44]

Frothingham recommended Edwards's *Humble Inquiry* as an improvement over Stoddardeanism, but complained that Edwards "writes in a misterious Manner, backwards and forwards, about this visibility."[45] While Stoddard extended charity to all because he could obtain no reliable knowledge about their souls, and Edwards limited visible sainthood because he could gain probable knowledge of grace in others, Frothingham insisted that the church was a communion of real saints who were certain of each other's godliness. If I ask for a sheep, Frothingham wrote, and someone brings me either a sheep or a goat, "is the Sheep visible, or is it not?" The answer was either yes or no, not a degree of probability. "[T]herefore to have a Thing visible that is requested amounts to a certain Knowledge of the thing thus presented."[46] However, what was presented had to be more than "a bare profession of Godliness" and good behavior. Candidates for admission in a Separatist church had to describe their experiences of God's grace upon their hearts, and tell the story of their conversion to Christ.

Edwards had had his fill of people publicly describing their trembling, trances, and visions, and he took great pains to distance himself from Separatist enthusiasm, denouncing those "slanderous" reports that said he "had fallen in with those Wild People."[47] The Stoddardean church did not do enough institutionally to recognize conversions, but the Separatist church placed too much emphasis on personal experience, and fostered spiritual pride. He argued that the pastor should be the one to decide when a particular conversion narrative might edify the whole congregation. Regular professions should not describe the details of conversion. The candidate's words and deeds, in fact, need not even signify that he is assured of his own conversion. But they do need to signify that he has experienced the essence of Christian piety: believing with his heart, loving God with all his soul, and loving his neighbor as himself. The simple language of the kind of profession Edwards would accept did not describe how the person came to be "born again;" it *referred* to the experience of godliness as an unspoken context and necessary precondition for the candidate's appearance before the church. Edwards did not want the focus to be on the subjective sensations of fear or joy but on "the Supreme holy Beauty, and Comliness of divine Things, as they are in themselves, or in their own Nature"—a beauty that human signs can only gesture toward.[48]

When Williams read Edwards's discussion of an individual's examination of his own heart prior to profession, he thought that he had found the fatal flaw to the whole scheme. If coming to the Lord's Supper without saving grace is a damning sin (as Edwards claimed), how could anything short of certainty about conversion induce a person to come? A man believes the gospel and sincerely desires to do his duty before Christ. But he hesitates. What if this belief and sincerity, which he knows he has, is "no more than moral Sincerity, the effect of common Grace and Illumination?"[49] Common and saving grace are often hard to distinguish, and all but those wild Separates acknowledge that assurance is hard to come by. On the other hand, any sane person with a healthy conscience *must* know whether he is being morally sincere or not. Such an awareness is essential to moral agency, and distinguishes the man from his sheep and goats. Therefore, the awakened person who still doubts whether he has saving grace should be allowed to make "such a Profession as he finds he can truly make."[50] Williams's church rested on the rock of the awakened conscience.

But in the next step, as this morally sincere candidate offers himself to the church, Williams went beyond Stoddard. Williams argued that the church, listening to the candidate's profession of belief and sincerity, must take his words in their highest sense, as a profession of saving grace. Whether the candidate thinks he is converted or not is beside the point, since he may be mistaken either way. The church, "without any metaphysical Speculations or abstruse Reasonings, upon the Nature of *Visibilities* and *Realities*," should treat the professor *as if* he were converted.[51]

Edwards found this more disturbing than anything in the bland rebuttal he had heard preached from his own pulpit by Jonathan Ashley of Deerfield in February 1750.[52] Ashley welcomed the merely moral to the Lord's Table, but at least did not then pretend that they were regenerate. After Williams set forth his position as an argument from "common sense," Edwards dismantled it with an argument based on three propositions about signification, summed up in a footnote citing Paul in 1 Corinthians 14:7, and then Locke's *Essay:* "He that uses Words of any Language without Distinct Ideas in his Mind . . . only makes a Noise without any Sense or Signification."[53] When a man says he has a king in his room, we do not know if he means George II or a chess piece. If he says he has metal in his pocket, we are not obliged by "charity" to assume it is gold and not brass. If a professor uses words allowed to signify either moral sincerity or real piety, he makes "no profession at all of *Gospel Holiness.*"[54]

Like Locke, Edwards knew that language becomes the "common Tye of Society" if the signs a person uses are held in common.[55] Locke distinguished between "ordinary" discourse, in which meanings established by "common use" and "tacit consent" usually served well enough, and "philosophical" discourse, which was more in need of an "Under-Labourer" in "The Commonwealth of Learning" who could point out abuses and demand more precision in the use of words.[56] Edwards, too, in his treatises on the will, true virtue, and original sin, tried to reform the vocabulary of the Commonwealth of Learning, aiming especially at points where ordinary and philosophical usage became confused. But before he left Northampton for the Stockbridge settlement where he would write those treatises, he was more immediately concerned with reforming a different community of discourse. He tried to correct the damage that common usage and tacit consent had done to terms like *professing* Christianity, *owning* the covenant, and *visible* sainthood.

THE NEW ENGLISH ISRAEL

Scholars have long appreciated the central place Edwards and his followers gave to the *individual's* relationship to God in the covenant of grace.[57] The public or national covenant, however, conspicuously absent from Edwards's published writings, was thought to have been repudiated or replaced by new forms of Christian union achieved through revivalism or concerts of prayer.[58] At any rate, New Divinity ministers, others said, were too caught up with metaphysics and the millennium to be distracted by the mundane social and political concerns that Puritan covenant sermons had so often addressed.[59]

Three recent studies of Edwards and New Divinity manuscript sermons have reassessed the importance of the public or national covenant in Edwardsian preaching. Harry Stout's initial investigation of Edwards's occasional sermons found plenty of references to the national covenant, and contended that the formula Edwards inherited had become a "taken-for-granted reality."[60] Stout further argued that neither Edwards nor any other eighteenth-century established minister denied "New England's attendant identity as a special people with a messianic destiny."[61] Mark Valeri's essay on Edwards's New Divinity followers and the American Revolution, however, suggested instead that Edwards's references to New England's covenant were "somewhat untypical" of his preaching.[62] More importantly, Valeri argued that after 1750 Edwards, Bellamy, and Samuel Hopkins replaced covenantal terminology with the language of moral law, and spoke of a God who did not give special treatment to an elect nation but ruled all through "impartial, universal moral standards."[63] Another study of Edwards's manuscript sermons detached the question of the prominence of covenant discourse per se from its ideological implications. Yes, Edwards preached about the national covenant, Gerald McDermott wrote, but he did so as a "pessimistic" critic and not as an endorser of New England's special errand or America's manifest destiny.[64] All three of these studies point toward the need to put Edwards's covenantal preaching in the context of both the Stoddardean church he inherited and the post-Awakening evangelical union he championed. Changes in emphasis and relative importance are revealed only when the national covenant is seen within a larger understanding of Edwards's language of corporate identity—a language which changed as Edwards's focus shifted from Northampton and New England to the revival movement within international Protestantism.

As we have seen, covenantalism was neither taken for granted nor untypical; it was an integral part of Edwards's pulpit language of corporate identity before 1750. Certainly Edwards's early preaching recognized New England's high spiritual privileges, if not with grandiose claims for New England's national election. But to castigate Northampton for its spiritual and moral declension after the 1735 revival and the 1740 Awakening, Edwards pointed to the outpourings of the Spirit that they had all so recently witnessed rather than to an "inheritance" from the New England founders or the town's pious forefathers.[65] During the communion controversy, even as Edwards discussed Israel's covenanting in Deuteronomy, he emphasized the *experience* of the people's religious revival rather than the legal *fact* of their covenantal status.

Some historians have contrasted the covenant preaching of Puritan fast-day Jeremiahs with the "New Light" calls for revival and evangelical union. Covenantal jeremiads, Alan Heimert wrote, had become conservative, backward-looking instruments of social control, trying to impose order "mechanically" through institutional discipline and calls for obedience. "New Lights" called instead for an "affectionate union" of Christian brethren in Christ, looking ahead to the millennial age.[66] In 1747, Edwards published *An Humble Attempt to Promote Explicit Agreement and Visible Union of God's People* and compared the two forms of public worship. A fast day proclaimed by the civil government of a Christian society and a concert of prayer promoted by private Christians differed only in "circumstances," he argued.[67] The union of Christians in either case depended upon joining for prayer at a fixed *time* rather than gathering in a single *place.* Although the precedent Edwards cites for the concert of prayer had been proposed for the *national* deliverance of Great Britain in 1712, the concert he promoted was to be "an *union* of Christians of distant places," from many different cities, countries, and nations.[68] Although the plan was proposed by pro-revival ministers in Scotland and encouraged by private praying societies that had sprung up during the Awakening, Edwards offered the plan as an attempt to heal the divisions the Awakening had spawned.[69] Nevertheless, the concert, which people joined voluntarily, much more than New England's public covenant, which fell to them because of where they lived, matched the transatlantic vision and personal appeal of midcentury Protestant revivalism.

Edwards in the 1740s also reordered the relationship between the national covenant and the covenant of grace. Seventeenth-century Congregationalists spoke of the covenant of grace for individual saints, church covenants for those who professed to be saints (and, in some sense, for their children), and the national covenant for a whole people who acknowledged Christianity as the established religion. Northampton's Solomon Stoddard had, in effect, conflated these covenants, speaking instead of the internal (individual) and external (corporate) aspects or articles of the covenant of grace, and placing public worship and especially the Lord's Supper as the central ritual for them all. Stoddard's model was the Old Testament "Jewish church," rather than the early Christian congregations that were set up before Christianity had been instituted as a national religion.[70] Edwards separated what Stoddardean practice had joined.

When Edwards defended his position on church membership before his congregation in 1750, he closed his argument by quickly dismissing any objections arising from a comparison to Israel's covenanting in the Old Testament.[71] But the senses in which the Jews—and like them, New Englanders—were "God's People" would loom larger in subsequent debates. Like Stoddard, Solomon Williams spoke of people keeping the external, public covenant by their natural powers and keeping the internal covenant by saving grace.[72] Edwards argued that outward covenanting must express an inward covenanting or it signifies nothing.[73] But did not Edwards himself preach that God makes a public covenant with a professing people, a covenant that does not require true piety but only religion and virtue in outward exercise and things visible? True, he had explained that this public or national covenant was one that God made with whole societies and not with particular persons; but then are not particular persons, as members of society and in respect to things external and temporal, *in* covenant, just as the Jews were?[74] The Jews, Williams wrote, gracious and moral alike, covenanted with their God, and "were alike called *the People of God, A chosen Generation, a royal Priesthood, an holy Nation, a peculiar People.*"[75]

Edwards argued "that such Appellations as God's *People,* God's Israel, and some other such Phrases, are used and applied in the Scripture with considerable *Diversity* of Intention."[76] There were appendages to Abraham's

Covenant of Grace, promises to his family and bloodline that ceased with the Gospel dispensation. Sometimes "God's People" referred to all Jews in this carnal aspect of the covenant, which did not literally apply to Christians. But Williams dismissed this as more blather about names and words. Christians are in covenant just as the Jews were, he contended.[77] All Christian Gentiles are grafted onto the root of Abraham, so God's promise extends to them and their seed—meaning that all the children of Christian parents are born into a state of "federal holiness," and are (at least externally) in the covenant with their parents.

Edwards at first seemed to concede the narrow doctrinal point to Williams, though he in no way surrendered the larger issue. He turned to "the Ambiguity of the Phrase, *Being in Covenant,*" and noted that it "signifies two distinct Things: either (1.) *Being under the Obligations* [and] *Bonds of the Covenant;* or (2.) *A being conformed to the Covenant, and complying with the Terms of it.*"[78] Many ungodly Jews and New Englanders can be said to be some of God's Covenant People in the first, weaker sense of that expression, he admitted. But—and here Edwards reduced Williams' federal theology to an empty husk—being People under Obligations of the Covenant is hardly a special privilege, for "so are all Mankind" in covenant in this sense. Unconverted New Englanders are "God's Covenant People" in no greater sense than are "*Mahometans,* or *Heathens.*"[79]

Thus Williams's "external covenant" seemed to be extended as the Moral Law of all mankind, and the title "God's People" became an empty phrase on the lips of the ungodly. Williams was horrified. Edwards's scheme denied morally sincere New Englanders under "the good Impressions of Convictions and Awakenings" their place alongside the truly godly; it classed them with the heathens and would perplex their tender consciences.[80] But that was precisely Edwards's point. Awakened sinners "are very ready to flatter themselves that they are willing to accept Christ," Edwards asserted, but they need to be driven to their knees. They need to see that they have not "the least spark of Love to God." Devils are even more convinced of the truth of the gospel; sinners roasting in hell have their consciences far more awakened than they ever had in this world.[81] Edwards warned that Williams's book might lead people to suppose that the Christless could be friends to Christ, when actually they were enemies who bore greater guilt than the heathens who had neither bibles nor preachers.[82]

Although the unregenerate living in a Christian nation could call themselves "God's People" in a very weak sense, Edwards wanted to strip them of their titles. "Now why is it looked upon so dreadful, to have great Numbers going without the *Name* and honourable *Badge* of Christianity[?]" Too many are "contented with the *Sign,* exclusive of the *Thing* signified!" They overvalue common grace and moral sincerity. "[T]his, I can't but think, naturally tends to sooth and flatter the Pride of vain Man."[83]

Here lies the crux of Edwards's rhetorical strategy, which his New Divinity followers would accentuate and develop. Names and "appellations" that flattered graceless men, even if there was some scriptural precedent for their use, were to be applied with great care or avoided. The verbal badges of Christianity must conform to doctrine and cut through the rhetorical fog obscuring the chasm between nature and grace. Edwards tried to sift through the ambiguities of being "in" or "under" the covenant; later Edwardsians such as Nathanael Emmons simply defined a covenant as a mutual contract requiring the personal consent of all parties, and declared all other uses of the term, even in scripture, to be figurative rather than literal. "If faith is the condition of the covenant of grace," Emmons wrote, "there can be no medium between being completely in and completely out of it."[84]

From what has been discussed here, it would seem that Stout and McDermott's arguments about the importance of the national covenant for Edwards might be more suited to Edwards before the communion controversy. Valeri's stress on God's impartial moral government of nations, coupled with Heimert's emphasis on the "affectionate union" of Christians within the international visible church, might be more appropriate for the later Edwards. But there are problems with this conclusion. Edwards's shift toward moral law terminology can be seen in his private notebooks, implied in some of his sketchy outlines to sermons preached to the Stockbridge Indians, and inferred, perhaps, from his endorsement of Bellamy's *True Religion Delineated* in 1750.[85] However, in the 1750s, Edwards repreached several sermons written in the 1740s or earlier. In 1755, he again explained that "God in a national Covenant promises prosperity to External duties."[86] In 1754 and again in 1757, he described the great difference between these externally covenanted "People of God" and others: though under the same moral law, God's People received more special favors and mercies.[87] How could he give such titles to those he so strenuously argued did not deserve them—to those inhabitants of a nation who did not *experience* union through *religious* affections? How could he now hand out the badges of Christianity?

One answer lies in the difference between doctrine and rhetorical strategy. After careful study of the scriptures, Edwards had determined what God's will was with regard to admitting people to full communion in the church. He sacrificed his pulpit to this doctrine. He never completely abandoned the idea of a national covenant, although he argued that it could be neither sealed by church ordinances nor inflated with pretensions of unique national election. He had strongly objected to the diverse use of signs that had become a local habit and to the common custom that gave distinguishing names and titles to the whole body public. But correcting those who abused the idea of a national covenant or obscured the distinguishing marks of godliness became less important when faced not by hypocrites sitting at the Lord's Table but by French and Indian minions of Antichrist who threatened to wipe Protestant churches off the continent. The rhetorical context had changed, not his doctrinal commitments.

It is not that Edwards, having moved to the Stockbridge frontier, had decided that a little flattering exhortation might help rouse the militia. Just the opposite: he blamed Braddock's defeat in 1755 upon those who had trusted their own power rather than committing all to God's hands. Still, he called the soldiers who marched off to war "God's People," and did so because they fought *for* Christ's church (though many of them may not have been fully *in* Christ's church) against its openly professed enemies. They were God's covenant people in this weaker sense because they lived in a land of family bibles and learned preachers who *offered* the covenant, rather than in a nation of priestly inquisitors with Latin bibles under lock and key.[88]

If, during the communion controversy, it had been Edwards's burden to clarify the ambiguities of New England's covenant discourse for the sake of the church, during the Seven Years War he would exploit those ambiguities once again as he exhorted the defenders of Protestant civilization in the New World. Just as the sacramental controversy had drawn attention to the language that distinguished (or failed to distinguish) between the church and society at large, the war weakened that rhetorical boundary line. Edwards did not live to see Quebec fall; Williams did, and chose the text for his thanksgiving sermon carefully.[89] In Exodus 15:2 Moses and the Israelites sing God's praises just after Pharaoh's army had been drowned in the Red Sea. "God had not yet explicitly taken them into Covenant with himself, as he did a little after this at *Mount Sinai,*" Williams explained.[90] But the Israelites could look back to the covenant God had made with their fathers, Abraham, Isaac, and Jacob, and the promises extending to their seed. This generation of Israelites, then, prefigured baptized but unconverted Christians: they lived under the *promises* of their fathers' covenant and had to engage those promises by honoring God and preparing "an habitation" for him. Williams applied this text "to *New-England,* and the rest of the *British subjects* in America." You too, he told his congregation, had pious and holy fathers in covenant.[91] You too have been saved from your enemies. As a vast British Empire in America opened for settlement, "every *English American*" ought to prepare his soul as God's habitation and resolve to cleave to God as the New England forefathers had. Williams also joined many others in calling for the country as a whole to prepare a habitation for Christ's church on the frontier by sending missionaries to Christianize the Indians. While Edwards's New Divinity disciples were abandoning the idea of the public covenant, others, like Solomon Williams, were recasting the rhetoric to fit new situations. Williams combined preparationism, Stoddardean institution building, and a dawning vision of the westward course of Anglo-American civilization.[92]

Edwards's attempt to regulate religious discourse involved fixing the meaning of particular words used in public professions, controlling how religious signs in general ought to refer to divine realities and signify commonly understood ideas, and placing this regulatory power firmly in the hands of ministers rather than parishioners. His own earlier preaching contained some of the "diverse use" of signs in regard to covenants and profession that he objected to during the communion controversy. His preaching during the Seven Years War employed the kind of ambiguous terminology for the imperial context that he had condemned in connection with the local church. Yet his New Divinity followers embraced his effort to bring moral order to a changing world by controlling the terms of public religious discourse. By asserting the authority to regulate an increasingly diverse use of signs, Edwardsians fueled antagonisms between laity and clergy. Like Edwards, of course, they believed that they were only trying to correct the ways that discourse had come to misrepresent the Word.

NOTES

1. Jonathan Edwards, *A Farewell Sermon* (Boston, 1751), iii.

2. Jonathan Edwards, *An Humble Inquiry* (Boston, 1749), 15–16. "And therefore whatever some of these words and signs may *in themselves* most properly and naturally import, they entirely cease to be significations of any such thing among people accustomed to understand them otherwise."

3. Perry Miller, *Jonathan Edwards* (Amherst, 1981; originally published 1949), 211.

4. Patricia J. Tracy, *Jonathan Edwards, Pastor: Religion and Society in Eighteenth-Century Northampton* (New York, 1980); Gregory H. Nobles, *Divisions throughout the Whole: Politics and Society in Hampshire County, Massachusetts, 1740–1775* (Cambridge, 1983).

5. Solomon Williams, *The True State of the Question* (Boston, 1751); Ebenezer Frothingham, *The Articles of Faith and Practice* (Newport, 1750). Hereafter, references to the "Discourse" following the "Articles" and "Covenant" will be referred to as Frothingham's *Discourse.*

6. Mark A. Noll has discussed the social, economic, and cultural conditions that may have made mid-eighteenth-century New England less receptive to the rhetoric of the national covenant. Noll, "Jonathan Edwards and the Transition from Clerical to Political Leadership in New England's Intellectual History," paper presented at the Writings of Jonathan Edwards: Text and Context, Text and Interpretation conference, Bloomington, Indiana, June 2–4, 1994.

7. Jonathan Edwards, letter to Peter Clark, May 7, 1750, quoted by Edwards in *Misrepresentations Corrected and Truth Vindicated* (Boston, 1752), 13.

8. Edwards, *Farewell Sermon,* vi.

9. Jonathan Edwards, MS Sermon on Ezekiel 44:9 [booklet one], delivered Feb. 15–March 22, 1750, Beinecke Rare Book and Manuscript Library, Yale University, New Haven. All manuscript sermons cited hereafter are from the Beinecke collection. For a brief discussion of this text, see Editor's Introduction, *The Works of Jonathan Edwards, 12, Ecclesiastical Writings,* ed. David Hall (New Haven, 1994), 88.

10. In a November 1746 lecture to young people, Edwards had tried to explain the various senses and different degrees behind a commonly used title like "God's Children." Spoken to the people of Israel in Isaiah 1:2, the words could also denote all mankind, since man was created in God's image, or refer to all who have been raised in "the House of God" among Christians. In a higher sense, the term could be limited to the saints, those "acknowledged as true born Children & not bastards" in God's family.

11. MS fast sermon on 2 Chronicles 23:16, March 1737, leaves 3r.–4v.

12. Ibid., leaf 13r. See also MS sermon fragment C, c. 1727.

13. MS fast sermon on 2 Chronicles 23:16, March 1737, leaves 3n.–4v. By "religious efforts" I mean the instituted "means of grace," i.e., prayer, preaching, and public worship. Under God's blessing, preaching successfully awakens and converts sinners and enlivens saints, prayers are answered, and public worship becomes a joyous communion with God.

14. MS sermon on Matthew 5:14, July 1736, leaf 4v.

15. MS sermon on Matthew 5:14, July 1736.

16. Ibid., 18r.

17. See C. C. Goen, Editor's Introduction, *The Works of Jonathan Edwards, 4, The Great Awakening,* ed. Goen (New Haven, 1972), 32–46.

18. MS fast sermon on 2 Chronicles 23:16, March 1737. Here Edwards again notes that Northampton has been exceedingly exalted "as a most honourable People in the Esteem & Eye of the world" (17v.), and "no Town this day on the Face of the Earth" was more obliged "Jointly & with one Consent to Resolve upon it that we will be the Lords People" (16r.).

19. Ibid., 8v.

20. Ibid., 7v., 9v.

21. Edwards included a copy of the 1742 covenant in his December 12, 1743, letter to Thomas Prince, who published it in the *Christian History,* 1 (January 14, 21, and 28, 1744): 367–81, reprinted in *The Great Awakening,* 550–54. The sermon Edwards preached for the occasion drew its doctrine from Joshua 24: 15–27: "A visible people of God on some occasions are called plainly and publicly to renew their covenant with God."

22. MS sermon on Ecclesiastes 5:4–6, October 1743, ll. 12v., 14v.

23. Ibid., 14v.

24. MS quarterly lecture on Joshua 24:21–22, August 1747, l. 5r.

25. MS sermon on Ps. 111:5, August 1745, l. 6r., and MS quarterly lecture on Joshua 24:21–22, August 1747, l. 6r.

26. Edwards, *Humble Inquiry,* 16, 76.

27. Solomon Williams, *The True State of the Question* (Boston, 1751), 20, 60.

28. Edwards, *Misrepresentations Corrected,* 80.

29. Ibid., 148.

30. See Jonathan Edwards, "Miscellanies," no. 338. For passages in Williams's *True State of the Question* related to owning the covenant, see pp. iv, 5, 8, 9, 11, 24, 28, 53, 81, 83, 111, 112, 122, 125, 130, 133, 134.

31. See Edwards, "Miscellanies," nos. 389, 393, 394. I am indebted to Kenneth P. Minkema for this reference. Thomas A. Schafer, as cited by Tracy in *Jonathan Edwards, Pastor,* 258, n. 1, points to an important discussion in "Miscellanies" no. 689, written in early 1736.

32. "Miscellanies" no. 617.

33. Edwards, MS fast sermon on 2 Chronicles 23:16 (1737), ll. 4v.–6v.

34. Ibid., 22r.

35. Williams, *The True State of the Question,* iv, 8–9.

36. Ibid., 53, 10.

37. Ibid., 134.

38. Edwards, MS sermon on Ezekiel 44:9 (1750), l. 17r.

39. Ibid., 17v.

40. Ibid., 18r.

41. Frothingham, *Discourse* (1750), 47; see also p. 37.

42. Edwards, *Humble Inquiry,* 71.

43. Ibid., 73.

44. Edwards, *Misrepresentations Corrected,* 10.

45. Frothingham, *Discourse,* 39.

46. Ibid.

47. Edwards, *A Farewell Sermon,* i–ii. See also the preface to *Humble Inquiry.*

48. Jonathan Edwards, *True Grace Distinguished from the Experience of Devils* (New York, 1753), 34.

49. Williams, *The True State of the Question,* 111.

50. Ibid.

51. Ibid., 11–14.

52. Jonathan Ashley, *An Humble Attempt to Give a Clear Account from Scripture* (Boston, 1753). These two sermons were first preached in Northampton, February 10, 1750.

53. The quotation from Locke is in Edwards's (7th) edition of Locke's *Essay concerning Human Understanding,* vol. 2, p. 103.

54. Edwards, *Misrepresentations Corrected,* 40–41.

55. John Locke, *An Essay concerning Human Understanding,* ed. Peter H. Nidditch (Oxford, 1975), Book III, chap. I, p. 402.

56. Ibid., 10, 476, 501.

57. Perry Miller incorrectly thought that Edwards had outgrown covenant theology altogether. See Conrad Cherry, *The Theology of Jonathan Edwards: A Reappraisal* (Garden City, N.Y., 1966), and Carl Bogue, *Jonathan Edwards and the Covenant of Grace* (Cherry Hill, N.J., 1975).

58. Alan Heimert, *Religion and the American Mind: From the Great Awakening to the Revolution* (Cambridge, Mass., 1966), 126. Harry S. Stout pointed to this interpretation as one of the few areas that had *not* been revised by post-Miller scholarship. See Stout, "The Puritans and Edwards," in Nathan O. Hatch and Harry S. Stout, eds., *Jonathan Edwards and the American Experience* (New York, 1988), 143.

59. Mark Valeri, "The New Divinity and the Revolution," *William and Mary Quarterly,* 3d Ser., XLVI (October 1989): 743, n. 4, notes that this older view can be seen in Edmund S. Morgan, "The American Revolution Considered as an Intellectual Movement," in Arthur M. Schlesinger, Jr., and Morton White, eds., *Paths of American Thought* (Boston, 1963), 11–33.

60. Stout, 157.

61. Ibid.

62. Valeri, 751, n. 18.

63. Ibid., 745. Valeri follows Norman Fiering, *Jonathan Edwards's Moral Thought and Its British Context* (Chapel Hill, 1981), in arguing that the moral philosophy of Francis Hutcheson had a great impact on Edwards. This interpretation has been challenged by Paul Ramsey in Appendix II, *The Works of Jonathan Edwards, 8, Ethical Writings* (New Haven, 1989), 692–93, n. 1.

64. Gerald McDermott, "Jonathan Edwards, The City on a Hill, and the Redeemer Nation: A Reappraisal," *Journal of Presbyterian History* (Spring 1991). See also McDermott, *One Holy and Happy Society: The Public Theology of Jonathan Edwards* (University Park, Penn., 1992).

65. Contrast, for example, William Williams, *The Duty and Interest of a People* (Boston, 1736), which was published with Edwards's account of the 1735 Northampton revival.

66. Heimert, 95, 100, 120, 157, 402, 425, and 470. See also Perry Miller, "From the Covenant to the Revival," *Nature's Nation* (Cambridge, Mass., 1967), 90–120.

67. Edwards, *Humble Attempt,* in *The Works of Jonathan Edwards, 5, Apocalyptic Writings,* ed. Stephen J. Stein (New Haven, 1977), 372–73, 428. Heimert, 115, claims that "the crucial premises of Calvinist rhetoric [of union] were disclosed in Edwards's argument for a concert of prayer."

68. Edwards, *Humble Attempt,* 430; see also 317, 371.

69. Ibid., 360–61, and 434.

70. See, for example, Solomon Stoddard, *An Appeal to the Learned* (Boston, 1709), 55, 68–69, 82. Like Stoddard, Congregationalists recognized that their individual, church, and national covenants were in fact merely the different aspects of the single covenant of grace. But their *practice,* as well as their rhetoric, often emphasized the *differences* between inhabitants in New England, members of particular churches, and saints qualified to attend the Lord's Supper. See Samuel Willard, *Covenant-Keeping the Way to Blessedness* (Boston, 1682), especially 26–28, 68–74, and 96–101. It is a mistake to assume that the individual and corporate aspects of covenanting created radically distinct covenants with incommensurate aims and logics; but one may err at the other extreme by arguing that "the boundaries between self and society" were always blurred by the "bipolar thrust" of a single unified doctrine (Theodore Dwight Bozeman, "Federal Theology and the 'National Covenant': An Elizabethan Presbyterian Case Study," *Church History* 61 [December 1992]: 394–407).

71. MS sermon on Ezekiel 44:9 (1750) l. 20r. Hypocrites though many of the Jews were, Edwards argues, they still promised to abide by the covenant with all their hearts and souls. Moses Mather argued in 1772, referring to Edwards's published writings, that "when the late President *Edwards* wrote upon this controversy, he kept this general [external] dispensation of the covenant of grace, out of both his own, and the reader's view, and predicated his arguments only upon the covenant of grace, taken in its most limited tenor." Mather, *A Brief View of the Manner in Which the Controversy about the Visible Church, Has Been Conducted, in the Present Day* (New Haven, 1772), 6.

72. Williams, in *The True State of the Question,* 129, quotes a passage from Stoddard's *Appeal to the Learned,* 84, and then amplifies it with his own remarks, 129–30. Technically, Williams acknowledged only a single covenant of grace that was exhibited in two ways: internally to those who are converted and externally to those who profess and enjoy church ordinances (23).

73. Edwards, *Misrepresentations Corrected,* 89.

74. Edwards, MS sermon on Leviticus 26:3–13, February 28, 1745, and MS sermon on Joshua 7:12, Fast on the Occasion of the war with France, June 28, 1744, and March 1755.

75. Williams, 9.

76. Edwards, *Humble Inquiry,* 84.

77. Williams, 87.

78. Edwards, *Misrepresentations Corrected,* 151.

79. Ibid., 152.

80. Williams, 133.

81. See Edwards, *True Grace Distinguished from the Experience of Devils* (1753). See also Edwards, *The Nature of True Virtue,* chap. 5, and Ramsey's discussion of the development of Edwards's concept of natural conscience in "Appendix II: Jonathan Edwards on Moral Sense, and the Sentimentalists," both in *The Works of Jonathan Edwards, 8, Ethical Writings,* 689–705.

82. Edwards, *Misrepresentations Corrected,* 169–71. Like the Pharisees of Christ's day, nominal Christians were at once closest to the kingdom of God and farthest from it. They enjoy the greatest of God's blessings, yet by so misimproving their privileges, they become more vile than heathens. Instead of taking pride in being members of God's privileged people, they should be confronting their own sin in fear and trembling. Nathaniel Appleton discusses this close-and-yet-far relationship in *Some Unregenerate Persons Not so Far*

from the Kingdom of God as Others (Boston, 1763). Appleton, however, unlike Edwards, argues that someone with a good understanding of doctrine *is* closer to the kingdom.

83. Edwards, *Humble Inquiry,* 128–29.

84. Nathanael Emmons (1745–1840), *A Dissertation on the Scriptural Qualifications for Admission and Access to the Christian Sacraments* (Worcester, Mass., 1793), 45. See also Emmons, *A Candid Reply to the Reverend Dr. Hemmenway's Remarks* (Worcester, Mass., 1795). Emmons studied under John Smalley (1738–1808), who in turn had been Bellamy's student.

85. Edwards, "Miscellanies," no. 1338, probably written after 1755 (see Ramsey, 692); MS sermon on Luke 16:19, June 1753.

86. Edwards, MS sermon on Joshua 7:12, "Fast on occasion of the war with France," June 28, 1744, preached again March 1755.

87. Edwards, MS sermon on Exodus 33:19, "Thanksgiving for victory over the Rebels," August 1746, preached again November 1754; MS sermon on 1 Kings 8:44–45, "Fast for success in Cape Breton expedition," April 4, 1745, preached again July 1755; MS Thanksgiving sermon on Jeremiah 51:5, December 5, 1745, preached again November 1757.

88. Cf. William Hobby's *Happiness of a People, Having God for Their Ally . . . on Occasion of an Expedition Design'd against Canada* (Boston, 1758).

89. Solomon Williams, *The Relations of God's People to Him* (New London, 1760). Cf. Eli Forbes, *God the Strength and Salvation of his People* (Boston, 1761), a sermon preached the following year on the same text (Exodus 15:2). Neither Forbes nor David Hall's *Israel's Triumph* (Boston, 1761), on Exodus 15:1, focuses on *how* the colonies "resemble" the tribes of Israel, as Williams does.

90. Williams, *Relations of God's People,* 10.

91. Ibid., 10–11.

92. This was Williams's version of what historian Nathan Hatch has termed the "civil millennialism" taking root after the wars with France. See Nathan O. Hatch, *The Sacred Cause of Liberty: Republican Thought and the Millennium in Revolutionary New England* (New Haven, 1977), chap. 1.

THREE

The Deist Connection

JONATHAN EDWARDS AND ISLAM

GERALD R. McDERMOTT

Toward the end of his life Jonathan Edwards launched a series of diatribes against Islam. This was not the first time, of course, that a Christian thinker had regarded Muslims with dismay. Edwards was continuing a long tradition of anti-Islamic sentiment that combined fear and loathing with curious fascination. Yet Edwards's hostility toward Islam evinced a new fervor and a new motive. His denunciations of Muhammad's tribe were unusually vitriolic because he considered Islam to be a foil for one of Reformed Christianity's most dangerous enemies: deism.

I

In some respects, Edwards regarded Islam with a certain ambivalence. For while he seemed to feel visceral hostility toward everything Islamic, he also wrote that Muslims are less blameworthy than wayward Protestants because the latter were brought up with greater light about Christ and true faith.[1] Since God's judgment of Muslims shall be "proportioned to their light," their condemnation shall be less severe than that of those who knew more.[2] Edwards also believed that Muslims have far more light about Christ than many "heathen" thinkers whom he roundly praised. The Qur'an, Edwards seemed happy to note, accurately portrays Jesus as a great prophet and messenger of God who was born of a virgin and without sin, healed the blind, and raised the dead. "The Alcoran" even recognizes Jesus as the Messiah "foretold in the law and the prophets." "Now, owning this," Edwards claimed, "is in effect owning the whole. This is the foundation of the whole, and proves all the rest."[3]

Yet, in typically Reformed fashion,[4] Edwards believed that the light given to Muhammad and Muslims only aggravated their condemnation, for they had shamelessly ignored or abused this light. Hence they deserved only contempt. Islam, he snarled, had a tendency "to debase, debauch, and corrupt the minds of such as received it." Muslims were "an ignorant and barbarous sort of people." The propagation of Islam showed "the extreme darkness, blindness, weakness, childishness, folly and madness of mankind in matters of religion . . . [and] how helpless mankind are, under ignorance and delusion in matters of religion." The Islamic faith contained things that "are too childish and ridiculous to be publicly mentioned in solemn assembly."[5]

The "heathen" philosophers, on the other hand, were given less light about the true God but taught it more faithfully. Despite conceding that they did not love God and were full of pride, Edwards fairly gushed with admiration for the religious truth they shared with Christians. Plato, he wrote, delivered "very noble and almost divine truths concerning the nature and attributes of the supreme God." Cicero was "the greatest and best philosopher that Rome or perhaps any other nation ever produced." Epictetus was an "admirable moralist." For a true sense of virtue, he had "no superior in the heathen world." Confucius knew by divine light that the heavens are not self-existent, and Lao Tzu that God is eternal and cannot be comprehended. Edwards believed that the Chinese knew of a Christ who would suffer and die to save the world.[6] Yet even they did not know, as Muhammad did, that *Jesus* was the Christ.

II

Edwards took up Islam's remarkable worldwide expansion in a section of his private notebooks (the *Miscellanies*) that was probably written after 1747—that is, in the last decade of his life.[7] In a 2,500-word essay he attempted to rebut the charge that "the propagation of Mahometanism" was "parallel with the propagation of Christianity."[8] More than half of his data are taken, both directly and indirectly, from Johann Friedrich Stapfer (1708–75), the German Reformed scholastic whose five-volume *Institutiones theologiae polemicae* (1743–47) served as one of his principal sources of knowledge about Islam. Edwards chose from Stapfer's material selectively to suit his own polemical purpose.[9] But while the form of his argument was somewhat creative, its content was conventional. Edwards was advancing nothing that contemporary orthodox controversialists had not already proposed.[10]

Edwards's first line of argument is that Islam represents intellectual regression and the suppression of free thought. Whereas Christianity advanced knowledge, Islam retarded its growth. Any increase of knowledge brought by Islam was "borrowed" from Christianity. Christianity was propagated in Jerusalem, "one of the greatest and most public cities in the world," among the Greeks and Romans, "the most knowing and learned in the world." The gospel encouraged "reasoning and inquiry." In contrast, Islam was developed in Arabia, "a dark corner of the earth" peopled by "an ignorant and barbarous sort." Their religion was promoted by "forbidding inquiry . . . [and] discouraging knowledge and learning."[11]

Second, Muhammad won followers because of the enticement of sensual rewards. While Christianity taught self-denial, Islam gratified human sensuality. Early Christianity did battle with ancient mores, but Islam simply accommodated itself to seventh-century cultural sensibilities. It encouraged the worst of human desires by permitting divorce on demand, blood revenge, and polygamy.[12] (This was several decades before Edward Gibbon's observation that in comparison to Solomon's appetite for wives, Muhammad was commendably modest!)[13]

Third, because it appealed to base human desires, Islam never encountered much opposition. Christianity, on the other hand, contended against the "strongest empire ever." But while the gospel triumphed by the power of meekness, Islam won conversions only by the power of the sword.[14]

Edwards's last line of argument was an appeal to the standard orthodox assumption (at least until the middle of the eighteenth century) that miracles are the best authentication of revelation.[15] He wrote that "Christianity is built on certain great and wonderful visible facts" such as Christ's resurrection and other miracles, but Islam has "no facts for its proof and foundation, . . . only Mahomet's pretences to intercourse with heaven, and his success in rapine, murder, and violence." While Christ's miracles were performed publicly and attested to by people writing near the time and places of those miracles, Muhammad's miracles were private and lacked "public attestations of heaven."[16]

III

Other religious leaders of the eighteenth century also showed considerable interest in Islam.[17] In part, this interest was the continuation of a long tradition in Christian apologetics, beginning with Thomas Aquinas's *Summa Contra Gentiles* (1259–64), a manual for Christian missionaries in Spain. It was also stimulated by traders' contacts with Muslims at Constantinople and in Hungary, the Turkish empire, Syria, Persia, and the East Indies. War had also played a role: in 1453 Constantinople fell to the (Muslim) Turks, and in 1683 Turkish forces were defeated outside Vienna. And there had been a general growth of interest in foreign cultures, particularly the mysterious and exotic East.

But why did leaders such as Edwards show such hostility?[18] There was little or no fear of Muslim military power or of conversions in the West to Islam. There was historic memory of the Crusades, but this seemed to play little or no role in Edwards's thinking.[19] What *did* figure in Edwards's thinking, however, was eschatology. Edwards believed that Islam was one of the devil's two world-historical forces stalking the earth in the latter days. It was one of the two great works fashioned by the devil in the Middle Ages (the other, of course, was the Roman papacy) that had become, since that time, twin Antichrists. Catholicism had taken over the Western empire, while Islam had swallowed up the Eastern empire. The first is the kingdom of the "beast" and the second is the kingdom of the "false prophet," both described in John's Revelation. "Heathenism" (meaning, for most eighteenth-century orthodox writers, all non-Christian religion beyond Judaism and Islam) is the kingdom of the "dragon," a third demonic power in Revelation. This false trinity will work in concert near the end of the world to destroy the truth, but will finally be vanquished at the battle of Armageddon.[20]

In the meantime one could scan secular history with Bible in hand to plot the course of the eschaton. Edwards did just that, of course, and recorded his copious observations in his notebooks. There he wrote that the Turks, who "have been the most terrible scourge to Christendom, that ever divine providence made use of," were the 200 million mounted troops who, according to John, were released to kill a third of humankind by three plagues of fire, smoke, and sulfur.[21] At the very beginning of that same chapter in Revelation Edwards found Muhammad himself. He is the star that fell to the earth (for Edwards, this described Muhammad's fall from Christianity) in verse 1 and released locusts which sting like scorpions. Those stung, writes John, will seek death but will not find it.[22]

For Edwards, it was clear that Muhammad and Islam are the referents of this passage. After all, it was a wind that blew from Arabia to bring locusts to Egypt, so Arabia is obviously the country of locusts. The poison in the tail of the locusts is therefore Islam, because Muhammad's religion will kill the soul. The tormenting pain is the pain of the afflicted conscience being tempted to convert to Islam. Seeking death, then, is wishing to be convinced of the truth of Islam so that the painful cries of the conscience will no longer be heard.[23]

If that interpretation seems tortured, Edwards was simply the latest in a long line of Western interpreters to be so pained. As early as the ninth century two Spaniards, one a priest and the other a layman (Eulogius and Paul Alvarus), developed the idea that the rule of Islam was a preparation for the final appearance of Antichrist. In the eleventh century Abbott

Joachim of Fiore proclaimed that the end of the world was at hand and Antichrist's chief instruments were the Saracens. Martin Luther also believed the end was at hand, but was perhaps even more pessimistic about Islam. It was Gog (the papacy was Magog), Muhammad was the little horn in Daniel's vision (7:8), and the expansion of Islam was the little horn's crowding of the other horns. Christendom, Luther despaired, would probably be engulfed by Islam. Interestingly, although Calvin judged Muhammad to be an apostate, he refused to speculate about the eschatological significance of Islam. But then Revelation was one of the few books on which Calvin never wrote a commentary, and the only book on which Edwards did![24]

Edwards's eschatological vision of Islam differed in two respects from that of most of his predecessors. First, he did not believe the end of the world was imminent. Instead, he foresaw a 250-year period of conflict and revival to come before the millennium.[25] Intriguingly, he predicted that the two most formidable religious forces still on the scene in the twentieth century would be Roman Catholicism and Islam[26]—not far from the truth.

Second, as I have argued elsewhere, eschatology was more important to Edwards than to most Reformed thinkers. Though not the center of his theology, it was consistently prominent in, and even essential to, much of his thought.[27] Therefore his designation of Islam as one of the Antichrist twins means that "Mohametanism" played a larger role in the history of redemption for Edwards than for others in his tradition.

IV

Islam's role in eschatological history, however, does not fully explain Edwards's hostility. After all, other Christian thinkers had known this eschatological tradition but nevertheless regarded Islam with considerable favor. Pope Gregory VII, for example, speculated that because of their obedience to the Qur'an, Muslims might have eternal salvation in the bosom of Abraham.[28] Dante placed Avicenna, Averroes, and Saladin in limbo as the only moderns among the sages and heroes of antiquity.[29] William of Tripoli said that Muslims were not far from salvation.[30] For John Wycliffe, the church was full of the same vices as Islam, but to a greater degree. Muslims could be saved if at the moment of death they "believe in the Lord Jesus Christ."[31] Some of the Radical Reformers saw Muslims as members of an interfaith church of spiritual Semites with three covenants—Judaic, Christian, and Muslim.[32] And seventeenth-century Reformed divine Richard Baxter was willing to grant salvation to those (outside the "Jewish church") who did not have "knowledge of Christ *incarnate*." Edwards, however, was not so willing.[33]

What made Edwards unwilling were the deists.[34] They were using Islam as a stick to shake at their orthodox opponents. Deist Thomas Chubb, for instance, argued that "the great prevalence of *Mahometanism*" was *not* due primarily to the sword, but that the sword may have assisted its later growth. Then, in a move that perturbed his orthodox readers and may have incited Edwards's criticism of Islam's propagation, Chubb alleged that Christianity's propagation was no different.[35] Matthew Tindal celebrated the "*Moammarites,* a famous sect among the *Mahometans,*"[36] who knew that reason is the only reliable tool for interpreting the metaphors and allegories of the Qur'an. If other Muslims ignored the Law of Nature (given to humans by reason alone) in blind submission to the words of the Qur'an, Tindal went on, they were no worse than Christians who made the same mistake. John Toland concluded that Muslims were really "a sort or sect of Christians," and closer to the original gospel than the historical church. An anonymous author in a 1745 issue of *The American Magazine* wrote that Christians' treatment of other religionists was no better than that of Muslims. Christianity had "prov'd as brutal, bloody and inhuman as Mohametanism."[37] By the last decades of the century, it had become a characteristic deist move to quote Islamic sources or praise Islam in contradistinction to Christianity.[38]

If the intellectual atmosphere of the eighteenth century is evidence that Edwards may have had deism in the background when he wrote about Islam, his actual arguments against Islam contain compelling internal evidence that his thinking about—and therefore hostility toward—Islam was shaped in large part by deistic challenges to Protestant orthodoxy. In a long series of intricate arguments against deism in his *Miscellanies,* Edwards makes two principal arguments. For each argument he uses Islam as a star witness to substantiate his claims.[39]

The deists were claiming the capability of human reason to discover the truths of natural religion, which alone are sufficient for salvation. Therefore, they said, revelation is not needed to guide humans to virtue in this life and happiness in the next.[40] The first argument which Edwards used to counter these claims was the assertion that pagan religion is derived from revelation—what might be called the trickle-down theory of revelation. What is true in non-Christian religions came not from unassisted reason but from revelation, by tradition from the ancient founders of nations[41] or from the Jews. The notion of sacrifice to atone for sin, for example, was given to all nations through Noah and his descendants. Noah had received this by tradition from his ancestors, who heard it in turn from God himself. Plato learned that idolatry is wrong only after traveling to the East, where he heard it from the Jews. It is no wonder, Edwards reasoned, that those furthest from revelation—such as the American Indians and remote tribes of Asia and India—are the "most brutish." Their traditions are "more worn out and they are more distant from places enlightened with revelation."[42]

For Edwards, Islam was a perfect illustration of this pattern. It was only because of the revelation provided by Christianity that the Islamic world condemned polytheism, and all the truth found in Islam was directly taken from Christianity. Whatever light the pre-Islamic Arabian tribes had was derived from "the glimmerings of the gospel which had been diffused over great part of the world." Islam itself had no truth of its own; hence the propagation of Islam may be considered a part of the propagation of Christianity. Therefore, Edwards concludes, "the great propagation of the Mahometan religion," far from being evidence of natural religion, "is confirmation of revealed religion."[43] Edwards thereby turned the deists' appropriation of Islam upside down to prove that deist claims could not stand.

The second argument which Edwards used to rebut deist claims was that nature and reason can never produce true religion. Edwards charged that reason is unreliable in matters of religion. The philosophers searched for clear knowledge of God for thousands of years, but in vain. Their search was relatively fruitless because unassisted reason will lead only to absurd notions. Many great philosophers, for example, have concluded that the world is eternal. This absurd conclusion is evidence that it is almost impossible for naked reason to prove a creation. Even Cicero, the "greatest and best philosopher," said good and evil persons have the same destiny in the next life. If he was so wrong, Edwards asked, what about the rest of humanity, who are far less intelligent than he?[44]

But even if natural reason were somehow able to penetrate the divine mysteries, it would be overwhelmed by the human "inclination to delusion in things of religion."[45] Human nature is such that it tends to pervert what little religious truth it is given and turn it into idolatry. As evidence for this claim, Edwards pointed to American Indians, Tartars, and Chinese peasants, who still worship "stocks and stones and devils"[46] despite trying to perfect their religions for five thousand years. There is no innate sense of God, at least "clear and sure knowledge of his nature and relation to us." Nature may be able to teach us how to continue in favor with God, but not how to regain it after we have lost it.[47]

Edwards argued that history had demonstrated this human tendency to turn revelation into idolatry. This happened after the flood, and after revelations had been given to Abraham and Isaac, Melchizedek, Job, Jacob and Joseph, and Moses. It also happened after the apostolic era. And the cardinal example in church history was Islam. The Islamic part of the world had been given revelation through the Christian church and had accepted it to such a degree that it became largely Christian. After Muhammad, however, this region turned to the idolatry of Islam. In Edwards's words, it "fell away to Mohametanism."[48] Once more, then, Islam was used by Edwards as a principal illustration for his most important arguments against the deists.[49]

V

Edwards's hostility to Islam, fired by his struggle against deism, demonstrates that his view of significant religious others was shaped in large part by internal apologetic demands. Islam as a living faith deserving appreciation seemed to be beyond his ken. He looked at Islam through the eyes of a determined apologist for strict Reformed doctrine and New Light experience in a culture that was making enlightened reasonableness the criterion of faith.

Edwards's treatment of Islam also suggests the remarkable degree to which Western knowledge of Islam since the eighteenth century has been distorted. Edwards slavishly followed his sources, who were seventeenth- and eighteenth-century controversialists. Their reports contained an astonishing number of inaccuracies and distortions. For example, their term for Islam—Mahometanism—reflected the mistaken belief of some in that era that Muslims worshiped Muhammad. They tiresomely repeated the misleading charge that most or all Muslim conversions occurred at the point of a sword.[50] They ignored the distinguished tradition of Islamic learning that sometimes encouraged rational inquiry,[51] and the fact that Jews and Christians often have been treated tolerantly and respectfully by Muslims, perhaps more than could be said of non-Christians in predominantly Christian lands over the same centuries or even of minority Christian bodies that lived independently of Rome.[52] Edwards's sources never mentioned that most Muslims were not polygamists or that in Muslim folklore lustful looking at another person is equivalent to fornication, in precisely the same sense Jesus intended in the Sermon on the Mount.[53]

They never mention that Muslim restrictions on polygamy were not simply indulgences to Arab passion but also restrictions on the loose and unregulated practices of the Jahiliya period in Arabia. Nor do they recognize that divorce was said by Muhammad to be the most detestable of permitted things, or that the Qur'an counsels immediate arbitration between spouses when there is danger of a split. Muslim laws on marriage and divorce cannot be rightly considered mere accommodation to Arab sensuality.[54]

Despite Edwards's hostility and misunderstanding, his treatment of Islam suggests ways in which he could contribute to interreligious understanding. Unlike many of his later disciples, Edwards asserted confidently that there is substantial and genuine truth in non-Christian religions. He believed that Islam, for example, teaches much truth about Christ, that the Holy Spirit inspired Socrates and Plato, and that the Chinese were given hints of the Trinity by revelation.

But in contrast to his deist contemporaries and some interreligious dialoguers today, Edwards rejected the possibility of any true religion arising from reason or religious consciousness. Edwards was too convinced of reason's relative inability in matters of religion and of human nature's inclination to idolatry to affirm any natural human capacity to find the true God. However, Edwards's treatment of non-Christian religions points to a kind of interreligious dialogue in which a Christian can learn from non-Christian traditions. Although Edwards never explicitly conceded the point, in practice he learned from religious others. For example, there are indications that the central thesis of his religious project, the notion that true religion is based on a vision of God's beauty, was shaped less by the Bible or the Reformed tradition than by Neoplatonic influences. So while holding to the finality of Christ as the only ontological way to God, he nevertheless demonstrated in practice that a non-Christian religious tradition can help Christians better understand their own tradition. Perhaps if he had not been battling deism, Edwards could have learned something from Islam as well.

NOTES

1. See John Wilson, ed., *A History of the Work of Redemption,* vol. 9 of *The Works of Jonathan Edwards* (New Haven, 1989), 489–90, and Jonathan Edwards, "Man's Natural Blindness in Religion," in Edward Hickman, ed., vol. 2 of *The Works of Jonathan Edwards* (London, 1834; reprinted Edinburgh, 1974), 250.

2. Jonathan Edwards, "On the Medium of Moral Government," in Hickman, ed., *Works,* 2:488.

3. Jonathan Edwards, "Mahometanism compared with Christianity—particularly with respect to their propagation," in Hickman, ed., *Works,* 2:493 [hereafter referred to as "Mahometanism"]. These quotes are taken from a slightly edited transcription of a 2,500-word discussion of Islam in Edwards's private notebooks (no. 1334 in the *Miscellanies*). See notes 8 and 9 below. Most scholars of Islam would hold that affirming Jesus as the Messiah does not "prove all the rest," for Muhammad did not mean by Messiah what Edwards meant by the term. Besides denying both the crucifixion and resurrection, Muhammad denied that anyone, even a Messiah, could save anyone from his or her sin; Qur'an 82.17–19; 40.18–20; 4.157–159; 4.158–59. The Qur'an teaches that Jesus was "raised up" to Allah. A common Muslim interpretation is that he never died a human death but was translated to Paradise, like Enoch.

4. See, for example, John Calvin, *Institutes of the Christian Religion,* ed. John T. McNeill (Philadelphia, 1960), Book I, chap. iv.

5. Edwards, "Mahometanism" 492, 493; "Man's Natural Blindness," 249.

6. Edwards, *Miscellanies,* nos. 979, 1162, 1181, 1236.

7. Dating is based on the work of Thomas A. Schafer, editor of the Yale University edition of the *Miscellanies.* Most of Edwards's reflections on the world religions were recorded in his last decade, most of which he spent at Stockbridge. One wonders if his firsthand contact with "heathen" Indians may have prompted this interest.

8. The differences between Edwards's original essay and its transcription in nineteenth-century editions of his works are largely stylistic. When the nineteenth-century editor thought Edwards's language too coarse, he substituted a new word or eliminated Edwards's

word: e.g., "promulgated" was substituted for "sounded out," "existed" for "was," and "blinding the eyes" for "hoodwinking mankind and blinding the eyes." Only one section, approximately 300 words, is omitted from Edwards's notebook. It does not contain anything substantially different from the printed text, but it amplifies and dramatizes Edwards's conviction that Islam opposes critical inquiry and was propagated by the sword. In the omitted section, for instance, Edwards quotes Johann Friedrich Stapfer (1708–75), the German Reformed scholastic: "Omnes enim infideles, qui religionem illam non amplecterentur interficere jubet Mahamet" (For Mohammad ordered the destruction of all those who did not embrace that religion). The result is that Edwards's printed comments on Islam are less vitriolic than what he actually wrote in his private notebooks. All quotations from this section are identical to Edwards's original words.

9. Stapfer's section on Islam is fifty-two pages long, approximately 16,000 words. In contrast, Edwards's discussion in no. 1334 of the *Miscellanies* takes up about 3,000 words. But while Stapfer treats many aspects of Islamic belief and history, no. 1334 focuses exclusively on Islam's propagation.

10. It is evident from Edwards's catalogue of reading that Edwards was familiar with the following works which were anti-Muslim in whole or in part: Philip Skelton, *Deism Revealed* (1749); James Miller, *Mahomet the Imposter. A Tragedy* (1744); Robert Millar, *History of the Propagation of Christianity* (1731); Daniel Defoe, *Dictionarium Sacrum or a Dictionary of All Religions* (1704); Thomas Broughton, *Bibliotheca Historico Sacra* (1737–39, reissued as *An Historical Dictionary of All Religions* (1742); George Sale's translation of and preface to *The Koran* (1734); and the above-mentioned Stapfer theology. We don't know if he read all of these works, but his arguments are very similar to theirs.

11. Edwards, "Mahometanism," 492. In *Notes on the Scriptures* no. 241, Edwards wrote, "The Arabs were above all nations a wild People and have been so through all ages . . . [with] fierce qualities . . . [they] have ever lived in professed Enmity with all mankind . . . and they have continued in a state of perpetual Hostility with the Rest of their Brethren." He went on to note that no one has been able to subdue them—neither the Romans nor the Parthians, nor any of their successors.

12. Ibid.

13. Edward Gibbon, *The Decline and Fall of the Roman Empire* (New York, n.d.), 3: 116.

14. Edwards, "Mahometanism," 492.

15. John Locke, "A Discourse of Miracles," *The Works of John Locke* (London, 1768), IV: 226–27. See David A. Pailin, *Attitudes to Other Religions: Comparative Religion in Seventeenth- and Eighteenth-Century Britain* (Manchester, 1984), 86.

16. Edwards, "Mahometanism," 492–93. The notion that Muhammad was an imposter was common to Christian attacks on Islam and was spread most widely by Humphrey Prideaux's *True Nature of Imposture Fully Display'd in the Life of Mahomet with a Discourse annexed, for the Vindicating of Christianity from this Charge; Offered to the Consideration of the Deists of the Present Age* (2nd London ed., 1697).

17. See, for instance, John Wesley, sermon LXVIII, "The General Spread of the Gospel," in *Works*, IX; and, more generally, Pailin, *Attitudes to Other Religions.*

18. Wesley, for instance, found "all the principles of pure religion" in a story written by a Muslim, but determined Muslims themselves to be "as void of mercy as lions and tygers, as much given up to brutal lusts as bulls or goats; so that they are in truth a disgrace to human nature." George Sale, a London lawyer who translated the Qur'an in 1734, said that Muhammad gave the Arabs the best religion that was possible in the circumstances—monotheism to replace idolatry and some moral and divine virtues "not unworthy even a Christian's perusal." But he also said that its conquests by the power of the sword provide "one of the most convincing proofs that Mohammedism [sic] was no other than a human invention." Wesley, "The General Spread of the Gospel," 234; see Pailin, 48; Sale, "Preliminary Discourse," in *The Koran* (New York, 1984), 45, 77, 35.

19. Edwards by and large ignored the Crusades. Of the twenty-five-odd discussions of Islam that I have found in his published writings and *Miscellanies,* only one has any possible reference to the Crusades; even that is debatable. Hickman, ed., *Works,* 1:471. The only explicit reference to the Crusades does not mention Islam; instead it criticizes the papacy. Stein, ed., *Apocalyptic Writings,* 237–38. In Edwards's reviews of redemption history in both his *History of the Work of Redemption* and *Apocalyptic Writings,* there is no mention of the Crusades.

20. *History of the Work of Redemption,* 410–11, 463. For surveys of Edwards's eschatology, see Stephen J. Stein, introduction to Stein, ed., *Apocalyptic Writings,* vol. 5 of *The Works of Jonathan Edwards* (New Haven, 1977), and Gerald R. McDermott, *One Holy and Happy Society: The Public Theology of Jonathan Edwards* (University Park, 1992), 37–92.

21. *History of the Work of Redemption,* 415–16; *Apocalyptic Writings,* 407.

22. *Apocalyptic Writings,* 103.

23. Ibid., 103.

24. R.W. Southern, *Western Views of Islam in the Middle Ages* (Cambridge, 1962), 22–26, 40–42, 105; George Huntston Williams, "Erasmus and the Reformers on Non-Christian Religions and *Salus Extra Ecclesiam,*" in Theodore Rabb and Jerrold Seigel, eds., *Action and Conviction in Early Modern Europe: Essays in Memory of E. H. Harbison,* 344, 361.

25. I have argued this thesis in my *One Holy and Happy Society,* 50–60, 77–90.

26. See McDermott, *One Holy and Happy Society,* 82. Edwards believed that evangelical Protestantism would also be on the scene, struggling with these two religions.

27. Ibid., 41–50, 90–92.

28. Gregory, letter (ca. 1076) to the Moorish ruler al-Nasir ibn Alennas, contained in Migne, *Patrologia Latina,* CXLVIII, cols. 450ff.; cited in *The Declaration on Non-Christian Religions* in Walter M. Abbott, S.J., ed., *The Documents of Vatican II* (New York, 1966), 663 n. 14.

29. Dante, *Inferno,* iv, 129, 143–44.

30. William of Tripoli, *Tractatus de Statu Saracenorum,* cited in Southern, 62.

31. Southern, 80–82; Wycliffe, *De Fide Catholica (Opera Minora),* 112, cited in Southern, 82.

32. Williams, 363–65.

33. Richard Baxter, *The Reasons of the Christian Religion* (London, 1667), 201–2; see also Sidney H. Rooy, *The Theology of Missions in the Puritan Tradition: A Study of Representative Puritans: Richard Sibbes, Richard Baxter et al* (Delft, 1965), 89. Edwards flirted with the possibility of the salvation of non-Christians since the days of Christ, but never explicitly allowed for it. He wrote that they "have not been left utterly destitute of all benefit of divine revelation. They are not so entirely and absolutely cast off, but that there is a possibility of their being reconciled." He speculated that revelations given to ["heathen"] might be of "great benefit . . . to their own souls" without stipulating the nature, mode or result of that benefit. In his *History of the Work of Redemption* he suggested that some humans were saved without explicit knowledge of Jesus Christ, for "souls . . . were saved before Christ came," and God has justified souls "in all ages." Edwards, "On the Medium of Moral Government," Hickman, ed., *Works,* 487; *Miscellanies,* no. 1162; *History of the Work of Redemption,* 128–29, 120.

34. For British deism (the deism with which Edwards was most familiar), see John Redwood, *Reason, Ridicule and Religion: The Age of Enlightenment in England, 1660–1750* (Cambridge, Mass., 1976). For surveys of Enlightenment deism, see "The Religion of Nature," in John Herman Randall, Jr., *The Making of the Modern Mind: A Survey of the Intellectual Background of the Present Day* (Boston, 1926), and Alfred Owen Aldridge, "Deism," in Gordon Stein, ed., *The Encyclopedia of Unbelief* (Buffalo, 1985). On American deism, see Kerry S. Walters, *Rational Infidels: The American Deists* (Wolfeboro, N.H., 1992), and *The American Deists: Voices of Reason and Dissent in the Early Republic* (Lawrence, 1992). James Turner, *Without God, without Creed: The Origins of Unbelief in America* (Baltimore, 1985), is

particularly incisive. On the English deists who particularly concerned Edwards, see chap. 3 of Peter Harrison, *"Religion" and the Religions in the English Enlightenment* (Cambridge, 1990). Turner has recently shown that the orthodox fear that deism would undermine theism in America was unjustified. The danger that deism would threaten Christian theism was real, but greatly exaggerated. See Turner, *Without God, without Creed,* 44–49. This is particularly true when Edwards was writing about Islam in the 1740s and 1750s, at least three decades before deism came into its own in America. Turner, 52.

35. Chubb, *The Posthumous Works of Mr. Thomas Chubb,* vol. II, 48. The notion that the propagation of Islam and Christianity were very similar was fairly common in the eighteenth century. William Paley, for example, pronounced that the success of Islam is "the only event" in the history of humanity that bears comparison with the spread of Christianity. Thomas Stackhouse added that "of all false Religions, the *Mahometan* came nearest to the *Christian* in the swift Manner of its Propagation; for in a small Time it over-ran a great Part of the *eastern* World." William Robertson gasped, "There is nothing similar in the history of mankind" to the rapidity of Islam's spread. It was probably because of the prevalence of this claim that Edwards spent 2,500 words trying to refute it. Paley, *Evidences of Christianity,* 3rd ed. (Cambridge, 1901), 341; Stackhouse, *Compleat Body of Divinity,* 720; Robertson, *Historical Disquisitions of India,* 92; both Stackhouse and Robertson cited in Pailin, 100.

36. Tindal, *Christianity as Old as the Creation* (orig. ed. 1730; reprint New York, 1978), 202–3. The Moammarites were probably Mu'tazilites, since Mu'ammar was the oldest of the four principal founders of the Mu'tazili school. M. Montgomery Watt, *Islamic Philosophy and Theology* (Edinburgh, 1962), 59, 69.

37. John Toland, *Nazarenus: or Jewish, Gentile and Mahometan Christianity* (1718), 4; "Eusebius," "The Unreasonableness of Persecution," *The American Magazine* (June 1745), 256.

38. Herbert M. Morais, *Deism in Eighteenth-Century America* (New York, 1960), 144. In 1771 Ezra Stiles met Theophilus Cossart, a German printer who had lived in Cairo, who appeared "to be a Freethinker & Philosopher" and thought "the morals of the Mahometans superior to those of the Christians in general." Franklin B. Dexter, ed., *The Literary Diary of Ezra Stiles, D.D., LL.D* (New York, 1901) 1:179–80.

39. Edwards's essay on the propagation of Islam (*Misc.* 1334), which I discussed in section II, is one of a large number of long entries in his *Miscellanies* aimed directly or indirectly against deism. Typically their titles include the words "Christian religion," and they argue that it is true, despite the protests and arguments of deists. See, e.g., nos. 125, 443, 986, 1230, 1236, 1297, 1314, 1337.

40. Deists also claimed that revelation is full of unreasonable and therefore preposterous mysteries. See, for example, John Toland, *Christianity Not Mysterious* (London, 1696).

41. Edwards frequently repeats this claim in his private notebooks but rarely explains it beyond saying that Greek, Roman, and Chinese philosophers believed the same. See, for example, *Misc.* 959, 960, 962, 977. In his *Notes on the Scriptures,* however, he explains that the antediluvians got instructions from Adam (which he presumably received from God), and those after the flood were instructed by those who "came out of the ark." Note 111 on Job 8:8. Edwards also says that revelation came directly from the Holy Spirit to such as Socrates, Plato and other wise philosophers; *Misc.* 1162.

42. *Misc.* 977; *History of the Work of Redemption,* 134–37; "Observations on the Scriptures," in Hickman, ed., *Works* 2:479; "Observations on the Facts and Evidences of Christianity, and the Objections of Infidels," in Hickman, ed., 2:463.

43. "Observations on the Facts and Evidences," 464; "Mahometanism," 492, 493, 493.

44. "Observations on the Facts and Evidences," 461; "Observations on the Scriptures," 475, 476, 478; *Misc.* 979.

45. "Man's Natural Blindness," 250.

46. "Observations on the Scriptures," 476. This was an idiomatic expression common in the eighteenth century; Edwards may have derived this argument from Philip Skelton's *Deism Revealed* (p. 76), to which he referred repeatedly in his *Miscellanies.*

47. "On the Medium of Moral Government," in Hickman, ed., 2:491.

48. "Man's Natural Blindness," 249.

49. Edwards was not alone in his concerns about deism. A Philadelphia newspaper column worried in 1735, for example, that deism was poisoning the minds of the young. *The American Weekly Museum,* October 9–16, 1735 (no. 824), cited in Morais, *Deism in Eighteenth-Century America,* 79. In the following decade evangelist George Whitefield noted anxiously that deists were trying to convert "moral men," and he seemed relieved when a deist yielded to his evangelical preaching. At about the same time Jonathan Dickinson, the New Side Presbyterian pastor, was concerned that guests at inns and coffeehouses were entertaining deistic notions. Whitefield, *A Continuation of the Rev. Mr. Whitefield's Journal. etc.* (London, 1744), 66–67; Dickinson, *Familiar Letters* (Glasgow, 1775), 2. Cited in Morais, 80.

50. Islamicist Frederick M. Denny writes, "Throughout the Near East and North Africa, conversion was generally a voluntary affair, but at times non-Muslims suffered persecution, discrimination and other indignities." *Islam and the Muslim Community* (San Francisco, 1987). See also Norman Daniel, *Islam and the West* (Edinburgh, 1960); Fred McGraw Donner, *The Early Islamic Conquests* (Princeton, 1981); M. A. Shaban, *Islamic History A.D. 600–750 (A.H. 132): A New Interpretation* (Cambridge, 1971); Albert Hourani, *A History of the Arab Peoples* (Cambridge, Mass., 1991).

51. See W. Montgomery Watt, *The Formative Period of Islamic Thought* (Edinburgh, 1973).

52. One thinks, for example, of Rome's persecution of the Cathars, Patari, Humiliati, Waldensians, Albigenses, and Huguenots. On Muslim treatment of other religions, see Frederick M. Denny, *An Introduction to Islam* (New York, 1985), 125–29; Nehemiah Lavtzion, ed., *Conversion to Islam* (New York, 1979); and Richard Bell, *The Origin of Islam in Its Christian Environment* (London, 1926), 185–86.

53. Denny, *Introduction to Islam,* 302.

54. Ibid., 303, 305; Qur'an 4.35.

FOUR

The Other Unfinished "Great Work"

JONATHAN EDWARDS, MESSIANIC PROPHECY, AND "THE HARMONY OF THE OLD AND NEW TESTAMENT"

KENNETH P. MINKEMA

In his famous letter of October 19, 1757, to the trustees of the College of New Jersey, Jonathan Edwards outlined his reasons why he should *not* accept their offer of the presidency. Besides his delicate constitution, Edwards cited his "course of employ in my study," which he feared would be permanently interrupted in governing a college. Too often he had been forced to put aside favorite projects—by the revivals of the 1730s and 1740s, by the communion controversy that ended in his dismissal from Northampton in 1750; now he wished to spend as much time as possible in his beloved study, before his giant "scrutore."

Edwards did not live to see any more of his books in print, but his unpublished writings reveal that, like another great philosopher before him, Isaac Newton, Edwards in his mature years found a rejuvenated interest in his lifelong love, the Bible, and became absorbed in the esoteric realm of precise scriptural exegesis. John F. Wilson writes that, shortly before his death, "Edwards was at a transitional point in his career as a theologian, preparing to return to exposition of strictly biblical themes but in a more rationalistic manner."[1] Many of his late "Miscellanies" and other manuscript notebooks, devoted to defending the truth of the Christian revelation, represent a much larger, though largely unappreciated, vein in Edwards's thought.[2]

Most significant among Edwards's later projects is a virtually unknown treatise—described thus far only by Stephen J. Stein—that explicates the messianic focus of biblical prophecy, where "prophecy" for Edwards comprehends promises concerning the Messiah already fulfilled and yet to come.[3] In its parts and method, as in the writers and trends it was addressing, the work was to be Edwards's contribution to the transatlantic debate over biblical messianic prophecy and the trustworthiness of the Bible.

Here we shall begin by briefly considering the place of this treatise within Edwards's larger corpus and by sketching its relation to the history of Christian scriptural exegesis. Though Edwards does not specifically name any of his opponents in the treatise, it is a polemical work; the second section therefore identifies authors and trends that Edwards was criticizing, particularly Deists, or "free thinkers," as well as those writers who eschewed a historical and literal interpretation of Scripture. And the concluding section reconstructs the structure and method of its component parts, focusing in turn on the themes of prophecy and fulfillment, typology, and harmonization. In combining his copious observations on these themes, Edwards wished to demonstrate not only the authenticity and unity of the Scriptures but also that biblical prophecies, types, and harmonies find their ultimate meaning in the person of the incarnate Logos as Messiah.

In his letter to the trustees, Edwards describes this treatise as one of two "great works" currently occupying his attention. The first, *A History of the Work of Redemption,* is well known among scholars of colonial America. Edwards then goes on to describe the other work at some length:

> I have also for my own profit and entertainment, done much towards another great work, which I call *the Harmony of the old and new Testament* in three Parts—The first considering the prophecies of the Messiah, his Redemption and Kingdom; the Evidences of their Referrences to the Messiah &c. comparing them all one with another, demonstrating their agreement and true scope and sense; also considering all the various particulars wherein these prophecies have their exact fulfillment; shewing the universal, precise, and admirable correspondence between predictions and events. The second Part: Considering the Types of the old testament, shewing the evidence of their being intended as representations of the great things of the gospel of Christ: and the agreement of the type with the antitype.—The third and great Part, considering the harmony of the old and new testament, as to doctrine and precept.—In the course of this work, I find there will be occasion for an explanation of a very great part of the holy scripture; which may, in such a view be explained in a method, which to me seems the most entertaining and profitable, best tending to lead the mind to a view of the true spirit, design, life and soul of the scriptures, as well as to their proper use and improvement.[4]

If size is any indication, "The Harmony of the Old and New Testament" was truly a major effort for Edwards, over 500 pages in manuscript. More important than sheer length, however, was the prodigious amount of labor that went into the work, which represents Edwards's accumulated knowledge on the subject. Alongside his repository of scriptural commentary consisting of "Notes on the Scripture" and the "Blank (or Interleaved) Bible," "The Harmony of the Old and New Testament" is the result of decades of close biblical study and reflection. But where the "Blank Bible" follows canonical order, the "Harmony" arranges biblical exegesis according to a preconceived method.

The interpretive methods Edwards planned to utilize in "The Harmony of the Old and New Testament" were as old as Christianity itself. The disciplines of delineating the fulfillment of prophecy, of finding typological links between the testaments, and of harmonizing the holy texts began in the second century after Christ. Some early commentators argued that the testaments were irreparably contradictory, while others held that prophecy and fulfillment were important links between the testaments that confirmed their divine origins.[5] Over the centuries, Christian exegetes came to rely increasingly on symbolism and allegory to demonstrate the unity of the testaments. But there were some who were hesitant about allegorization, chief among them Augustine, who attached increasing importance to the historical sense of Scripture, which included the prophetic and typological dimensions. During the Reformation, John Calvin reemphasized the parity of the testaments rather than follow other Protestant leaders such as Martin Luther in relegating the Old Testament to an inferior status.[6] Together the Augustinian sense of Scripture and the Calvinist view of the inner relationship of the Bible were part of the English dissenting tradition that Edwards inherited.

Surprisingly, similar issues still prevailed in the eighteenth as in the fifth century, though now filtered through the Reformation and under vastly different historical circumstances. In biblical interpretation as in doctrine, the first half of the eighteenth century was the Age of Rationalism and the Age of Deism. It was largely agreed that revelation was agreeable to reason, yet orthodox and liberal exegetes came to very different conclusions about the truth of traditional Christian doctrines, the reliability of the Christian Bible, and the nature and meaning of its central figure, Jesus of Nazareth.

In his classic study, *The Eclipse of the Biblical Narrative,* Hans Frei traces the changes that occurred in biblical hermeneutics during the eighteenth century, culminating in the modern higher critical approach. During the "precritical" period, Frei states, figural interpretation confirmed that the meaning of the biblical texts and the story they told were one. However, as a result of Deist challenges and rationalist adjustments, a wedge was driven between meaning and story, between the biblical world and the real historical world, so that the author's intention and the meaning of what the author wrote became different things. Orthodox exegetes like Edwards, while wholly sharing in the assumption that religion was in accord with reason, sought for ways to affirm the intended meanings of the texts *and* their historical reality by demonstrating the overall integrity of the Scriptures.[7]

It is this larger struggle against Deism or free thought, along with an antihistorical approach to Scripture, a struggle that occupied some of the best minds of England—including Addison, Berkeley, and Butler—that the "Harmony" addresses. The "Harmony," a lone voice from the colonial wilderness, was to join all of the traditional Protestant strands of scriptural interpretation into a synthetic proof of the unity and factuality of the Bible. Like Calvin, the hermeneutic linchpin for Edwards was Jesus Christ as Messiah, whose coming to earth and the particularities of whose life, death, and resurrection were foretold of old. The christocentric meaning of creation is illustrated in "Miscellanies" no. 837, where Edwards writes:

> The whole of Christian divinity depends on divine revelation, for though there are many truths concerning God and our duty to him that are evident by the light of nature, yet no one truth is taught by the light of nature in that manner in which it is necessary for us to know it: for the knowledge of no truth in divinity is of any significance to us, any otherwise than it some way or other belongs to the gospel scheme, or has relation to Christ the Mediator. It signifies nothing for us to know anything of any one of God's perfections, unless we know them as manifested in Christ.[8]

In response to those who argued that the "light of nature" alone was sufficient to teach morality and virtue, Edwards insisted that an experience of the excellency of Christ was essential. Only in Christ could the unity of Scripture be understood and the higher unity of all creation be achieved.

As a number of historians have pointed out, the modern critique of the Christian revelation began in 1695 with John Locke's *Reasonableness of Christianity.*[9] Locke reacted against the creedal and confessional strife of the Interregnum by attempting to boil down Christianity to what he saw as the fundamental, reasonable teachings on which all Christians could agree. During the following seven decades or so, authors followed Locke's lead with efforts to prove or disprove that Scripture was within the bounds of reason and empirical evidence. These included Edwards, who, though he emulated Locke's methodology, was intent on demonstrating that revealed religion was not merely a "republication" of natural religion.

Along with Enlightenment notions of toleration and reason, new attitudes toward religion were shaped by the Scientific Revolution. Many theologians sought to incorporate Isaac Newton's mechanical philosophy into their approach, including Edwards, who wrote that God had sent Newton "to make way for the universal setting up of Christ's kingdom."[10] But advocates of natural religion such as Samuel Clarke used Newton's writings to support their criticisms of revealed religion.[11] Human observation and reason alone, they argued, could prove the existence and wisdom of God and the superiority of natural law. The new authority given to scientific method threatened to deprive orthodox exegetes of their traditional appeals to biblical evidence and metaphysical argumentation, which were both subject to increasing ridicule.[12]

Some of Locke's and Newton's professed disciples took their ideas further than the masters themselves would have gone. Among them was John Toland, who in 1696 published *Christianity Not Mysterious.* If, Toland concluded, reason was the standard to which everything, especially revelation, was to be subjected, then many things in Scripture were suspect, including the credibility of inspiration, the reliability of the biblical narrative, its prophetic content, and its accounts of miracles—all subjects which Edwards defended extensively in his private notebooks.[13] Scripture was attacked in several notorious books, with Matthew Tindal's *Christianity as Old as Creation* (1730) leading the way. Christianity, Tindal held, was "as old as creation" only insofar as it mirrored natural reason. On this basis, he dismissed much of the Old Testament and prompted a torrent of criticism, including some from Edwards.[14] In an essay toward a treatise on the mysteries of religion aimed at Tindal and his allies, Edwards attempts to explain the proper relation between reason and revelation:

> Multitudes of the free thinkers of late ages deceive themselves through the ambiguous or equivocal use of the word REASON. They argue as though we must make reason the highest rule to judge of all things, even the doctrines of revelation, because reason is that by which we must judge of revelation itself—'tis the rule by which the judgment of the truth of a revelation depends, and therefore undoubtedly must be that by which particular doctrines of it must be judged—not considering that the word *reason* is here used in two senses: in the former case, viz. in our judging of a supposed revelation, the word means the *faculty* of reason taken in the whole extent of its exercise; in the other case, 'tis the *opinion* of our reason or some particular opinions that have appeared rational to us. Now there is a great difference between these two.

Edwards goes on to assert that "divine testimony" is necessary and cannot be "contradistinguished" from other equally valid forms of evidence or argument. Resorting to one of his favorite tactics, he claims that making reason a higher rule than revelation is "making sounds without understanding or fixing any distinct meaning."[15]

Beside the Deist threat, the Bible was also being attacked by those who opposed an Augustinian or historical interpretation of Scripture. These "antihistoricists" comprehended a wide range of writers who argued that the Bible could not be taken as an accurate account of events, that its books—most prominently the Pentateuch[16]—were not written by the attributed authors, and that an historical approach to Scripture led on the one hand to Puritan dogmatism and on the other to enthusiasm. While there was no concerted effort during Edwards's life to reintroduce the extravagant allegorizing that had characterized the works of the metaphysical preachers such as Lancelot Andrewes and John Donne, there were those, including Collins and the French Catholic priest Richard Simon, who favored it over the literal-historical hermeneutic that had prevailed during the Puritan era. Most prominent among those who did call for a return to an allegorical approach was the English theologian Conyers Middleton, who found that efforts to defend Christianity through a literal exposition of the Bible only created embarrassing "difficulties."[17]

Though the "Harmony" was to be a work of apologetic theology par excellence against such antihistorical writers, it contains hardly any polemical statements. We must go to Edwards's other notebooks to find his unabashed, unedited condemnations of the antihistoricists and their treatment of Scripture. He bristled at his opponents' claims that many biblical passages could not be understood by uneducated readers and that only those versed in the original languages could hope to interpret the sacred texts correctly. In one series of notebooks, Edwards castigates the new critics' approach and "their MAGISTERIAL, CONTEMPTUOUS, SOVEREIGN, ASSURED, SUPERCILIOUS, OVERBEARING, INSULTING, OVERLOOKING AIRS." In contrast, he defends the accessibility of the Scripture to all believers, both learned and unlearned:

> SCRIPTURE EXPRESSIONS are everywhere exceeding contrary to their scheme, according to all use of language in the world these days. But then they have their refuge here: they say the ancient figures of speech are exceeding diverse from ours, and that we in this distant age can't judge at all of the true force of expressions used so long ago but by a skill in antiquity, and being versed in ancient history, and critically skilled in ancient languages—never considering that the Scriptures are written for us in these ages, on whom the ends of the world are come, yea, were designed chiefly for the latter age of the world, in which they shall have their chief and, comparatively, almost all their effect, and they were written for God's people in these ages, when at least 99 out of an hundred must be supposed incapable of such knowledge.

Edwards goes on to condemn "their vast pretenses to an accurate and clear view of the SCOPE and DESIGN of the sacred penmen and a critical knowledge of the ORIGINALS," concluding, "'Tis easy to refine and criticize a book to death."[18] Though Edwards was firmly against lay interpretation of Scripture, neither could he brook the elitist, exclusionary view of his opponents.

Such were the forces against which Edwards set himself when he laid out the tripartite structure of the "Harmony." With this background, we can better understand the purpose behind the treatise as a whole as well as its separate parts.

Following Edwards's synopsis in his letter to the trustees, the components of the "Harmony"'s first section are entitled "Prophecies of the Messiah" and "Fulfillment of the Prophecies of Messiah." "Prophecies" comprises a series of "Miscellanies" entries, nos. 891, 922, and (by far the longest) 1067, while "Fulfillment" is no. 1068.[19] As arrangements of the texts pertaining to the coming of Christ, Edwards's "Prophecies" and "Fulfillment" are strikingly reminiscent of Handel's *Messiah* (1742), which reflected the contemporary debate over Scripture. The librettos of "Prophecies" and "Fulfillment" both feature numbered sections (101 and 181 respectively), with each section considering a different passage. Throughout, Edwards engages in detailed textual study, dissecting the words of the text, exhaustively citing related texts, and gathering evidence from both ancient and modern authorities, from Josephus, Tacitus, and Cyrus to Jacques Basnage, Hugo Grotius, and Johann Stapfer. Like many other authors of his time, Edwards found these sources useful in marshaling confirmation for events related in the Bible and in searching into the actual or multivalent meanings of Hebrew and Greek words.

The "Prophecies" considers significant Old Testament passages describing the Messiah. Section 91, for example, considers Dan. 9:24–27, which Edwards believed to be "a great prophecy of the messiah . . . one of the most remarkable and plain of all in the Old Testament."[20] In this lengthy and detailed article, Edwards seeks to show that the "Great King" often promised in prophecy is the same as the Messiah, or Anointed One, mentioned by Daniel. The "Fulfillment" explicates the Messiah's time of coming, his descent, his manner of person, the benefits of his death, and the many things relating to his church, his kingdom, his judgment, and the fate of his enemies. Section 3 takes up the same passage in Daniel, contending that the things prophesied in the Old Testament are literally embodied in the person of Jesus and contain mystical meanings for the church of God.[21]

For the revisionists with whom Edwards was so dissatisfied, among the most "irrational" elements of Christianity were the prophecies and their interpretation—topics very close to Edwards's heart. Controversial books that criticized the canon of Scripture included Thomas Woolston's *Six Discourses on Miracles* (1727) and William Whiston's *Essay towards Restoring the True Text of the Old Testament* (1722). While Whiston's method of "restoring" the original text was viewed by nearly everyone as eccentric, Collins and Woolston agreed with Whiston that the Old Testament texts were corrupt and untrustworthy, which rendered their literal interpretation irrelevant, even dangerous.[22]

Another seminal book was Anthony Collins's *Discourse of the Grounds and Reasons of the Christian Religion* (1724). Edwards's "Catalogue" of his reading shows his immersion in the avalanche of apologetic literature that surrounded Collins's work. Among other volumes he cites Edward Chandler's *Defence of Christianity, from the Prophecies of the Old Testament* (1725), which linked prophecy and types in much the same way Edwards does; Thomas Sherlock's *Use and Intent of Prophecy* (1725), which he frequently cited to affirm the fulfillment of the prophecies in Christ; and Arthur Ashley Sykes's *Essay upon the Truth of the Christian Religion* (1725), which maintained that Christianity had its "real foundation" in the Old Testament and that Christ's claim to fulfill prophecy was among several proofs of the authenticity of Scripture.[23]

Literary scholars in particular will recognize Edwards's description of the second part of "Harmony," "considering the Types of the old testament," as "Types of the Messiah," which in the "Miscellanies" follows "Fulfillment" as no. 1069. This entry was first published by Sereno Dwight in his 1829 edition, without any indication that it was part of a larger work.[24] Only when viewed in the light of Edwards's letter to the trustees, however, do we understand the essay's true place and full function.

Edwards's aim in "Types of the Messiah" is to show that the Old and New Testaments cannot be understood apart from each other; the former prophetically and typologically anticipates the latter and the latter interprets the former. For Edwards, all of the things of the Old Testament are typical; it was, he says, "a typical world." Of utmost importance for understanding God's plan is that the Old Testament "abundantly prefigured and typified . . . the Messiah and things appertaining to his kingdom." "The introducing of the Messiah and his kingdom and salvation," Edwards continues, "is plainly spoken of in the Old Testament as the great event which was the substance, main drift and end of all the prophecies of the Old Testament, to reveal which chiefly it was that the Spirit of prophecy was given."[25]

Alongside messianic prophecy and fulfillment, typology became for Edwards one of the primary means of comprehending "the Messiah and things appertaining to his kingdom." Here Edwards was joining the argument against critics like Collins, Tindal, Woolston, and Simon in advocating the inseparable link between the testaments. Numerous works arose from the conservative camp that emphasized this "connection," among them Humphrey Prideaux's *Old and New Testament Connected* (1716), William Harris's *Practical Discourse on the Principal Representations of the Messiah throughout the Old Testament* (1724), and most importantly for Edwards, Samuel Clarke's *Discourse concerning the Connexion of the Prophecies in the Old Testament, and the Application of Them to Christ* (1723).[26] Eclectically pulling arguments and illustrations from Nonconformist typologists as well as from the more philosophical Clarke, Edwards ends his lengthy consideration of the Old Testament types of the Messiah with a corollary that sums up for him the meanings of the types:

> Seeing it is thus abundantly evident by the Old Testament itself that the things of the Old Testament were typical of the Messiah and things appertaining to him, hence a great and most convincing argument may be drawn that Jesus is the Messiah, seeing there is so wonderful a correspondence and evident, manifold and great agreement between him and his gospel and these types of the Old Testament.[27]

It is in this light as well that we can more fully understand Edwards's theoretical statements about typology in "Types of the Messiah," which were aimed at the natural religionists and anti-historicists. Edwards affirms an Augustinian approach to Scripture when he says that "the material and natural world is typical of the moral, spiritual and intelligent world, or the City of God."[28] In posing an objection concerning "the abuse that will be made of this doctrine of types," Edwards replies:

> We have as good warrant from the Word of God to suppose the whole ceremonial law to be given in order to a figurative representing and signifying spiritual and evangelical things to mankind, as we have to suppose that prophetical representations are to represent and signify the events designed by them, and therefore as good reason to endeavor to interpret them.[29]

That Edwards had these same commentators in mind for his expanded theory of typology is also clear from his thesis in the "Types" notebook: "To show how there is a medium between those that cry down all types, and those that are for turning all into nothing but allegory and not having it to be true history; and also the way of the rabbis that find so many mysteries in letters, etc."[30]

Edwards's thesis as stated in the "Types" notebook does not apply to the entire "Harmony" project but rather to one discrete section of it. Nonetheless, his statement does point to his new way of viewing typology. Edwards, who saw all of creation as the "shadows of beings," found direct correspondences with divine things in history, nature, and human experience as well as in Scripture. To draw merely moralistic lessons from Scripture and observable phenomena, as did the antihistoricists, did not go far enough for Edwards; on the other hand, cabalistic claims concerning "mysteries in letters" went too far in his estimation. Where his fellow ministers in the dissenting and Reformed camps largely refused to venture outside of the Bible itself for types and antitypes, Edwards advocated stepping beyond the written Word for representations of divine things. "It would be on some accounts as unreasonable to say that we must interpret no more of them than the Scripture has interpreted for us, and than we are told the meaning of in the New Testament, as it would be to say that we must interpret prophecy, or prophetical visions and types, no further than the Scripture has interpreted it to our hand."[31]

With Edwards's thesis for the "Types," too, it becomes clear that "Images of Divine Things" and the notebook on "Types," which contain the more innovative elements of Edwards's typology, were actually grist for the "Harmony" mill. In these notebooks he criticizes natural religionists for limiting the meaning of the created world by making it an end in itself rather than a source of references to divine truths. Throughout "Images" Edwards insists, as for example in no. 8, that "there is a great and remarkable analogy in God's works," and that "the whole outward creation . . . is so made as to represent spiritual things." And in "Miscellanies" no. 760, Edwards reiterates the christocentric focus of the realm of the types when he writes:

> Things that appear minute in comparison with the work of creation are much insisted on in Scripture, for they become great by their relation to Christ and his redemption, of which creation was but a shadow. And the history of Scripture, which gives an account of the works of providence, are all taken up in the history of Christ and his church; for all God's works of providence are to be reduced to his providence towards Christ and his church.

Thus the "Images" and "Types" notebooks, with their shared ascription of the meaning of signs to things relating to the Messiah, unexpectedly find their home in a treatise about biblical prophecy.

While the previous sections of the treatise have survived intact, the final one, "considering the harmony of the old and new testament," is fragmentary. Only one quarto-sized notebook (not a part of the "Miscellanies") has survived, entitled "The Harmony of the Genius, Spirit, Doctrines and Rules of the Old Testament and the New."[32] Since this notebook deals with Genesis through Psalms, we can only speculate that there were further notebooks toward this "great," or largest part of the treatise, taking us from Proverbs onward, that are no longer extant.

Edwards begins here by grouping Old Testament texts under the "signs of godliness," a rubric that underlies his revival works. These signs include faith in God, the Messiah, and a future state; love to enemies, humility, and selling all for Christ; sympathy for others, not being anxious, and not laying up earthly treasures. He then abandons this method and begins to go canonically through the Old Testament, noting how passages "harmonize with doctrines, precepts, etc. of the New." For instance, Edwards couples God's command to Abram to leave his home (Gen. 12:1–4) with Jesus' injunction that the Christian is to "forsake father and mother, brethren and sisters, and all that he hath" (Luke 14:26). Thus this biblical exercise becomes for Edwards a means of illustrating the central features of his theology, particularly his interest in Christian behavior as the primary "mark" or "sign" of true sainthood.

Just as in typology Edwards was forging a new way of viewing types, so in harmonizing the testaments he was also at the forefront of Reformed hermeneutics. Here Edwards could draw on a long tradition of Protestant writers who "harmonized" scriptural accounts, particularly the four gospels; but his aim was much more ambitious, comprehending the entire Bible and employing a unique organizing principle. This principle was what Stephen J. Stein has called the "spiritual" or "spirit-given" sense, the meaning available only to the regenerate by indwelling grace.[33] Through the spiritual sense, Edwards linked all the meanings of biblical texts through an "analogy of faith" by conforming them to the saving doctrines of Christianity, stressing, as Frei puts it, "the similarity of the effect all the parts of the Bible have on the devoutly inquiring mind."[34] The important point for Edwards was not the direct inspiration or literal wording of the Bible, but rather its *matter* or subjects and their agreement; the congruity of the whole was more important than the sum of its parts. Here Edwards was a leader, with German theologians such as Matthaus Pfaff, Johann Jacob Rambach, and Sigmund Jacob Baumgarten, in forging what Emanuel Hirsch has called the transition from "Bible faith" to "revelation faith."[35] It is yet another testimony to Edwards's genius that he developed this approach, emphasizing the unity and harmony of the testaments and the spiritual sense, virtually on his own.[36]

Yet we cannot ignore that "harmony" was a packed word for Edwards; it connoted for him an element of the excellency of the saint as well as Scripture, and so was integral to his philosophical theology. Moving from the testimony of prophecy and the created world, Edwards in this final section is considering not just the harmony of Scripture per se but also describing the necessary harmony, congruity, and correspondency of perceiving minds to Christ. The similarity and consent of God's Word to itself finds its analog in the similarity and consent of the soul to Christ. "The more the consent is, and the more extensive," Edwards wrote in "The Mind" no. 1, "the greater is the excellency."[37] So in the section on "Harmony," Edwards's emphasis is on following what he calls "the way of universal holiness." The extent of consent applied as much among God's means of revealing his will—Scripture, nature, and the Spirit—as to the soul's accepting the revelation.

As a whole, "The Harmony of the Old and New Testament" was to combine the various sorts of internal and external proofs available to Edwards—prophecy and fulfillment, typology, and harmonization—into one work. Scripture, creation, and rational being, Edwards wished to argue, together found their ultimate meaning and unity in the person of Christ. Whether Edwards saw any problem with reconciling his traditional treatment of prophecy with his revisionist approaches to typology and harmonization is not clear. Two things, however, are clear: that at the end of his life Edwards had embarked on a new direction into biblical exposition; and that his unifying concept was Jesus Christ as the reference point of all promises, whether they had already been fulfilled through the incarnation of the Logos or were yet to be accomplished through the ongoing work of redemption.

NOTES

1. *The Works of Jonathan Edwards, 9, A History of the Work of Redemption,* ed. John F. Wilson (New Haven, 1989), p. 554.

2. Among Edwards's late notebooks is "Subjects of Inquiry" (Beinecke Rare Book and Manuscript Library, Yale University, Edwards Papers, Box 21, f. 1251), which contains memoranda in which he directs himself to read through the Old Testament, the Evangelists, and the Epistles for confirmation of prophecies; his late "Miscellanies" contain a disproportionate amount of entries on such topics as Revealed Religion, the Necessity of Revelation, the Spirit of Prophecy, and the Prophecies of the Old Testament; and to facilitate his understanding of the Old Testament, Edwards was even attempting to improve his Hebrew. For example, he tells the trustees that he cannot teach languages, "unless it be the hebrew tongue, which I should be willing to improve my self in, by instructing others" (Samuel Hopkins, *The Life and Character of . . . Jonathan Edwards* [Boston, 1765], p. 78). In "Subjects of Inquiry," Edwards notes to himself that he should read the Scripture through and make a list of Hebrew words, which resulted in the notebook "Hebrew Idioms" (Box 16, f. 1211).

3. Stephen J. Stein, "Spirit and the Word: Jonathan Edwards and Scriptural Exegesis," in Nathan O. Hatch and Harry S. Stout, eds., *Jonathan Edwards and the American Experience* (New York, 1988), pp. 118–28.

4. Hopkins, *Life,* pp. 77–78. "Harmony" was to deal with the period up through the early church, while the *History* was to take the story of redemption to the end of time. In this way, they were related. Nevertheless, at the time of his letter, the *History* still lay at loose ends in several books of notes, in scattered "Miscellanies," and in the unrevised sermon series preached nearly two decades earlier, while the first two parts of the "Harmony" had been drawn up into nearly final form and the third section was well under way. The manuscript evidence suggests that the *History* may have reached publication first because of the interests of Edwards's disciples rather than because of any stated preference of his own.

5. *The Cambridge History of the Bible,* vol. 1, *From the Beginnings to Jerome,* ed. P. R. Ackroyd and C. F. Evans (New York, 1963), pp. 76, 258, 276, 330–31, 486.

6. Ibid., pp. 552–54; *Cambridge History of the Bible,* vol. 3, *The West from the Reformation to the Present Day,* ed. S. L. Greenslade, pp. 16–17.

7. Hans Frei, *The Eclipse of Biblical Narrative: A Study in Eighteenth and Nineteenth Century Hermeneutics* (New Haven, 1974), pp. 1–16.

8. Quotations from the "Miscellanies" are taken from Thomas A. Schafer's transcript on deposit at the Beinecke Library. On the christocentrism of the "Harmony," see Stein, "Spirit and the Word," pp. 124–27.

9. Mark Pattison, "Tendencies of Religious Thought in England, 1688–1750," *Essays and Reviews* (London, 1860), pp. 259–60; Leslie Stephen, *History of English Thought in the Eighteenth Century,* vol. 1 (London, 1876; rep. 1927), 91–96; Gerald R. Cragg, *Reason and Authority in the Eighteenth Century* (Cambridge, 1964), pp. 13–14; John Redwood, *Reason, Ridicule and Religion: The Age of Enlightenment in England, 1660–1750* (Cambridge, Mass., 1976), pp. 101–3.

10. Beinecke Library, Edwards Papers, Box 16, f. 1212, "Work of Redemption" Book I, p. 5.

11. J. P. Ferguson, *An Eighteenth-Century Heretic: Dr. Samuel Clarke* (Kineton, 1976), pp. 106–18, 210–25; Cragg, *Reason and Authority,* p. 50.

12. Cragg, *Reason and Authority,* pp. 13, 16–18, 46; Redwood, *Reason, Ridicule and Religion,* pp. 94–95; John Gascoigne, *Cambridge in the Age of the Enlightenment: Science, Religion and Politics from the Restoration to the French Revolution* (Cambridge, 1989), pp. 115–23, 164.

13. Among Edwards's notebooks is one defending the authenticity of the Pentateuch as a work of Moses (Beinecke Library, Edwards Papers, Box 15, f. 1204; see also notes on the Books of Moses, Box 15, f. 1204a), an extension of "Notes on the Scripture," no. 415. On

Christ's miracles, see "Miscellanies" nos. 1306, 1311, 1319, and the sermon on John 10:37 f. (Jan. 1740). See also "On the Christian Religion" (Box 21, f. 1257), which contains materials relating to all of these topics.

14. Redwood, *Reason, Ridicule and Religion,* pp. 134–55.

15. Beinecke Library, Edwards Papers, Box 15, f. 1203, "Controversies" Notebook, pp. 190, 193. The "Controversies" essay on mysteries is linked by Edwards to "Miscellanies" no. 1340, entitled "Reason and Revelation," which is a direct response to Tindal's *Christianity as Old as Creation.*

16. See Edwards's manuscript notebook on Moses's authorship of the Pentateuch (Beinecke Library, Box 15, f. 1204), where he collected evidence that these books could not have been forged. The most famous work defending the Pentateuch as a work of Moses was William Warburton's *Divine Legation of Moses Demonstrated, On the Principles of a Religious Deist* (2 vols. London, 1737–38), which was listed by Edwards in his "Catalogue" of reading and used by him in teaching at Stockbridge. But Edwards's approval of the book was not without exceptions; his small manuscript entitled "Places of the Old Testament that Intimate a Future State" (Edwards Collection, ND5.4–5, the Franklin Trask Library, Andover Newton Theological School, Newton Center, Massachusetts) may have been in response to Warburton's argument that the Old Testament did not contain proof of an afterlife.

17. Frei, *Eclipse,* pp. 120–22; W. Fraser Mitchell, *English Pulpit Oratory from Andrewes to Tillotson: A Study of Its Literary Aspects* (London, 1932), pp. 148–49; *The Works of Jonathan Edwards, 11, Typological Writings,* ed. Wallace E. Anderson and Mason I. Lowance, Jr. (New Haven, 1993), pp. 20–24. On Father Simon, see Dean Freiday, *The Bible: Its Criticism, Interpretation and Use in Seventeenth and Eighteenth Century England* (Pittsburgh, 1979), pp. 105–6.

18. Beinecke Library, Edwards Papers, Box 15, f. 1207, "Efficacious Grace," Book II, pp. 62–63.

19. "Miscellanies," Book 6, containing nos. 1067 and 1068, is at the Trask Library (ND6A-C); the remainder of the "Miscellanies" are at the Beinecke Library. The length of these entries is unparalleled among Edwards's unpublished writings: "Prophecies" and "Fulfillment" together amount to nearly 300 neatly written folio pages bound in their own cover. Each even has its own "table," or index.

20. See, for example, the early note in the Blank Bible (Beinecke Library, Edwards Papers, Box 17, f. 1216) on Dan. 9:23–24, which Edwards states is the angel's answer to Daniel's prayer concerning the Messiah.

21. On the mystical meaning, see Stephen J. Stein, "The Quest for the Spiritual Sense: The Biblical Hermeneutic of Jonathan Edwards," *Harvard Theological Review* 70 (1977): 99–113.

22. Stephen, *History of English Thought,* vol. 1, 210 ff., 228; Frei, *Eclipse,* pp. 68–70.

23. Edwards's manuscript "Catalogue" of reading (Beinecke Library, Edwards papers, Box 15, f. 1202) contains numerous titles relating to miracles (Sherlock), harmony of the evangelists (Lightfoot, Cradock, Fisher), Deism (Leland, Skelton), Scripture chronology (Hoar, Bedford, Lardner), and other current issues that show his involvement in the debate over Scripture.

24. Sereno E. Dwight, ed., *The Works of President Edwards,* vol. 9 (New York, 1829–30), pp. 9–111. The Yale Edwards Edition does only a little better, for though the connection of the piece to the larger project is made clear in the introduction to vol. 11, *Typological Writings* (pp. 12–13), the tradition of separate publication begun with Dwight is perpetuated.

25. *Works of Jonathan Edwards, 11,* pp. 202, 203.

26. Answering Collins on the nonliteral meaning of prophecies of the Messiah, Clarke cites typology as an important buttress for the claim of Jesus's messiahship: "The Correspondences of *Types* and *Antitypes,* though they are not themselves proper *Proofs* of the Truth of a doctrine, yet they may be very reasonable *Confirmations* of the *Foreknowl-*

edge of God; of the uniform View of Providence under *different Dispensations*; of the *Analogy, Harmony, and Agreement* between the *Old Testament* and *the New.*" Samuel Clarke, *A Discourse concerning the Connexion of the Prophecies in the Old Testament, and the Application of Them to Christ* (London, 1729), p. 32.

27. *Works of Jonathan Edwards, 11,* p. 321.

28. Ibid., p. 191.

29. Ibid., pp. 321, 323–24.

30. Ibid., *11,* p. 151. Although his "Catalogue" of reading contains several items relating to rabbinic learning and cabal, Edwards most likely understood "the way of the rabbis" through Christian expositors such as the Cambridge Platonists rather than through primary sources.

31. *Works of Jonathan Edwards, 11,* pp. 147–48.

32. Beinecke Library, Edwards Papers, f. 33.

33. See Stein, "Quest for the Spiritual Sense," pp. 106–7, and "The Spirit and the Word," p. 123.

34. Frei, *Eclipse,* p. 92.

35. Ibid., p. 91.

36. See W. R. Ward, *The Protestant Evangelical Awakening* (Cambridge, 1992), chap. 1, which discusses the Pietist influence in the American colonies through immigration.

37. See "The Mind" no. 1, in *The Works of Jonathan Edwards, 6, Scientific and Philosophical Writings,* ed. Wallace E. Anderson (New Haven, 1980), pp. 332–38. See also the manuscript entitled "Christ's Example" (Beinecke Library, Edwards Papers, Box 21, f. 1259), which details the ways in which the believer should conform to Christ.

Part II

CONTEXT

INTERPRETING TEXTS AND IDENTIFYING INFLUENCES

FIVE

"The Death of the Prophet Lamented"

THE LEGACY OF SOLOMON STODDARD

PAUL R. LUCAS

It is not fashionable today to speak of a Puritan legacy. Perry Miller's *New England Mind,* with its rise, reign, and fall of the New England Way, is a dusty artifact.[1] Indeed, during the last several decades, the focus of the historiography of colonial America has drifted away from New England and reduced New England's importance in the American story. The southern colonies had slave societies; the middle colonies had many immigrant groups living side by side. Both often appear far more important in shaping the American experience than a handful of zealous, idealistic Puritans. Many scholars of colonial New England don't believe that New England was cast by Puritans. Instead, they argue, English avarice, folk ways of the British Isles, and the mixing of white, red, and black cultures were the major forces which molded the development of New England.[2]

So what am I going to do—rescue the Puritans? I'm going to try. Twenty years ago my view of Solomon Stoddard cast doubt about the plausibility of Perry Miller's New England Way.[3] Today an examination of the legacy of Solomon Stoddard will cast doubt on our attempts to write the Puritans out of the American story. I propose to show that despite the renunciation by Jonathan Edwards of the most notable features of Stoddard's legacy—his "Instituted Church," his use of "converting ordinances," and his adoption of "open communion,"—Stoddard's legacy, as much as Edwards's, anticipates and helps explain the religious revivalism of the nineteenth-century United States and the amazing successes of Protestant denominations.[4]

Stoddard's life and his intellectual legacy were molded by a number of factors. Some are well known. Historians have in the past examined Stoddard's character, personal charisma, and intellect and his experiences in Northampton.[5] What has not been fully explored or known, however, is the extent to which Stoddard's thought was molded by the peculiar character of the Connecticut Valley and the strong influence exerted by a seventeenth-century English lawyer and activist, William Prynne, and the Christian imperialism and nationalism of John Knox and Samuel Rutherford. Stoddard embraced the ideas of these men and then masterfully adapted them to meet the daily concerns of colonial New England.

This essay will sketch, first, the climate of the Connecticut Valley in the late seventeenth century and examine how it affected Stoddard's theology and ecclesiology. Thereafter, attention will turn to the pivotal role of William Prynne, John Knox, and Samuel Rutherford in the development of Stoddard's thinking. Finally, we will look at Stoddard's impact upon Jonathan Edwards and his legacy to evangelical Christianity in nineteenth-century America.

The key to understanding Stoddard is to be found in part in the peculiar circumstances of the Connecticut Valley in the late seventeenth and the first half of the eighteenth century. The peculiar quality of the Connecticut Valley is suggested by these interesting facts. In the fall of 1675 Northampton built a wall around part of the town. The wall was enlarged in 1689 and then remained in some form until 1763. The wall was built to protect the town from Indians; then, later, it provided protection from French and Indians. It remained for nearly a century, for almost five generations.[6] For most of Stoddard's tenure, the Connecticut Valley was a scene of war between Indians and English, then French and Indians and English and Indians. These wars were genocidal wars—wars of extermination. When war did not rage, there were frequent rumors of war.[7]

During the seventeenth and eighteenth centuries, combatants in the valley did not conduct warfare with pitched battles between large armies. Instead, they fought dirty, guerrilla wars in which small bands attacked the weak and the defenseless more often than they attacked the strong and well fortified. Historians know well the stories of white captives carried off to Quebec over a period of generations.[8] What has not been considered and what these stories suggest is how the inhabitants of the Connecticut Valley lived in constant fear of a family member's being killed or taken captive in a field or on the way to school, never to be seen again. Stories abounded of destroyed farmsteads in King Philip's War, of dazed pets guarding the wreckage until they became wild animals. Such scenes remained common until the end of the French Empire in North America.

Guerrilla warfare meant atrocities on both sides. People, both white and Indian, were not simply killed or abducted; they were brutalized and tortured. Everyone knew some family in which a loved one had died an agonizing death. It was not uncommon to travel the woodland trails of the valley and find a family member on a stake, horribly mutilated and disfigured. Colonials were just as barbaric. Colonial bands of irregulars, or "scouts," roamed Indian country killing all they encountered. Women and children were especially prized to prevent future "warriors" from maturing. From 1675 it was normal for troopers to cut off the heads of their victims and bring them back in sacks to be displayed like trophies in the villages of New England.[9]

The Connecticut Valley was a dark and bloody ground for five generations. No other region of New England was quite as grim—certainly not prosperous, commercial Boston. Moreover, the valley people of Northampton and western Massachusetts dealt with the Indian threat on their own. Not part of Connecticut, they could expect little help from that colony. They were 120 miles from Boston through woods and over Indian trails. They could expect little help from the Bay or from its government. The people of the valley lived a risky frontier existence. They were alone, they were a long way from help, and they lived with constant fear of violent death.[10] This was the environment in which Solomon Stoddard lived and ministered.

Stoddard developed theological, psychological, and ecclesiastical principles to help his people cope with their situation and win their struggles. Stoddard's life and his intellectual legacy, including his presbyterianism and his Instituted Church, were connected with and molded by the agony of his parishioners and the people of the upper Connecticut Valley. He helped begin an evangelical revival tradition which produced the Great Awakening.

Some time between King Philip's War (1675–76)—when loss of life (one in eight) among whites and Indians was the highest in the history of the United States—and 1700, when Stoddard published his *Doctrine of Instituted Churches,* Stoddard decided that the people of the upper Connecticut Valley and the people of New England needed guidance and discipline in their lives to get them through protracted wars with Indians and the French. They needed guidance and discipline from a great institution because their churches and their government could not cope with their desperate situation and England was too far away to provide relief. Colonists were thrown on their own devices, and they needed a church system to give them moral and spiritual strength.

Stoddard found such a church within the ideas of a seventeenth-century English lawyer and activist, William Prynne, amid the Independent-Presbyterian controversy over church government in England in the 1640s; in the English clerical debates over the nature and function of the sacraments; and in the Christian imperialism and nationalism of John Knox and Samuel

Rutherford. Stoddard embraced the ideas of these men and these events and then masterfully adapted them to colonial New England. Simply stated, Stoddard extracted from these English influences a solution to the daily problems his people faced.[11]

To understand fully the Stoddard legacy, one must begin with the religious struggles of seventeenth-century England. Perry Miller believed that the bedrock of New England Puritan society was formed in England before the English Civil War. In Miller's view, New England Puritans considered their society and church to stand as an alternative for England during the turmoil of the 1640s.[12] Philip Gura has amended that notion, arguing that Civil War religious radicalism infused New England.[13] Stephen Foster also explained New England connections to the Civil War era.[14] Nevertheless, colonial historians do not cite the English Civil War as one of the benchmarks of Anglo-American civilization. We acknowledge that English opposition thought, what has been called radical whiggery, emerged first during the 1640s and 1650s among "classical" republicans like John Milton, James Harrington, and Algernon Sydney, but our magnificent discussions of the origins of American revolutionary thought do not dwell long on the Civil War era.[15]

In Solomon Stoddard's case, one cannot ignore the importance of the intellectual heritage of the English Civil Wars without peril. In a 1700 attack on Stoddard, Increase Mather, then president of Harvard College as well as minister of First Church in Boston, noted the important influence upon Stoddard of "Mr. Prin."[16] This "Prin" was none other than the noted English Civil War activist, nationalist, and reformer, the man who lost his ears protesting Archbishop William Laud's excesses, the lawyer, William Prynne, the man they called "marginal Prynne." An examination of William Prynne's writings of the 1640s and 1650s reveals ideas repeated, in an Americanized form, by Solomon Stoddard in 1700. Stoddard's Presbyterian "Instituted Church" came in part from Prynne. The same is true of Stoddard's famous "open communion" and the "converting ordinances."

Prynne's biographer, William Lamont, writes that like most seventeenth-century Puritans, Prynne endorsed a prophetic, even apocalyptic vision of a world divided between good and evil in which Catholicism was the central evil force. The pope was Antichrist and Catholic monarchs were his henchmen. Church of England bishops who argued that their positions came not from election or appointment but from divine approbation perpetuated Catholicism—and evil—in England. Catholicism thus tainted both the English church and English society. Immorality was rampant in English society. The state of decay in England was God's terrible judgment for her moral laxness. Catholicism, aided by the activities of divine right bishops such as William Laud, was at fault for England's troubles.[17]

Lamont argues that although Prynne began as a Church of England man and ended as one, he went through many twists and turns along the way. A lawyer, Prynne believed in the ancient constitution of king, lords, and commons, the concept of balanced and limited government, and the notion of fundamental law. The king's power, and its limitations, came from an ancient agreement between king and people. Following the lead of John Foxe, Prynne also believed that England held a special position in God's eyes. England was a new Israel which, like the old Israel, had entered into a national covenant with God. English kings and queens were "Christian emperors." As with Foxe, Prynne articulated an English nationalism with millennial overtones.[18]

Catholicism's influence, through the bishops, poured into English politics and English life. Puritans cried for a reformed England. At first Prynne feared the bishops would undermine the Crown. By the early 1640s Prynne saw King Charles I as England's main problem. He advocated the sovereignty of Parliament and turned to that institution to undertake moral reformation. When Parliament would not or could not act, he turned to Presbyterianism. Lamont argues that throughout his life, Prynne had one great concern: God's plan and England's pivotal role in fulfilling that plan. His debt to John Foxe never wavered. Also, Prynne never lost his belief that to achieve greatness England had to undertake moral reform. Moral reform preceded spiritual awakening. Both were tied to the destruction of Catholicism.[19]

During his Presbyterian phase in the 1640s and 1650s Prynne participated in great arguments between Presbyterians and Independents, as well as the internal debates among Presbyterians. Essentially Presbyterians called for parishlike churches in which the visibly godly were admitted to communion with a minimum of difficulty. Church courts would guarantee adherence to biblical law among both members and nonmembers. Some Presbyterians urged strict admission standards for full membership and admission to communion. This type of Presbyterian imitated Independents who called for churches of saints separated from the reprobates of the world. Independents rejected courts and hierarchies, opting for discipline exercised by the congregations of the elect. Both Independents and these Presbyterians sought to remove the taint of Catholicism and restore the purity of primitive Christianity.[20]

Other Presbyterians rejected discipline for doctrine, i.e., they rejected the search for primitive purity in church form and the ecclesiastical disputes it produced. They argued that a church pattern could be found in both the Old and the New Testaments. What was important, they believed, was not arguments over elders' authority but the spiritual power unleashed by Christ's life and death. That spiritual power was in the Word and sacraments. Baptism and communion were means through which people might receive God's grace.[21]

Prynne followed this second brand of Presbyterianism. He broke with Independents and other Presbyterians by saying that all decent people should be brought to the Table because the Lord's Supper was a "converting ordinance." For Prynne, and for others, the converting ordinances unleashed spiritual power vital in winning souls and bringing about moral reform. Spiritual awakening and moral reform meant a huge setback to Catholicism, the advancement of England, England's Protestant allies, and God's plan. For Prynne, and for many Puritans who admired John Foxe, spiritual awakening, moral reform, and earthly politics were inextricably linked. Every preacher, every godly layman, was a reformer and a politician committed to God's cause and to England's. In summary, then, William Prynne was a Christian imperialist as well as an English imperialist and nationalist who argued that England's millennial role was imperiled by domestic immorality and corruption fomented by bishops and a king tainted by Catholicism.[22]

While no republican, William Prynne shared with the English republicans of his day a strong belief in the need to limit power. Prynne believed that England's ancient constitution protected the people's civil liberties and the Protestant religion through its balanced system of divided authority. Prynne's millennial views made him almost obsessive in his belief in a papal plot to undermine English liberties and the Protestant church. To Prynne, Catholicism was identified with and by "tyranny." If tyranny existed, Antichrist was afoot. Election of representatives to Parliament and the election of bishops in the church were the means to limit power and thus protect against tyranny.[23]

In addition to adopting many of the ideas of William Prynne, Solomon Stoddard owed a great debt to John Knox, the architect of Scottish Presbyterianism, and to Samuel Rutherford, one of Knox's ablest seventeenth-century exponents. Stoddard learned of the theology, ecclesiology, and political thinking of Knox through his studies of Samuel Rutherford while at Harvard. Stoddard knew that Knox spent much of his life seeking to overthrow Catholicism in Scotland. He understood that Knox and Rutherford argued that Christianity was divided into nations, with each nation having a covenant with God to Christianize its own people. Stoddard found the Christian imperialism of Knox and that of his student, Rutherford, to be especially applicable to New England.[24]

At the end of the seventeenth century, Stoddard fashioned an amalgam of the ideas of Prynne, Foxe, Knox, and Rutherford which bore a distinctly "American" imprint. In *The Doctrine of Instituted Churches,* Stoddard framed his "Instituted Church" for a transatlantic audience. The Instituted Church was national in scope and evangelical in nature. It utilized open communion, communion as a "converting" ordinance, church courts, and powerful preaching to foster spiritual awakening and moral reformation among all Anglo-Americans, as well as blacks and Indians.[25]

Stoddard did not live or think in a vacuum. In his Instituted Church he attempted to mold and adapt the Scottish and English reformation heritage to his situation and that of his people in the Connecticut Valley.

The year, 1700, is instructive. Stoddard's charges had lived through two terrible eras of Indian warfare. Now there were rumors of a third. His people were very frightened. Stoddard knew that church members, a minority in New England, found strength and solace in each other and in their God. But what of nonmembers? What of the society at large? Many during this era could not or would not become members. Ministers reported that many New Englanders had scruples against joining. Largely, these individuals considered themselves unworthy. The clergy had railed against these people for forty years, telling them that they were sinners bound for hell. Their "sins" were the reason God unleashed the Indians, and now the French. Reformation, that is, behavior modification, was needed before God would turn his frown to a smile.[26]

So Stoddard faced people who were frightened, people who were told that their sad plight was their own doing. Stoddard had told them so himself. By 1700, though, New England faced a social calamity. Ministers and magistrates recorded the signs of societal disintegration—drunkenness, profanity, lack of respect for elders among children, lack of concern for children among parents, divorce, suicide. New England society, it was argued, had come loose from its moorings. It had abandoned the ways of the founders.[27]

Historians have accepted this view of "declension" and the "reformation of manners" the clergy created to try to fight it. In looking for a reason for declension, historians suggest the decline of Puritan ways and the arrival of a secular, capitalistic, typically English society.[28] That is an extreme and fundamentally artificial explanation. A simpler explanation, and one which reflects the reality of the Connecticut Valley, is the cumulative effect of war and fear of war on a society unable to cope. By 1700 New England institutions—churches, governments, even families and kinship networks—were breaking down and people were being left without these societal supports at a time when they were needed badly.

Stoddard moved to meet this situation, and to do more. He believed that God had sent Europeans to America to convert the Indians. The English had failed miserably. Left without God and English ways, the Indians became the devil's disciples and the disciples of the devil's own: the Catholic French. Thus the devil used French and Indians to punish the English for their sins and for their failure to convert the heathen.

Stoddard believed that New Englanders had a duty to fulfill God's plan to convert the multitudes and bring civilization and Christianity to the Indians. The Indians were at the heart of all of Stoddard's visions. He foresaw a unique American nation with a unique American church. That church and that nation would be multiracial. Indians, whites, and, presumably, blacks would live together in communities all over the continent. Their religion would be Protestant and their civilization would be English. Missionaries would carry the message everywhere, and God's enemies, French Catholics in particular, would be vanquished.[29]

Stoddard concluded that the small, self-governing communities and churches of New England in 1700 were not sufficient for the task he envisioned. He also concluded that the state needed help as well. A larger, commanding institutional structure—a national church connected to the state and a parish structure reflecting European patterns—was needed to fulfill God's plan for America.[30]

Stoddard adapted the nationalist and ecclesiastical views of Knox, Rutherford, and Prynne to the American scene, a scene of chronic warfare. He posited an American church and an American nation in covenant with God and founded for the specific purpose of converting the heathen within its boundaries. American colonials were not the only people with such a covenant, but it was clear that Satan's forces, especially the French, were strongly at work in America. Therefore the colonists engaged this enemy. Stoddard anticipated that French Catholicism would be defeated as the colonists advanced steadily across the vast areas of North America.[31]

To fulfill God's plan, Stoddard proposed the creation of his "Instituted Church." It copied a pattern found in the Old and New Testaments, but the importance of the church's ecclesiastical structure was more practical than millennial. Like his mentor Prynne, Stoddard anticipated that the Christian-English conquest of America would be built around a moral-spiritual reformation and the defeat of Catholicism. His Presbyterian system promised courts for discipline, admission of professed Christians to the sacraments, "converting" ordinances, and powerful preachers spreading the Word. As conversions took place there would be an explosion of spiritual power which would lead to the fulfillment of God's plan through political action and social reform.[32]

Stoddard also made the same strong connection as Prynne between Catholicism and tyranny. Like Prynne, Stoddard looked first to the political arm of the society to lead the moral reformation. If that did not happen, the Instituted Church would take over. Further, the Instituted Church, with its national synod of elected delegates and its moral authority, would protect the people from the state.

Prynne believed Catholicism had tainted the bishops and the government of Charles I, thus creating a tyranny. Stoddard, like Prynne, believed the people had liberties to protect. Therefore Stoddard advocated election for both political representatives and church officials. He emphasized again and again how all officers in his church were elected and how closely his church reflected prevailing attitudes and practices in New England of limiting the authority of the clergy. He was "whiggish," but his model was not the English "country" party. His model was Prynne.[33]

Stoddard's vision of church and state, if implemented, was intended to conquer America for God and advance the world toward the inevitable victory of righteousness. Stoddard's conception of America's historic role in the unfolding of God's plan and his Instituted Church evolved, probably originating between the 1660s and 1670s and King William's War and Queen Anne's War. It was not until 1700, however, that his *Doctrine of Instituted Churches* appeared. Then it was published in London, not Boston.[34]

Why 1700? Perhaps earlier Stoddard feared the censor. No doubt he knew what was happening to the rebellious Covenanters in Scotland in the late seventeenth century.[35] It is more likely, however, that by 1700 Stoddard's vision of a state-led "reformation of manners" had simply faded. Certainly by 1700 Stoddard was more convinced than ever that New England needed spiritual awakening and moral revitalization, just as England had needed reformation in the 1640s. In fact, it is likely that chronic warfare had created a desperate situation in the Connecticut Valley.

Not a part of Connecticut and too far from the Bay government, the upper valley towns were on their own. The people, especially the majority outside the churches, were panicky. To whom could they turn for help and safety? By 1700, probably no one. The scrupulosity argument so apparent in those years among nonmembers was often a mask for depression and melancholy. Truly depressed, melancholy people know they cannot help themselves.

Stoddard confronted those feelings of helplessness daily. He and Edwards both wrote at great lengths on the "melancholy" of the people. In the nineteenth century melancholy would be considered a virtue. In the seventeenth century it was an invitation to the devil. As an antidote to war-induced helplessness and melancholy, as a defense against the machinations of the devil as well as a long-range plan for denying the devil his henchmen (French and their victims, the Indians), Stoddard proposed his Presbyterian system. Just as Prynne had once done, Stoddard abandoned hopes for a state-led revival. The people would reform themselves.

Stoddard attacked New England Congregationalism precisely because it advanced an inward-looking, "small church" concept. The written exchanges between Stoddard and Increase Mather during the early 1700s echoed the arguments of English Independents and Presbyterians in the 1640s while reflecting the need to adapt Puritan ideals and the church to the New England environment. Mather espoused several positions. Mostly, however, he asserted that it was the millennial role of New England's churches to identify and gather the elect. New England's founders understood this, but subsequent generations had declined to follow the lead of the first generation and New England had gone awry as a result.[36]

In contrast, Stoddard declared that the founders erred from the beginning. Instead of forming an exclusive communion of saints, the church in New England should have sought out all willing to listen. As a result of the closed, inward-looking quest for a pure body of saints, New England's churches had now become semi-heathenish gatherings solely for the wealthy and the members of a few chosen families. By 1700 Congregationalism stood forth as a defense for the behavior of the privileged few. At that moment, Stoddard argued, sons and daughters of church members were being admitted to full communion automatically, whereas newcomers, poor people, or the otherwise unprivileged had to undergo New England's famous public examination of one's religious experience.[37]

Worse, Stoddard pointed to New England's abysmal record with the Indians. Beyond lip service and John Eliot and a few others, New England had done nothing to advance God's cause with the Indians. Thanks to New England's neglect and then its program to push them out of the colonies, the Indians had fallen under the spell of the French and Spanish Catholics, but especially the French. Stoddard, ever the Christian imperialist and English nationalist and imperialist, urged immediate attention to converting both colonists and Indians and beating the French, lest God's plan and England's future fall to the dark forces. Stoddard minced no words. The Indians had to be converted and the Catholics had to be defeated.[38]

Stoddard's "big church" view, with its imperialist and nationalist tones, found few friends in New England outside of the Connecticut Valley. Northampton endorsed it after years of argument, and Hampshire County ministers formed the Hampshire Association of ministers in 1714. That group was considerably less than a church court, but it did provide guidance for Hampshire County churches. Connecticut ministers formed the Saybrook Platform in 1708. Stoddard helped shape the Platform through "Stoddardeans" and Presbyterians like Gurdon Saltonstall of New London, Timothy Woodbridge of Hartford First Church, and Timothy Edwards, Stoddard's son-in-law and Jonathan's father, in East Windsor.[39]

Jonathan Edwards grew up hearing about the ideas of his grandfather. In 1726 Northampton invited Edwards to become Stoddard's assistant. In 1729, upon Stoddard's death, Edwards assumed the pulpit of one of New England's most famous congregations. He led the church for twenty years, through the great revivals of 1734 and the early 1740s and through more years of war and terror. In 1749 Edwards broke with Stoddard's legacy by closing the church to all but those who could give evidence of a true conversion. He did it because of "Antinomianism" among some converts during the Great Awakening. Edwards became convinced that those converts were really led by the devil, not God. Within a year he was fired by the Northampton Church.

Jonathan Edwards was a "Stoddardean" for most of his career. So was much of the Connecticut Valley, a region dominated by the Williamses, more of Stoddard's relatives. Although Edwards's ministry began with peace which lasted until the 1740s, his parishioners still carried with them memories of the terrible wars. Even in peace, rumors of war were frequent. In Edwards's era the valley served as a major trade route to and from Canada. When war returned in the 1740s, the valley became a highway for Indians and French coming south from Quebec and for friendly forces headed north.[40]

Both Stoddard and Edwards ministered to frightened, often panicky people who lived with terrible stress. In 1749 Edwards rejected Stoddard's notions of open communion, his converting ordinances, and his Presbyterianism and returned to a Congregationalism more consistent with the majority position in New England.[41] Although Edwards ultimately diverged from Stoddard, they both developed theological, psychological, and ecclesiastical principles to help their people cope with their situation and to win their struggles.[42]

Modern scholars might call their programs a "revitalization movement."[43] They were similar to movements among desperate Indians from King Philip to the Prophet to the Ghost Dance of the late nineteenth century. Stoddard and Edwards exhorted their people to look to God for spiritual help to overcome fear, melancholy, and the sin both spawned. Both sought to isolate the reasons for God's anger and to seek solutions. Both called for rebirth and renewal. It was a desperate call for a "shower" of grace, as Stoddard labeled it, that would change people and bring them together in love, sharing, and common purpose. Both Stoddard and Edwards espoused a program for revival for people who had no other help at hand.

Nonetheless, and despite the 1749 communion controversy, Edwards's thought and behavior continued to show the Stoddard stamp. Edwards worked hard to advance missionary work among the Indians, and he had the same sense of the evangelical "church militant" that guided Stoddard. Like Stoddard, Edwards observed and responded to the climate of crisis in the Connecticut Valley. Like his grandfather before him, Edwards ministered to his parishioners and sought to provide answers for their fears and anxieties. By 1749, however, Edwards saw a church of visible saints as the right solution to the problems of the Connecticut Valley and elsewhere.

By the end of the eighteenth century Edwards was synonymous with Calvinism. Building on his 1749 break with Stoddard, Edwards's disciples wrote New England history as the rise and fall of a regenerate church membership with Edwards as the defender of church purity and Stoddard as a leader of the "Arminian" faction eager to encourage laxness.[44] Stoddard's reason for advocating open communion was the alleged deterioration of the New Englander's devotion to a regenerate membership marked by the Half-Way Covenant of 1662. Supposedly, nonmembers knew they were not worthy of church membership. They had "scruples"; they feared closing with a church lest they bring about God's wrath. Stoddard supposedly lowered standards and encouraged a free-will posture to make it easier for the nonelect to join. By the nineteenth century Stoddard was largely forgotten, while Edwards's theology and the work of his followers forged a powerful evangelical movement.

Edwards's disciples may have written New England history as they did because they had no recollections of the terror of those times. New England was quiet and peaceful by 1800.[45] The French were gone and so were most Indians. The Connecticut Valley had ceased to be a dark and bloody ground decades earlier. The hopelessness and terror many people felt was unknown in 1800. Looking back, interpreters no longer saw that the "scruples" of unregenerates were really the cries for help of people rendered helpless by real fears of sudden death. Stoddard knew that, and he tried to help. So did Edwards. That later generations would forget part of the story should not be surprising.

Nonetheless, the ideas championed by Stoddard reemerged among many nineteenth-century evangelicals confronting situations similar to those in the Connecticut Valley of the late seventeenth and early eighteenth centuries. Many Presbyterians and Methodists, for example, shared with Stoddard the same sense of nationalism, of mission, and of militant Christianity. God's church on earth was an institution open to all and a vehicle for transforming society. In the nineteenth century, churches in the United States looked again, as had Stoddard, to preaching and the ordinances as means to convert the ungodly.

Stoddard's exact nineteenth-century influence has not been charted, but it is clear that in his own era he was ahead of his time. Many historians identify a connection between Christian imperialism and nineteenth-century revivalism, missionary efforts, and social reform.[46] They speculate about the origins of the imperialist, reformist impulse. None have shown an awareness of the Stoddard-Prynne link or the war-ravaged Connecticut Valley that made Stoddard look to Prynne. If they did they would recognize, immediately, a major source for the tradition they describe, the tradition of American evangelicalism and revivalism.

NOTES

1. Perry Miller, *The New England Mind,* 2 vols. (New York, 1939, and Cambridge, Mass., 1953).

2. See, for example, David Hackett Fischer, *Albion's Seed: Four British Folkways in America* (Oxford, 1989); David Cressy, *Coming Over: Migration and Communication between England and New England in the Seventeenth Century* (New York, 1987); and Jack P.

Greene, *Pursuits of Happiness: The Social Development of Early Modern British Colonies and the Formation of American Culture* (Chapel Hill, N.C., 1988).

3. Paul R. Lucas, "An Appeal to the Learned: The Mind of Solomon Stoddard," *William and Mary Quarterly,* 30 (1973), 257–92, and *Valley of Discord: Church and Society along the Connecticut River, 1636–1725* (Hanover, N.H., 1976).

4. Lewis O. Saum, *The Popular Mood of Pre–Civil War America* (Westport, Conn., 1980), 65–66; Patricia Tracy, *Jonathan Edwards, Pastor: Religion and Society in Eighteenth-Century Northampton* (New York, 1980), 3–11; Michael J. Crawford, *Seasons of Grace: Colonial New England's Revival Tradition in Its British Context* (New York, 1991), 47–51, 246–47; Annabelle S. Wenzke, *Timothy Dwight* (Lewiston, N.Y., 1989), 221 ff. There is another, very important phase of Stoddard's career—the charismatic preacher seeking spiritual revival or awakening—that emerged after 1708. That phase formed a separate part of the Stoddard legacy as well as another important layer of influence on Jonathan Edwards's thought and behavior. It is not my intent to discuss the "charismatic" Stoddard here, just his advocacy of the "Instituted Church." Readers interested in the charismatic Stoddard may consult my "Appeal to the Learned," 283–92; my *Valley of Discord,* 195–202, and Crawford's path-breaking study, *Seasons of Grace,* 70–123.

5. For Stoddard's life and thought, see Perry Miller, "Solomon Stoddard, 1643–1729," *Harvard Theological Review,* 34 (1941), 277–320; Thomas A. Schafer, "Solomon Stoddard and the Theology of the Revival," in Stuart C. Henry, ed., *A Miscellany of American Christianity: Essays in Honor of H. Shelton Smith* (Durham, N.C., 1963), 328–61; Patricia Tracy, *Jonathan Edwards, Pastor: Religion and Society in Eighteenth-Century Northampton* (New York, 1980), chap. 1; Lucas, "Appeal to the Learned"; and Crawford, *Seasons of Grace,* chap. 2.

6. James R. Trumbull, *History of Northampton, Massachusetts, from Its Settlement in 1654* (Northampton, Mass., 1902), vol. 1, 275–77.

7. The wars are described in detail in Trumbull, *Northampton,* vols. 1 and 2.

8. See, for example, John Demos, *The Unredeemed Captive: A Family Story from Early America* (New York, 1994).

9. The details of genocidal warfare are recounted in Douglas Leach, *Flintlock and Tomahawk: New England in King Philip's War* (New York, 1958); Russell Bourne, *The Red King's Rebellion: Racial Politics in New England, 1675–1708* (New York, 1990); Ian K. Steele, *Warpaths: Invasions of North America* (New York, 1994); and Francis Jennings, *The Invasion of America: Indians, Colonialism and the Conquest* (Chapel Hill, N.C., 1975).

10. See Leach, *Flintlock and Tomahawk,* vii–viii, 84–88. The effects of war on the towns and peoples of the Connecticut Valley during these years were recorded by nineteenth- and early twentieth-century local historians. See, for example, Trumbull, *History of Northampton*; Henry R. Stiles, *The History of Ancient Windsor* (New York, 1859); Sherman W. Adams and Henry R. Stiles, *The History of Ancient Wethersfield,* 2 vols. (Wethersfield, Conn., 1904); Sylvester Judd, *History of Hadley* (Springfield, Mass., 1905); and J. Hammond Trumbull, *Memorial History of Hartford County, 1633–1884,* 2 vols. (Boston, 1886).

11. E. Brooks Holifield first connected Stoddard to the English sacramental debates of the 1640s and 1650s in his doctoral dissertation and in his book, *The Covenant Sealed: The Development of Puritan Sacramental Theology in Old and New England, 1570–1720* (New Haven, 1974). I learned from Holifield (*Valley of Discord,* chap. 7).

12. See Perry Miller, "Errand into the Wilderness," *Errand into the Wilderness* (New York, 1964). Miller's argument became familiar to generations of college students through Edmund Morgan's *Puritan Dilemma: The Story of John Winthrop* (Boston, 1958).

13. Philip Gura, *A Glimpse of Sion's Glory: Puritan Radicalism in New England, 1620–1660* (Middletown, Conn., 1984).

14. Stephen Foster, *The Long Argument: English Puritanism and the Shaping of New England Culture, 1570–1700* (Chapel Hill, N.C., 1991).

15. See Bernard Bailyn, *The Ideological Origins of the American Revolution* (Cambridge, Mass., 1967; enlarged ed., 1992), and *The Origins of American Politics* (New York, 1968).

16. Increase Mather, *The Order of the Gospel, Professed and Practised by the Churches of Christ in New England . . .* (Boston, 1700), 22.

17. William M. Lamont, *Marginal Prynne, 1600–1669* (London, 1963), 1–85, 200, 229–230.

18. Lamont, *Marginal Prynne,* 16–21, 92ff., 175–204; J. G. A. Pocock, *The Ancient Constitution and the Feudal Law: A Study of English Historical Thought in the Seventeenth Century* (Cambridge, 1957), 155–56; William Prynne, *The First Part of an Historical Collection of the Ancient Parliaments of England . . .* (London, 1648); and Prynne, *A Plea for the Lords . . .* (London, 1648). For John Foxe, see Katharine R. Firth, *The Apocalyptic Tradition in Reformation Britain* (Oxford, 1979), esp. chap. 4, and Paul Christianson, *Reformers and Babylon: English Apocalyptic Visions from the Reformation to the Eve of the Civil War* (Toronto, 1978), chaps. 1 and 2.

19. Lamont, *Marginal Prynne,* 68–84, 108–48, and William Prynne, *Canterburies Doome . . .* (London, 1646), 57; *The Popish Royall Favourite . . .* (London, 1643), preface and passim; and *Romes Masterpiece . . .* (London, 1644).

20. Lamont, *Marginal Prynne,* 79–80. For Presbyterian-Independent distinctions, see George R. Abernathy, Jr., "The English Presbyterians and the Stuart Restoration, 1648–1663," *American Philosophical Society Transactions,* 55, part 2; Geoffrey Nuttall, *Visible Saints: The Congregational Way, 1640–1660* (Oxford, 1957); and C. G. Bolam et al., *The English Presbyterians from Elizabethan Puritanism to Modern Unitarianism* (London, 1968).

21. Lamont, *Marginal Prynne,* 92ff., 197–200.

22. Ibid., 92ff.

23. Ibid., 175–204. See also William Prynne, *True and Perfect Narrative* (London, 1659), 20, and *The First Part of an Historical Collection of the Ancient Parliaments of England. . . .* Examples of English Republicans' assessments of Prynne are John Rogers, *Mr. Pryn's Good Old Cause Stated and Stunted 10 Years Ago . . .* (London, 1659), and John Streater, *The Continuation of This Session of Parliament Justified . . .* (London, 1659).

24. "Solomon Stoddard's Commonplace Book," microfilm copy, Widener Library, Harvard University. Samuel Rutherford, a Scot and professor of divinity at the University of St. Andrews, was the leader of the Presbyterian faction in revolutionary England and was an architect of the Westminster Assembly (1642–48) and the Westminster Confession. He was a noted polemicist and controversialist. Increase Mather hinted that Rutherford flirted with "converting ordinances" at some point in his life. He may have, but he was on the other side of the argument from Prynne in the 1640s and 1650s. Nonetheless, for Presbyterian political and ecclesiastical thinking he was the acknowledged master. In 1664 Stoddard owned *The Due Right of Presbyteries* and *The Divine Right of Church Government and Excommunication . . .* (London, 1646). For an introduction to Knox's political and ecclesiastical thinking and his Christian "imperialism," see Richard Kyle, "John Knox and Apocalyptic Thought," *Sixteenth Century Journal,* 15, no. 4 (Winter 1984), 449–70; W. Stanford Reid, "John Knox's Theology of Political Government," *Sixteenth Century Journal,* 19, no. 4 (Winter 1988), 529–40; and Richard Greaves, *Theology and Revolution in the Scottish Reformation,* (Grand Rapids, Mich., 1980). See also Marvin A. Breslow, ed., *The Political Writings of John Knox,* (Cranbury, N.J., 1985), introduction, and J. D. Mackie, *A History of Scotland,* 2nd ed., rev. and ed. Bruce Lenman and Geoffrey Parker (New York, 1978), 154–83.

25. Solomon Stoddard, *The Doctrine of Instituted Churches* (London, 1700). For the Synod of 1679 and the "Reformation of Manners" in the late seventeenth century, see Richard P. Gildrie, *The Profane, the Civil, and the Godly: The Reformation of Manners in Orthodox New England, 1679–1749* (University Park, Pa., 1994), 1–59.

26. Crawford reviews ministerial calls for moral and spiritual revival in *Seasons of Grace,* 19–51. See also David Hall, ed., *The Works of Jonathan Edwards, 12, Ecclesiastical Writings* (New Haven, 1994), 37–39.

27. Cotton Mather, *The Present State of New England* (Boston, 1690), 23–41, 47–52 (rep. Haskell House, 1972); *The Public Records of the Colony of Connecticut, 1636–1776* (Hartford, Conn., 1850–1890), vol. 4, 468.

28. This is an argument that began with Perry Miller. Gildrie, in *The Profane, the Civil, and the Godly,* offers both a restatement and a correction; see 1–15.

29. Solomon Stoddard, *Some Answers to Cases of Conscience* (Boston, 1722), 11–14, and *Question: Whether God Is Not Angry with the Country for Doing So Little towards the Conversion of the Indians?* (Boston, 1723), 6–12. Stoddard's position should be compared to that of the most famous New England missionary to the Indians, John Eliot; see Eliot, *The Christian Commonwealth* (London, written in 1651 but not published until 1659). Eliot's millennialism is discussed in Timothy J. Sehr, "John Eliot: Millennialist and Missionary," *The Historian,* 46, no. 2 (February 1984), 187–203.

30. Stoddard, *Instituted Churches,* 1–8, 26–34. Massachusett's "independence" ended in 1684 when the original colonial charter was revoked by an English court. From that date Massachusetts was a royal colony with a royal governor. A new colonial charter was issued by England for Massachusetts in 1692.

31. Richard Greaves, *Theology and Revolution in the Scottish Reformation: Studies in the Thought of John Knox* (Grand Rapids, Mich., 1980), chap. 6; Stoddard, *Instituted Churches,* 7–8, 25–29; Lamont, *Marginal Prynne,* 92ff.

32. Stoddard, *Instituted Churches,* 20–22.

33. Ibid., 9–15; Stoddard, *An Examination of the Power of the Fraternity* (Boston, 1718), 1–3.

34. Obviously, Stoddard hoped for a wider audience than New England. However, the English audience he sought wasn't interested in left-over ideas from the discredited Civil War era, especially not those of William Prynne. No Englishman or Scot responded to Stoddard. Instead, he heard from Boston's Increase Mather (*Order of the Gospel,* Boston, 1700), and what he probably hoped might be a transatlantic debate became, instead, a local squabble.

35. Charles II's government tried to impose Anglican bishops on Presbyterian Scotland. Rebellious Scottish "Covenanters" took to the woods and were often slaughtered by English troops. Stoddard may have encountered exiled Scots in his years in Barbados (ca. 1667) when he was chaplain to the governor. The Covenanters' story is recounted in Leigh Eric Schmidt, *Holy Fairs: Scottish Communions and American Revivals in the Early Modern Period* (Princeton, N.J., 1989), chap. 1.

36. I described this debate among some of New England's leading ministers in *Valley of Discord,* chap. 8. Perry Miller lists all of the pamphlets which appeared at the time in his article "Solomon Stoddard," 303 and 304. Stoddard's *Doctrine of Instituted Churches* and Increase Mather's *Order of the Gospel* have been reprinted in *Increase Mather vs. Solomon Stoddard: Two Puritan Tracts* (New York, 1972).

37. Stoddard was called the minister to the poor and the lowly, and his writings show that he was aware of the emergence of class distinctions in New England. See Lucas, *Valley of Discord,* chap. 6. Stoddard also revealed that many churches were admitting their children to full membership automatically while forcing newcomers and outsiders (the poor) to provide a narrative of religious experience. This discrimination based on standing in the community clearly infuriated Stoddard. See Stoddard, *An Examination of the Power of the Fraternity,* 7, 14–16; *Efficacy of the Fear of Hell, to Restrain Men from Sin* (Boston, 1713), 5–10; *The Inexcusableness of Neglecting the Worship of God under a Pretense of Being in an Unconverted Condition* (Boston, 1708), preface, 11–17, 25–27; *An Appeal to the Learned . . .* (Boston, 1709), 1–5; *Doctrine of Instituted Churches,* 1–10. See also Stoddard, *To Preach the Gospel to the Poor,* an undated sermon bound with the *Efficacy of the Fear of Hell . . .* (1713); and the preface written by an unidentified person for the 1772 Boston edition of Stoddard's *Nature of Conversion and the Way Wherein It Is Wrought* (1719).

38. Stoddard, *Some Answers to Cases of Conscience,* 11–14, and *Question: Whether God Is Not Angry,* 6–12.

39. Lucas, *Valley of Discord,* 189–202.

40. The Connecticut Valley's strategic importance may be seen in Steele, *Warpaths,* chaps. 7–8. See also Douglas Leach, *The Northern Colonial Frontier* (New York, 1960), 125.

41. See Jonathan Edwards, "Narrative of Communion Controversy," in *Works, 12,* 507–619.

42. See Crawford, *Seasons of Grace,* chap. 2; Lucas, *Valley of Discord,* 203–6. In his introduction to *Works, 12,* David Hall writes that "Jonathan Edwards pursued the program of Stoddard and the Williamses in his Northampton ministry in part because he faced the same pastoral situation as his grandfather" (44).

43. Anthony F. C. Wallace, "Revitalization Movements: Some Considerations for their Comparative Study," *American Anthropologist,* 58 (May 1956), 264–81. See also Anthony F. C. Wallace, *The Death and Rebirth of the Seneca* (New York, 1969, 1972), chaps. 8–10.

44. *Works, 12,* 38–44; Conrad Cherry, *The Theology of Jonathan Edwards: A Reappraisal* (Bloomington, Ind., 1990), chap. 11; Mark Valeri, *Law and Providence in Joseph Bellamy's New England: The Origins of the New Divinity in Revolutionary America* (New York, 1994), 3–8, 11.

45. One of Edwards's disciples was Yale president Timothy Dwight, whose *Travels in New England and New York* (Barbara Miller Solomon, ed., 4 vols., Cambridge, Mass., 1969) provides an enormous amount of information about New England in 1800. Dwight was a descendant of both Stoddard and Edwards. He wrote that Stoddard had "probably more influence than any other clergyman in the province during a period of thirty years" (vol. 1, 240–41), but he offered no reason for that influence. He also wrote that Edwards had "enlarged the science of theology [more] than any divine of whom either England or Scotland can boast" (vol. 4, 228).

46. The literature is voluminous. Outstanding examples include Charles H. Hopkins, *The Rise of the Social Gospel in American Protestantism, 1865–1915* (New Haven, 1967); Robert L. Berkhofer, *Salvation and the Savage: An Analysis of Protestant Missions and American Indian Response, 1787–1862* (Lexington, Ky., 1965); Timothy L. Smith, *Revivalism and Social Reform: American Protestantism on the Eve of the Civil War* (Baltimore, 1980); Henry Warner Bowden, *American Indians and Christian Missions: Studies in Cultural Conflict* (Chicago, 1981); Nathan O. Hatch, *The Democratization of American Christianity* (New Haven, 1989); Jon Butler, *Awash in a Sea of Faith: Christianizing the American People* (Cambridge, Mass., 1990); and esp. William R. Hutchison, *Errand To the World: American Protestant Thought and Foreign Missions* (Chicago, 1987).

SIX

The Godly Will's Discerning

SHEPARD, EDWARDS, AND THE IDENTIFICATION OF TRUE GODLINESS

WILLIAM K. B. STOEVER

Specification of "true Christian experience" and, in relation to it, identification of the true "matter" of the church, were persistent, characteristic issues in the Puritan religious tradition. These issues figured prominently in the New England Antinomian Controversy of the 1630s and in Jonathan Edwards's contention with his Northampton congregation in the 1740s. The *Treatise concerning Religious Affections* (1746), produced in the controversial retrospect of the Great Awakening, was Edwards's fullest and most pointed statement about the nature and expression of true godliness. In the later 1730s Edwards began to address this subject publicly, in his sermon series on Matt. 25 and 1 Cor. 13. In his treatment, he turned in part to Thomas Shepard (1604–49), an important participant in the Antinomian Controversy and in shaping the New England "way" respecting professed godliness as the basis of church membership. In the Antinomian affair, a central issue was how truly converted persons could be distinguished, in their own consciousness and in public probability, from persons affected by transient fancies and emotions. In different but analogous circumstances, Edwards found Shepard instructive. There is more in Edwards than is derivable simply from his Puritan antecedents. He maintained substantial continuity with them, however, in theological conceptions, and drew upon them in relation to circumstances that he encountered. This essay explores continuities between Shepard and Edwards respecting evidence of a godly estate, in relation to development and implications of Edwards's thought on the subject, chiefly with reference to the sermons from 1738 published as *Charity and Its Fruits* and to *Religious Affections.* It argues that Edwards developed his position with conscious attention to Shepard's, which, in the charged circumstances of post-Awakening Northampton, he asserted in a particularly rigorous and provocative way.

Shepard and Edwards both encountered people who offered special experiences of the Holy Spirit, and therein of God's good will to themselves, as ground for conclusions about their own and others' godliness. Both men responded, by way of distinguishing true Christian experience, in terms of an understanding of the nature of conversion that was conventional in seventeenth-century Reformed Protestant Orthodoxy. Here the crucial locus is that concerning sanctification, the new inner quality that makes "saints" saintly. In conversion, individuals are considered to undergo both a relative and a substantive change. In the first, God pronounces the person free from the guilt of sin and from the sentence of condemnation upon it. In the second, God infuses habitual grace into the soul, where it remains as a principle of "indwelling holiness," altering the soul's character. This gracious transformation affects preeminently the will, the active, elective faculty, which acquires thereby a fundamental antipathy toward sin and an unqualified commitment to the will of God as the rule of Christian life. On this ground William Ames (1576–1633), the theological doctor of New England Puritans, characterized theology as essentially practical, as "the doctrine of living to God," i.e., "in accord with the will of God, and to the glory of God." Peter van Mastricht (1630–1706), whose theological handbook Edwards greatly admired, said the same. Like Ames, Mastricht arranged his work in two great divisions, comprising "faith," the establishment in the soul of a principle of spiritual life, and "observance," the active expression of that principle in holy duty. Observance, said Ames, as "submission to the will of God, . . . is . . . called *Holiness* because it takes the pure form and shape of that will"; as such, it objectifies the conformity of human to divine nature that is the goal of the work of redemption.[1]

In the Orthodox conception, reliable knowledge of the substantive change in conversion derives from the soul's ability to know its own motives. Such knowledge is the work of conscience, which Ames characterized, in this connection, as a "reflect act of the understanding" whereby a person reviews and judges "his own actions with their circumstances." In its judgment, Christian conscience is guided by the rule of God's will for human action, expressed partly in the principles of natural morality but declared comprehensively in scripture. The objects of its judgment are the individual's external and internal actions, together with "the inclinations, and dispositions, . . . whence [they] flow." Outer and inner acts are inseparable in this consideration, inasmuch as an inclination of the will tends naturally to action. In the work of introspection, conscience proceeds via a "practical syllogism," in which the "proposition" derives from the divine law, the "assumption" concerns a finding respecting the individual, and the conclusion concerns the relation arising from the finding in respect of the law.[2] Francis Turretin (1623–87), whose compendious polemical divinity Edwards recommended, adduced the practical syllogism, relating declarations of scripture and effects of conversion perceived in the soul, as the ordinary means of obtaining assurance about one's estate in grace. For Turretin (who was reflecting a commonplace), as for Ames, assured knowledge of estate comes not by special revelation of God's mind respecting the individual but by apprehension of faith and love in oneself, confirmed by the witness of conscience, according to the rule of Scripture. For both men, "a necessary condition" for obtaining assurance is "zeal for sanctification."[3]

This is essentially the conception that Edwards filled out and applied, with increasingly critical force, to the phenomena of the New England Awakening manifest in his own congregation. It is laid out formally in his favorite dogmatic handbooks. In Shepard, however, it is elaborated and applied in a pastoral and ecclesiological situation similar to Edwards's own. Edwards's use of Shepard in *Affections* is well known. Less appreciated is the degree of continuity between Edwards's developed view and Shepard's respecting inherent sanctification and the extent of Edwards's familiarity with Shepard. Edwards's acquaintance with Shepard appears to have begun in the early 1720s; and, it may be suggested, his understanding of the nature of conversion, its effects, and their manifestation developed in cognizance of the earlier man's.[4] It is pertinent, accordingly, to look more closely at Shepard.

Shepard's major work, *The Parable of the Ten Virgins Unfolded* (1660), a sermon cycle of 1636–40 on Matt. 25:1–13, focuses on characteristic differences between the persistent acts and dispositions of the truly godly and the transient fancies, emotions, resolutions, and endeavors by which hypocrites assume and sustain a pretense of godliness.[5] Underlying and comprehending the distinction—indeed the *substance* of the difference—is the assumption that sanctification inheres in the converted. Shepard's pastoral treatise, *The Sound Believer* (1645), and his controversial tract, *Theses Sabbaticae* (1649), make the same point.

Believers, says Shepard, are endowed with two correlative graces: that of spiritual illumination, "whereby the soul . . . beholds such a glory of Christ's person, as that he esteems him in all his glory, as his present, greatest, and only good"; and that of sanctification, "whereby the soul beholding the glory of Christ, and feeling his love, hereupon closeth with the whole will of Christ, and seeketh to please him, as his happiness and utmost end."[6] The unregenerate characteristically make themselves their last end, and make their own happiness their chief good, to which they subordinate God and grace. They seek Christ, if at all, to quiet fears, ease consciences, gain repute among the neighbors, but not to change their own natures. Saving grace, however, does exactly that, and terminates, in both its illuminating and sanctifying modes, in the will. Gracious renovation is evident, fundamentally, in change of the will's chief end, "which . . . appears in making the Lord the utmost end of all that we do" "in the room of self-seeking." The sanctified, unlike the only apparently godly, " . . . love and will holiness and the means thereto, as God doth; they hate . . . sin, as God doth; they . . . delight in the whole law of God." In this transformation, the person is renewed "unto the image of God"; and Christ's glory, his love to the soul and the soul's reciprocation of it, and holy obedience as the soul's own "beauty," "excellency," and "glory," all coincide.[7]

Beholding Christ, the soul sees "a glory in the government, and commands, and will of Christ," and in all his "ordinances." Feeling Christ's love, the soul loves in return. It closes with Christ's whole will, as pleasing to him whom it loves, and because it sees Christ's holiness as the pattern of its own.[8] Inclined by excellency beheld, and tending naturally whither it now inclines, the soul, which before " . . . desired God and Christ only to keep his sores from aching, . . . now . . . makes the life of the Lord its happiness to live unto him." The Lord's "whole will" is revealed in the moral law, the comprehensive rule of Christian life. Its epitome is the Decalogue, "Christ's pandects," and its "end and scope" is love to God for his own sake and glory. Sanctification "is nothing else but our habitual conformity to the law," between which and the "new nature . . . in a believer" "there is a sweet agreement." Saints are both called to and enabled to live "the life of love, in fruitful and thankful obedience," in return of Christ's love received.[9] Such obedience is necessarily "universal" respecting scope and motive. It embraces all of Christ's commands as such, great and small, easy and onerous, in circumstances comfortable and not; and it does so with a whole heart. The unregenerate pick and choose commands, obey out of self-interest, scant obedience when they obtain comfort or meet difficulty. Saints, in contrast, perceive Christ's glory and holiness, and their own, in all the law without distinction, all of which they willingly undertake.[10]

In the present life, holy exercises are necessarily imperfect and variable. They spring, however, from an abiding "inward principle of the Spirit of life" that unbelievers cannot have. The effects of this principle in the soul are distinctive, and by the testimony of scripture regarding them, applied in introspection, "the true believer may know the blessedness of his estate" by the working of grace in himself, specifically in the distinctiveness of his ends and motives.[11] Scripture does not name the elect, nor are they identified personally by immediate revelation; but they *are* identified mediately, through the exercise of conscience, applying the word and rule of scripture to the individual's acts and intentions. The Lord ordinarily "speaks peace" to the heart via a syllogism, in which "the major is the word, the minor experience, and the conclusion [is] the . . . Spirit's work, quickening your spirit [i.e., conscience] to it." Only God can discern particular hearts, and hypocrites can counterfeit acts of obedience. Churches, as public institutions, must rest upon "judgments of rational charity" based on public observation. Individuals, however, may know their minds without special revelation. The marks of Christian character are accessible to ordinary cognition, and scripture is plain: "Whom doth the Lord Jesus love? You need not go to heaven for it; 'the word is nigh thee.' Those that love Christ: who are those? 'Those that keep his commandments . . .'"—per John 14:5 (with 1 John 2:3) the chief scriptural locus for the doctrine.[12]

Formal obedience and external conformity to the law abound; but they differ from saints' obedience, which arises from love to Christ and pleasure in his ends. Unsound hearts exhibit "much reformation, much affection, many duties; but their end is not changed, though their lives be, and hearts seem to be." "Angels," however, "know that they are not devils" because the Lord's will is their own. So saints are able to know their own hearts by "experience and sense." Their lives are subject to much variation and trial, but their end and intention do not shift. Hypocrites, in trial and temptation, return to the ungodly ends that they truly love, and never really left. In contrast, through the vicissitudes of spiritual and common life, saints' new "bent and bias of the soul" remain, as loving conformity of will with God's will; and they live spiritually and practically from "a little spring" of inner holiness, running ceaselessly unto eternal glory.[13]

It is a fairly direct route from these formulations to the significance given to "holy practice" in Edwards's sermons on Christian charity and to "universal obedience" as the culminating sign of *Religious Affections.*

In the winter of 1738, in a sermon series on the parable of the virgins in Matt. 25, Edwards distinguished true from counterfeit godliness in terms of an indwelling principle of spiritual life. In a longer series on 1 Cor. 13, beginning the same spring, he developed this distinction in terms of the spiritual principle's characteristic expression in godly love.[14] Much of the Charity sermons' practical force, in light of the preceding series, lies in their "uses" of self-examination respecting the indwelling of holiness. In this connection, the Charity sermons appear as an application of Shepard's position on manifest sanctification and the difference between genuine "virgin Christians" and false "gospel hypocrites," with sermon no. 10, on "holy practice," the focus of the series.

In regeneration, says Edwards, the soul receives spiritual insight, enabling it to behold God's excellency, beauty, and holiness, and Christ's excellency and sufficiency as Savior. Such insight elicits love to God for his own sake as "supreme good," which disposes the soul to "hearty" "acquiescence in" God's will, out of desire to please him.[15] The believer closes with Christ as King as well as Savior, i.e., "with subjection to his laws, and obedience to his commands." God's will respecting "the duty of mankind" is expressed in his law, comprehended in the Decalogue, the sum of which is Christ's dual command to love God and neighbor. The soul's submission to God's will is comprehensive, in that it esteems God as highest good entirely in place of self and world. It is thereby motivated to "constant and universal respect to [all] God's commands" as such; it enters "most cordially" upon "the whole of duty" respecting God and man; and it strives earnestly "to be universally holy."[16] Holy love necessarily issues in "holy practice," as the natural result of an active principle seated in the will. Such practice is abiding and consistent, and appears as conscientious living to God through the course of a lifetime. It is not "a mere incidental thing" beside other concerns, but is the "great aim" and "business" of a person's life.[17]

As the substance of Christian life, holy practice is the decisive evidence of sincere godliness. Herein, the Spirit's gracious indwelling of the soul is distinguished from his merely transient influences upon it. By the former, the soul's nature is altered, being conformed to the image of God. The latter, as sudden affections, intuitions, visions, and voices, are not evidence of this transformation. Saving grace is apprehended, accordingly, not in such experiences, but in and by acts of love, discerned in introspection, and judged by scripture, which acts, as expressions of grace, are "evidential of" its presence. Scripture "abundantly" insists on "Christian practice" as evidence of "sincerity in grace," inter alia, in John 14:23ff, where love to Christ is manifest in keeping his commandments. Accordingly, "we . . . are to argue . . . by discerning the exercises of grace in our hearts, some exercise of . . . divine charity, and comparing this with the rule of God's word, and so to conclude our good estate." True godliness is discovered via a practical syllogism (though Edwards did not use the term) based on the findings of conscience.[18]

Self-examination necessarily encompasses inner motives along with outward acts. Humans are voluntary intelligent beings and, as such, God especially considers their intentions, in particular whether their obedience is "cordial" or grudging. Outward practice, in any case, is inevitably imperfect, such that sincerity must be sought inwardly in motives and dispositions. Motives alone, however, are insufficient evidence without corresponding action. Grace, per definition, "is a principle of holy action" subsisting in the will, whose inclination to serve its highest good issues naturally in particular action. The "most proper evidence" of the reality and sincerity of an inner principle "is its being effectual" outwardly.

> So if we see a man who by his constant behavior shows himself ready to take pains and lay out himself for God, . . . this is an evidence of love to God more

> to be depended on than if he only professes that he feels great love to God in his heart.[19]

The clearest evidence of "a title to heaven," accordingly, is "in feeling that which is heavenly in the heart." "Heavenly feeling," however, that is not motivated by divine love, is inconclusive; and such feeling that does not carry forth in holy action is suspect. Truly "clear" evidence is to be found in "the continual and lively exercises" of a "*life* of love," lived wholly "unto God."[20]

From the waning of the Northampton awakening of 1734–35, Edwards was concerned about the transitoriness of religious stimulation, especially its effects on personal behavior, in light of his understanding of sanctification. This matter was on his mind in his Ten Virgins sermons, and it motivated, in part, the Charity sermons. In the *Treatise on Religious Affections,* it became the focus of a searching examination of visible sainthood. In this respect, Part III of *Affections* may be viewed as the summation of Edwards's progressive effort, begun already in the 1720s, to specify the content and character of true godliness.[21] Part III may also be seen as a deliberate filling out of the Orthodox dogmatic locus on the substantive change that occurs in conversion, constructed on the formula articulated by Shepard. As in no. 10 of the Charity sermons, the conclusive "sign of signs" (no. 12), "which confirms and crowns all other signs of godliness," is a settled course of "Christian practice" that is "universally obedient" to God's revealed will.[22]

Here, Edwards became thorough and emphatic. Because the sanctified soul is comprehensively renovated, Christian obedience is also comprehensive. It is "universal" in scope, motive, and activity. Obedience encompasses all the duties of God's law, as represented in both tables of the Decalogue. It springs from the "full, steadfast, determination of the will for God and holiness," elicited by holy affections. It exhibits, therefore, entire aversion from moral evil, and is without any admixture of subordinating self-interest. Its activity encompasses "the whole of religion," including the difficult parts, sustainedly prosecuted as the main "business" of a Christian's entire life. It is "strict, universal, and constant obedience."[23] As such, it is the preeminent evidence of a gracious estate, to others and to oneself.

Early in Part III, Edwards scouted all confidence of a person's estate arising from "impressions on the imagination," including the "voice of Christ," the "witness of the Spirit," and "immediate suggesting of words of scripture to the mind," all perceived as "inward testimony of the love of Christ to the soul." Such confidence is founded upon misapprehension about the nature of the experiences involved, and about God's communication with saints.[24] God does not reveal his mind to individuals by "an inward immediate suggestion, as though . . . by a . . . secret voice," such that they may conclude their blessedness from the experience itself. On the contrary, God applies the scriptural promises respecting blessedness by effecting in the soul that to which the promises refer, in the form of "sensible actings of grace," which conscience "receives and declares" in their evidential significance. From the effects of the love of God infused into the heart, persons "may argue [and prove] that they are children of God." "Scripture reveals the . . . persons who are beloved . . . by revealing the qualifications of persons that are beloved of God." The Spirit "witnesses" in and through a reasoned conclusion, founded on the rule of scripture and the testimony of conscience; which conclusion—not extraordinary "spiritual" experiences—is the proper basis of Christian profession.[25]

The nature of such profession is a prominent issue in *Affections* (and the subject also of Edwards's Virgins sermons, as of the later communion controversy). Though Christian profession may be false, and may, if true, be tentative, it is not speculative respecting nature or object. It is, Edwards insisted, fundamentally an assertion of actually *being Christian,* of which a "visibly holy life" "in universal obedience to Christ's commands" is the concrete manifestation. This is *the* distinguishing mark of godliness, and visible holiness is the basis for being charitably accounted a professing Christian by one's neighbors. The indispensable element in profession, however, is invisible to neighborly eyes: what "the professor understandingly and honestly . . . is conscious of in his own heart." The "obedience . . . of the soul" necessarily includes the "aim or intention" upon which visible action depends. Outward obedience is to be judged, accordingly, in respect to "the end acted for, and the respect the soul then has to God, or service done to him," as object of "supreme love." Sincere profession is distinguished by its motives. The crucial interest is "that in our practice which is visible to our own consciences."[26]

The evidential significance of mental acts, however, is not distinct from their consistent expression in outward acts of obedience. As in the Charity sermons, Edwards stressed the inseparability of intention from action. In this connection, toward the end of *Affections,* he distinguished purely subjective religious experience from "Christian experience" properly so called. The former comprises the "great discoveries" and high emotions prominent in the revival, and also the "immanent exercises" of holiness (e.g., in meditation) that remain within the soul. The latter is not limited to inward acts, but "consists . . . in those operative exercises of grace in the will" that "have outward behavior immediately connected with them"—i.e., in "Christian practice" in the large sense of Sign 12. In face of the wildly experiential religion of the Awakening, Edwards asserted a severely practical religion: the experience that counts is "practical" experience, in the sense that the "highest and most proper evidence" that a tree is a fig tree, "is that it actually bears figs." Objective Christian "fruit," as the effectual exertion of holy intention, is diagnostic to *conscience,* and is given "from the beginning of Genesis to the end of Revelations" as "the [chief] sign of the holy principle and good estate" *to ourselves.*[27] Accordingly, says Edwards (echoing Shepard),

> If God were now to speak from heaven to resolve our doubts concerning signs of godliness, and should give some particular sign, that by it all might know whether they were sincerely godly or not, . . . should not we look upon it as a thing beyond doubt, . . . as . . . [an] eminently distinguishing note of true godliness? But this is the very case with respect to [Christian practice]; God has again and again uttered himself in his Word in this very manner; . . . "He that hath my commandments and keepeth them, he it is that loveth me."[28]

Shepard was engaged chiefly with people who held that assurance of salvation depends on an extraordinary "witness of the Spirit" "speaking peace to the soul," and who regarded use of the law as the rule of Christian life as contrary to "free grace." The first, he said, was no more than Balaam and his ass experienced; the second is a devilish plot to save people *in* their sins. In response, he invoked the "ordinary" spiritual principle of inherent sanctification, acting in holy obedience discerned by conscience, as manifesting the elect. Edwards, encountering the psychosomatic phenomena, transient personal effects, congregational contentiousness, and antinomian tendencies of the Awakening, invoked the same principle. The blessed are not revealed in sudden illuminations and raised affections, but in practical conformity of will to the whole will of God as chief end. For both men, the godly will is discerned in the character of its inner acts expressed.

For Shepard, however, the sanctified will, in gracious experience, was the complement of trusting reliance on Christ alone as Savior; fiducial faith and holy love, alternately and together, sustain the true saint. For Edwards, in the texts considered here, sanctification is the chief preoccupation, as the substantive expression of saving grace. Sanctification of particular persons, he maintained, is the aim of the decree of election, the goal of Christ's redemption, the end of effectual calling and of all the gracious stimulations of religious life.[29] These were commonplaces of Reformed Orthodoxy; in Part III of *Affections,* Edwards brought them to systematic application. The conception of Part III, respecting the new abiding spiritual principle, its manifestation in universal obedience, and the implications thereof for church members' conduct, is present but undeveloped in nos. 5–8 of the Virgins sermons. There, the focus is studied contrast between the mutual resemblances of saints and hypocrites in the visible church, and their decisive differences, though the sermonic "uses" bring the differences home in terms of outward behavior as well as subjective perception and intention. In the Charity sermons, scope and development are directed by Paul's text and by the classic topic of divine love; but both the text and the homiletical occasion converge on love exercised in practice, not only "felt." As in Charity no. 12 all graces are "concatenated together"—such that any one elicits others and love stimulates them all; so in *Affections* Part III all the signs of godliness, arising from the new spiritual principle, concur in practice as their natural expression. Both tracts indicate that hopeful saints may evidence other graces from apprehension of one of them, and also that all graces are perfected, and validated, in practice.[30] Though Part III early addresses the question of how to know one's estate (in Sign 1), its focus is not assurance of election (though that is involved), but the new spiritual principle as an *abiding* change of personal *character*, i.e., the sanctification that ought to be evident if people really are the children of God that they claim to be. In this, the challenge to professing Christians in the visible church—present in the Virgins sermons, and explicit in the Charity sermons and the Northampton covenant renewal—is central, and the development is thorough and pointed.[31] Edwards's interest is not counsel to weak, imperfect Christians, but the unwarranted presumption of professors.

Herein, in relation to the Puritan tradition, Part III presents both a paradox and a problem. The paradox is the familiar one of Puritan experiential piety, respecting the simultaneity of divine efficacy in regeneration and its subjective elusiveness in the beneficiaries. How is it that so momentous and comprehensive an event as spiritual rebirth—a new creative act by the same almighty power that made the world and will raise the dead, a thorough renovation of the whole soul in all its faculties, a radical reorientation of its conscious ends, effected by the revelatory and transforming influx of divine and supernatural light—as actually experienced is often so slight and tenuous that those in whom it has happened may be unaware of it, and, having once recognized the event, may come nonetheless to doubt it? How can so great a change be so little evident to the subjects of it? (A variant of this question frames *Affections.*)[32] Yet such is manifestly the case, in the experience of people and pastors. Puritan preachers had a standard answer: God ordinarily works indirectly and by degrees. He drops grace into the soul rather than floods it. He allows the saints to experience their remaining corruption, and their weakness against it, so that they may appreciate his graciousness and learn reliance on him alone. Wherefore the effectualness of calling is usually concluded retrospectively by degrees, from cumulative recognitions of a changed attitude (though "much mixed with sin").[33] A little grace, however, truly recognized, is sufficient to conclude a gracious estate; for a little grace implies the whole, whose ultimate perfection is guaranteed by God's immutable will and irresistible power. True saints doubt, but do not despair; they fall but their frail new love remains fixed. In this respect, sermonic delineations of true godliness served to instruct about the range of possibilities wherein evidence of regeneration might be sought, and worked to reassure by depicting the glorious whole that fragmentary finding reliably implied. This conception of gracious life corresponded to the ambiguous, "mixed" character of Christian experience, and in a measure contained the radical contrast between the "new being," as homiletically defined, and the "old," personally familiar one.

The problem in Part III lies in the thoroughness of Edwards's characterization of true godliness. *Affections* is a polemical and theoretical work, but the content of its delineation of godliness is the standard stuff of Puritan pastoral discourse. Shepard, an accomplished pastor, and Edwards (presumably in another mood) would have said (in effect) that the delineation in its fullness is an abstract ideal, and is, therefore, to be applied to particular cases only with care and judiciousness, by ministers versed in the variousness of God's working and of recipients' experience. In Shepard's *Parable,* "uses" of encouragement and comfort, directed to the weak and doubtful, tend to balance pointed "uses" of examination, directed at the overhopeful. In *Affections,* the former sort drop out. Part III presents a rigorous, systematic program of self-examination, in which the formulation is full and particular, and the language correspondingly emphatic: conversion is "a great and remarkable, abiding change," not only of the "present exercise, sensation, and frame of the soul," but of its "very nature"; it is a "great and universal change of the man, turning him from sin to God." The regenerate "have the whole image of Christ upon them" in the "universality of their sanctification"; they "are sanctified throughout, in spirit, soul, and body," and have "a new conversation and practice." Conversion entails "thorough conviction of the judgment, of the reality and certainty of divine things," and of all "the great doctrines of the gospel." It engenders in the person a "sense of [his] own utter insufficiency, despicableness, and odiousness, with an answerable frame of heart." It produces "such a spirit of love, meekness, quietness, forgiveness and mercy, as appeared in Christ." The converted are not "religious only by fits and starts," but abidingly and in due proportion to all their varying circumstances. Conversion expresses itself lifelong in constant and insatiable "longings after God" as the object of supreme desire. Practically, conversion is manifest in "strict, universal and constant obedience" to all the commands of Christ, prosecuted as that "business which [the person] is chiefly engaged in, devoted to, and pursues with highest earnestness and diligence"; and which he persists in, without intermission, "through all changes, and under all trials, as long as he lives."[34] This is a formidable schedule.

In part, this heightening of definition arose from the polemical situation. In Edwards's estimate, "hypocrites" in the Awakening seem to have the really good effects. They claim visions, voices, and transports, and scripture verses given directly to their minds. They discourse impressively on the manner and occasion of their conversions, and on the affecting special communications that God gives them personally. They have great confidence, and quite positive views about their own, and others', godliness. In comparison, what poor doubting real saints, enmeshed in their "mixed" condition, have to offer appears pale and weak. To undercut the hypocrites, Edwards elaborated the specification of godliness so as to display unmistakably its radical contrast with current counterfeits. But *Affections* was, in a sense, a pastoral as well as a polemical exercise, directed not only at the New Lights, but also at Edwards's congregation. In this connection, its force lay, not primarily in its definition of "religious affections," and not only in its repudiation of New Light excesses, but in its challenge to self-deception on the part of particular people. Part III, in its formidable, comprehensive specificity, calls into question virtually all pretense to inherent godliness.[35]

Part III also poses a significant ecclesiological problem, in that the force of Edwards's delineation of true godliness threatens to undercut attainment of it as a real possibility. Dwight, apparently without irony, likened Edwards's trial of godliness in *Affections* to that of the Last Day, and declared that "who[ever] can endure [it] . . . will stand unhurt amidst a dissolving universe." Practically, however, what empirical congregant could hope to meet the schedule of godly action and intention that Edwards prescribes—however judiciously applied, by an astute and sympathetic minister (in private)? It would seem seriously presumptuous to present oneself for church membership, if conscientious, on Edwards's terms (as no one in Northampton did after 1744). In the searching thoroughness of his delineation, Edwards appears, almost, to remove true godliness from the realm of practical realization. At least, he severely circumscribed that realm, and therein proportionately circumscribed the "matter" of the visible church.[36] Edwards seemed to confirm this impression when he observed to a correspondent that, in New England, the number of converts who, from "their conversation," may be "suppose[d]" actually to be "true converts," is like "the proportion of the blossoms on a tree which abide and come to mature fruit, to the whole number of blossoms in the spring." Herein, he echoed Shepard's observation, early in *The Parable,* about the "many hundreds [who] drop away," though they were "exceeding forward . . . for a year or two." From this judgment, implicit in *Affections,* the admission controversy was but a step away.[37]

NOTES

1. William Ames, *The Marrow of Theology,* trans. and ed. John D. Eusden (Boston, 1968), I.i, ii, xxvii, xxix; II.i, ii; Peter van Mastricht, *Theoretico-Practica Theologia* (Amsterdam, 1715), 50, 1102. On Edwards's estimate of Mastricht, see Stanley T. Williams, ed., "Six Letters of Jonathan Edwards to Joseph Bellamy," *New England Quarterly,* 1 (April 1928), 228–32.

2. William Ames, *Conscience with the Power and Cases Thereof* (London, 1643), I.i.8–11, ii.1, 3–9; viii.1–2, 4; II.i.7–14; *Marrow,* I.xxvii, xxx, II.iii.

3. Francis Turretin, *Institutio Theologiae Elenchticae* (New York, 1847), Loc. IV.xiii.4–9, 19, xviii.26; Loc. XV.xvii.6–8, 12, cf. xviii. Cf. Ames, *Cases,* II.v.1–10, *Marrow,* II.i.13, 16; cf. Mastricht, *Theologia,* VI.viii.31. For a summary of the "common places" of Reformed Orthodox doctrine, see Heinrich Heppe, *Dogmatik der evangelisch-reformierten Kirche, dargestellt und aus den Quellen belegt,* ed. Ernst Bizer, 2nd ed. (Neukirchen, 1958); for Edwards's estimate of Turretin, see Williams, ed. "Six Letters," 229–30.

4. Edwards's Miscellanies 4, 43, and 45 (ca. 1723), inter alia, on the "morality of the sabbath" appear to coincide with Edwards's interest, noted in his "Catalogue" of reading in Shepard's *Theses Sabbaticae;* see Jonathan Edwards, *The "Miscellanies,"* ed. Thomas A. Schafer, *The Works of Jonathan Edwards, 13* (New Haven, 1994), and MS leaf in "Catalogue," Beinecke Rare Book and Manuscript Library. The principal section of Shepard's *Theses,* on "the morality of the sabbath," includes discussion of the moral law as incumbent on Christians and a long interjection on inherent sanctification as evidence of a justified estate, in opposition to antinomians; see *The Works of Thomas Shepard,* ed. John Albro (1851–53; rpt. New York, 1967), vol. 3, 80–88, 92–133. Other Miscellanies on faith and the Spirit's operation in conversion suggest Edwards's occupation, in the 1720s, with "spiritual understanding" as formulated by Shepard in *The Parable of the Ten Virgins* and *The Sound Believer;* Edwards elaborates the formulation in terms of his recension of empiricist psychology (e.g., Misc. aa, 123, 201, 239, 397; *Parable, Works, 2,* 200–201, 235–36, 309–17; *Believer, Works, 1,* 126–29). Edwards's handling, in his sermon series on Matt. 25 in 1738, of similarities and differences among "true" and "false" "virgins" in the visible church follows Shepard's handling of the same subject in *Parable.* Virtually all of Edwards's characteristic vocabulary in *Affections* respecting spiritual understanding and illumination, the beauty, excellency, and amiableness of holiness, the soul's esteem thereof, holy affections, and universal obedience appears in *Parable* and *Believer.* Cf. also Shepard's ecclesiological assumptions in *Parable* (esp. Pt. I, ch. 19) and Edwards's later position (see intro., Jonathan Edwards, *Ecclesiastical Writings,* ed. David D. Hall, *Works, 12* [New Haven, 1994], pp. 44–63, 80–85). Cf. intro., Jonathan Edwards, *Religious Affections,* ed. John E. Smith, *Works, 2* (New Haven, 1959), pp. 53–57.

5. See *Parable,* Part I, chaps. 13–22; Part II, chaps. 9–13.

6. Shepard, *Parable,* 44, 86–88, 313, 333; cf. *Believer,* 199–200.

7. *Parable,* 113, 139, 176–79, 241, 332–33, 438–41; *Believer,* 211–13, 256–57, 262.

8. *Parable,* 241, 314–15, 321, 334–36, 437–38, 465–70; *Believer,* 207–8, 257.

9. *Parable,* 126, 139–40, 171–72, 337, 535–36, 560; *Theses,* 51–52, 84–88, 98, 102–3, 119, 154; *Believer,* 275–79.

10. *Parable,* 82, 113, 266–67, 357–58; *Theses,* 98, 120, 130. Shepard routinely entered the standard Protestant qualification: obedience to the law is not ground and matter of justification, being excluded by the *sola gratia;* but the law as rule of life is part of the gospel, is the "law of Christ," to which obedience is possible only as fruit of prevenient, renovating grace. Christ in the gospel provides the rule to guide us and provides us grace to follow it (*Theses,* 91–92).

11. *Parable,* 206–10, 212–17, 222–23, 238, 261–62, 268–69, 580–82, 586–87; *Theses,* 119–20; *Believer,* 238–39, 259–61.

12. *Parable,* 215–16, 222, 521–22; *Believer,* 226; *Theses,* 119.

13. *Parable,* 215–16, 226–27, 279, 322–23, 326, 337–38, 359, 362; *Believer,* 256, 262, 279.

14. Edwards, Sermon series on Matt. 25:1–12, no. 5, Beinecke Library (I am indebted to Ava Chamberlain for examination of the transcript of these MSS). The Charity sermons are an important expression of Edwards's ethical thinking, and also of his homiletical practice; see introduction, Jonathan Edwards, *Ethical Writings,* Paul Ramsay, ed., *Works, 8* (New Haven, 1989), 1–3.

15. Edwards, *Charity and Its Fruits, Works, 8,* 133–35, 137, 145–46, 296–97, 299–300; cf. 302–3.

16. *Charity*, 137–39, 176, 182, 264–65, 300–301, 333, 388–89.

17. *Charity*, 297–99, 311–12, 349.

18. *Charity*, 145–48, 157–61, 164–66, 168–70, 181–83, 227, 309–12.

19. *Charity*, 178–80, 182–83, 213, 259, 264–65, 297–98, 302, 309–11.

20. *Charity*, 396 (italics added). What Edwards meant concretely by "holy practice" appears in the public covenant renewal that he exacted from his congregation in March 1742, after the peak of religious excitement in Northampton. As an explicit program of outward carriage and inner intent for "professing Christians"—respecting persevering neighborliness, honesty, equity, religious duty, self-examination, and "Christian humility, gentleness, quietness, and love" in private and public conduct—his "covenant" is a remarkable document; Edwards to Thomas Prince, December 12, 1743, in Jonathan Edwards, *The Great Awakening*, ed. C. C. Goen, *Works, 4* (New Haven, 1972), 549–54.

21. Edwards's interest in the "matter" of the church and its identification appears well before the Northampton revival, e.g., in Misc. 462 on the visible church (ca. 1730), and in his Signs of Godliness notebook (begun in 1728) (see Schafer, *"Miscellanies,"* 100, 104); these together anticipate the fully developed position of *Affections* and *An Humble Enquiry*.

22. *Affections*, 383–84, 444. In *Affections* more than usually, Edwards acknowledged his sources; in Part III, Shepard is the principal author cited, thirty-one times in ten of the twelve Signs, including seven times in Sign 12. The Shepardian frame in Part III may be traced as follows. (1) The foundation of true religious affections is a distinctive abiding transformation of mind; assurance respecting estates is not, therefore, obtained from striking "immediate suggestions" allegedly from God, but from particular evidence of inner transformation, discerned by "the eye of conscience" and judged according to the declaration of Scripture (Sign 1). (2) Holy affections, arising as love to God, are elicited by spiritual sight and knowledge of the reality, "loveliness," and "moral excellency" of God, considered in himself; this excellency is his holiness, of which the "grand expression . . . and prescription of holiness" to creatures is "God's law" (Signs 2, 3, 4). (3) Love to God as he is in himself amounts to a "great and universal change" of the person, "from sin to God"; as such, it is wholly the effect of God's creative power, altering the nature of the soul, restoring it to the divine image in which it was created (Sign 7). From this qualitative change others flow, in the "exercise, sensation and frame of the soul" (delineated in Signs 8, 9, 10, 11). (4) Of these changes, the sum and "crown" is "universal obedience" to Christ's commands (Sign 12).

23. *Affections*, 383, 387–89, 393–94, 396–97, 418–19, 429–30, 434, 437–39. For his "doctrine" respecting "universal obedience," Edwards adduced Solomon Stoddard (*Affections*, 384, n. 8). In the local circumstances, Stoddard was a pertinent authority, and he is pointed on the topic; he was articulating a Puritan commonplace (cf. Peter Bulkeley, *The Gospel Covenant* [London, 1646], 376–77, and Shepard, passim). Stoddard figures in the conception and content of *Affections* beyond what appears from citations; see his trilogy on conversion, *A Guide to Christ* (Boston, 1714), *A Treatise concerning Conversion* (Boston, 1719), and *The Way to Know Sincerity and Hypocrisy* (Boston, 1719).

24. *Affections*, 210–13, 218–26.

25. *Affections*, 225–26, 231–34, 239, 268, 294; cf. 426, 441–43.

26. *Affections*, 413–17, 418–19, 420–21, 423–24, 430–31, 434–35.

27. *Affections*, 420, 422–24, 426–27, 436–38, 443–53. Edwards's insistence on the necessary reciprocity of inner and outer godliness closely parallels Ames's treatment of godly virtue; *Marrow*, II.iii.

28. *Affections*, 438; cf. Shepard, *Parable*, 222.

29. *Charity*, 161–62, 169–70; *Affections*, 376–79, 398–99.

30. *Charity*, 299–308; *Affections*, 392–99, 444–50.

31. E.g., *Charity*, 172–73.

32. *Affections*, 85–86.

33. For each man's experience with the "mixed" condition of converted life, see Shepard's "Journal," in Michael McGiffert, ed., *God's Plot: The Paradoxes of Puritan Piety* (Am-

herst, 1972), 81–238, and Edwards's "Diary," in Sereno Edwards Dwight, *Life of President Edwards* (New York, 1829), 76–94, 99–106.

34. *Affections,* 291–92, 311, 340–41, 344–45, 365, 372–73, 376–78, 383–84, 391, 395, 396.

35. Dwight said that Edwards preached the contents of *Affections* to his congregation ca. 1742–43 (*Life,* 223); if so, they can scarcely have missed his point. The vehemence of their repudiation of him in the admission controversy and their categorical refusal to countenance his public defense seem hardly spontaneous. Conceivably, these reactions were prepared in the interval between the covenant renewal and the appearance of *Affections.* In the first, in a sense, Edwards called his constituents out; in the second, he wrote them off.

36. His clerical opponents in 1750–51 appear to have read him in approximately these terms. See introduction, Edwards, *Ecclesiastical Writings,* 54, 72–73, 80; cf. Edwards, *Misrepresentations Corrected,* Pts. I.2, II.2 in idem. Edmund Morgan suggested perceptively that heightened conscientiousness might account for the relatively few full communicants in some Edwardsian and Stoddardian churches; "New England Puritanism: Another Approach," *William & Mary Quarterly,* 18 (1961), 236–42.

37. Edwards to John Erskine, June 28, 1751, in Dwight, *Life,* 460 (I am indebted to Kenneth Minkema for the source of this remark); Shepard, *Parable,* 40; cf. introduction, Edwards, *Ecclesiastical Writings,* 57–58, 84, on the relation of *Affections* to Edwards's subsequently expressed views on admission.

SEVEN

Did Berkeley Influence Edwards?

THEIR COMMON CRITIQUE OF THE MORAL SENSE THEORY

RICHARD A. S. HALL

> This Gentleman and Mr. Thwackum scarce ever met without a Disputation; for their Tenets were indeed diametrically opposite to each other. Square held human Nature to be the Perfection of all Virtue, and that Vice was a Deviation from our Nature in the same Manner as Deformity of Body is. Thwackum, on the contrary, maintained that the human Mind, since the Fall, was nothing but a Sink of Iniquity, till purified and redeemed by Grace. In one Point only they agreed, which was, in all their Discourses on Morality never to mention the Word Goodness. The favourite Phrase of the former, was the natural Beauty of Virtue; that of the latter, was the divine Power of Grace.
>
> —Henry Fielding, *Tom Jones*

Following Edwin S. Gaustad's lead, I shall here bring to light some evidence that George Berkeley may very well have influenced Jonathan Edwards, though in a way hitherto unsuspected, thereby reviving the long dormant argument for that influence. The evidence consists of some remarkable continuities of thought between Edwards's *Nature of True Virtue* and Berkeley's *Alciphron* with respect to their common critique of the moral sense theory. Accordingly, this essay addresses the issue of Berkeley's alleged influence on Edwards; how *Alciphron* and *True Virtue* each fits into its respective author's life and thought; their public reception; some similarities between these works, together with their differences; the issue of Berkeley's influence on Edwards in the light of them; what can be concluded about Berkeley's influence on Edwards; and the larger significance of the parallels between *Alciphron* and *True Virtue* beyond the question of the former's influence.

I

Georges Lyon proposed that Berkeley influenced the youthful Edwards in order to account for the latter's precocious idealism.[1] There is no evidence for this, however. The current wisdom is that Edwards more than likely derived his metaphysical idealism from the Cambridge Platonists and Malebranche—presumably the very sources from which Berkeley might have derived his own. Norman Fiering thinks that Wallace Anderson "has argued convincingly that Edwards, too, may have adopted the idealist or immaterialist position from premises in Henry More and in Newton."[2] Moreover, Perry Miller confidently declared, "there is no evidence whatsoever that Edwards read Berkeley, . . . ; his journals meticulously acknowledge his debts to every philosopher he managed to read, and nowhere is there any sign of his first-hand acquaintance with Berkeley."[3]

Now though it is quite unlikely that Edwards's idealism owed anything to the Irish bishop, this may not be the case with other philosophical positions of his. Gaustad intriguingly suggests, but does not elaborate, that *Alciphron,* in particular, "showed evidence of its influence in his [Edwards's] later writing." Gaustad detects evidence of its influence on Edwards's *True Virtue.* Specifically, he cites the fact that "Edwards, like Berkeley, found beauty a useful analogue, or more, in attempting to understand the nature of virtue," and that "against Shaftesbury, both men agreed that virtue was more than sentiment or innate sense, more than an accident of taste or an arbitrariness of manners. Virtue, in short, was built into the very nature and purpose of the universe."[4] Fiering thinks that Edwards must have read Berkeley, for "his reading in ethics undoubtedly began to broaden by the mid-1730s" to include, among other things, the "third dialogue in Berkeley's *Alciphron* with its careful discussion of Shaftesbury."[5] As evidence, Fiering notes that both men agree, against Shaftesbury's exalted Platonism, that virtue's being its own reward is an insufficient inducement to virtue for the vast majority of men and women who require the inducements of carrot and stick.

II

Sojourning in Newport, Rhode Island, between 1729 and 1731 while awaiting funds from Parliament for the purpose of founding in Bermuda what would have been St. Paul's College, the then dean of Derry and the Somers Islands (now Bermuda) wrote the bulk of seven dialogues published in 1732 as *Alciphron, or the Minute Philosopher.* George Berkeley had long cherished the hope of planting in the Caribbean a "Utopian Seminary" for the express purpose of training missionaries and pastors for the New World.[6] He thought Bermuda a propitious place for this endeavor because of its sizable population of natives and black Africans from whom seminarians might be recruited; he speculated that they would be more effective than Caucasians in evangelizing the indigenous peoples of North America and be better received by their auditors.[7]

Berkeley doubtless saw the mercantile and political advantages to Britain of establishing an English college there that might prove decisive in soliciting monies from the Crown. The Caribbean was a crucial nexus in the trade between the New and the Old Worlds. Moreover, an Anglican seminary in Bermuda would serve as a strategic outpost for the Protestant cause in offsetting the looming Catholic hegemony in the region—Spain to the south and France to the north.[8]

But Berkeley's evangelical scheme was impelled by a larger purpose. He had come to lament what he saw as the precipitous moral and spiritual decline of British society in the Age of Enlightenment, which was undoubtedly exacerbated by the financial crash of the South Sea Company in October 1721.[9] So bad was it that the dean was moved to say that "other nations have been wicked, but we are the first who have been wicked upon principle,"[10] a clear augury, he thought, of Britain's demise as a civilization. And since, in his conception, Great Britain was the bulwark of the Protestant Reformation, the future no less of Christianity and Western civilization itself was in dire peril. The only hope of redeeming British piety and virtue and so of safeguarding Christian civilization, as he saw it, was to look west.[11] "Westward the Course of Empire takes its Way," Berkeley proclaimed in the last stanza of his only poem.[12] "I have determined to spend the residue of my days in the Island of Bermuda, where," he confides, "I may be the mean instrument of doing good to mankind."[13] Thus animated by this philosophy of history and with a royal charter in hand, Berkeley set sail for Rhode Island, where he would begin establishing his new "Athens of the World."[14]

In 1731, Parliament reneged on its promised grant because of political intrigues, and Berkeley's dream was dashed. He did not hesitate to lay the blame on the freethinking and deistic spirit of the times: "What they foolishly call free-thinking seems to me the principal root or source not only of opposition to our College but of most other evils in this age."[15] He alludes to "the affair which brought me into this remote corner of the country" in *Alciphron,* a work which he saw as a way of helping to redeem the miscarriage of his philanthropic scheme. "The course and event of this affair gave opportunity for reflexions that make me some amends for a great loss of time, pains, and expense."[16] If he was prevented from fighting infidelity and vice in the field, then he would do so from the press. This is exactly what he undertook in this series of dialogues which bears the tendentious subtitle "Containing an Apology for the Christian Religion, against those who are called Free-Thinkers." It was a spark, as Gaustad aptly expresses it, "to arise from the ashes of Bermuda."[17]

What place does *Alciphron* occupy in Berkeley's oeuvre? The answer in part depends on one's estimate of the work in its own right, and these estimates have ranged from outright dismissal to panegyric. A contemporary historian, William Douglass, scored it for its "obscurantism" and for evincing "a certain enthusiasm in human nature."[18] John Stuart Mill adjudged that "were it not the production of so eminent a man, it would have little claim to serious attention," though he did commend its literary style and dialectical skill.[19] Leslie Stephen wrote, "Berkeley's 'Minute Philosopher' is the least admirable performance of that admirable writer," but, echoing Mill, allowed that parts of it are "expressed in a style of exquisite grace and lucidity."[20] And most recently, J. O. Urmson thinks "there is little in this work which still has philosophical or religious importance."[21] G. J. Warnock complains that the work is more a caricature of strawmen than a fair criticism of the actual views of Berkeley's opponents, and is too much preoccupied with obsolete disputes in theology instead of substantive issues in philosophy. Furthermore, unlike *Alciphron's* other detractors, Warnock does not even concede the work's literary merits, declaring that "the comparative tedium of the debate as a whole is not relieved by any new philosophical matter, not even by the grace of Berkeley's style."[22] It is noteworthy, I think, that the critics of *Alciphron* by and large hold no brief for religion, especially Christianity, and so their low estimates of a work in Christian apologetics is quite predictable.

On the other hand, M. R. Ayers does find some "new philosophical matter" in the form of "an interesting discussion of theoretical terms in theology as well as in science, in which the flavour of pragmatism is pronounced."[23] David Berman deems it "Berkeley's most substantial work in philosophical theology."[24] For T. E. Jessop, "he comes next to Plato in the easy and lively shaping of philosophical dialogue." Finally, Jessop's estimate of *Alciphron* is, "As a work of art it stands supreme in the whole body of our English literature of philosophy, and perhaps supreme also in our literature of religious apologetics [this latter comment being especially noteworthy in light of the greater popularity of Butler's *Analogy* in the tradition of English apologetics]." Jessop goes on to say, "Some of his [Berkeley's] passages read as though they were transcripts of a Socratic conversation in a new Attic tongue." And he suggests something of its significance for our own age in saying, "The dialogues go beyond philosophy as Natural Theology to the vindication of a particular revealed religion against the current apostacy of both belief and practice."[25]

But the place accorded *Alciphron* among Berkeley's works also depends on how one construes the general drift of his thought. Thus "Berkeley's system," in Jessop's construal, "was plainly a piece of religious apologetics. . . . The intention was unconcealed; it is explicit in his texts, confessed in his prefaces, and flourished on his title pages." If so, then *Alciphron* must surely be considered the capstone of the whole and equal in rank to Berkeley's more highly esteemed "philosophical" productions. For Jessop, it is "in content and avowed intention a piece of outright and forthright apologetics, in which he strides beyond a general theism to a defense of religion in its Christian form."[26] Whatever others' opinions of the work, laudatory or not, *Alciphron* did bear some practical fruit for Berkeley. Since it came to Queen Anne's approving attention, it may very well have helped his preferment in 1734 to the bishopric of Cloyne.[27] If Jessop is right, then *Alciphron* richly deserves to rank with Joseph Butler's better-known *Analogy* and William Paley's *Evidences* as contributing to the "Enlightened" defense of Christianity in the Age of Enlightenment. Interestingly, *Alciphron's* apologetic intent was not lost on Timothy Dwight, Jonathan Edwards's grandson. He turned to it—not, significantly, Butler's better-known work—to spearhead his attack on the deists and freethinkers of his day. In his preface for its first American edition of 1803, Dwight commended it as "a storehouse, whence many succeeding writers have drawn their materials, and their arguments."[28] One wonders if his illustrious grandfather was one of them.

Edwards's *True Virtue* is the second part of a two-part inquiry—the first being *Concerning the End for Which God Created the World*—which was posthumously published in 1765. It is a classic dissertation in axiology which, significantly, is grounded in the metaphysics of its twin. Here Edwards returned for the last time to the great question that had haunted him from his youth—what is the nature of true religion?—though he now formulated it as what is the nature of true virtue?[29] But Edwards's last answer differs significantly from the one he formulated earlier in *A Treatise concerning Religious Affections.* There he defined "piety" as essentially complacence, i.e., loving God principally for the sake of his holiness or benevolence; but in *True Virtue* he defined it as benevolence, i.e., loving God principally for the sake of his being. He came to see that his earlier answer was circular, and too self-interested to qualify as genuine virtue.[30]

True Virtue was not initially received with approbation. William Hart complained that by conceiving of God as being in general Edwards had substituted for the God of Abraham the god of the philosophers. Edwards's God was a mere metaphysical abstraction bereft of personality and the moral capacities that go along with it—Being as such is hardly the sort of thing which can be adored, petitioned, or supplicated. Robert Hall, on the other hand, questioned the soundness of Edwards's moral psychology, which rooted true virtue in benevolence to general being and then only had to branch out to particular beings. Hall argued that it was more psychologically plausible that virtue should grow from benevolence to individual beings, like one's relatives and friends, and thence to a more general benevolence inclusive of humanity and God. Moreover, the members of the

Princeton Review scored Edwards for placing the essence of virtue too much in benevolence, to the neglect of justice, and for equating vice with mere selfishness.[31]

Like *Alciphron, True Virtue* had to wait for the twentieth century to have its true worth assayed. This was undertaken by Perry Miller, who saw revealed in this work "Edwards at his very greatest," the purest play of his speculation, and a teasing glimpse of the *summa* that was never to be.[32] This dissertation, far from being dismissed as heterodox, is now appreciated for what it really is: an uncompromising theocentric Christian ethics in flat opposition to the anthropocentric ethics, then in vogue, of Shaftesbury, Hutcheson, et al. Again, like Berkeley in *Alciphron,* Edwards in *True Virtue* has an explicitly apologetic intent.

III

Before weighing in detail some of the striking thematic continuities between these two books as evidence for the influence of *Alciphron* upon *True Virtue,* let us review their grosser similarities. Both are apologetical and polemical in design, the dialogues being more stridently and explicitly so than the dissertation. Berkeley and Edwards alike expose the internal inconsistencies of the so-called moral sense theory of ethics, and diagnose its adequacy as the lack of a theological, and metaphysical, grounding—which they do so, interestingly, in purely philosophical terms. Unlike Berkeley in *Alciphron,* though, Edwards in *True Virtue* develops a fully fledged theological ethics of his own as an improvement on the secular ethics of Shaftesbury and Hutcheson. And, incidentally, both texts were long underrated or misunderstood; but now each is rightly deemed a major work that goes to the very heart of its author's thought.

In the third dialogue of *Alciphron* and the fifth chapter of *True Virtue,* Berkeley and Edwards respectively criticize the moral sense theorists, and for exactly the same reasons: (1) misunderstanding the fundamental nature of beauty; (2) reducing ethics to aesthetics; (3) overlooking the role of reason in judgments of value; (4) failing to ground their ethics in teleology; (5) supposing naively that a mere taste for moral beauty is sufficient for motivating us to virtue; (6) the redundancy of the moral sense; and (7) sundering morality from religion. We shall now consider each of these points in turn, noting the similarities in their critiques though without ignoring their not insignificant differences.

The Nature of Beauty

Berkeley and Edwards, though accepting Hutcheson's analysis of beauty into proportion, further analyze proportion itself into utility and consent respectively. Both agree in affirming the autonomy of the moral and its irreducibility to the aesthetic; instead, Berkeley and Edwards reduce the aesthetic itself to something deeper, namely utility and love respectively. Where they disagree is over which—the moral or the aesthetic—is the more fundamental: for Berkeley, it is moral value, since utility determines proportion; whereas for Edwards it is aesthetic value, since proportion determines utility.

Berkeley uses the character Alciphron, the representative freethinker or "minute philosopher," to expound the moral sense theory of beauty.[33] He states that beauty inheres as much in certain kinds of moral behavior, motives, and attitudes as in paintings and landscapes. Such moral beauty is but a species of aesthetic beauty: "As this beauty is found in the shape and form of corporeal things; so also is there analogous to it a beauty of another kind, an order, a symmetry, and comeliness, in the moral world." And just as physical beauty requires an outward eye for its perception, so moral beauty requires an analogous inward "eye" for its apprehension. This "sixth" sense belongs uniquely to the mind. "As the eye perceiveth the one, so the mind doth, by a certain interior sense, perceive the other," avers Alciphron. "Thus, as by sight I discern the beauty of a plant or an animal, even so the mind apprehends the moral excellence, the beauty, and decorum of justice and temperance."[34]

After some floundering in their attempt to define clearly and precisely "moral beauty," the interlocutors eventually agree unanimously that beauty is something which is intrinsically "amiable" or pleasurable, though not everything enjoyable, like certain tastes and smells, is deemed beautiful. Beauty is more than a subjective feeling or sentiment; specifically, the pleasure we associate with and derive from beauty is uniquely elicited by "the idea of order, harmony, and proportion."[35] Beauty, then, is as much an objective quality, like shape and size, inherent in external objects of vision among other things. Objectively considered, beauty is proportion and so a quantifiable relation. This identification of beauty with mathematical relations like proportion and harmony was a commonplace of eighteenth-century aesthetic theory.

However, speaking through Euphranor, Berkeley replies that the essence of beauty does not lie in proportion and analyzes proportion itself into something more fundamental which he thinks is adaptation to an end, or utility. According to Euphranor, what makes a thing's structure proportional is how well the relationships among its parts are adapted to its function: "The parts, therefore, in true proportions must be so related, and adjusted to one another, as that they may best conspire to the use and operation of the whole." Thus, the proportionality of a racehorse's anatomy is determined wholly by its function. But transfer the equine anatomy to, say, a badger, then it would utterly cease to be proportional since this structure would be ill-suited to the badger's function of digging and burrowing. Or take an arch, which is perfectly proportional to its function of allowing access to pedestrians or traffic. But merely invert that arch, and it ceases altogether to be proportional because now it is maladapted to its use: "There is no beauty without proportion, so proportions are to be esteemed just and true, only as they are relative to some certain use or end, their aptitude and subordination to which end is, at bottom, that which makes them please and charm."[36] That the essence of beauty lay in utility was another widespread tenet of eighteenth-century aesthetics which was in explicit opposition to the idea that it lay instead in proportion.

Alciphron accedes to Euphranor's definition of beauty as utility—thereby providing the latter with the leverage for a two-fold critique of the moral sense theory. First, if beauty is essentially utility, continues Euphranor, then beauty cannot be perceived by anything like a moral sense because a thing's purpose or end is not always immediately apparent. We can look at a machine but not "see" its use. This is something that we need to *understand* either by being told or figuring it out for ourselves: "But the comparing parts one with another, the considering them as belonging to one whole, and the referring this whole to its use or end, should seem the work of reason." Understanding something's end and determining its proportionality relative to that end can be done "only by reason through the means of sight." Beauty, then, "is an object, not of the eye, but of the mind."[37] Consequently, since the moral sense cannot explain our experience and enjoyment of moral beauty, because the latter is not an object of direct sensation but the result of ratiocination, then there is no need to posit its existence.

Second, if beauty is essentially "adaptability," then, argues Euphranor, so is moral beauty. Our actions, motives, dispositions and characters are beautiful (virtuous) only if they are relative to some larger purpose which they help serve. But that purpose presupposes the existence of some intelligent agent who can frame, desire, and seek it. The only agent who can frame a purpose large enough to warrant our realization of it is God. However, freethinking and deistic moral sense theorists like Alciphron who want to divorce moral values from religion, i.e., from theological sanctions for moral actions, give short shrift to God and his purposes in their conception of the moral life. Hence, even if they concede that moral action is beautiful only insofar as it helps realize some divine purpose, they do not take the existence of such purposes seriously. Thus they are committed to the absurdity of ascribing beauty or utility to actions which are bereft of any purpose: "What beauty can be found in a moral system," Euphranor protests, "governed by chance, fate, or any other blind unthinking principle? Forasmuch as without thought there can be no end or design; and without an end there can be no use; and without use there is no aptitude or fitness of proportion, from whence beauty springs."[38]

Early on Hutcheson published a rejoinder to Berkeley's reduction of beauty to utility. He maintained that they are distinct because beauty is not always reducible to utility. He cites three cases by way of illustration: First, we prefer a similarity or uniformity among the parts of a design to its contrary despite its uselessness: "*Similitude* of parts is regarded, where unlike parts would be equally useful: thus the feet of a chair would be of the same use, though unlike, were they equally long; though one were strait, and the other bended." Second, the imitation of organic forms in architecture is deemed beautiful, though deprived of any natural function they once had: "And then what is the *use* of these *imitations of nature* or of its works, in *architecture*? Why should a pillar please which has some of the human proportions? Is the *end* or *use* of a pillar the same as of a man?" Third, some organisms are deemed beautiful though their functions are unknown: "And is there no beauty discerned in plants, in flowers, in animals, whose use is to us unknown?"[39]

Edwards effects a reconciliation of Hutcheson's aesthetics with Berkeley's. He initially claims that Hutcheson's definiens for "beauty," i.e., "regularity, order, [and] harmony,"[40] simply expresses in different terms his own understanding of beauty as consent. Thus, "a mutual consent and agreement of different things, in form, manner, quantity, and visible end or design" are "called by the various names of regularity, order, uniformity, symmetry, proportion, harmony, etc.," so that Edwards thinks his own theory of beauty "is the same that Mr. Hutchinson [sic], in his Treatise on Beauty, expresses by uniformity in the midst of variety. Which is no other than the consent or agreement of different things in form, quantity, etc."[41] For Edwards, then, Hutcheson's "proportion" is simply a synonym for his "consent." However, Edwards thinks that consent underlies utility as much as it does proportion. "The beauty which consists in the visible fitness of a thing to its use, and unity of design, is not a distinct sort of beauty." A thing's fitness or adaption to its use exemplifies the consent or agreement of means to end: "The answerableness of a thing to its use is only the proportion and fitness of a cause or means to a visibly designed effect."[42]

Edwards thus subsumes both Berkeley's and Hutcheson's theories of beauty under his own theory of beauty as consent, thereby disclosing their essential compatibility. Hutcheson rejects entirely Berkeley's utilitarian aesthetic, affirming that utility has nothing to do with beauty. However, Berkeley, far from rejecting the centrality of proportion to beauty—"there is no beauty without proportion"—only argues that proportion *depends* upon utility—"so proportions are to be esteemed just and true, only as they are relative to some certain use or end." Edwards, like Berkeley, understands that utility and proportionality are not antithetical positions in aesthetics.[43]

Edwards, though, goes further than Berkeley in his critique of the moral sense theory. He agrees with Hutcheson and Berkeley that the beauty of moral behavior—whether analyzed as proportion, utility, or consent—is the very same beauty displayed in works of human art and of nature. It is all aesthetic beauty and gratifying to us. But for this Puritan Neoplatonist, aesthetic or "secondary" beauty is merely a shadow of "primary" or real beauty. Primary beauty is "that consent, agreement or union of being to being" or "the union or propensity of minds to mental or spiritual existence"; that is, it is agapistic love, a relation among persons. Secondary beauty, on the other hand, is "some image of this" and "not peculiar to spiritual beings, but is found even in inanimate things"; that is, it is "a mutual consent and agreement of different things." Take justice, for example, which moral sense theorists along with Berkeley and Edwards all agree is an example of moral beauty. Retributive justice is beautiful and gratifying because it represents a proportion or consent between one action and another as when the punishment perfectly fits the crime. "There is a beauty in the virtue called justice," says Edwards, consisting in "an agreement in nature and measure" as "when he that loves has the proper return of love." Justice as an aesthetic relation is aptly represented to sight by the equipoise of a scale and is no different from the balance displayed in a Palladian building. Yet Edwards emphatically denies that the natural agreement exhibited in just requital, no more than the symmetry of the Parthenon, however valuable and pleasant it is to us, is in itself an instance of true moral virtue: "This kind of beauty [secondary] is entirely diverse from the beauty of true virtue [primary], whether it takes place in material or immaterial things [e.g., justice]." Nor is our appreciation or enjoyment of it a sign of our being genuinely virtuous, since "who will affirm, that disposition to approve of the harmony of good music, or the beauty of a square or equilateral triangle, is the same with true holiness?"[44]

Why, then, for Edwards is the aesthetic beauty of proportion or utility (as exemplified in the moral beauty of justice) inferior and secondary beauty? He explains that proportion represents the consent or agreement among inanimate things, which he calls "natural" consent; because physical things like mortices and tenons or abstractions like reward and punishment lack will, they cannot literally "consent" or "agree" between themselves since literal consent or agreement is a volitional exercise. Thus the consent fundamental to aesthetic proportion—whether exhibited in physical, abstract, or moral things—is merely figurative consent which Edwards distinguishes from real or "cordial" consent. The latter is "a concord and union of mind and heart," or an agreement among minds or persons, who have will. Now just as natural consent constitutes secondary or aesthetic beauty, cordial consent constitutes primary beauty. And "cordial consent," as an exercise of the will that binds persons in heart-inspired agreement or concord, is another name for love. Thus the aesthetic or secondary beauty of proportion or utility is less real than primary beauty because it is constituted by natural consent which is but a copy of cordial consent. Thus the beauties, say, of nature, architecture, and justice are but images or shadows of love or primary beauty. Proportion is only figurative or "typical" love, not vital and archetypal love.[45]

Thus for Edwards, not just Hutcheson's proportion as displayed in moral beauty, the object of his moral sense, but Berkeley's beauty of utility as well, are no more instances of primary beauty or true virtue (benevolent love) than is the symmetry of Jefferson's Monticello; but like that of Monticello, the proportion or utility of justice is but a semblance of genuine beauty or love. Moreover, a "taste" for the beauty of justice, that interior sense which has moral beauty as its object thereby enabling us to perceive and enjoy it, is no more indicative of a truly virtuous temper or disposition in the person possessing it than is a taste for eighteenth-century English watercolors.

To summarize: Berkeley and Edwards agree that Hutcheson's theory of beauty as proportion stops short of the essence of beauty, which they think is utility and consent respectively. Unlike Hutcheson, they further agree that proportion and utility are not at odds; where they disagree is over which is the more fundamental. Edwards, moreover, goes beyond Hutcheson and Berkeley in thinking that aesthetic beauty—whether proportion, utility, or consent—even when displayed in the moral order in acts of justice, is but a shadow of real beauty. Yet they are fundamentally agreed that the moral, though it, like a piece of architecture, may very well please and be deemed beautiful, cannot be reduced to the aesthetic. Indeed, they both think that the converse is true. Berkeley ultimately dissolves beauty into utility, which is more a practical, moral value than a purely aesthetic one like proportion. And if, as Berkeley believes, the utility or merit of human actions ultimately lies in the divine end they serve, then it has religious value as well. Edwards dissolves beauty into agapistic love or disinterested benevolence, the archetypal or primary beauty from which aesthetic or secondary beauty ultimately derives any worth it might have, which is of course a moral and religious value as well. In short, then, Berkeley and Edwards are equally nonreductionist: for them both, the moral sphere is *sui generis* and is itself rooted in teleology.

Reason and Value

Berkeley and Edwards concur in criticizing the moral sense theory's intuitionism and subjectivism, but they differ as to the scope of reason in aesthetic and moral evaluations. This difference arises from their different conceptions of beauty. For Berkeley, since a thing's beauty depends upon its adaptiveness to its end, and understanding this requires knowing or inferring that end, the experience of beauty is essentially ratiocinative. For Edwards, though there is an objective "ground" or basis for our enjoyment of beauty requiring an exercise of reason for its apprehension, the experience of secondary beauty is wholly intuitive; and, unlike that of secondary beauty, the experience of primary beauty requires direct knowledge of its ground, but this too results from intuition, though of a spiritual kind.

According to moral sense doctrine, beauty, as the object of an internal sense, is directly intuited and needs no assistance from thought for its discovery and appreciation. "A man needs no arguments to make him discern and approve what is beautiful," says Alciphron; "it strikes at first sight, and attracts without a reason." But in Berkeley's view, the discernment of beauty requires thought: If beauty is utility, then it, as Euphranor notes, "is an object not of the eye, but of the mind" since "the comparing parts one with another, the considering them as belonging to one whole, and the referring this whole to its use or end, should seem the work of reason."[46]

Unlike Berkeley, Edwards is somewhat sympathetic to the moral sense theory's intuitionism. Our sense of beauty is "founded in sentiment" inasmuch as "that form or quality is called beautiful, . . . the view of which is *immediately* [italics mine] pleasant to the mind." Furthermore, he seems to exclude reason entirely from the experience of beauty since our "being affected with the immediate presence of the beautiful idea, depends not on any reasonings about the idea after we have it, before we can find out whether it be beautiful or not." Secondary beauty may be enjoyed without its ground, i.e., "mutual agreement and proportion," being understood, "but in many instances, persons who are gratified and affected with this beauty, do not reflect on that particular agreement and proportion which, according to the law of nature, is the ground and rule of beauty in the case, yet, are ignorant of it." Music, for example, may be aesthetically enjoyed without knowledge of acoustics, since "a man may be pleased with the harmony of the notes in a tune, and yet know nothing of that proportion or adjustment of the notes, which by the law of nature is the ground of the melody." We can enjoy secondary beauty without understanding its physical basis, explains Edwards, because there is no necessary connection between the objective nature of beauty and its pleasantness. "The cause why secondary beauty is grateful to men, is only a law of nature which God has fixed, or an instinct he has given to mankind; and not their perception of the same thing which God is pleased to regard as the ground or rule by which he has established such a law of nature."[47] However, though our aesthetic pleasure does not depend on our understanding the mathematical structure of beauty, it is still possible to do so. Thus we can enjoy an Italian Renaissance painting without knowledge of the complex theory of perspective underlying it; however, that knowledge is available. By allowing that we might "reflect on that particular agreement and proportion which, according to the law of nature, is the ground and rule of beauty in the case," Edwards allows some scope to reason in aesthetic experience, albeit an inessential and more restrictive one than that allowed by Berkeley. By contrast, we can enjoy primary beauty only by understanding its "ground or rule," i.e., "a spiritual union and agreement": "What makes [primary beauty] grateful, is perceiving the [cordial] union itself. It is the immediate view of that wherein the beauty fundamentally lies, that is pleasing to the virtuous mind." Still, even its apprehension, like that of secondary beauty, is an intrinsically enjoyable intuition, though a "spiritual" one, and not the result of ratiocination: "They who see the beauty of true virtue do not perceive it by argumentation on its connections and consequences, but by the frame of their own minds, or a certain spiritual sense given them of God—whereby they immediately perceive pleasure in the presence of the idea of true virtue in their minds."[48]

Edwards, then, with his aesthetic intuitionism, allies himself with Hutcheson and Shaftesbury. However, by allowing that aesthetic experience, though intuitive, has at a deeper level an intelligible "ground or rule" (known always to God) the apprehension of which, in the case of secondary beauty, requires thought, Edwards allies himself with Berkeley. His synthesis of Berkeley's and Hutcheson's disparate aesthetic theories is yet another instance of Edwards's synthetic impulse.

The Metaphysics of Value

As discussed above, Berkeley and Edwards alike—though Berkeley more so than Edwards—locate beauty in utility. But it is not just human purposes that play a role in their moral economy. They further agree that moral beauty ultimately has to do with the conformity of human voluntary actions to God's purposes, not merely human ones. Both, then, ground their axiology in teleology, an implicit criticism of moral sense theorists who were reticent in doing so. Thus for Berkeley, the moral beauty of human acts, motives, and attitudes depends wholly on their conformity or adaptation to a transcendent purpose: "In a system of spirits, subordinate to the will, and under the direction of the Father of spirits, governing them by laws, and conducting them by methods suitable to wise and good ends, there will be great beauty."[49] The same is no less true for Edwards, for whom "the true goodness of a thing must be its agreeableness to its end, or its fitness to answer the design for which it was made."[50] And the true goodness of human beings is the agreeableness of their dispositions and actions to God's end in which consists their highest good and happiness.

Beauty as Moral Motive

Berkeley and Edwards concur in faulting the moral sense theorists for their overly sanguine view of human nature in supposing that a mere taste for moral beauty, however defined, is a strong enough motive for virtue. "Where there is this natural taste, nothing further is wanting, either as a principle to convince, or as a motive to induce men to the love of virtue," Alciphron assures his companions, "and more or less there is of this taste or sense in every creature that hath reason." The only proper, or moral, motive for our being morally good is moral goodness itself; its intrinsic merit or beauty alone is what draws us to moral virtue. Echoing Socrates, the moral sense theorists insist that to know virtue is to be virtuous. Therefore, being moral or virtuous, or acting so, must be purely disinterested to qualify as such. If our principal incentive for being moral is either the threat of punishment for not being, or the promise of reward for being so, then we are no more moral than any circus animal who performs its tricks from fear of the whip or desire of food, "it being a mean and selfish thing to be virtuous through fear or hope."[51] Anticipating Kant, Shaftesbury and Hutcheson insist that a moral action, to be moral at all, must be performed autonomously.

An implication of the moral sense theory for religion, particularly disquieting for Christian divines like Berkeley and Edwards, and which Alciphron is eager to draw out, is the moral bankruptcy of religious sanctions for moral behavior. Since we all are naturally endowed with an infallible sense of moral beauty, the idea of which is sufficient to induce us to behave virtuously, we do not need to be "frightened into virtue, a thing so natural and congenial to every human soul" that "it follows that all the ends of society are secured without religion."[52] Now if, as Alciphron believes, the chief function of religion is to provide the ultimate moral sanctions with its eschatological scheme of divine rewards and punishment, then religion is not only redundant in the moral life but actually subverts it by undermining our moral autonomy.

Berkeley's and Edwards's doubts about the efficacy of moral beauty as a disinterested motive for virtue echo Hobbes's cynicism as to the likelihood of human beings acting from any motive other than self-interest. Even if such as Shaftesbury and Hutcheson had formulated a coherent idea of moral beauty which might serve as a disinterested motive, it would scarcely be sufficient to actuate the majority of men and women to virtuous action, given the corruption of human nature. "In this country of ours," cautions Euphranor, "reason, religion, and law are all together little enough to subdue the outward to the inner man; and that it must argue a wrong head and weak judgment to suppose that without them men will be enamoured of the golden mean." "In no case," he continues, "is it to be hoped that *to kalos* will be the leading idea of the many, who have quick sense, strong passions, and gross intellects."[53] Because of its inadequacy as an incentive to virtue, Euphranor (Berkeley) concludes that moral beauty needs to be supplemented by an appeal to the prospect of either reward or punishment.

For Edwards, moral beauty is not so much a weak motive for acting virtuously as hardly a motive at all, since the complacent love of beauty is self-interested and so can scarcely be a motive for disinterested action. Doing anything from love of moral beauty qualifies, to be sure, as natural virtue but not true virtue—it is to behave on the lower plateau of aesthetics instead of the summit of authentic morality and religion. Furthermore, Edwards makes the telling remark that the remorse of conscience, i.e., our being pained by our untoward behavior toward another, which is partly a function of our recognizing its aesthetic deformity, is not the same as repentance. "If conscience, approving duty and disapproving sin, were the same thing as the exercise of a virtuous principle of the heart, in loving duty and hating sin, then remorse of conscience will be the same thing as repentance," says Edwards. But in fact, "some men, through the strength of vice in their hearts, will go on in sin against clearer light and stronger convictions of conscience than others,"[54] which hardly evinces a penitent hatred of sin. The implication is clear: moral beauty not only cannot begin to impel us to true virtue; it often fails to prompt us to natural virtue.

The Redundancy of the Moral Sense

Berkeley and Edwards similarly criticize the designation "moral sense" for its redundancy, since it does not designate any such distinctive faculty but is simply a new name for one that is already familiar. According to Berkeley, moral sense is nothing other than sympathy or, in Euphranor's words, "a fellow feeling with the distressed, and tenderness for our offspring, an affection towards our friends, our neighbors, and our country, and indignation against things base, cruel, or unjust." In the same verbally parsimonious vein, Crito, Euphranor's ally in the discussion, suggests alternatively that the "conscientious joy, which a good Christian finds in good actions, would not be found to fall short of all the ecstasy" which is "supposed to be the effect of that high and undescribed principle,"[55] or moral sense, thereby implying the identity between the so-called moral sense and common grace.

Whereas Berkeley reduces moral sense to either sympathy or something like common grace, Edwards reduces it to conscience. "The sense of moral good and evil," writes Edwards, "which men have by natural conscience, is that moral sense so much insisted on in the writings of many of late." This enables him to show that though moral sense counterfeits true virtue, it is nevertheless quite distinct from it, as it is distinct from self-love: "There is a moral taste," he says, which does "not properly arise from self-love," but it is not "of the nature of a truly virtuous taste."[56]

Value and Religion

Finally, Berkeley and Edwards agree in criticizing the moral sense theorists for sundering morality from religion and giving mere lip service to God in their ethical theory. Indeed, this criticism has been implicit all along in their other criticisms discussed above: in the inadequacy of the moral sense theorists' idea of moral beauty, which they define independently of God's purposes, and in making an eschatological scheme of reward and punishment redundant.

Their criticism that such as Shaftesbury and Hutcheson had divorced ethics from theology had grounds. Shaftesbury himself had declared, "It is possible for a Creature capable of using Reflection, to have a Liking or Dislike of moral Actions, and consequently a Sense of Right and Wrong, before such time as he may have any settled Notion of a God."[57] By also suggesting that human nature is not morally corrupt from the Fall but, on the contrary, is perfectly capable of making sound moral choices through reason alone without the need of the ameliorative effects of saving grace, thereby making unnecessary the intervention of the Holy Spirit in the human heart, Shaftesbury neatly expresses the spirit of deism.

Berkeley retorts by asking, "A consciousness of virtue . . . not regarded or rewarded by God, . . . , where is the beauty of this scene?"[58] But Edwards, ever the acute logician, exposes the inconsistency of moral sense theorists who acknowledge God's existence but give scant place to him in their moral systems: "There seems to be an inconsistence in some writers on morality, in this respect, that they do not wholly exclude a regard to the Deity out of their schemes of morality, but yet mention it so slightly, that they leave me room and reason to suspect they esteem it a less important and a subordinate part of true morality." His rejoinder is, "If true virtue consists partly in a respect to God, then doubtless it consists chiefly in it." Hence, "those schemes of religion or moral philosophy" that "have not a supreme regard to God, and love to him laid as the foundation," affirms Edwards, "are fundamentally and essentially defective."[59]

IV

The evidence of *Alciphron's* influence in *True Virtue* is to be found in the latter's iteration of Berkeley's very objections (albeit with qualifications) to the moral sense theory. This, of course, is only evidence of that influence, not conclusive proof. In lieu of any influence of *Alciphron* on *True Virtue,* how else might we explain their thematic continuities? One way is by reference to their authors' common faith, which was unalterably opposed to deism's reduction of religion to morality and its belief in a deity which did not intervene in the world. As Stephen Neill writes, "The defect of all forms of deism was that they treated religion as being a system of ideas and a code of moral precepts. The heart of the Christian faith is personal communion with a living God, redemption from sin, and the redemption of history through the personal interposition of God himself in it through the incarnation."[60] And, more specifically, Berkeley and Edwards, though

Anglican and Congregationalist respectively, were Calvinist, as were their denominations. According to John F. H. New, "Both Anglicans and Puritans accepted the doctrine of total depravity, the Fall from Grace, and its attendant consequence, the doctrine of justification by faith alone."[61] Edwards, Conrad C. Cherry writes, "presupposes a radical doctrine of original sin in his ethic."[62] Berkeley's estimate of human nature is scarcely more sanguine: "Man is an animal formidable both from his passions and his reason; his passions often urging him to great evils, and his reason furnishing means to achieve them."[63] This statement would not be out of place in Edwards's *Original Sin.* Finally, both men's ethics were thoroughly theocentric. "The theocentric line of thought decidedly prevails in the [Berkeley's] ethics of immaterialism. . . . It is the will of God that supports the universe and that through the laws of nature, furnishes the norm of good and evil."[64] And for Edwards, too, "God is the first, last and ultimate fact about the universe. The wishes, hopes, and ethical norms which men entertain concerning their own nature and destiny must bend to the will of this supreme Being."[65]

Their Calvinism is more than sufficient to account for Edwards's and Berkeley's general opposition to a naturalistic and secular ethical theory (moral sense) which divorced the moral order from the religious—indeed, deemed religion, at best, as irrelevant to morality and, at worst, actually detrimental to it, and for all but three of the criticisms that they bring against the moral sense theory. Edwards's critique of moral sense ethics in *True Virtue* could just as well be derived from the theological heritage he happened to share with Berkeley as from *Alciphron,* just as his idealism, as we now know, was derived not from Berkeley but from a source common to both. But this leaves three of Edwards's criticisms of moral sense theory still unaccounted for: (1) its overlooking the role of reason in normative judgments; (2) its reducing ethics to aesthetics; (3) its misunderstanding the fundamental nature of beauty, the redundancy of the moral sense. The most promising lead, perhaps, in support of Berkeley's influence is with respect to the nature of beauty. Gaustad recognizes this in saying that "Edwards, like Berkeley, found beauty a useful analogue, or more, in attempting to understand the nature of virtue," though this is better explained, I think, by the influence of Shaftesbury and Hutcheson, who earlier drew the analogy between virtue and beauty and had inspired Berkeley's own discussion of it. Berkeley's influence is most likely, I think, in Edwards's emendation of his theory of beauty by taking pains in showing its essential compatibility with the utilitarian theory of beauty espoused by Berkeley, thereby demonstrating "an organic relationship between the principle of utility or commodity and Hutcheson's formula of uniformity amidst variety."[66] Since he emended his theory in light of Hutcheson,[67] it stands to reason that he might have done so in light of Berkeley as well.

Berkeley was the chief exponent of the principle of utility in aesthetics, and presents his case for it in a book which Edwards must have read. But why, if Edwards did read Berkeley, does he not cite him as well in *True Virtue*? After all, he does not fail to acknowledge Hutcheson's influence in this work in the course of emending his theory. This could well have been an oversight; Edwards did not live long enough to give final form to his posthumously published dissertation on virtue.

Now the continuities (offset by significant discontinuities) traced above between Edwards's *True Virtue* and Berkeley's *Alciphron* with respect to their common critique of the moral sense theory, even if they are insufficient to establish once and for all the latter's influence on the former, are nevertheless noteworthy for these reasons: First, they constitute nothing less than a trenchant Christian apologetics directed against deists and freethinkers, with the two books in which they can be detected being fully worthy to join the more popular apologetic efforts of Butler's *Analogy* and Paley's *Evidences.* Second, they indicate something more of Berkeley's possible influence in the New World, justifying Richard Popkin's claim that he is "America's first philosophical friend" and "must be re-read, re-studied, and re-digested with each stage of the intellectual evolution of America."[68] Third, they further embed Edwards's thought in its European context and invite a more positive interpretation of him as no less an Enlightened and philosophically adroit Christian than his Irish compatriot. The linkage with Berkeley helps show that Edwards is not the theological aberration that he has too often been portrayed as being. Indeed, he is well within the pale of Christian orthodoxy and did nothing more eccentric than defend the faith, as did Berkeley, Butler, and Paley. Curiously, opprobrium is not heaped on their heads for their theology as it is on Edwards.

NOTES

1. See Georges Lyon, *L'Idealisme en Engleterre* (1888), pp. 429–33, as cited by Wallace E. Anderson in *Jonathan Edwards, Scientific and Philosophical Writings, The Works of Jonathan Edwards, 6* (New Haven, 1980), p. 325.

2. Norman Fiering, *Jonathan Edwards's Moral Thought and Its British Context* (Chapel Hill, N.C., 1981), pp. 39–40.

3. Perry Miller, *Jonathan Edwards* (New York, 1949), pp. 61–62.

4. Edwin S. Gaustad, *George Berkeley in America* (New Haven, 1979), pp. 159, 160. I have found other possible influences of *Alciphron* on Edwards's works other than *True Virtue* with respect to the topics of freedom of the will, philosophical psychology, typology, and faith and reason; but their discussion would exceed the limits of this essay, and so must be deferred.

5. Fiering, *Moral Thought,* pp. 65, 170. We do know that the book had come to Edwards's attention, since he cited it in his catalogue of reading. Thomas Schafer estimates the

date of the citation to be within a year or so of 1732, the date of *Alciphron's* publication in England. See Gaustad, *Berkeley,* p. 159.

6. Gaustad, *Berkeley,* p. 49. It is noteworthy, I think, that both Berkeley and Edwards, two magisterial philosophers, were active and practical philanthropists who took risks for the betterment of non-European peoples. Edwards, in midlife, turned his back on a brilliant ecclesiastical career to become a missionary to the Housatunnocks and Mohawks on the Massachusetts frontier. Among other things, he promoted their children's education in the liberal arts and went to Boston to defend in court their land claims—which he did successfully—against the predatory encroachments of his fellow white settlers. Like Berkeley, he envisioned native Americans becoming church leaders in their own right: "How happy will that state be when neither divine nor human learning shall be confined and imprisoned within only two or three nations of Europe, but shall be diffused all over the world, . . . ; when the most barbarous nations shall become as bright and polite as England, when ignorant heathen lands shall be packed with most-profound divines and most-learned philosophers" (from Harvey G. Townsend, ed., "Miscellanies," *The Philosophy of Jonathan Edwards from his Private Notebooks* [Westport, Conn., 1977], p. 207.)

7. Ibid., p. 24.

8. Ibid., pp. 33–34.

9. Winston S. Churchill, *A History of the English-Speaking Peoples,* vol. 3, *The Age of Revolution* (New York, 1957), pp. 110–12.

10. George Berkeley, *Essay towards Preventing the Ruin of Great Britain,* in *The Works of George Berkeley, Bishop of Cloyne,* ed. A. A. Luce and T. E. Jessop, vol. 6 (1950), p. 84.

11. Gaustad, *Berkeley,* pp. 23, 50.

12. *Verses by the Author on the Prospect of Planting Arts and Learning in America,* in Berkeley, *Works,* vol. 7, p. 373. This poem became virtually a motto for advocates of Manifest Destiny in the next century. Daniel Webster quoted it in a speech on July 4, 1851, to commemorate the laying of the cornerstone in an addition to the Capitol. See Gaustad, *Berkeley,* p. 204.

13. Gaustad, *Berkeley,* p. 24.

14. The site of the college was changed from Bermuda to Rhode Island, which was thought more suitable. For a discussion of the reasons for the change, see ibid., pp. 29–51.

15. Berkeley, *Works,* vol. 8, p. 212.

16. Berkeley, *Alciphron, or the Minute Philosopher in Works,* vol. 3, p. 31.

17. Gaustad, *Berkeley,* p. 142.

18. Ibid., p. 179, n. 34.

19. J. S. Mill, "Berkeley's Life and Writings," *Fortnightly Review,* 59 (1871), 519–20, as cited in George Berkeley, *Alciphron, or the Minute Philosopher in Focus,* ed. David Berman (London, 1993), p. 175.

20. Leslie Stephen, *History of English Thought in the Eighteenth Century,* vol. 2 (New York, 1962), p. 37.

21. J. O. Urmson, *Berkeley* (Oxford, 1982), p. 79.

22. G. J. Warnock, *Berkeley* (Notre Dame, Ind., 1982), p. 220.

23. M. R. Ayers, ed., *George Berkeley: Philosophical Works* (London, 1975), p. xxiii.

24. Berkeley, *Alciphron,* ed. Berman, p. 1.

25. T. E. Jessop, Editor's Introduction, in Berkeley, *Works,* vol. 3, pp. 2, 3, 4.

26. T. E. Jessop, "Berkeley as Religious Apologist," in Warren E. Steinkraus, ed., *New Studies in Berkeley's Philosophy* (New York, 1966), pp. 98, 107. Jessop's construal of Berkeley as fundamentally a Christian apologist seems not exceptional. Earlier, J. S. Mill wrote, "The war against Freethinkers was the leading purpose of Berkeley's career as a philosopher" (cited in Joseph Tussman, "Berkeley as a Political Philosopher," in *George Berkeley,* ed. S. C. Pepper, K. Aschenbrenner, and B. Mates [Berkeley, 1957], p. 123.) And Ingemar Hedenius claimed, "It is no exaggeration to say that Berkeley's life was . . . a tireless search for morality and practical Christianity. Nor is it merely accidental that most of his philosophical writings are direct or indirect attacks on the so-called free-thinkers" (see Hedenius, *Sensa-*

tionalism and Theology in Berkeley's Philosophy [Uppsala, 1936], p. 143). Moreover, Berkeley's wearing the mantle of Christian apologist accords well with F. J. McConnell's characterization of him as "a Christian of unmistakable devotion, a veritable saint" (see Francis John McConnell, *Evangelicals, Revolutionists, and Idealists: English Contributors to American Thought and Action* [Port Washington, N.Y., 1972], p. 134). Interestingly, Edwards too was reputed no less for his piety than for his intellect.

27. Berkeley, *Alciphron,* ed. Berman, p. 6.

28. Timothy Dwight, "Character of the Work," in George Berkeley, *Alciphron, or the Minute Philosopher* (New Haven, 1803). Moreover, even the place of its composition enjoyed a vogue for a while in the larger American culture of the nineteenth century. According to local legend, Berkeley composed some of it while sitting beneath a rocky ledge on Sachuest Beach in Newport. This rock formation, which is variously known as Hanging Rock and Paradise Rock, became known also as Bishop's Seat, in honor of the future bishop of Cloyne. This beach actually became something of a tourist attraction in the 1800s. One tourist visiting it in 1836 happened to be William Ellery Channing, the proto-Transcendentalist, who said of it, "No spot on earth has helped me to form so much as that beach." And Worthington Whittredge and John F. Kensett, landscape painters associated with the Hudson River School, both did two views of the Bishop's Seat (see *American Paradise: The World of the Hudson River School* [New York, 1987], pp. 191–92). Berkeley himself could not resist painting pictures in words of the beach and its environs. At the beginning of the second dialogue he writes, "Whereupon, after breakfast, we went down to a beach about half a mile off, where we walked on the smooth sand, with the ocean on one hand, and on the other wild broken rocks, intermixed with shady trees and springs of water, till the sun began to be uneasy. We then withdrew into a hollow glade, between two rocks" (from Berkeley's *Works,* vol. 3, p. 65).

29. Both questions concern the nature of the Good, his attention to which puts Edwards squarely within the tradition of American philosophy. "In the end," remarks John E. Smith, "the spirit of philosophical thinking in America represents another outcropping of that ancient tradition established by the reflective genius of Socrates and Plato in which the Good is the dominant category" (Smith, *The Spirit of American Philosophy* [Albany, 1983], p. 188).

30. In the treatise Edwards wrote, "The first objective ground of gracious affections, is the transcendentally excellent and amiable nature of divine things" (*A Treatise concerning Religious Affections,* in *The Works of Jonathan Edwards,* ed. John E. Smith, II [New Haven, 1959], p. 240). Compare this to what he later wrote in the dissertation: "The first object of a virtuous benevolence is being, simply considered." (From *The Nature of True Virtue,* ed. by William K. Frankena (Ann Arbor, 1960), p. 8.) For a fuller discussion of Edwards's reconception of moral goodness as benevolence rather than complacence, see R. A. S. Hall, *The Neglected Northampton Texts of Jonathan Edwards: Edwards on Society and Politics,* Studies in American Religion, Vol. 52 (Lewiston, 1990), pp. 170–74; and Nancy Manspeaker, "Did Jonathan Edwards' Thought Develop? A Comparison of the Doctrine of Love Expressed in His First and Last Writings" (Ph.D. dissertation, Institute of Christian Thought, University of St. Michael's College, Toronto, 1983), p. 60.

31. Clyde A. Holbrook, *The Ethics of Jonathan Edwards: Morality and Aesthetics* (Ann Arbor, 1973), pp. 114, 124, 126.

32. Miller, *Jonathan Edwards,* p. 285.

33. Two questions occur here. First, which moral sense theorist does Alciphron represent? Gaustad seems to agree with Jessop's claim that "Alciphron here faithfully outlines the philosophy of Shaftesbury" (see Berkeley, *Works,* vol. 3, p. 116). However, Urmson thinks otherwise. "It is surely wrong for Jessop to claim," he thinks, "that Alciphron either faithfully presents or is meant faithfully to present the ideas of Shaftesbury" (see J. O. Urmson, "Berkeley on Beauty," in Berkeley, *Alciphron,* ed. Berman, p. 180). Furthermore, both L. A. Selby-Bigge and David Berman identify Alciphron as Francis Hutcheson. "Some of Berkeley's criticisms would be closer to the mark if aimed against Hutcheson rather than

Shaftesbury," writes Berman. "Hence, it seems plausible that Berkeley had Hutcheson at least partly in mind" (see Berman, in Berkeley, *Alciphron,* p. 4, and L. A. Selby-Bigge, ed., *British Moralists,* vol. 1 [New York, 1965], pp. xlii–xliii). Second, does Berkeley misrepresent the moral sense theory? If indeed it is Hutcheson whom Alciphron represents, then Berkeley neglects to have him make Hutcheson's distinction between the "internal sense of beauty," i.e. "our power of perceiving the beauty of regularity, order, harmony," and the "moral sense," i.e. "the determination to be pleased with the contemplations of those affections, actions, or characters of rational agents which we call virtuous" (see Francis Hutcheson, "An Initial Theory of Taste," in *Aesthetics: A Critical Anthology,* ed. George Dickie and R. J. Sclafani [New York, 1977], p. 570). For a discussion of Alciphron's conflation of Hutcheson's two senses, see Urmson, "Berkeley on Beauty," p. 183.

34. Berkeley, *Alciphron,* ed. Berman, pp. 59–60.

35. Ibid., pp. 65, 66.

36. Ibid., pp. 66–67, 71.

37. Ibid., p. 67.

38. Ibid., p. 71.

39. Francis Hutcheson, *An Inquiry into the Original of Our Ideas of Beauty and Virtue,* in Berkeley, *Alciphron,* ed. Berman, p. 169. J. O. Urmson iterates and adds to Hutcheson's criticisms. His first is that Berkeley's positing a cosmic and divine purpose to complete his theory of beauty as utility is contrived and unconvincing. How can we, in our finitude, presume to know what that is? His second criticism is that Berkeley's aesthetics is confined to visual beauty, as displayed by the spatial arts and nature, and so to more obviously functional objects; conspicuously, it leaves out music and poetry, arts whose function if any is less obvious, and neither of which, interestingly, Berkeley considers. See Urmson, "Berkeley on Beauty," p. 182. However, Berkeley restricts the interlocutors' discussion of beauty to visual beauty, specifically natural beauty and architecture, since he thinks it is the most accessible—though some, but certainly not all, that they say about beauty applies equally well to music and poetry. But there are perhaps other reasons that are unmentioned. First, Berkeley lived in an age of burgeoning interest and research in optics, and he himself had contributed a work in philosophical optics called *An Essay towards a New Theory of Vision* (1709). Second, since Berkeley was committed to a theory of beauty as utility, it is little wonder that he would illustrate his doctrine with such visual objects as hammers and hammer-beam ceilings whose utility is obvious, rather than with things like sonatas and sonnets whose usefulness is hardly evident. Third, Berkeley himself was a practicing architect who drew up a plan for St. Paul's College and had some hand in designing Whitehall, his residence in Newport. He thus anticipated that other great philosopher-architect, Ludwig Wittgenstein. For a fascinating discussion of Berkeley's involvement with architecture, see Gaustad, *George Berkeley in America,* pp. 68–71. Edwards, interestingly, includes music in his discussion of beauty.

40. Hutcheson, "An Initial Theory of Taste," p. 570.

41. Edwards, *True Virtue,* p. 28. Edwards is here paraphrasing Hutcheson's statement: "The figures which excite in us the ideas of beauty seem to be those in which there is uniformity amidst variety." See Hutcheson, "An Initial Theory of Taste," p. 578.

42. Edwards, *True Virtue,* pp. 28–29.

43. Edwards's reconciliation of Hutcheson's theory of beauty with Berkeley's has been noted by A. Owen Aldridge, who writes, "Edwards demonstrates an organic relationship between the principle of utility or commodity and Hutcheson's formula of uniformity amidst variety." Moreover, Aldridge detects in Edwards's demonstration "an anticipation of Kant's principle of 'adherent beauty.'" See Alfred Owen Aldridge, "Edwards and Hutcheson," *Harvard Theological Review,* 44 (1951), p. 45. However, Berkeley, I think, had already hinted at that "organic relationship" when he explained that proportion (Hutcheson's "uniformity amidst variety") *depended* on purpose, i.e., "there is no beauty without proportion, so proportions are to be esteemed just and true, only as they are relative to some certain use or end."

44. Edwards, *True Virtue,* pp. 27–28, 36, 40.

45. Ibid., pp. 31–32.

46. Berkeley, *Alciphron,* ed. Berman, pp. 59, 67.

47. Edwards, *True Virtue,* pp. 98, 99, 32–33.

48. Ibid., pp. 33, 99.

49. Berkeley, *Alciphron,* ed. Berman, p. 7. Edwards holds to the same holistic conception of the world as a moral system under God's governance: "The whole world is one commonwealth and kingdom, all made of one blood, all under one moral head, one law, and one government; and all parts of it are joined in communication one with another" (from Jonathan Edwards, "The Propriety of a General Judgment, and a Future State," *Miscellaneous Observations on Important Theological Subjects, Original and Collected,* in *The Works of President Edwards,* ed. E. Williams and E. Parsons, vol. 8 [London, 1817], p. 167). For a detailed discussion of Edwards's conception, see Hall, *Neglected Northampton Texts,* pp. 287–90.

50. Edwards, *True Virtue,* pp. 24–25, 16. Berkeley's and Edwards's common insistence that the moral order requires some sort of theological and eschatological sanction anticipates Kant's understanding of God and immortality as postulates of that order. See John H. Hick, *Philosophy of Religion* (Englewood Cliffs, N.J., 1990), pp. 28–29.

51. Berkeley, *Alciphron,* ed. Berman, pp. 59, 60.

52. Ibid., p. 61.

53. Ibid., p. 74.

54. Ibid., pp. 71–72.

55. Ibid., pp. 63, 65.

56. Edwards, *True Virtue,* pp. 70, 71.

57. Selby-Bigge, *British Moralists,* vol. 1, p. 23. Jessop thinks that Shaftesbury was not as irreligious as Berkeley supposed: "But he [Berkeley] misrepresented Shaftesbury by leaving the impression that the latter had nothing more to say than that morality can do without religion. . . . His writings show that he was religious by temperament, both naturally and reflectively reverent." See Jessop, Editor's Introduction, in Berkeley, *Works,* vol. 3, pp. 10–11.

58. Berkeley, *Alciphron,* ed. Berman, p. 72.

59. Edwards, *True Virtue,* pp. 16–17, 26.

60. Stephen Neill, *Anglicanism* (Baltimore, 1965), p. 183.

61. John F. H. New, *Anglican and Puritan: The Basis of Their Opposition, 1558–1640* (Stanford, 1964), p. 6.

62. Conrad C. Cherry, *The Theology of Jonathan Edwards: A Reappraisal* (Gloucester, Mass., 1974), p. 182.

63. George Berkeley, *A Discourse Addressed to Magistrates and Men in Authority,* as cited in Tussman, "Berkeley as a Political Philosopher," p. 136.

64. Hedenius, *Berkeley's Philosophy,* pp. 230–31.

65. Holbrook, *Jonathan Edwards,* p. 5.

66. Aldridge, "Edwards and Hutcheson," p. 45.

67. Aldridge detects and carefully traces Hutcheson's influence on Edwards: "Evidence of the extent of Hutcheson's influence may be found by comparing Edwards' dissertation [*True Virtue*] with his earlier work on The Mind. . . . In the later work, probably because of the influence of Hutcheson, he discards equality as the basis of esthetic pleasure, [and] substitutes a formula of uniformity amidst variety." See Aldridge, "Edwards and Hutcheson," pp. 35–36.

68. R. H. Popkin, "Berkeley's Influence on American Philosophy," *Hermathena* 82 (1953), p. 136, as cited in Gaustad, *Berkeley,* pp. 207–8.

EIGHT

Perception and Love in Religious Affections

WAYNE PROUDFOOT

Recent philosophical analysts of religious experience have portrayed it as a kind of intuition or perception.[1] This is in part the influence of William James's *Varieties of Religious Experience*.[2] Though *Varieties* includes much more, James throughout identifies religious experience with a sense or feeling, and when he comes to assess its noetic value he focuses on the analogy with ordinary sense perception.

At first glance Jonathan Edwards's *Treatise concerning Religious Affections* appears to be a distinguished predecessor in the same tradition. James cites Edwards approvingly at crucial points in his argument.[3] Though the term "religious experience" is somewhat anachronistic when applied to *Religious Affections,* Edwards has provided a rich and subtle account of experiential religion. His striking use of Lockean language to describe "some new sensation or perception of the mind, . . . or . . . what some metaphysicians call a new simple idea," and his analogy with the taste of honey, are among the best-known passages in the book.[4]

Closer inspection reveals, however, that the parallel with James and the use of Locke are misleading. The new sensation, and the analogy with the deliverances of the other senses, plays no epistemic role in Edwards's criteria for distinguishing genuine from spurious affections. Despite the fact that Perry Miller's characterization of Edwards as an enthusiastic Lockean has been discredited, the references to sense and taste continue to influence readers in ways that can detract from the main argument of the book. Edwards is well aware that sincere first-person reports of a new sensation or perception carry no guarantee that affections are "truly spiritual and gracious" (197). To discriminate genuine from spurious affections, Edwards turns away from the analogy with sense perception and toward the practice of moral appraisal. This turn leads to a more sophisticated understanding of self-examination and of experience than can be found in *Varieties.*

I want to examine the argument in *Religious Affections* in order to call attention to the sophistication Edwards brings to the description and examination of religious experience. By attending to the practice of moral inquiry and to the ways in which we attribute character traits to others and to ourselves, Edwards captures and contributes to the complex and reflexive self-consciousness that is constitutive of much religious experience. The reflexive character of this experience, with its attention to ubiquitous forms of self-deception and subtle changes in the moral will, is left unexplored by those who portray the experience chiefly as intuition or perception. At the outset and at the conclusion, I will contrast Edwards's approach with that of James's in *Varieties* in order to cast Edwards's contribution into greater relief. I have tried to lift the structure of Edwards's argument out of its theological context, not to claim that for him it was or could be independent of that context but to demonstrate its sophistication.

PERCEPTION AND LOVE

Edwards and James both examine both the perceptual and moral components of religious experience. Each builds his account chiefly around two aspects of that experience, the new sense or insight and the virtues of the saint or the fruits of the religious life. Both reflect at length on methods for assessing claims made on behalf of and by appeal to religious experience.

Given their very different contexts, it is not surprising that the claims they consider differ greatly. Edwards was a theologian, preacher, and pastor in the midst of a period of revivals of religion during which he had been attacked by both liberal rationalists and radical evangelicals. *Religious Affections* is the culmination of a series of polemical writings in which he addressed both groups, though the chief adversaries against whom this text is directed are the radical evangelicals.[5] Edwards was convinced that the Holy Spirit was at work in these events and tried to identify criteria that would distinguish genuine spiritual affections from spurious ones, those that are the result of divine operation from the raised affect and excitement that are artifacts of the revival and of other natural causes.

James wrote as a psychologist, a philosopher, and a member of a university faculty. He collected autobiographical accounts of religious experiences from classical religious literature, contemporary pamphlets, journalism, and other documents of personal testimony. As a philosopher, he wanted to determine to what extent such testimonies provide evidence for belief in an unseen order, a More that is continuous with the moral life and is not exhausted by natural causes. While Edwards was convinced that the divine was at work and tried to identify its effects, James asked whether the religious dimension of human experience could be accounted for by natural explanations alone.

It might appear that the distinction between Edwards's task as a theologian and James's as a psychologist and philosopher is sufficient to account for the differences in their approaches to religious experience. Edwards's initial appeal is to Scripture, and to what that can tell us about the operations of the Spirit of God. This is almost always followed by consideration of what reason can tell us on the particular topic at hand. James says that he approaches his subject as a psychologist and rejects any appeal to authority or tradition. But much of both treatises is occupied with what we might call philosophy of mind. Both authors reflect carefully and subtly on perception, moral appraisal, and varied components of the religious life. The sophistication in *Religious Affections* to which I want to call attention is in this reflection and analysis.

Both authors examine the moral life and the revelatory quality of religious experience. James inquires whether religious practice, or the life of the saint, contributes to or detracts from human flourishing. But the noetic quality of religious experience, its claim to truth or insight, rests for him on a sense that is analogous to our other senses. He considers this noetic component and assesses its epistemic value in the chapter on mysticism. As a sense analogous to the five senses, it cannot be impugned. Its deliverances are on as firm a foundation as our other knowledge. But, as is the case with those other senses, its results must be tested against our prior beliefs. If I seem to see something that I believe to be impossible or untrue, I may doubt the evidence of my own senses. Further inquiry will be required to resolve the matter.

Edwards takes quite a different tack. He does attribute to the saint a new sensation and perception that is wholly unlike anything available to natural men or women. "And if there be in the soul a new sort of exercises which it is conscious of, . . . then it follows that the mind has an entirely new kind of perception or sensation; . . . and something is perceived by a true saint, in the exercise of this new sense of mind, in spiritual and divine things, as entirely diverse from anything that is perceived in them, by natural men, as the sweet taste of honey is diverse from the ideas men get of honey by only looking on it, and feeling of it" (205–6). But this new sense serves no epistemic function. Religious affections comprise both love and joy, and it is love that is the source of both perception and practice. In order to distinguish genuine love from spurious, Edwards attends not to sense or perception but to practice. *Religious Affections* is a treatise about love and the assessment of loves. With talk of love, we are in the domain of the moral life, of will and inclination. The affections are "the more vigorous and sensible exercises of the inclination and will of the soul" (96). By locating religious affections in this domain, Edwards can avail himself of the complex and subtle language of character and moral assessment.

TESTING THE SPIRITS

Edwards opens *Religious Affections* with reference to the trials of the faith of the early Christians. Spirits are tested by trials, as gold is tried by fire. But spiritual trials not only reveal; they also purify and enhance. "True virtue never appears so lovely, as when it is most oppressed: and the divine excellency of real Christianity, is never exhibited with such advantage, as when under the greatest trials . . ." (93). Conditions of oppression and hardship enable us to distinguish those who give lip service to the gospel from those whose virtues or faith can stand the test. Later he draws a parallel with testing in science. "As that is called experimental philosophy, which brings opinions and notions to the test of fact; so is that properly called experimental religion, which brings religious affections and intentions, to the like test" (452).

Edwards's publications on the revival show a development from the relatively uncritical enthusiasm exhibited in *Faithful Narrative* (1737), with its citation of numerical evidence ("more than 300 souls") and naive descriptions of dramatic changes in behavior, to their culmination in the substantial and critical treatise *Religious Affections* (1746). *Distinguishing Marks* (1741) is a proposal for testing the spirits, and *Some Thoughts* (1742) a reflection on the multiple causes of a single effect and a redirection of attention toward spiritual growth.[6]

Even in *Faithful Narrative,* Edwards acknowledges some skepticism about the conversions he reports. He assures the reader that the people of Northampton and the surrounding county are free "from error and variety of sects and opinions" that might lead to enthusiasm, and that the revival appears to be not subjective experience alone "but the influence of God's Spirit with their experience, that attains the effect. . . ."[7] In *Distinguishing Marks,* Edwards takes as his text the New Testament injunction to test the spirits and offers five marks, of which the fifth is the most eminent: it operates as a spirit of love, not self-love but true benevolence.[8] This is the only mark the devil cannot counterfeit. The next year, in *Some Thoughts,* Edwards notes that a revival ought not to be dismissed because of its excesses or of the role of psychological and social causes in bringing it about. An effect may differ in kind from the occasional causes that contributed to its occurrence. He also includes a case study that is more extensive than those in *Faithful Narrative,* focusing now not on external behavior but on an inner life of moral and spiritual growth.[9]

In the preface to *Religious Affections,* Edwards states that this treatise differs from its predecessors in that he was formerly concerned "to show the distinguishing marks of a work of the Spirit of God, including both its common, and saving operations; but what I aim at now, is to show the nature and signs of the gracious operations of God's Spirit, by which they are to be distinguished from all things whatsoever that the minds of men are the subjects of, which are not of a saving nature" (89). True virtue, love of God, and holy affections are consequent upon the gracious operations of the Spirit.

The first part of *Religious Affections* is prefaced with a text from 1 Peter, set by Edwards in the context of the trials of the early Christians, and characterizing true religion as love and joy: "Whom having not seen, ye love: in whom, though now ye see him not, yet believing, ye rejoice with joy unspeakable, and full of glory" (1 Peter 1:8, 93). Love and joy, but especially love, are the objects of Edwards's scrutiny. His problem is that of how to distinguish genuine spiritual love and joy, which have God for their object, from natural affections that might appear to be indiscernible from them, but upon analysis reduce to love of self and joy in one's experiences for their own sake.

UNDERSTANDING AND WILL

The soul, Edwards writes, has been endowed by God with two faculties, the understanding, by which it discerns and judges, and the will, by which it is inclined or disinclined. Affections are "the more vigorous and sensible exercises of the inclination and will" (96). By employing this distinction between the two faculties, Edwards makes available for his analysis the language of belief and desire. Affections are a form of desire, or love. Love is not independent of belief. Love that is premised upon false beliefs about the lover, that does not perceive her as she really is, is inferior love. But love and desire are not reducible to belief.

This language of belief and desire structures our interpretations of other persons, our attempts to understand them, attributions of character traits, and moral appraisal. From my observation of someone's behavior in a variety of situations, I attribute to him a set of beliefs and desires. If a person moves a dial on a thermostat, I understand what she is doing by attributing to her a desire for more heat and a belief that this action will bring that about. When Edwards constructs a sermon around a powerful image, I attribute to him the desire to move his congregation and a belief that this rhetorical device will contribute to that end. This attribution of beliefs and desire by inference from behavior and context is at the heart of our understanding and appraisal of the actions of others and, as Edwards makes clear, of ourselves as well.

The practice of moral appraisal includes resources for testing the spirits. Patterns and continuities in beliefs and desires are marked by ascribing traits of character. Character, whether virtuous or vicious, shows itself in a person's actions and attitudes. Someone may appear courageous, but a particular situation reveals him to be timid and cowardly. Kindness, humility, selfishness, and hypocrisy are all traits that are ascribed on the basis of observation of behavior and responses on different occasions, and especially under trying conditions. "Reason shows that men's deeds are better and more faithful interpreters of their minds, than their words. The common sense of all mankind, through all ages and nations, teaches 'em to judge of men's hearts chiefly by their practice . . ." (409–10). Edwards proposes to put religious affections to such a test.

Love is the chief of the affections, the fountain of all other affections. Edwards finds it evident from Scripture "that the essence of all true religion lies in holy love; and that in this divine affection, and an habitual disposition to it, and that light which is the foundation of it, and those things which are the fruit of it, consists the whole of religion" (107). In *Distinguishing Marks,* Edwards had said that love was the most eminent mark of the work of the spirit of God. Here, where the subject is restricted to gracious affections, love is no longer a mark of true religion, but is identical with it. The task, then, is to distinguish between genuine love and spurious, between love of God and self-love, between true virtue and counterfeit. It is the task of moral appraisal, and it is a task for which the language of understanding and will, or belief and desire, is well suited.

SYMPTOMS AND CRITERIA

The bulk of *Religious Affections* is devoted to commentary on twelve uncertain and twelve certain signs, those that are insufficient to identify gracious affections and those that are sufficient. In fact, Edwards uses the term "sign" very sparingly in his commentary on the sufficient characteristics.[10] There are no distinguishing marks of gracious affections if we mean by that something that can be empirically observed and that will clearly distinguish those affections that are genuine from those that are not. What are the marks of love? How do I know whether John loves Sarah, or even whether I am really in love? There is no decisive empirical evidence. Behavior that seems to express concern for the other and delight in her successes may or may not be an expression of genuine love. We must look at patterns of behavior, at responses to the presence and absence of the loved one, with particular attention to actions not governed by convention or determined by external circumstances. Even this evidence is not infallible.

The two sets of signs Edwards offers differ in kind, as symptoms differ from criteria.[11] The uncertain signs are symptoms. They can be observed empirically, but are insufficient to identify genuine religion. The certain signs are sufficient, but it is not possible to determine with certainty whether or not they obtain. Their identifying descriptions incorporate criteria that guarantee their success.[12] For example, an appearance of love is one of the insufficient signs, but a genuine loving disposition is sufficient.

Insufficient signs, which Edwards calls no certain signs, include intensity of affections, great bodily effects, fervent talk of religion, involuntary behavior, conformity to a certain pattern, attractiveness to the saints, and devotion to the external duties of religion. These are phenomena Edwards cited with enthusiasm in *Faithful Narrative* and include many that had been used in the Puritan tradition. A morphology of conversion had been employed, for instance, and testimonies and behavior of candidates were compared with that pattern to ensure that each component was included, and in the proper order.[13]

Edwards states his criterion for genuine religious affections in the first sufficient sign, and it is a causal one. "Affections that are truly spiritual and gracious, do arise from those influences and operations on the heart, which are spiritual, supernatural and divine" (197). If it holds, the affections are genuine. The Spirit of God "communicates himself in his own proper nature" to the saints, and "dwells in their souls" (200). But how are we to determine whether affections, my own or another's, arise from influences that are spiritual, supernatural and divine? This contrasts with the insufficient signs or symptoms, which are detectable by the observer.

THE NEW SENSE

Edwards introduces the new sense and the new simple idea in his commentary on the first sign, in which true religious affections are said to arise from spiritual, divine, and supernatural operations. He uses them chiefly to make the point that this is "an entirely new kind of perception or sensation" that differs completely from the deliverances of the natural senses (205). Like the taste of honey to one who has only seen honey, it is inaccessible to someone without the Spirit. The saint's idea of and delight in the loveliness of God "is peculiar and entirely diverse from anything that a natural man has, or can have any notion of" (208). It is qualitatively, not merely quantitatively, unlike anything that could result from natural causes or from common grace.

But the new sense does not play any role whatsoever in Edwards's inquiry into what distinguishes true religion from false. The saint does come to know divine things in a new way through this sense, but it is of no help for determining whether or not someone is a saint. How can this be? Edwards's chief reason is theological. Though the certain signs are infallible, no living saint can know his or her status with certainty, because of a twofold defect due to sin: a defect in the object, because grace may be feeble and mixed with corruption, and a defect in the eye, because these same factors cloud and distort perception (194–95).

As in other instances, though, Edwards's theological argument is supplemented by a consideration of the ways in which we do resolve doubts about such matters. Consider the epistemic status of sense impressions. Were a person who had never tasted honey to have a striking new taste of what she took to be honey, how would she know that this was genuine honey? She would know only by its provenance, and by criteria outside the initial tasting. Even more, a person captivated by what she takes to be a new sense of God's glory has no way of knowing whether this is the genuine work of the Spirit, or the result of natural causes. Persons with raised affections may sincerely report a new sense of the excellency of divine things, but this sense may be spurious, derived from self-love (252). Sincere first-person reports are not necessarily reliable.

The second sign addresses this point. "The first objective ground of gracious affections, is the transcendently excellent and amiable nature of divine things, as they are in themselves . . ." (240). The objective ground of a taste of honey must be authentic honey. A sense or taste of the divine must be objectively grounded in the divine nature, not in the illusions of self-love. The third sign is similar, but more specific. "Those affections that are truly holy, are primarily founded on the loveliness of the moral excellency of divine things" (253). Love is the chief and source of genuine religious affections, and the proper object of love is not natural beauty, but moral beauty, the beauty of moral agents, of beings with mind and will. That beauty is holiness.[14]

The fourth and fifth signs follow suit. "Gracious affections do arise from the mind's being enlightened, rightly and spiritually to understand or apprehend divine things" (266). "Truly gracious affections are attended with a reasonable and spiritual conviction of the judgment, of the reality and certainty of divine things" (291). This is like saying that true sentences must be grounded in reality rather than illusion, must derive from correct apprehension and must grasp the real with certainty. If the mind apprehends divine things, as opposed to misapprehending them, it has succeeded in grasping those things. But these considerations are of no help in deciding which sentences are true, or which claims to have apprehended divine things are valid.

CHARACTER AND VIRTUE

For signs 6–11, Edwards shifts into a new key. He identifies particular virtues as evidence of genuine religious affections. The Spirit of God dwells in the true saints, providing a new foundation for the exercise of the faculties of understanding and will, thus giving rise to a new sense and a new disposition (206). As we have seen, this new sense is of no help in testing the spirits, but we can look for evidence of the new loving disposition. Again there is no definitive mark. A person may appear to be humble, kind, or loving, while actually being motivated by self-love. But in ordinary moral inquiry, we are constantly called upon to make such judgments of character, and we make them by observing behavior over time and gradually coming to understand the particular structure of beliefs and desires that constitute that person.

The virtues and moral characteristics Edwards lists include humility, a loving spirit, a soft heart, beautiful and symmetrical affections, heightened spiritual appetite, and an abiding change of nature. In each case an adjective is included to assure that the virtue is genuine. For instance, gracious affections are attended with evangelical, as distinct from legal, humiliation. A change of nature is abiding rather than transient.

These are all thick terms of moral appraisal. While we can never be sure that our judgments applying them are correct, we make them all the time. We make them on the basis of our observation of moral practice. We attribute beliefs and desires to others on the basis of what they say and do, correcting for what we take to be disingenuous or self-deceptive and for exigencies of circumstance and constraints of convention. The moral distinctions available to us are subtle, and we are attentive to signs of illusion or self-deception. Edwards is able to bring all of this to bear on his analysis of religious affections.

Genuine religious affections are founded on love of God, and their false counterparts are founded on self-love. Much enthusiastic religion is the product of self-love. Hypocrites who are taken with the beauty of their own experiences engage in a kind of idolatry in which those experiences are loved for their own sakes (251). This provides Edwards with ample opportunity to call attention to self-deception. Liberation from love based on illusion comes from increased self-knowledge, from critically examining the illusions. Moral self-scrutiny exposes hypocrites. If they could see into their own hearts "it would knock their affections on the head; because their affections are built upon self, therefore self-knowledge would destroy them" (253).

The faith of the saints, on the other hand, is not only revealed but enhanced by increasing self-knowledge. In his discussion of humility, Edwards calls for relentless and recursive self-examination: "Let not the reader lightly pass over these things in application to himself. If you once have taken it in, that it is a bad sign for a person to be apt to think himself a better saint than others, there will arise a blinding prejudice in your own favor; and there will probably be need of a great strictness of self-examination, in order to determine whether it be so with you. If on the proposal of the question, you answer, 'No, it seems to me, none are so bad as I.' Don't let the matter pass off so; but examine again, whether or no you don't think yourself better than others on this very account, because you imagine you think so meanly of yourself. Haven't you a high opinion of this humility? And if you answer again, 'No; I have not a high opinion of my humility; it seems to me I am as proud as the devil'; yet examine again, whether self-conceit don't rise up under this cover; whether on this very account, that you think yourself as proud as the devil, you don't think yourself to be very humble" (336).

Moral self-scrutiny, proceeding from skepticism and doubt about the state of one's soul, is not only something that the faith of the saint can survive, but is essential to that faith, as it is to the examined moral life more generally.

PRACTICE

The criterion for gracious affections, as given in the first sign, is that they arise from spiritual, supernatural, and divine influences on the heart. We have seen that this condition is incorporated into the identifying description of each of the first eleven signs. The affections must be grounded on objective reality, proceed from a right apprehension, and must issue in true humility and a genuinely loving nature. But how can a person know whether or not these criteria are fulfilled? What evidence will enable him to distinguish apparent love from a loving nature? How does he test the genuineness of trust, humility, fear of God, gratitude, and an abiding change in nature? By attending to behavior, or practice.

When we say of someone that he or she is humble, selfish, courageous, or has undergone a change in character, the evidence we employ is practice. We observe how the person acts and responds over time and under a variety of conditions. This is the point of Edwards's twelfth sign: "Gracious and holy affections have their exercise and fruit in Christian practice" (383). While attributions of virtues and other traits of character are always underdetermined by the evidence, this is the only evidence we have, and it is generally reliable. He recapitulates each of the first eleven signs, showing that they all culminate in Christian practice (392–97).

In all other matters, Edwards writes, we judge a person's heart chiefly by her practice, and we should do the same here (410). Words are not excluded; they are also a form of practice. But the mind is better known by deeds than by words. Voluntary actions, where a person was free to choose among alternatives, are more revealing than actions determined by external circumstances (426). Compliance with prescribed form is not sufficient; the person must understand what she is doing (416–17). Behavior under trying circumstances is particularly revealing (434). This is the proper evidence by which to make judgments of character and attributions of virtue. It is not merely a concession to our ignorance. God will employ this kind of evidence on the Day of Judgment (441).

Edwards goes further, and sees that the situation is not radically different in the first person case. Practice is the only evidence I have not only for judging others, but also for myself. It is "the chief of all the signs of grace, both as an evidence of the sincerity of professors unto others, and also to their own consciences" (406). It is, he says, "much to be preferred to the method of first convictions, enlightenings and comforts in conversion, or any immanent discoveries of grace whatsoever, that begin and end in contemplation" (426).

Am I really in love? I reflect on my behavior and my response to the presence or absence of the object of my affections. Am I humble or proud, selfish or considerate? In my own case, I have data not available to others. I can attend to private thoughts and associations, and to feelings and reactions that may be imperceptible to another. Edwards refers to these as acts and practices of the soul (422). To this extent, I am better placed to judge than others are. But self-interest may cloud my vision and influence my conclusions. A person is often not the best judge of whether he is jealous, angry, courteous, or kind. Reliable ascription of such traits requires a certain disinterestedness that one is seldom able to attain in his own case, and attention to patterns of behavior and their persistence over time. I may be the last to see that my behavior issues from self-love rather than from genuine regard for the other or from love for God.

Moral appraisal is no different, in principle, in the first-person and third-person cases. It requires an inference from practice to the attribution of particular virtues, vices, or other traits of character. Such inferences are always corrigible; they are underdetermined by the evidence. That, and the distorting effects of sin or self-love, lead Edwards to preface his commentary on the sufficient signs with the disclaimer that he cannot provide signs that will enable anyone with certainty to distinguish true affections from false in others, or for saints who are low in grace or hypocrites to judge accurately in their own cases (195–97). The signs are sufficient, but there is no algorithm for their application.

PROFESSION

In 1750 Edwards was dismissed from his church in Northampton as the result of controversy following his proposal to restrict church membership and communion to "such as are in profession, and in the eye of the church's Christian judgment, godly or gracious persons."[15] In *An Humble Inquiry*, published in 1749, he criticized the "half-way covenant" and Stoddardeanism, calling for "credible profession" and "a visibility to the eye of a Christian judgment" as qualifications for communion.[16] The emphasis here on profession might seem to differ from the position taken in *Religious Affections.*

In fact, Edwards's stand in the communion controversy does not conflict with, and is informed by, the argument in *Religious Affections.* He calls for profession of belief and visible evidence that it is grounded in the proper foundation, but he knows that there can be no certainty on this score. Edwards is suspicious of traditional narratives of spiritual experience. He criticizes those who attend to inessential articles "such as impressions on the imagination, instead of renewing influences on the heart; pangs of affection, instead of the habitual temper of the mind; a certain method and order of impressions and suggestions, instead of the nature of things experienced, etc."[17] Sincere profession and visible indications of character are far more reliable than these impressions.

Edwards does not say that only true saints, with genuine religious affections, can be admitted to membership in the church and to the sacrament of the Lord's Supper. "The question is not, whether Christ has made converting grace or piety *itself* the condition or rule of his people's admitting any to the privileges of members in full communion with them: there is no one qualification of mind, whatsoever, that Christ has properly made the term of this; not so much as a common belief that Jesus is the Messiah, or a belief in the being of a God. 'Tis the credible *profession* and *visibility* of these things, that is the church's rule in this case."[18]

Neither the minister, other members of the church, nor the person herself can know with certainty who is a true saint. Edwards is concerned that prospective members have made lax and insincere professions of belief in order to gain membership in the church and to insure that their children will be baptized. He wants credible professions and visible evidence, but he knows that error can never be precluded. Edwards's insistence on sincere profession does not privilege the first-person perspective, but warns both professors and observers to attend to evidence regarding the fit or lack of it between statement and character.

COMPARISON WITH JAMES

James also examines both the perceptual component and the fruits of religious experience, what he calls the sense of immediate luminousness and the moral life of the saint. Unlike Edwards, however, he examines and evaluates each independently of one another. He cites *Religious Affections* in support of his claim that religious experience should be evaluated only by its fruits, not by its roots or causes.[19] James does not understand that Edwards turns to consequences as the only way we have of assessing whether or not affections arise from operations that are spiritual, supernatural, and divine.[20] In contrast, he wants to evaluate the consequences for their own sake, in order to discern whether they are beneficial or detrimental to human welfare. James proposes, then, to assess religious experience by attending to three components: the immediate feeling of luminousness, the moral helpfulness of the experience, and its philosophical reasonableness.[21] He does not explore the possibility of any internal relation between these, but considers each in turn.

After sketching a composite picture of saintliness ("the collective name for the ripe fruits of religion"), James examines what he takes to be its practical consequences: asceticism, strength of soul, purity, and charity.[22] In each case, he asks whether this ideal or character trait is conducive or detrimental to human flourishing. While deploring the ways in which asceticism and purity, for instance, can degenerate into paltry ideals when taken to extremes, his considered judgment is that, on the whole, "the saintly group of qualities is indispensable to the world's welfare."[23] The evaluation is frankly utilitarian, and benefits are assessed from the perspective of turn-of-the-century liberal values.[24] James does not consider self-deception, complexities of the moral will, or other perspectives on the inner moral life.

In the following chapter, under the heading "Mysticism," James focuses on the noetic quality in religious experience, the sense of intuition or insight into a higher truth. After another attempt at a composite sketch or core description, he asks how we should assess the validity of claims to such insight, and he answers in terms of the analogy with ordinary sense perception. Our "rational" beliefs are based on the same kind of evidence, he says, so we have no right to dismiss these claims out of hand. They are unassailable from without, though the most they can do for those of us who do not share the experiences is to establish a presumption. But they must be sifted and tested in the context of our other beliefs, just like the deliverances of the senses.[25] Their provenance alone should not be used either to dismiss them or to endow them with special authority.

These descriptions and evaluations of saintliness and the noetic sense in religious experience are completely independent of one another. From James's analysis, there is no reason to think that mystical intuition or insight might not equally well accompany distinctly unsaintly qualities, which are inimical to the world's welfare. In part, this is a consequence of James's methodological decision to keep completely separate the description and explanation of religious experience, on the one hand, and the evaluation of that experience on the other.[26] In part, it is a consequence of the attention to sense or perception on one hand, and benefits and deficits on the other, without any exploration of how they might be internally or grammatically related to one another.

The result is a sharp separation between explanation and evaluation, and another between the third-person perspective, from which James evaluates the moral qualities of the saint, and the first-person perspective, from which he evaluates the religious sense. As a consequence, he cannot portray moral and spiritual inquiry with the accuracy that Edwards achieves. In particular, he is not able to explore subtle forms of self-deception or the reflexive character of moral self-examination. Edwards makes the concept of love central and carefully considers the ways in which love is related to its object and its manifestations. In this way, he ensures that the internal relations between perception and action will be addressed.

By attending to the practice of moral inquiry and to the ways in which we attribute character traits to ourselves and to others, Edwards has brought a sophistication to the description and evaluation of religious experience that is lacking in much contemporary literature. The complexity of his analysis of self-knowledge, his exploration of subtle forms of self-deception and of the vagaries of the moral will, and his nuanced descriptions of the virtues of the saint are more akin to the thought of Augustine, Calvin, and Kierkegaard than they are to that of *Varieties.*

This difference is in part due to the fact that Edwards is a theologian and James a philosopher. But Edwards's descriptions of, and critical reflection upon, diverse practices of moral appraisal and self-examination are striking even apart from the theology in which they are embedded, and capture a dimension of religious experience that is missing from James's account.

Modern epistemology since Descartes has been hampered by overreliance on introspection and the first-person perspective. Edwards was right to see that the ways in which we come to know ourselves are not so different from the ways in which we come to know others. By shifting the focus of inquiry from scrutiny of first-person accounts of a new sense or perception of the divine that is not accessible for comparison or criticism to the practice of appraising character and identifying virtues, Edwards has provided a model for the proper study of religious experience.

NOTES

1. See, for example, William Alston, *Perceiving God* (Ithaca, 1991).

2. William James, *The Varieties of Religious Experience,* in *The Works of William James* (Cambridge, 1985).

3. James used the Ellerby edition, which was popular in the nineteenth century: Jonathan Edwards, *A Treatise on Religious Affections,* abridged by W. Ellerby (New York,

n.d.). See James, *Varieties*, p. 433. This edition is highly abridged, and lacks the philosophical and literary sophistication of the original text.

4. *The Works of Jonathan Edwards, 2, Religious Affections*, ed. John E. Smith (New Haven, 1959), p. 205. Parenthetical references in the text are to this volume.

5. For a good sketch of the polemical context of *Religious Affections*, along with attention to the theological dimension of the issues dealt with here, see Ava Chamberlain, "Self-Deception as a Theological Problem in Jonathan Edwards's *Treatise concerning Religious Affections*," *Church History* 63 (1994): 541–56.

6. Edwards writes from within a tradition of Puritan and Reformed piety, with its attention to the need for constant introspection and to its fallibility. See Charles Hambrick-Stowe, *The Practice of Piety* (Chapel Hill, 1982), and Charles Cohen, *God's Caress* (New York, 1986).

7. *The Works of Jonathan Edwards, 4, The Great Awakening*, ed. C.C. Goen (New Haven, 1972), p. 144. Isaac Watts and John Guyse, editors of the first edition (London, 1737), assure readers that the sermons that occasioned the revival were "common plain Protestant doctrine of the Reformation," and that the revival was not a response to an earthquake or some other calamity; ibid., pp. 130–37. They also question the significance and appropriateness of Edwards's two case studies.

8. Ibid., pp. 255–59.

9. The case is that of his wife, Sarah Edwards, edited to serve his purposes. Ibid., pp. 331–42. For a discussion of the differences between Sarah's narrative and Jonathan's selective paraphrase of it, and a setting of her narrative in historical and social context, see Julie Elison, "The Sociology of 'Holy Indifference': Sarah Edwards' Narrative," *American Literature* 56 (1984): 479–95.

10. Edwards uses the term "sign" only in the introduction to Part III and in his commentary on the twelfth "sign."

11. For discussion of this distinction, see my "From Theology to a Science of Religion: Jonathan Edwards and William James on Religious Affections," *Harvard Theological Review* 82 (1989): 149–68.

12. The formulations of these signs contain what Gilbert Ryle called "achievement words." See Ryle, *The Concept of Mind* (London, 1949), pp. 149–53.

13. For a discussion of this morphology, see Edmund Morgan, *Visible Saints* (New Haven, 1963), pp. 66–73.

14. "The moral excellency of an intelligent being, when it is true and real, and not only external, or merely seeming and counterfeit, is holiness. Therefore holiness comprehends all the true moral excellency of intelligent beings: there is no other true virtue, but real holiness. Holiness comprehends all the true virtue of a good man . . ." (255).

15. *The Works of Jonathan Edwards, 12, Ecclesiastical Writings*, ed. David D. Hall (New Haven, 1994), p. 174. For a good discussion of the communion controversy and its context, see Hall's introduction, pp. 1–90.

16. Ibid., pp. 176–77.

17. Ibid., p. 310.

18. Ibid., p. 176.

19. James, *Varieties*, p. 25.

20. For a criticism of James's reading of Edwards, see my *Religious Experience*, pp. 166–67.

21. James, *Varieties*, p. 23.

22. Ibid., p. 221.

23. Ibid., p. 299.

24. Ibid., pp. 263–66.

25. Ibid., p. 338.

26. Ibid., p. 13. For a criticism of this separation, see my discussion of James in *Religious Experience*, pp. 156–79.

Part III

INTERPRETATION

IDENTIFYING AND CLAIMING THE EDWARDSIAN TRADITION

NINE

Nathaniel William Taylor and the Edwardsian Tradition

A REASSESSMENT

DOUGLAS A. SWEENEY

Nathaniel W. Taylor, the Dwight Professor of Didactic Theology at Yale from 1822 to 1858, was arguably the most influential and the most frequently misrepresented American theologian of his generation. The author of a few published sermons and doctrinal treatises and a great number of polemical reviews and essays in religious journals, he never published a systematic work. He probably did not have much right, then, to complain that his opponents had misinterpreted him. But complain he did—and he was largely correct. His friends published his lectures on the moral government of God and several more of his essays and sermons soon after he died, but by then it was too late. Taylor's foes had made up their minds and his reputation had been muddied for good.

Taylor and his associates always claimed to be Edwardsian Calvinists. Unfortunately for their image in posterity, however, relatively few people, then or since, have believed them. As critics like Ezra Stiles have succeeded in defining the New Divinity for most twentieth-century historians, so Taylor's opponents, the Tylerites in New England and the Princetonians and other Old School Presbyterians to the south, have succeeded in defining Taylor and his New Haven Theology. They have set him apart from their own, allegedly authentic Calvinism, repudiating his claims of allegiance to New England's legitimate Edwardsian tradition. Not all subsequent scholars have shared the animus of the Tylerites or the Princetonians against Taylor and his followers, but virtually all have shared the notion that

Taylor must be distinguished from the Edwardsians as a man of an essentially different spirit. Indeed, most recent scholars have portrayed Taylor not as he portrayed himself but in one of two different ways: as the inveterate, rationalistic Arminianizer of the Edwardsian tradition or as the leading exponent of a resurgent Old Calvinism that co-opted New England's Edwardsian tradition and undermined its claim to represent "*the* New England Theology."[1] These historiographical trends have not been entirely infelicitous. There are important differences between Taylor and Jonathan Edwards and, in what follows, I do not aspire to discredit those studies that distinguish Taylor from others who patterned their doctrines more reverentially after the articulations of Edwards. However, I will address a large body of evidence which suggests that, in many significant ways, Taylor did build upon, engage, and forward New England's Edwardsian legacy. I will argue that Taylor was neither an Arminian nor an Old Calvinist. He was an Edwardsian whose claims to be doing theology in an Edwardsian mode were neither intentionally nor unintentionally deceptive.

While it is fruitful to debate the ways in which Edwards's ideas could have or should have unfolded in the rarefied air of logical possibility, it is also important to understand how Edwardsianism actually did develop on the ground. In order to make sense of the claims of dispossessed Edwardsians like Taylor to continuity with the Edwardsian tradition, we will need to expand our methodological purview and reconsider what it meant to be an Edwardsian in the nineteenth century. For quite some time now, a rather narrow doctrinal understanding of the Edwardsian tradition has governed most historians' perceptions of the development of the New England Theology. Though specialized doctrinal histories have comprised only a small minority of the studies treating the Edwardsians, Joseph Haroutunian's notion of "the passing of the New England Theology" has become paradigmatic for a wide variety of intellectual and cultural histories that discuss the fate of Edwardsianism in the revolutionary, early national, and antebellum periods.[2] Those who claimed to have been carrying forward Edwards's mantle are typically measured against their eponymous predecessor in terms of genius, stature, and especially fidelity to Edwards's phraseology and the language of high Calvinism. Frequently they are found wanting. While this method of charting the development of New England Theology has its advantages (particularly for those trying to demonstrate the singular brilliance of Edwards or the dangers of Edwardsian "moralism"), on the whole it has not proved to be a very effective way to study the dynamics of later Edwardsian thought. In fact, it has tended to restrict our conception of New England Edwardsianism to the New Divinity school. When defined in thin, doctrinal terms, the Edwardsian tradition remains susceptible to the power of the declension model of religious history. People such as Samuel Hopkins and Timothy Dwight, not to mention Taylor, Lyman Beecher, and Edwards

Park, can be shown to differ in certain respects from Edwards, and the New England Theology can be assumed to have declined to the vanishing point by about 1830. When defined in thick, cultural terms, however, it becomes clear that Edwardsianism actually gained momentum during and after New England's Second Great Awakening. It included not only those approved by self-appointed Edwardsian gatekeepers, but all who participated in and took their primary religious identity from the expanding social and institutional network that supported and promoted Edwardsian thought. This network survived and supported Taylor's doctrinal adjustments much as it had those of his predecessors, and Edwardsianism thrived well into the antebellum period.

Beginning gradually after Edwards's death and growing rapidly by the end of the eighteenth century, a uniquely Edwardsian theological culture emerged, surrounding and grounding the development of Edwardsian thought. An example of what Thomas Bender has called "cultures of intellectual life," this theological culture was constructed originally by the New Divinity clergymen, a group knit closely together by a common, largely rural demographic background, a connection to Yale College, an intricate kinship network, and regular correspondence and social contact. The members of this theological culture sought to promote Edwardsian theology through education, ecclesiastical reform, publication, and cooperative revivalism. Their success with "schools of the prophets" is well known. By taking post-baccalaureate ministerial hopefuls into their homes as pastoral apprentices, New Divinity theologians such as Joseph Bellamy and Nathanael Emmons trained the lion's share of New England's future pastors.[3] Other New Divinity achievements have garnered less attention. In the realm of ecclesiastical reform, Edwardsians gained control of many of New England's ministerial associations by the end of the eighteenth century and thereby played a major role in examining, licensing, and dismissing the region's pastors. This enabled them to further the quintessentially Edwardsian cause of pure or gathered church polity as well. As Allen Guelzo has remarked, "the New Divinity desired nothing so much as to repudiate the notion of a church-in-society . . . which embraced all members of a community as a covenantal entity." This desire came to fruition by century's end when the Half-Way Covenant all but disappeared, Edwardsian polity triumphed, and Edwards's clerical reputation received a belated vindication.[4] As scholars, these New Divinity pastors attempted to shape New England thought by means of the print media. Not only did they publish hundreds of sermons and treatises, but they also undertook the publication of many of Edwards's unpublished manuscripts.

Though historians have usually misrepresented New Divinity preaching as dry and metaphysical, the Edwardsian theological culture expanded most rapidly as a result of the New Divinity–led revivals of New England's

Second Great Awakening. Having prepared for a special outpouring of divine grace through concerts of prayer and circular fasts, the Edwardsians nurtured this awakening with pulpit-swapping itinerancy and special evangelistic conference meetings. Before they knew it, thousands of New Englanders were flooding their churches with applications for membership. The result was that, beginning in the late 1790s, Edwardsian preaching, polity, institutions, and theology infiltrated the region to such an extent that it would not be inappropriate to speak of an Edwardsian enculturation of Calvinist New England during the first third of the nineteenth century. Contemporary accounts from observers all across the religious spectrum suggest that friends and foes alike recognized the extent to which Edwardsianism had captivated New England's Calvinist imagination. The liberal William Bentley admitted with regret in 1813 that Hopkins's theology stood as "the basis of the popular theology of New England." Berkshire clergyman Sylvester Burt wrote in 1829 that the main contours of Hopkinsianism, "waiving a few points," had become standards for "the orthodox and evangelical clergy of N. England." Princetonian Archibald Alexander testified in 1831 that "Edwards has done more to give complexion to the theological system of Calvinists in America, than all other persons together. This is more especially true of New-England; but it is also true . . . in regard to a large number of the present ministers of the Presbyterian church." His colleague Samuel Miller affirmed in 1837 that "for the last half century, . . . no other American writer on the subject of theology has been so frequently quoted, or had anything like such deference manifested to his opinions, as President Edwards." Bennet Tyler claimed in 1844 that the Edwardsians comprised the "standard theological writers of New England." And as Samuel Worcester noted in 1852, "within fifty years past," Edwardsian theology had "so pervaded the orthodoxy of New England, . . . that there are hundreds of very good Hopkinsian ministers, who may never have given any more particular attention to Hopkins's 'System of Divinity,' than to the 'Aphorisms' of Confucius." By 1853, the Edwardsian Mortimer Blake could boast that Edwardsian theology had "modified the current theology of all New England, and given to it its harmony, consistency, and beauty, as it now appears in the creeds of the churches and the teaching of the ministry."[5]

Edwardsians took advantage of this exposure throughout the nineteenth century to reprint Edwards's works dozens of times in runs that totaled in the hundreds of thousands. The unprecedented success of Edwards's *Life of Brainerd* (1749) signaled the burgeoning of Edwardsian achievements in missions, education, and benevolent reform as well. David Brainerd's grave became a shrine visited by evangelistic admirers from both sides of the Atlantic. His spirit pervaded the Connecticut and Massachusetts Missionary Societies, which arose with the Edwardsian revivals and whose magazines disseminated news of revivals and conversions throughout the region. The American Board of Commissioners for Foreign Missions (1812), the American Tract Society (1814), the American Home Missionary Society (1826), and many other agencies, though not all constituted on strictly Edwardsian terms, were imbued with the millennial fervor of Edwardsian revivalism. Edwardsians ensconced themselves at many of New England's leading schools—from Amherst, Dartmouth, Mount Holyoke, and Williams to Yale and Bangor Seminary—thereby acquiring the means to enculturate future generations of the region's leaders. Even the founding of Andover Seminary (1808), though the result of a compromise with Old Calvinists, provided them with a favorable medium for instilling their values in New England churches throughout the century.[6]

This notion of an Edwardsian enculturation of Calvinist New England calls into question what has become a near-standard argument in recent years, the argument for Edwardsian decline in this period in the face of a resurgent Old Calvinism. Initially used negatively as a term referring to the opponents of Edwardsian or "New" Divinity in New England, the moniker "Old Calvinist" was never very clearly defined. As long as those who upheld the label could continue to marginalize the New Divinity clergy and withstand their theological and ecclesiastical reforms, they would succeed in their attempts to invent an aura of tradition for "Old" Calvinism, portraying themselves as the party of mainstream Congregationalism and historic New England orthodoxy. But in the face of tremendous Edwardsian successes in the heyday of New England's Second Great Awakening, the region's Joseph Lathrops, David Tappans, and Jedidiah Morses became a dying breed. As one historian has noted of Morse, his liberal opponents increasingly considered him an Edwardsian; and Morse, upon retiring from public life, in fact "relinquished the leadership of the orthodox to his Hopkinsian friends." Bangor Seminary's Enoch Pond explained in his *Sketches of the Theological History of New England* (1880) that as Edwardsians and Old Calvinists joined forces early in the nineteenth century to combat both social and religious infidelity, the Edwardsians proved more energetic. Their union "retain[ed] the better, the more essential parts of both" parties. "It embrace[d] all the leading features of the soundest Calvinism" and "it adopt[ed], to a considerable extent, the improvements of Edwards and his followers." But there was the rub. The Edwardsians had never repudiated "the soundest Calvinism." Thus to adopt Edwardsian improvements was to unite largely on Edwardsian terms. The theology of New England's united orthodox front became that "which was taught by such men as Bellamy, Hopkins, and the younger Edwards, and West, of Stockbridge, and Smalley, Spring, Emmons, Austin, Griffin, Worcester, and Dwight. This is the theology which has been preached in nearly all our revivals during the last sixty or seventy years, which has filled up our churches . . . , which has aroused and sustained the spirit of missions, which has fostered and directed nearly all the charitable enterprises of the day."[7]

In this light, it makes better sense to speak of an Edwardsian absorption of Old Calvinism than to argue for an Old Calvinist co-optation of Edwardsianism. Andover Seminary provides a further case in point. Guelzo cites the Edwardsian–Old Calvinist compromise at Andover as a major stage in the Old Calvinist co-optation of Edwardsianism. However, there is plenty of evidence to suggest that the Edwardsians carried the day at the first modern seminary in the United States. While a few of the most stringent followers of the radical Hopkinsian Nathanael Emmons began complaining by the late 1810s that the seminary was going to the Old Calvinist dogs, there were others who complained that the school had become too Edwardsian. There were outsiders, for example, who deemed this institutional legitimation of Hopkinsianism ridiculous. After perusing a "Review of the Constitution & Associate Statutes of the Theological Seminary in Andover" printed in the liberal *Anthology* for December 1808, William Bentley concluded that Andover's "Calvinists have been made to play into the hands of the Hopkinsians."[8] Insiders, as well, resented the Edwardsian domination of the seminary. It is said that founding Old Calvinist theologian Eliphalet Pearson resigned the Bartlet chair of natural theology after only a year because he felt disappointed that Hopkinsianism had become so dominant at Andover. Pearson's disappointment was not unfounded. The vast majority of Andover's leading faculty members—from Leonard Woods to Edward Dorr Griffin, Moses Stuart, Ebenezer Porter (the seminary's first president), and Edwards A. Park—shared Edwardsian sentiments. All were required to subscribe to the school's Hopkinsian "Associate Creed," a doctrinal standard for the seminary insisted upon by Edwardsian founders not content to repose on Westminster's Shorter Catechism alone. Furthermore, Andover's powerful, Edwardsian, and self-perpetuating Board of Visitors, established at the seminary's founding to placate Hopkinsians fearful of cooptation by Old Calvinists, ensured that the Edwardsians would maintain a consistently strong presence at Andover for years to come. In short, while the fears of Emmonsists may not have been groundless (Hopkinsianism did give way to a broader Edwardsianism in the thought of Woods and at Andover generally as time wore on), their claim that the seminary had gone over to the Old Calvinists was alarmist. As Leonard Bacon would summarize at Andover's semicentennial commemoration, "in a little while the Old Divinity leaven was quietly purged out, and Andover theology had become (quite to the discontent of a few extremists on both sides) a moderate Hopkinsianism."[9]

While Sidney Mead and others have argued that Taylor's mind was incubated in an Old Calvinist climate, it becomes clear upon inspection that Taylor's thought and religious identity matured in the context of this powerful, uniquely Edwardsian theological culture. Taylor's prepubescent years were spent under the Old Calvinist ministry of his grandfather's church in New Milford, Connecticut, but his later childhood and early adulthood were dominated by Edwardsian influences. He prepared for college under the tutelage of Azel Backus, the New Divinity clergyman who succeeded Joseph Bellamy in 1791 to the Congregational pulpit in Bethlehem, Connecticut. While Mead noted this connection, he did not acknowledge Backus's New Divinity commitments and he underestimated the role of Litchfield County generally in shaping Taylor's early predilections.[10]

Taylor spent his teenage years and early adulthood under the forceful influence of Yale's Edwardsian president Timothy Dwight, the very man Taylor's grandfather had voted against when the Yale Corporation sought a successor to divinity professor Samuel Wales in 1793. While Dwight's Edwardsian credentials have been contested by more people than Mead, and while it is true that he was not a radical Hopkinsian, Dwight did remain strongly devoted to the theology of his grandfather Jonathan Edwards and his uncle and New Divinity mentor Jonathan Edwards, Jr. He wrote two years before his death that "the two Edwardses, father and son, have exhibited as high metaphysical powers, as Europe can boast; and have thrown more light on several abstruse subjects, of the highest importance, than all the Philosophers of that continent and [Great Britain], united." In his well-known *Travels in New England and New York,* Dwight declared that he had "not a question" concerning the "truth" of his grandfather's theology, claiming that "the late President Edwards has more enlarged the science of theology than any divine of whom either England or Scotland can boast; and the loss of his works would occasion more regret than . . . the whole literary world, would feel for the loss . . . of the whole works of half the ancient authors now extant." In a letter to an English correspondent in 1805 Dwight had clarified that he objected to Hopkinsian extremes precisely because he thought Edwards had "gone as far" theologically "as the Bible warrants." Dwight had shown himself a faithful Edwardsian upon his ordination and installation at Greenfield, Connecticut, by eradicating the Half-Way Covenant there. And his ministerial students at Yale took in a diet consisting almost entirely of Edwardsian theology. Dwight exerted a tremendous influence over Taylor during Taylor's intellectually formative years. He took a special interest in Taylor as a college student, oversaw his conversion during Taylor's junior year at Yale, boosted his self-confidence, served as his post-baccalaureate mentor in theology, and hired him as an amanuensis, a position coveted by all students of Yale's weak-eyed president. Taylor never tired of showing his gratitude for these fatherly ministrations. He oversaw the conversion of Dwight's son, the attorney Sereno Dwight, and he prided himself throughout his career on his fidelity to Dwight's theology.[11]

Taylor received his license to preach in 1810 from the New Haven West Association, the clerical association toward which most of New Haven's Edwardsians gravitated. He then demonstrated his break with his family's Old Calvinist past by showing clear signs that his own ministry would be characterized by the theologically rigorous and revivalistic strains of the Edwardsians. He preached one of his first sermons at his home church in New Milford, after which many opposed his "faith and fervor."[12] He took his first full-time job in 1812 as pastor of New Haven's prestigious Center Church, a congregation which had taken a marked Edwardsian turn in 1806 when its young supply preacher Moses Stuart wrested control of its pulpit and its people dismissed their ailing and embittered Old Calvinist pastor, James Dana. Stuart had initiated what Taylor's clerical successor Leonard Bacon would call a revivalistic "revolution" at the church, winning it over for Edwardsianism. By January 26, 1809, when the church adopted a new "Confession, Covenant, & Articles of Practice," Stuart had succeeded in abrogating the Half-Way Covenant there, reserving membership for professing Christians only and barring the children of nonmembers from baptism. Taylor himself carried on Stuart's Edwardsian revolution, preaching revivals there in 1815, 1816, and 1820–21 and adding nearly 400 members to the church roll in just ten years.[13] In fact, nearly everything Taylor and his New Haven school did arose from and perpetuated the Edwardsian theological culture. After accepting his post at Yale's Theological Department, Taylor maintained an active commitment to preaching that made a clarion Edwardsian call for immediate repentance. So did his colleagues in the New Haven Theology, best friends Lyman Beecher and Chauncey Goodrich, and theological counterpart at the College Eleazar Fitch. To be sure, Old Calvinists had a place for revivalism as well. But the Taylorites' radical commitment to 180-degree conversions and immediate repentance distanced them from the more thoroughly covenantal and means-oriented spirituality of Old Calvinism. Taylorite involvement in New England's religious periodicals also proceeded along Edwardsian lines. Beecher's guiding hand in New Haven's *Christian Spectator* and Boston's *Spirit of the Pilgrims* ensured that both journals granted space to Taylorite authors while promulgating revivalistic, Edwardsian theology. New Haven's *Spectator* ranked Edwards as the best American theologian ever and then, "leaving a blank space, as is sometimes done in the English Universities, to indicate the comparative standing of candidates for academical honours," ranked Edwards, Jr., next. When Goodrich bought the *Spectator* in 1828 to make it the official organ of the New Haven Theology, it maintained its Edwardsian focus, devoting a great deal of copy to the Taylorites' intra-Edwardsian battles. Taylor, Goodrich, and Fitch, in the tradition of Timothy Dwight, gave Yale's Theological Department, too, a heavy Edwardsian flavor. Between the fall of 1834 and the spring of 1840, for example, students withdrew Edwards's *Works* from the Yale library nearly twice as often as the next most popular volume.[14]

None of this should prove surprising when we bear in mind that the Taylorites and those closest to them always deemed the New Haven Theology fundamentally Edwardsian. Taylor's daughter Rebecca Taylor Hatch, his son-in-law and colleague Noah Porter, his Center Church successor Leonard Bacon, and his student and colleague George P. Fisher all testified to Taylor's Edwardsianism. Lyman Beecher defended his own and Taylor's fidelity to Edwardsianism on many occasions, distancing their thought from Old Calvinists and Arminians alike.[15] Taylor himself, though less concerned with theological labels than most of his peers, did not fail to confess his own allegiance to the Edwardsian tradition, working almost exclusively with Edwards and the Edwardsians as his authorities at hand, and defending Edwardsianism constantly from the criticisms of Unitarians, Methodists, and other Arminians.[16] In other words, Taylor's theology emerged from and perpetuated the discursive structure of the Edwardsian theological culture. His "linguistic horizons," or "rhetorical world," were uniquely Edwardsian. He expanded his rhetorical world, to be sure, but he did so in an effort to contextualize his Edwardsian heritage for his own day and age. One finds continuity with Edwardsian discourse throughout his writings, but I will confine the remarks that follow to Taylor's best-known teaching, his doctrine of original sin.[17]

Like most Edwardsians before him, Taylor forsook the forensic notion of original sin so prevalent among confessional Protestants since the Reformation. Moreover, like most Edwardsians before him, he did so from a commitment to the emblematically Edwardsian distinction between moral and natural depravity or, viewing the distinction from another angle, between moral and natural ability. William Breitenbach has referred to this differentiation as "undoubtedly the most important mark of the New Divinity," the "shibboleth of their tribe."[18] Edwardsians had been wielding it since its American codification in Edwards's *Freedom of the Will* (1754) to combat liberal foes attempting to smear traditional Calvinists with the claim that their doctrine of sin damned people for an inborn, natural depravity that did not lie within their power to change. But while Edwards's disciples stoutly resisted this caricature, finessing a concept of depravity based on voluntary (moral) rather than physical (natural) inability, their liberal foes remained skeptical. The liberal claim against Calvinism only intensified in the 1810s with the coming of age of American Unitarianism; by the early 1820s it had culminated in the debate between Harvard's Henry Ware and Andover's Leonard Woods over the moral merits of Calvinism. Unfortunately for New England's Calvinists, Ware seemed to many observers to have bested Woods. Taylor and his colleagues certainly thought so, and soon entered the fray themselves to salvage what they could.[19]

Goodrich and Fitch spoke out first in lectures to the Yale students. In a move that proved quite controversial, they began making larger claims than usual that the liberal critique of the Calvinist doctrine of depravity rested largely on a common misapprehension of New England orthodoxy. The best of the New England theologians had never presented sin as an innate or concreated property of human nature that makes us sinful before we actually sin. They had always portrayed sin not as a natural necessity but as a moral or voluntary activity committed by agents who possessed within themselves genuine (natural) power to do otherwise. Edwardsians like Asahel Nettleton and Bennet Tyler balked. For while no self-respecting Edwardsian would ever have said the former, few would have portrayed human natural ability so optimistically, either. It was one thing to say that sin was in the willing, that the wayfaring sinner "can" turn to God if only "he will," and thus to deny that sinners were compelled to sin by natural force; but it was quite another to suggest that this natural ability to obey God could really ever overcome our moral inability to do the same, especially when sin was described as a moral act. Both leading parties within the Edwardsian ranks, the "Tasters" and "Exercisers," had been denying that for years, Tasters such as Asa Burton and Nathaniel Niles on the grounds that all moral acts spring from motives and that before God renovates the affections in regeneration they are governed ineluctably by our moral taste for sin, and Exercisers such as Nathanael Emmons and Samuel Spring on the grounds that, while humans bear responsibility as the agents of their sin, no moral act (of any kind) ever occurs without direct divine efficiency. When questioned, however, the Taylorites appealed to Edwards himself on moral and natural ability, claiming to have applied his distinction faithfully. In a letter to Lyman Beecher, Goodrich stated that his and Taylor's understanding of original sin was "the necessary result of the immovable principles established in [Edwards'] treatise on 'Freedom of Will.'" Likewise, in his *Two Discourses on the Nature of Sin* (1826), Fitch explained that he had based his own view of sin on the moral / natural ability distinction and asserted that this Edwardsian distinction should be applied "over the broad field of moral agency."[20]

Enter Taylor, who recognized that many fellow Edwardsians would resist New Haven's claim that its own view of sin derived by direct logical descent from Edwards on natural ability. He continued to claim allegiance to Edwards as "the most distinguished orthodox writer on the subject" of sin and moral agency. In response to the suggestion that he had abandoned Edwards's distinction between natural and moral ability, he retorted, "we fully believe in that distinction; and we believe also with Edwards, that 'moral necessity may be as absolute as natural necessity.'"[21] Indeed, he believed himself more authentically Edwardsian than his opponents, whose articulations of original sin he thought too often lapsed into the non-

Edwardsian language of inborn physical depravity. But Taylor also felt it incumbent to clarify the extent to which he and his colleagues, in true Edwardsian form, had improved upon the traditional Edwardsian solutions to the question of original sin and provided "the only" doctrine defensible in their own day and age "against Pelagian or Arminian objections."[22]

Taylor felt that, while Edwards had succeeded in demolishing the "absurdities" of the Arminian notion of "self-determination," he had not gone far enough in extrapolating his own view of moral agency. By the 1820s, the currency of the time-honored Edwardsian catch phrase "he can if he will" had depreciated significantly. Arminians and Old Calvinists had been calling the Edwardsians' bluff for some time, pressing them to come clean as to whether they really held out anything worthy of the name ability at all. The old Edwardsian notion of moral inability, founded as it was on the ineluctable inclination toward self-centered sin in the soul destitute of the indwelling Holy Spirit, seemed vastly to outweigh the merely theoretical promise of natural ability. It was not enough anymore to respond to the perplexities of troubled seekers with glibly rehearsed stock phrases like "he can if he will." Taylor described this phrase to his students as a "mere truism, nonsense, or absurdity" since, from an Edwardsian point of view, "*willing* is the thing to be done." At an installation sermon for his son-in-law Noah Porter, Taylor insisted that preachers who take human natural ability seriously must assert that "he can" even "if he won't." Further, faced with the declining purchase of the older, easily distorted rhetoric of moral inability, Taylor coined his own soon-to-be-classic catch phrase, "certainty without necessity." Conceived as a way to articulate the traditional Edwardsian doctrine of moral inability without undoing the sinner's sense of obligation, Taylor substituted this phrase whenever possible for the older Edwardsian distinction (moral / natural ability), employing the two distinctions synonymously and admitting when pressed that this innovation expressed no new doctrine but only enhanced the effectiveness of the older rhetoric.[23]

While Taylor was a proud and independent spirit, he always perceived his modifications of Edwardsian phraseology as faithful enhancements of Edwards's legacy, as changes in orthodox New England's *modus loquendi* and not in the substance of its doctrines. For Taylor and his fellow Taylorites, the manner in which one chose to articulate Calvinist doctrine made a great deal of difference. But they almost always claimed that the divisions caused in New England's orthodox community by New Haven views were unnecessary. When understood properly, the differences had everything to do with semantics and very little to do with substance. This was not to say that semantics were unimportant; rather semantics were worth fighting for. But Taylorite innovations in the manner of expressing orthodoxy should not be mistaken for departures from orthodoxy.[24]

This was certainly the logic behind the Taylorites' rearticulation of original sin. Taylor, along with Goodrich, Fitch, Beecher, and others, lamented the unhealthy extremes to which many recent Edwardsians had taken the doctrine. The split between Exercisers (who argued that sin existed, not in any innate psychological faculty or inbred sinful "taste," but only in individual sinful "exercises") and Tasters (who insisted that all are born with an insatiable, inherent taste for sin) had left them with an impoverished religious psychology, rendering the discussion of human sin tenuous and frequently incredible and leaving New Englanders with so low a view of human capacities that evangelistic appeals often seemed perfunctory and even futile. Both the Exercisers and the Tasters had abandoned the unique blend of neo-Platonic, rationalist, and empirical metaphysics that had made the philosophy of Edwards's private notebooks rather esoteric but had reinvigorated evangelical Calvinist theology with a fascinating preachability.[25] The Exercisers radicalized Edwards's occasionalist approach to causation by neglecting the fullness of what Sang Lee has aptly termed Edwards's "dispositional ontology" and respect for secondary causes. In the process, they offended and even appalled many of their colleagues by making God appear to be the only real cause of human sin. The Tasters, on the other hand, tried to maintain Edwards's appreciation for human affections without sufficient recourse to his doctrine of continuous creation, making the human taste for sin appear like an inborn, propagated faculty determined by natural corruption.[26]

The Taylorites lamented the whole dispute and worked toward a less dubious *modus loquendi*. They approved of the Exercisers' famed notion that sin is in the sinning (i.e., that sin does not exist in the soul prior to or apart from individual sinful exercises), but agreed with most other critics that the Exercisers' impoverished psychology yielded divine determinism. Rather than return to Edwards's own essentially Augustinian psychology, however, they substituted a conservative, Calvinist version of Scottish faculty psychology, though making clear, unlike the Tasters (who had also moved toward a modern faculty psychology), their rejection of propagated depravity. They wound up with what might be called a modified exercise scheme, heralding the doctrine that sin is in the sinning but depicting humans rather than God as the efficient causes of their own sin. While deprived of original righteousness and thus born with a certain tendency to sin, humans are not created inherently sinful. Their faculties remain free of any positive sinful charge and stand fully capable of doing what is right. The Taylorites affirmed, in other words, "that the entire moral depravity of mankind is by nature," while denying the vitiation of our natural constitution itself.[27] Their Scottish realism did give the doctrine of sin a different flavor than Edwards's Augustinian realism, but it is important to recall that almost everyone in New England, including the most ardent Edwardsians, employed the Scottish Philosophy by this time.[28] No one maintained Edwards's own eclectic metaphysics, though all, in one way or another, tried to maintain its powerful homiletical effects.

As the Taylorites stated repeatedly, they emphasized ability only to dispel the complacency generated by their forebears' emphasis on inability. As Beecher once wrote to Ebenezer Porter, when he began his ministry it seemed to him as though hyper-Calvinism and philosophical necessitarianism ruled the day. "The people did not need high-toned Calvinism on the point of dependence; they had been crammed with it, and were dying with excessive ailment, and needed a long and vigorous prescription of free agency to . . . render the truth salutary by administering the proper portions in due season." Taylor reiterated this pragmatic theme in print three years later: "I believe, that both the doctrines of dependence and moral accountability, must be admitted by the public mind, to secure upon that mind the full power of the Gospel. I also believe, that greater or lesser prominence should be given to one or the other of these doctrines, according to the prevailing state of public opinion." Taylor noted that his forebears focused intently on dependence due to the prevalence of Arminianism. "But the prominence given to the doctrine of dependence . . . was continued, until . . . many fell into the opposite error of quietly waiting for God's interposition." As might have been expected, this error led to a notable decline in revivals and conversions. For Taylor, however, this historical lesson did not teach simply that ministers ought to abandon "high-toned Calvinism" and Edwards's doctrine of moral inability. He went on: "nor would it be strange if the latter kind of preaching [accountability-oriented preaching] should in its turn prevail so exclusively and so long, that the practical influence of the doctrine of dependence should be greatly impaired, to be followed with another dearth of revivals, and a quiet reliance of sinful men on their own self-sufficiency." There was a delicate balance to be cherished between the doctrines of natural ability and divine dependence that required constant redress. "When both doctrines are wisely and truly presented, the sinner has no resting place. He cannot well avoid a sense of guilt while proposing to remain in his sins. . . . [and] he cannot well presume on his resolution of future repentance. . . . He is thus shut up to the faith—the immediate performance of his duty."[29]

For Taylor, then, the proof of one's doctrinal phraseology lay in the preaching.[30] Faced with heightened criticism from theological liberals and a spiritual lethargy among the people, he sought effective new ways to communicate the Calvinist doctrines of grace. Though he undoubtedly was a theological innovator, his innovations were neither Arminian nor Old Calvinist. Rather, they emerged from and perpetuated a rapidly expanding Edwardsian theological culture. Taylor's pragmatic perpetuation of this culture clearly favored the preachers of the future over the guardians of the past. But while it has angered faithful guardians ever since, and while it helped expand the boundaries of a previously united and coherent Edwardsian theological culture beyond the point of no return, it also contributed considerably to the diffusion and accessibility of Edwards's influence throughout American culture in a manner unprecedented among more cautious Edwardsian protectors.

NOTES

1. The former interpretation has been the most popular, shaped in large measure by Joseph Haroutunian's classic work, *Piety versus Moralism: The Passing of the New England Theology* (New York, 1932). For a brief sampling of its proponents, see William G. McLoughlin, *Revivals, Awakenings, and Reform: An Essay on Religion and Social Change in America, 1607–1977* (Chicago, 1978), 113ff.; Joseph W. Phillips, *Jedidiah Morse and New England Congregationalism* (New Brunswick, 1983), 7–8; John H. Gerstner, *The Rational Biblical Theology of Jonathan Edwards,* vol. 1 (Powhatan, Va., 1991), 552–63; Julius H. Rubin, *Religious Melancholy and Protestant Experience in America* (New York, 1994), 131–32, 125–55, and passim; and Paul K. Conkin, *The Uneasy Center: Reformed Christianity in Antebellum America* (Chapel Hill, 1995), 220, 264. Sidney Mead put forth the latter interpretation in *Nathaniel William Taylor, 1786–1858: A Connecticut Liberal* (Chicago, 1942). It has been held with minor variations by most recent specialists in the history of the New England Theology. See Mark A. Noll, "Moses Mather (Old Calvinist) and the Evolution of Edwardseanism," *Church History* 49 (1980): 273–85; Allen C. Guelzo, *Edwards on the Will: A Century of American Theological Debate* (Middletown, 1989), 218–71; David W. Kling, *A Field of Divine Wonders: The New Divinity and Village Revivals in Northwestern Connecticut 1792–1822* (University Park, 1993), 91–93, 232–43; and William R. Sutton, "Benevolent Calvinism and the Moral Government of God: The Influence of Nathaniel W. Taylor on Revivalism in the Second Great Awakening," *Religion and American Culture* 2 (1992): 28–29, 40.

2. For only the most influential of many studies that, in one way or another, bear Haroutunian's imprint, see Edmund S. Morgan, "The American Revolution Considered as an Intellectual Movement," in *Paths of American Thought,* ed. Arthur M. Schlesinger, Jr., and Morton White (Boston, 1963), 18–22; Donald Meyer, "The Dissolution of Calvinism," in ibid., 71–85; Conrad Cherry, *Nature and Religious Imagination from Edwards to Bushnell* (Philadelphia, 1980); James Turner, *Without God, without Creed: The Origins of Unbelief in America* (Baltimore, 1985), 60, 67–68, 90, 113; and Richard Rabinowitz, *The Spiritual Self in Everyday Life: The Transformation of Personal Religious Experience in Nineteenth-Century New England* (Boston, 1989), 3–151.

3. Thomas Bender, "The Cultures of Intellectual Life: The City and the Professions," *Intellect and Public Life: Essays on the Social History of Academic Intellectuals in the United States* (Baltimore, 1993), 3–15. On the demographic ties of the New Divinity clergymen, see Joseph A. Conforti, *Samuel Hopkins and the New Divinity Movement: Calvinism, the Congregational Ministry, and Reform in New England between the Great Awakenings* (Grand Rapids, 1981), 9–22, 41–58; and Kling, *Field of Divine Wonders,* 16–42. On the Edwardsian schools of the prophets, see David Kling, "By the Light of His Example: New Divinity Schools of the Prophets, 1750–1825," in R. Albert Mohler and D. G. Hart, eds., *Theological Education in the Evangelical Tradition* (Grand Rapids, forthcoming); Mary Latimer Gambrell, *Ministerial Training in Eighteenth-Century New England* (New York, 1937), 101–41; Roland H. Bainton, *Yale and the Ministry: A History of Education for the Christian Ministry*

at Yale from the Founding in 1701 (New York, 1957), 49–61; and Conforti, *Samuel Hopkins,* 23–40.

4. Guelzo, 124. Several of Connecticut's leading associations, such as Hartford North, Litchfield (which Bellamy is said to have ruled "with an iron hand"), and, later, Litchfield South, bore a marked Edwardsian stamp. In Massachusetts, Emmons presided as senior member of the powerful Mendon Association for nearly twenty-five years. Edwardsians also played leading roles in the Hampshire, Berkshire, and Essex Middle Associations and, when liberal clergy began to dominate the Salem Association, its Edwardsians pulled out and formed their own Salem Ministerial Conference. See Kling, *Field of Divine Wonders;* Michael P. Anderson, "The Pope of Litchfield County: An Intellectual Biography of Joseph Bellamy, 1719–1790" (Ph.D. diss., Claremont Graduate School, 1980), 289–90; Conforti, *Samuel Hopkins,* 58; Albert Hopkins, "Historical Discourse," in *Proceedings at the Centennial Commemoration of the Organization of the Berkshire Association of Congregational Ministers* (Boston, 1864), 5–6; Richard D. Birdsall, *Berkshire County: A Cultural History* (New Haven, 1959), 53–54; Samuel M. Worcester, *The Life and Labors of Rev. Samuel Worcester* (Boston, 1852), 2: 24–25; *The Diary of William Bentley* (Gloucester, Mass., 1962; 1905), 3: 113; Mortimer Blake, *A Centurial History of the Mendon Association of Congregational Ministers* (Boston, 1853), 29–34, 62–72; and John T. Dahlquist, "Nathanael Emmons: His Life and Work" (Ph.D. diss., Boston University, 1963), 174–75. On the triumph of pure church polity, see James Patrick Walsh, "The Pure Church in Eighteenth Century Connecticut" (Ph.D. diss., Columbia University, 1967); Joseph Tracy, *The Great Awakening: A History of the Revival of Religion in the Time of Edwards and Whitefield* (Carlisle, Pa., 1976; 1842), ix–xiii, 406–13; and Samuel W. S. Dutton, *The History of the North Church in New Haven, from Its Formation in May, 1742, during the Great Awakening, to the Completion of the Century in May, 1842* (New Haven, 1842), 97, who gloried, "now among the orthodox Congregational churches of New England, there is not one, which does not require experience of the renewing grace of God, as the qualification for admission to . . . any of the priviledges of its members."

5. *Diary of William Bentley,* 4:302; David D. Field, ed., *A History of the County of Berkshire, Massachusetts* (Pittsfield, 1829), 229; [Archibald Alexander], "An Inquiry into That Inability under Which the Sinner Labours, and Whether It Furnishes Any Excuse for His Neglect of Duty," *Biblical Repertory and Theological Review,* n.s., 3 (1831): 362; Samuel Miller, *Life of Jonathan Edwards* (Boston, 1837), 215; Bennet Tyler, *Memoir of the Life and Character of Rev. Asahel Nettleton,* 2nd ed. (Hartford, 1845), 274; Worcester, 1: 211; and Blake, 31. The best general treatment of New Divinity preaching is Kling, *Field of Divine Wonders,* 110–43. But see also Conforti, *Samuel Hopkins,* 175–90, on Hopkins; Mark R. Valeri, *Law and Providence in Joseph Bellamy's New England: The Origins of the New Divinity in Revolutionary America* (New York, 1994), on Bellamy; and Donald Weber, *Rhetoric and History in Revolutionary New England* (New York, 1988). On New Divinity methods of cooperative revivalism, see Richard Douglas Shiels, "The Connecticut Clergy in the Second Great Awakening" (Ph.D. diss., Boston University, 1976), 40–86; and Kling, *Field of Divine Wonders,* 67–73.

6. For statistics on the publication of Edwards's works, see Conforti, "Antebellum Evangelicals," and Thomas H. Johnson, *The Printed Writings of Jonathan Edwards, 1703–1758: A Bibliography* (Princeton, 1940), who notes that the American Tract Society alone "must have distributed approximately a million Edwards items before it ceased, in 1892, to list them among its publications" (p. xi). Cf. "Review of the Works of President Edwards," *Christian Spectator* 3 (1821): 298–99, which noted that the first American edition of Edwards's works (1808) "[placed] a useful body of divinity in the library of almost every young clergyman, in this part of the country." On the significance of Brainerd's grave, see William B. Sprague, ed., *Annals of the American Pulpit* (New York, 1857–69), 3: 116. For Brainerd's influence in the rise of American missions, see Oliver Wendell Elsbree, *The Rise of the Missionary Spirit in America, 1790–1815* (Philadelphia, 1980; 1928), 17–20, 57. For the influence of Edwardsianism

generally on the missions movement, see Samuel Hopkins to Andrew Fuller, 15 October 1799, in Edwards A. Park, *Memoir,* in *The Works of Samuel Hopkins, D.D.* (Boston, 1852), 1: 236; Elsbree, 138–42, 146–52; R. Pierce Beaver, "Missionary Motivation through Three Centuries," in *Reinterpretation in American Church History,* ed. Jerald Brauer (Chicago, 1968), 121–26; Clifton Jackson Phillips, *Protestant America and the Pagan World: The First Half Century of the American Board of Commissioners for Foreign Missions, 1810–1860* (Cambridge, 1969), chap. 1; Charles L. Chaney, "God's Glorious Work: The Theological Foundations of the Early Missionary Societies in America, 1787–1817" (Ph.D. diss, University of Chicago, 1973); and William R. Hutchison, *Errand to the World: American Protestant Thought and Foreign Missions* (Chicago, 1987), 49–51. On Edwardsian influence at New England's schools, see Claude M. Fuess, *Amherst: The Story of a New England College* (Boston, 1935), 30; Leon Burr Richardson, *History of Dartmouth College* (Hanover, N.H., 1932), 1: 239–40; Joseph Conforti, "Mary Lyon, the Founding of Mount Holyoke College, and the Cultural Revival of Jonathan Edwards," *Religion and American Culture* 3 (1993): 69–89; Frederick Rudolph, *Mark Hopkins and the Log: Williams College, 1836–1872* (New Haven, 1956), 89–132; and David Kling, "The New Divinity and Williams College, 1793–1836" (unpublished).

7. James King Morse, *Jedidiah Morse: A Champion of New England Orthodoxy* (New York, 1939), 40–41, 121–49, 148, 160; and Enoch Pond, *Sketches of the Theological History of New England* (Boston, 1880), 55–59, 74–75. Cf. David Harlan, *The Clergy and the Great Awakening in New England* (Ann Arbor, 1980), 5 and passim; William Breitenbach, "The Consistent Calvinism of the New Divinity Movement," *William and Mary Quarterly,* 3d ser., 41 (1984): 242; and Elsbree, 91–93, who wrote that the Edwardsians grew so strong "that there was soon no middle ground possible between the liberalism of the Boston Unitarians and the dogmatism of the New Calvinists. Forced to make a choice, the Old Calvinists, for the most part, cast in their lot with the revivalists."

8. *Diary of William Bentley,* 3: 403. Cf. "Theological Seminary," *Monthly Anthology* 5 (1808): 602–14.

9. Leonard Bacon, *A Commemorative Discourse, on the Completion of Fifty Years from the Founding of the Theological Seminary at Andover* (Andover, 1858), 39. On the Board of Visitors, see Henry K. Rowe, *History of Andover Theological Seminary* (Newton, Mass., 1933), 16, 20, 48–58. On Andover's early years, cf. William B. Sprague, *The Life of Jedidiah Morse* (New York, 1874), 110; Leonard Woods, *History of the Andover Theological Seminary* (Boston, 1885), 93–131, 257–60, 333–52; Edwards A. Park, *Memoir of Nathanael Emmons; with Sketches of His Friends and Pupils* (Boston, 1861), 209–10; Morse, 114, who notes that "in conference after conference . . . between the two groups . . . the moderate Calvinists yielded before the . . . Hopkinsians"; and Harold Young Vanderpool, "The Andover Conservatives: Apologetics, Biblical Criticism and Theological Change at the Andover Theological Seminary, 1808–1880" (Ph.D. diss., Harvard, 1971), 348.

10. New Milford sat in southwestern Litchfield County, the heart of New Divinity country. See Arthur Goodenough, *The Clergy of Litchfield County* (n.p., 1909), 10–17, 29–38, 40–42; and Kling, *Field of Divine Wonders,* 14–15, 145–47, 183–85, 244–50. On Taylor's grandfather and his church (which succumbed to Edwardsianism in 1810 and abrogated the Half-Way Covenant), see "Nathaniel Taylor," in Sprague, ed., *Annals,* 1: 467–69; and Samuel Orcutt, *History of the Towns of New Milford and Bridgewater, Connecticut, 1703–1882* (Hartford, 1882), 190, 265, 469–71. On Backus and his influence, see "Azel Backus, D.D.," in Sprague, ed., *Annals,* 2: 281–87; George P. Fisher, "A Sermon Preached in the Chapel of Yale College, March 14, 1858, the First Sunday after the Death of Rev. Nathaniel W. Taylor, D.D., Dwight Professor of Didactic Theology," in *Memorial of Nathaniel W. Taylor, D.D.* (New Haven, 1858), 26; S. W. S. Dutton, "A Sketch of the Life and Character of Rev. Nathaniel W. Taylor, D.D.," *Congregational Quarterly* 2 (1860): 246; and Goodenough, 42–43.

11. Timothy Dwight, *Remarks on the Review of Inchiquin's Letters* (New York, 1970; 1815), 107; Timothy Dwight, *Travels in New England and New York,* ed. Barbara Miller Solomon with Patricia M. King (Cambridge, Mass., 1969), 4: 227–31; and Dwight to John Ryland, 16 March 1805, Folder 3, Box 1, Dwight Family Papers, Sterling Memorial Library,

Yale University (hereafter SML). For Dwight's opposition to the Half-Way Covenant, see his *Theology Explained and Defended in a Series of Sermons,* 12th ed. (New York, 1858), 4: 338–54; and Charles E. Cunningham, *Timothy Dwight, 1752–1817: A Biography* (New York, 1942), 106–09. On his Edwardsian curriculum at Yale, see Lyman Beecher, *The Autobiography of Lyman Beecher,* ed. Barbara M. Cross (Cambridge, Mass., 1961; 1864), 1: 44–45. For Taylor's reverence for and fidelity to Dwight's theology, see the preface to Nathaniel W. Taylor, *Concio ad Clerum: A Sermon Delivered in the Chapel of Yale College, September 10, 1828* (New Haven, 1842; 1828); and George Park Fisher, "Historical Address," in *The Semi-Centennial Anniversary of the Divinity School of Yale College* (New Haven, 1872), 11, who wrote that Taylor "loved and honored" Dwight more than "any other mortal." For more on Dwight's moderate Edwardsianism, see John R. Fitzmier, *Such Lights and Shades: A Life of Timothy Dwight, 1752–1817* (Bloomington, forthcoming).

12. See Fowler, 50; Orcutt, 627; and Mead, 34–35.

13. Leonard Bacon, "A Sermon at the Funeral of Nathaniel W. Taylor, D.D., in the Center Church, March 12, 1858," in *Memorial of Nathaniel W. Taylor,* 5–6; Edwards A. Park, *A Discourse Delivered at the Funeral of Professor Moses Stuart* (Boston, 1852), 21–24; Dutton, "A Sketch," 248–49; Fowler, 47; John H. Giltner, *Moses Stuart: The Father of Biblical Science in America* (Atlanta, Ga., 1988), 2–3; and Harry S. Stout and Catherine Brekus, "A New England Congregation: Center Church, New Haven, 1638–1989," in James P. Wind and James W. Lewis, eds., *American Congregations: Portraits of Twelve Religious Communities* (Chicago, 1994), 52–54. For the Center Church's 1809 "Confession, Covenant, & Articles of Practice," consult the Records of the First Church of Christ and Ecclesiastical Society, New Haven, Conn., vol. 4, 1773–1840, 26–30, Connecticut State Library, Hartford (many thanks to Jim Walsh for tracking down the Center Church's adoption of pure church polity). While Taylor did not publish on the issue of church membership (by his day the Edwardsian pure church model had already triumphed), he did maintain an Edwardsian commitment to a membership of regenerate or "real" Christians only. See, for example, William H. Goodrich (Chauncey's son), "Notes of Lectures Delivered by Nathaniel W. Taylor, D.D. on Mental Philosophy, Moral Philosophy, Moral Government, Natural Theology, Evidences of Christianity, Revealed Theology, 1845–6," owned by John R. Fitzmier, Nashville, Tennessee, 204–5. For adherence to the pure church model in the Taylorites' *Quarterly Christian Spectator* (hereafter *QCS*), see "Review on the Early History of the Congregational Churches of New-England," *QCS* 2 (1830): 328–30; "Review of the Works of President Edwards," *QCS* 3 (1831): 349–50; "Review of Harvey's Inquiry," *QCS* 3 (1831): 552–56; and [Luther Hart], "A View of the Religious Declension in New England, and of Its Causes, during the Latter Half of the Eighteenth Century," *QCS* 5 (1833): 228–29.

14. Quotation from "Review of Edwards' Sermon," *Christian Spectator* 5 (1823): 39. On Taylor's ongoing revivalistic work in and around New Haven, see *Contributions to the Ecclesiastical History of Connecticut* (New Haven, 1861), 439–40; Bacon, "A Sermon," 7–10; Chauncey A. Goodrich, "Obituary Notice," in *Memorial of Nathaniel W. Taylor,* 41–43; Dutton, "A Sketch," 251–52; and Fisher, "A Sermon." While Goodrich taught a course on "Revivals of Religion" and instigated the many revivals occurring among Yale's student body between 1817 and 1858, Fitch superintended several revivals at Yale's College Church. See Chauncey A. Goodrich, notes of lectures on "Revivals of Religion," MS Vault File, Beinecke Rare Book and Manuscript Library, Yale University; John T. Wayland, *The Theological Department in Yale College 1822–1858* (New York, 1987; 1933), 99, 366, n. 53; and Rebecca Taylor Hatch, *Personal Reminiscences and Memorials* (New York, 1905), 41. For more on the shape of Beecher's influence in founding the *Christian Spectator,* see "Sketch of the Life and Character of the Rev. Luther Hart," *QCS* 6 (September 1834): 486; [Joseph Harvey], *Letters, on the Present State and Probable Results of Theological Speculations in Connecticut* (n.p., 1832), 15; and Beecher, *Autobiography,* 1: 245–47. On the demand for Edwards's *Works* at the Yale library, see Wayland, 238.

15. Out of many possible examples, see Hatch, 11, 28, 34; Noah Porter, "Dr. Taylor and His Theology," in *Semi-Centennial,* 92–97; Bacon, "A Sermon," 8; and Fisher, "A Sermon,"

32. For one of many instances where Beecher waved the Edwardsian flag, see his *Autobiography,* 2: 294. Even his cagey *Views in Theology,* 2nd ed. (Cincinnati, 1836), proved very Edwardsian, as he devoted over half of it to the Edwardsian distinction between moral and natural ability. For Beecher's repudiation of Arminianism, see his correspondence with Ebenezer Porter in June 1829, *Autobiography,* 2: 122–43. For his opposition to Old Calvinism, see his letters to Bennet Tyler (March 1830) and Benjamin Wisner (28 January 1833), *Autobiography,* 2: 153, 223–25.

16. See, for example, "On Heaven," in Nathaniel W. Taylor, *Practical Sermons* (New York, 1858), 190; Nathaniel W. Taylor, *Man, A Free Agent without the Aid of Divine Grace* (New Haven, 1818); and Nathaniel W. Taylor, "Letter from Rev. Dr. Taylor," *Spirit of the Pilgrims* 5 (1832): 175–76. For the work of Taylor's colleagues against Arminianism, see [Ralph? Emerson], "Review of Adam Clarke's Discourses," *QCS* 1 (1829): 575–80; [Chauncey Goodrich], "Review of High Church and Arminian Principles," *QCS* 2 (1830): 730–31; and [Eleazar T. Fitch], "Fisk on Predestination and Election," *QCS* 3 (1831): 597–640.

17. On the continuity of the other aspects of Taylor's theology with the Edwardsian theological culture, see my "Nathaniel William Taylor and the Edwardsian Tradition: Evolution and Continuity in the Culture of the New England Theology" (Ph.D. diss., Vanderbilt University, 1995). My employment here of linguistic analysis derives from the careful conceptual work of the English political historians J. G. A. Pocock and Quentin Skinner and their American counterparts, such as Gordon Wood and David Hollinger. See especially Pocock, "Languages and Their Implications: The Transformation of the Study of Political Thought," *Politics, Language and Time: Essays on Political Thought and History* (New York, 1971), 3–41; Gordon S. Wood, "Intellectual History and the Social Sciences," in John Higham and Paul K. Conkin, eds., *New Directions in American Intellectual History* (Baltimore, 1979), 27–41; and David Hollinger, "Historians and the Discourse of Intellectuals," in ibid., 42–63 (thanks go to Mark Noll and Brooks Holifield for guiding me to this literature). While not a partisan of the antifoundationalism in this school of interpretation, I have found useful its emphasis on the importance of language in forming and limiting our thought worlds. I have also benefited from its contention that such *functions* and *effects* of language prove more crucial historically than the alleged subjective meanings or intentions that propositions carry (often too difficult to determine anyway). Whatever Edwards may have meant by his doctrinal propositions, Edwardsian language gave birth to a rich and somewhat diverse theological culture. Rather than continue the debate over whether Taylor grasped the true meaning of Edwards's thought, I am trying to elucidate the ways in which Edwardsian language shaped Taylor's thought world and the ways in which, for better or for worse, Taylor carried forward the logic of the Edwardsian tradition.

18. See Breitenbach's "Consistent Calvinism," 257, and "Unregenerate Doings: Selflessness and Selfishness in New Divinity Theology," *American Quarterly* 34 (1982): 484. See also Mead, 105, and Guelzo, passim, who reveals how powerful the distinction proved to be in the unfolding of New Divinity doctrine. Taylor opposed the doctrine of imputation in both its classical Augustinian and later federalist forms. On the former, see Taylor, *Essays, Lectures, Etc.,* 171, and "Notes on the lectures of Nathaniel William Taylor. Copied by R. C. Learned, Edward Learned, and Joshua Learned in the years 1838–40 from the notes of another, unknown student," Yale Divinity School Library, 2: 117–18. On the latter, see especially *Essays, Lectures, Etc.,* 255–309. For the Taylorites' debate with Princeton over the doctrine of imputation, see "Inquiries Respecting the Doctrine of Imputation," *QCS* 2 (1830): 339–45; "Remarks of Protestant on the Biblical Repertory," *QCS* 3 (1831): 156–62; "Remarks on Protestant and the Biblical Repertory, Respecting the Doctrine of Imputation," *QCS* 3 (1831): 162–68; and "The Biblical Repertory on the Doctrine of Imputation," *QCS* 3 (1831): 497–512.

19. Bennet Tyler, *Letters on the Origin and Progress of the New Haven Theology* (New York, 1837), 6, noted that Taylor said that "Dr. Ware had the better of the argument, and that Dr. Woods had put back the controversy with Unitarians fifty years." For a blow-by-blow account of this and subsequent paper wars over original sin with comprehensive

bibliographical citations, see H. Shelton Smith, *Changing Conceptions of Original Sin: A Study in American Theology since 1750* (New York, 1955).

20. Goodrich introduced his students to the New Haven doctrine of sin in a lecture delivered on Saturday night, 15 December 1821. On his early lectures on sin, see Tyler's *Letters.* For his letter to Beecher, 6 January 1822, see Beecher's *Autobiography,* 1: 348. For his later, published view of original sin, see [Chauncey Goodrich], "Review of Taylor and Harvey on Human Depravity," *QCS* 1 (1829): 343–84. For Fitch's early contributions to this doctrine, see Eleazar T. Fitch, *Two Discourses on the Nature of Sin; Delivered before the Students of Yale College, July 30th, 1826* (New Haven, 1826), quotation from p. 38; and Eleazar T. Fitch, *An Inquiry into the Nature of Sin* (New Haven, 1827). For the commitments of other Taylorites to the moral/natural ability distinction, see "The Sermons of Dr. Samuel Clark," *Christian Spectator,* n.s., 1 (1827): 640–41; Lyman Beecher, *Dependence and Free Agency. A Sermon Delivered in the Chapel of the Theological Seminary, Andover, July 16, 1832* (Boston, 1832); and "An Inquiry into the True Way of Preaching on Ability," *QCS* 7 (1835): 223–57.

21. Taylor, *Essays, Lectures, Etc.,* 210; and [Nathaniel W. Taylor], "Review of Dr. Tyler's Strictures on the Christian Spectator," *QCS* 2 (1830): 195. See also Taylor, *Man, A Free Agent,* 10–11; Nathaniel W. Taylor, "Dr. Taylor's Reply to Dr. Tyler's Examination," *Spirit of the Pilgrims* 5 (1832): 428–29; and [Nathaniel W. Taylor], "Dr. Tyler's Remarks and Dr. Taylor's Reply," *QCS* 4 (1832): 458–64.

22. Quotation from *Essays, Lectures, Etc.,* 213. For Taylor's opposition to the language of physical depravity, which all Edwardsians repudiated whether or not they inadvertently lapsed into it, see especially his *Concio ad Clerum,* 5–6, 8, 14–15, 27; Nathaniel W. Taylor, "Dr. Taylor's Reply to Dr. Tyler," *Spirit of the Pilgrims* 6 (1833): 5–12, 16–18; Taylor, *Essays, Lectures, Etc.,* 135–36, 167–68, 183–94, 213–33; and Nathaniel W. Taylor, "The Peculiar Power of the Gospel on the Human Mind, as Determining the Mode of Preaching It," preached 12 January 1843 in Springfield, Mass. Folder 737, Box 19, Yale Misc. Mss., SML, p. 27.

23. For Taylor's desire to fill in where Edwards left off, see his letter to Beecher, 14 January 1819, in Beecher's *Autobiography,* 1: 284–87. For his response to the catch phrase "he can if he will," see J. A. Saxton, "Notes of Dr. Taylor's Lectures: Taken, in Part at the Lectures, and Compiled, in Part from the Notes of Dutton, Kitchel & Whittlesey" (1838), 2: 338, Folder 155, Box 32, Yale Lectures, SML; Taylor, "Peculiar Power," 26; and Taylor to Edward Dorr Griffin, 20 March 1832, in William B. Sprague, *Memoir of Rev. Dr. Griffin,* in Sprague, ed., *Sermons by the Late Rev. Edward D. Griffin* (New York, 1839), 1: 178. For examples of the synonymous use of the moral/natural ability and certainty/necessity distinctions, see Saxton, "Notes," 2:340; Sprague, *Memoir,* 1:174–83; and "Review of the Works of President Edwards," 337–57.

24. See, for example, [Taylor], "Dr. Tyler's Remarks," 456; Nathaniel W. Taylor, "Letter to the Editor from the Rev. Dr. Taylor," *QCS* 5 (1833): 448–69; and [Samuel R. Andrew], "What Is the Real Difference between the New-Haven Divines and Those Who Oppose Them?," *QCS* 5 (1833): 657–60. The Taylorites always regretted the divisions among the Edwardsians. They thought that the Tylerites had misunderstood them and they hoped for reunion among the New England theologians. For further examples, see Beecher to Ebenezer Porter, June 1829, *Autobiography,* 2: 128; Chauncey A. Goodrich to Bennet Tyler, 1 October 1832, MS Vault File, Beinecke Rare Book and Manuscript Library, Yale University; and Nathaniel W. Taylor to Asahel Nettleton, 4 June 1834, Folder 2851, Box 180, Nettleton Papers, Case Memorial Library, Hartford Seminary.

25. The best source on Edwards's metaphysics is Sang Hyun Lee, *The Philosophical Theology of Jonathan Edwards* (Princeton, 1988). On Edwards's occasionalism, see Norman Fiering, "The Rationalist Foundations of Jonathan Edwards's Metaphysics," in Nathan O. Hatch and Harry S. Stout, eds., *Jonathan Edwards and the American Experience* (New York, 1988), 73–101. But temper this with the arguments of Lee, 47–75, 107, and Clyde A. Holbrook, *Jonathan Edwards, the Valley, and Nature: An Interpretative Essay* (Lewisburg, Pa., 1987), 72 and passim, that Edwards did not hold to a pure occasionalism or even a pure idealism. He carved out a significant space for secondary causes, granting "finite habits and

laws . . . a relative and yet real causal function" (Lee, 107). On the philosophical background to Edwards's occasionalism, see especially Charles J. McCracken, *Malebranche and British Philosophy* (Oxford, 1983).

26. On the differences between the Tasters and the Exercisers, see William Kern Breitenbach, "New Divinity Theology and the Ideal of Moral Accountability" (Ph.D. diss., Yale University, 1978), 215–35; Guelzo, 108–11; and James Hoopes, *Consciousness in New England: From Puritanism and Ideas to Psychoanalysis and Semiotic* (Baltimore, 1989), 95–124.

27. This was the argument of Taylor's *Concio ad Clerum.* On the Taylorites' dissatisfaction with the Emmonsists, see Beecher's *Autobiography,* 1: 374–75; Taylor, *Essays, Lectures, Etc.,* 180–83; O. F., "On the Nature of Providence," *The Christian Spectator,* n.s., 1 (1827): 175–77, where the occasionalism of both Malebranche and the Emmonsists was criticized in favor of a "mediate" understanding of providence that allowed greater room for secondary causation; and the brief paper war between the Emmonsists and the Taylorites in the *QCS:* "The Mendon Association," *QCS* 8 (1836): 170–76; "The Mendon Association and Hopkinsianism," *QCS* 8 (1836): 327–36; and "Correspondence," *QCS* 8 (1836): 671–72. For the Taylorites' advocacy of a modified exercise scheme, see [Luther Hart], "Character and Writings of Dr. Strong," *QCS* 5 (1833): 337–63.

28. For the loose though consistent Taylorite employment of Common Sense Realism, see especially, "Review of Ernesti on Applying the Principles of Common Life to the Study of the Scriptures," *QCS* 3 (1831): 116–44; [Nathaniel W. Taylor], "Application of the Principles of Common Sense to Certain Disputed Doctrines," *QCS* 3 (1831): 453–76; and "On the Authority of Reason in Theology," *QCS* 9 (1837): 151–62. For the influence of this philosophy in America generally in this period, see Sydney E. Ahlstrom, "The Scottish Philosophy and American Theology," *Church History* 24 (1955): 257–72; and Mark A. Noll, "Common Sense Traditions and American Evangelical Thought," *American Quarterly* 37 (1985): 216–38. It is important to bear in mind here that, while this philosophy did emerge from Scotland's moderate Enlightenment and was usually attached there to a liberal religious sensibility, in America Common Sense thought was employed quite loosely by a wide range of thinkers. As Stanley Goodwin French, Jr., "Some Theological and Ethical Uses of Mental Philosophy in Early Nineteenth Century America" (Ph.D. diss., University of Wisconsin, 1967), 268, notes, "because of the lack or at least the relative unimportance of substantive metaphysical theory, the Scottish Philosophy could not be substantively employed as an apologetic philosophy for any particular theological views." Its use "did not determine theological differences between sects, but sectarian differences determined the manner in which mental philosophy was used." Taylor employed Scottish thought in support of a relatively *conservative* Calvinism. In fact, the Taylorites could prove quite critical of Enlightenment rationalism and its liberal anthropology. See, for example, Taylor, "On the Authority of Reason in Theology," 157, 161–62; Taylor, "The Peculiar Power of the Gospel," 1; and "Brown's Philosophy of the Human Mind," *Christian Spectator* 8 (1826): 141–55.

29. Beecher to Ebenezer Porter, June 1829, *Autobiography,* 2: 139; Taylor, "Letter from Rev. Dr. Taylor," 177–78. See also "Review of True Religion Delineated," *QCS* 2 (1830): 417–20; and "Views and Feelings Requisite to Success in the Gospel Ministry," *QCS* 5 (1833): 532.

30. On this theme, see, for example, Taylor, *Concio ad Clerum,* 37–39, and Fitch, *Two Discourses,* 32–34. Mead, *The Lively Experiment: The Shaping of Christianity in America* (New York, 1963), 124, contended (exaggeratedly) that Taylor "almost made 'preachableness' in revivals normative for doctrines."

TEN

Oberlin Perfectionism and Its Edwardsian Origins, 1835–1870

ALLEN C. GUELZO

"An impression has very generally prevailed," wrote James Harris Fairchild toward the end of his twenty-three-year presidency of Oberlin College, "that the theological views unleashed at Oberlin College by the late Rev. Charles Grandison Finney & his Associates involves a considerable departure from the accepted orthodox faith." It was an impression that Fairchild believed to be inaccurate, and he would probably be horrified to discover a century later that the prevailing impression the "Oberlin Theology" has made on historians of the nineteenth-century United States continues to be one in which Oberlin stands for almost all the progressive and enthusiastic unorthodoxies of the Age of Jackson, from Sylvester Graham's crackers to moral perfectionism.[1] But Fairchild, who was one of Finney's earliest students in the original Oberlin Collegiate Institute and who succeeded Finney as professor of moral philosophy and theology in 1858 and then as president of Oberlin College in 1866, was certain that he discerned a far different genealogy for Oberlin, one which ran back not to the age of Jackson but to the age of Jonathan Edwards. "The ethical Philosophy inculcated by Mr. Finney & his associates of later times is that of the elder Edwards," Fairchild repeatedly insisted, and the Oberlin Theology, far from being "original," was nothing less than "the theory . . . presented by various authors, especially by President Edwards . . . and by his pupil and friend Samuel Hopkins."[2]

This is a surprising claim, since the prevailing currents of interpretation of both Finney and Edwards meet more for the purposes of contrast than comparison, and also because the central doctrine of the Oberlin Theology—the attainability of moral perfection—seems too optimistic, too shallow, and above all too Pelagian to link with the most imposing apologist for Calvinism and human depravity in United States intellectual history. But Fairchild's claims are not easy to dismiss, if only because hardly anyone was in a better position to make an assessment of the intellectual dynamic of the Oberliners. Contrary to the conventional characterization of perfectionism at Oberlin as an enthusiastic aberration of the Jacksonian persuasion, Finney—along with his Oberlin co-adjutors, Asa Mahan, Henry and John P. Cowles, John Morgan, James Armstrong Thome, and Fairchild—owed a complex but clear reliance on Edwards and the particular evolution of Edwardsian theology known as the New Divinity, while Oberlin perfectionism was predicated in large measure on the Oberliners' explication of the famous natural ability/moral inability dichotomy in Edwards's great treatise *Freedom of the Will* and on the famous statement of "disinterested benevolence" articulated by Hopkins and the New Divinity. It was within this outline that Fairchild saw Oberlin as "Calvinistic in doctrine, after the New England type," and not Arminian, Jacksonian, or Wesleyan; and it was within that Edwardsian outline that Oberlin perfectionism represented a recoil from, rather than an embrace of, the democratized and sentimentalized piety of the nineteenth century.[3]

Perfectionism in English-speaking Christian theology is most often associated with John Wesley and Methodism, and later on, with what became known in American religious history as the "holiness movement." However, the term *perfection,* even in Wesley's hands, was a rather loose-fitting garment—Wesley actually used a bewildering cluster of synonyms, ranging from *entire sanctification* through *perfect love* to *the second blessing*—thrown over a collection of ideas which ranged from an instantaneous moment of divine sanctification of the soul to a gradual growth in stages of perfect love, and drawn from a conflicting array of sources that included both High-Church Non-Jurors and Moravian pietists.[4] Tracking down these disparities has drawn historical attention away from the underlying motive for Wesley's adoption of perfectionism, and that was the need, in an age of Enlightenment where the acceptance of truth depended on how well it could be proven by experience and demonstration, to make Christianity as empirically visible as any Lockean primary quality. "Faith implies both the perceptive faculty itself and the act of perceiving God and the things of God," Wesley insisted, employing a vocabulary of sensationalism which (as Frederick Dreyer and Richard Brantley have shown) owes more than a little to Locke. "It implies both a supernatural *evidence* of God, and of the things of God; a kind of spiritual *light* exhibited to the soul, and a supernatural *sight* or perception thereof. . . ." Perfection, by that reckoning, was the badge of those "who do not limit God"; to the contrary, perfectionists are the harbingers of a greater visibility of divine things "when a fuller dispensation of the Spirit is given, then there has ever been known before."[5] It is that relentless drive to promote the visibility of sanctity and to place it, through its visibleness, beyond the reach of question or doubt which clearly locates Wesley as a figure of the eighteenth century; and it is that same drive which links Wesley in the same century with another great promoter of the visibility of Christianity, Jonathan Edwards.

Whatever else separates Edwards and Wesley, they were utterly at one in this regard, for although Edwards would have shrunk from a claim to "perfection" per se as a species of enthusiasm, he and Wesley were united in making Christianity a matter of visible, perceivable experience. "The reasonable creatures are the eye of the world," Edwards wrote in his "Miscellanies," "and therefore it is requisite, that the beauty and excellency of the world, as God hath constituted it, should not be hid or kept secret."

> Since God has made the beauty and regularity of the natural world so publicly visible to all; it is much more requisite, that the moral beauty and regularity of his disposals in the intelligent world, should be publicly visible. . . . It is as reasonable to suppose, that these will be as publicly visible as the brightness and beautiful order and motions of the heavenly bodies . . . and the beauties of nature in the air and on the face of the earth.

And seeing that "spiritual beauty consists principally in virtue and holiness," Edwards made the famous and lengthy twelfth sign of "truly gracious and holy affections" in the *Religious Affections* (1746) to be "their exercise and fruit in Christian practice," since "the tendency of grace in the heart to holy practice, is very direct, and the connection most natural close and necessary."[6] The visibility of Christian holiness, however, depended in large measure on the power and abilities of the individual to make it visible. That presented fewer problems for Wesley than for Edwards; like his Non-Juror exemplars, Wesley freely embraced an Arminianism which preached the unfettered ability of sinners to be converted and lay hands on grace. Edwards, however, was fearful of the Arminian route for its potential for robbing God of his transcendence, and for the possibility that it would lead not to visibility and perfection but to stagnation. Edwards's route to visibility lay instead through his immaterialist ontology, while his route to action would lie through the ingenious formula he developed in *Freedom of the Will* (1754) for reconciling human willing and divine predestination through the famous dichotomy of human natural ability and moral inability.

The great treatise on *Freedom of the Will* gave to Edwards, and to his disciples Samuel Hopkins and Joseph Bellamy, the rhetorical equation they needed to preserve the most ultra definitions of divine sovereignty while at the same time justifying the most radical and direct address to the human will for repentance, conversion, and adoration. All humanity, argued Edwards, possesses a full natural ability to will and to do, in that all have the natural means—arms, legs, brains, reason—that they shall ever need for action. But just as no effect can exist without a cause, people only will to do things in response to what Edwards called *motives,* which only God controls. What is more, all humanity is afflicted with a moral inability to respond to truly sanctified motives, and that, without a divine initiative, ensures that the human will never actually makes use of those natural abilities. This guaranteed that the New Divinity of Hopkins and Bellamy would be forever wedded to a "consistent Calvinism" which nonetheless still held people accountable for the use (or nonuse) of their natural ability.[7]

It also led the New Divinity to blaze some new paths of their own: the possession of full "natural ability" led them to condemn in the harshest terms the false visibility of "Antinomianism," to call upon sinners to "change their own hearts," and to advocate a stern moral rigorism that promised that no matter what good sinners might try to do—prayer, Bible reading, charity—all was turned to sin by their unwillingness to fully use their "natural ability" to first become saints. Ultimately, that same logic was what drove New Divinity Calvinism to flirt with perfectionism. "Natural ability" was what rendered all human beings accountable, and able to obey God's laws; full "natural ability" ought then to require people to fully obey those laws. Natural ability, wrote Hopkins, requires "love exercised in a perfect manner and degree and expressed in all possible proper ways."[8] The naturally able will had no visible stopping point in the hands of New Divinity Calvinism, except in complete and perfect obedience.

The moment we look away from the New Divinity to Finney and Oberlin perfectionism, the kindred resemblance at once becomes apparent. Founded in 1833 by the Vermont missionary John Jay Shipherd, Oberlin had been organized in a tract of uncleared forest in Ohio's Western Reserve as a New England colony and settled by New Englanders from the western Massachusetts and Connecticut counties most heavily influenced by Edwardsianism (Fairchild's parents, for instance, had migrated to the Western Reserve along with a large group from Stockbridge, Massachusetts) who all solemnly bound themselves to a New England–style town covenant.[9] The Oberlin Collegiate Institute had been conceived by Shipherd as a missionary training enterprise, and it might not have amounted to anything more than that had not Shipherd managed to locate a source of funding (in the form of the evangelical philanthropists Arthur and Lewis Tappan), a president in the person of Asa Mahan (a New School Presbyterian pastor from Cincinnati who had cut his theological milk teeth on the most radical forms of the New Divinity), and the greatest catch of all, the celebrated revivalist, Finney.[10] Even so, the Panic of 1837 nearly wiped out the Tappans and Oberlin, and only by extraordinary self-sacrifice and the national reputation of Finney did the college survive, attract students, and recruit a faculty. As it did, the New England color of the institution deepened. Although Finney preferred to efface his early associations with Edwardsianism in his *Memoirs* at the end of his life, he was actually born in the thick of the Connecticut New Divinity country in 1792 and raised among the New Divinity–influenced "Presbygational" union churches of frontier New York; and he received his mature education in Warren, Connecticut, under the eye of the New Divinity minister Peter Starr, one of Joseph Bellamy's theological pupils. Henry Cowles was another western New Englander and a Yale College graduate, like his brother John; the Irish-born John Morgan came from Williams College to teach New Testament; and James Dascomb, the science instructor, was a graduate of Dartmouth, where the heavy hand of the New Divinity was still felt under the presidency of Bennet Tyler.[11]

In fact, the Oberlin faculty would have been surprised to discover that, by some accounts, they were less than Edwardsians. "It has never been our habit to commend our orthodoxy, by affirming our agreement with any human standards," wrote Henry Cowles in the *Oberlin Evangelist,* Oberlin's popular biweekly newspaper from 1838 till 1862. But if pressed to it, he cheerfully claimed "that we should choose to name the theology commonly known as that of New England . . . and as years ago, expounded by Edwards, Bellamy, and Hopkins." In contrast to the conventional image of the Oberlin Theology, the founders of Oberlin never seriously questioned the absolute sovereignty and transcendence of God; even Finney would speak of a free will only in the sense that a will is free when it has the moral ability to respond to motives for action which God places directly in the person's perception. "Human liberty does not consist in a self-determining power in the will," Finney wrote, but only in "the power which a moral agent possesses, of choosing in any direction, in view of motives." And if a will that moved only in response to divinely shown motives seemed to some critics to be something less than genuinely free, Finney was ready to explain the problem in terms of Edwards's great natural ability / moral inability dichotomy. "Natural ability relates to the powers and faculties of the mind," Finney explained to his New York City lecture audiences in 1836, and thus everyone has the natural ability to repent and at once; "moral ability" relates "only to the will," and can be exercised only by a divinely wrought change in the will. Finney acquired much of his notoriety in Calvinist circles from insisting on the grounds of natural ability that "a moral agent can resist any and every truth" and that moral agency "implies power to resist any degree of motive that may be brought to bear upon the mind"; what was less well noticed was how quickly Finney took it back on the grounds of moral inability by adding, "Whether any man ever did or ever will as a matter of fact, resist all truth, is entirely another question." Still, the possession by everyone of natural ability was enough to justify calls to repentance and enough to make the unrepentant accountable. "So it is explained," noted Finney, "by President Edwards, in his Treatise on the Will. . . ."[12]

It was this which launched Oberlin, as it had launched the pioneers of the New Divinity a generation before, on a trajectory which bent ineluctably toward perfectionism. In their preoccupation with establishing human accountability, the Oberliners began as the New Divinity had begun, by eliminating any excuses people might offer for why their wills could not be considered free or their choices responsible. People could not plead an absence of responsibility because of divine sovereignty because, while it was "essential to the very being and nature of God that in the depths of eternity, he should have planned and disposed all events," this did "not mean that he rules or in any wise acts capriciously." The whole purpose of the natural ability/moral inability dichotomy had been to show that no amount of divine control or decree concerning one's moral choices logically canceled out the natural ability to choose otherwise, and therefore the responsibility for choosing (or not choosing). As Henry Cowles explained, Oberlin believed "in the actual interworking of human and divine agency" which "takes place without any such friction as dislocates the system, or lessens liberty of will."[13] Nor could people complain that their "nature" or "constitution" predisposed them, through original sin or inherited depravity, to certain kinds of behavior or precluded an ability to repent. The Oberliners did not dispute that there were "appetites and propensities" or "impulses & Passions" which lay beneath the working consciousness and which might even be called "depraved." But none of these could be called *sinful*—in other words, none of this "depravation" was voluntary or moral and therefore could not be blamed for having caused one's volitions to become sinful. "These impulses & desires," argued Fairchild, "lying back of the will, are not sin—but are temptations to sin. The sin is in the voluntary action resulting." This, of course, clashed seriously with Old School Calvinism's doctrine of total natural depravity, but Oberliners like Samuel Cochran had long since come to the conclusion that this doctrine was "utterly absurd." It was true that "infirmities or constitutional tendencies to wrong action, temptations, may be transmitted" through natural generation, wrote Fairchild, and to that extent the Oberliners may be said to have believed in a notion of inherited original depravity in human beings. "But in strict thought and expression," Fairchild added, "sin belongs only to the agent who commits it, and cannot be transferred."[14] Anything which suggested that the will of the individual should or could be set aside in explaining moral conduct smacked to the Oberliners of yet another flight from accountability.

Natural ability not only removed any excuse from accountability; in the process it further paved the way to perfectionism by demanding the fullest possible exertions of that ability, in terms of both quality and quantity. In the first instance, the old Hopkinsian demand for an ethic of disinterested benevolence translated easily into a demand by Finney that converts give themselves over to "absolute and universal self-renunciation" in which "every sinful indulgence must be crucified, and Christ become all in all to our life and happiness." In fact, the Oberliners' preoccupation with natural ability only served to raise the Hopkinsian stakes even higher. Without sinful natural depravity to blame for one's failings, moral choices were no longer allowed to be mixed. "Moral character . . . must be either right or wrong," declared Fairchild, "No intermediate position is possible." If one possessed a natural ability to repent, one ipso facto possessed a natural ability to obey God up to the last degree of that ability at any given moment. "No partial becoming," warned Fairchild: "the sinner must give up sin wholly or he does not do it at all, no withholding is possible in this surrender to God. Any reservation is total reservation." Asa Mahan buttressed this by developing what became known as his doctrine of "the simplicity of moral action," which declared that, despite complex appearances, each volition was really simple in nature and guided by one basic object or consideration. In this case, each volition was entirely sinful or entirely virtuous, a proposition which (Mahan added) involves "our special attention" to "the remark of Edwards upon this subject" and which John Morgan was confident "agrees with that which President Edwards urges in his Treatise on the Will, Part III, Sec. IV. . . ."[15] The result, logically, was a "*universal* & *perfect good will*," and thus the Oberliners arrived at the possibility, predicated on natural ability, of moral perfection. As James Harris Fairchild remarked, by "forbidding the co-existence of sin and holiness . . . conversion becomes necessarily entire consecration, obedience, & faith."[16] It awaited only the trigger of a student revival at the college in October 1836 to propel Finney and Mahan into public proclamation of the availability and obligation of perfection. "That there is a natural ability to be perfect is a simple matter of fact," Finney announced for the first time to his New York City lecture audiences that winter. "It is self-evident that entire obedience to God's law is possible on the ground of natural ability. . . ."[17]

The image of Oberlin perfectionism which emerges from these texts spreads itself far wider than a simple frontier progressivism, and includes at its core a series of rigidly logical constructs, demanding a self-critical life of the most exhausting and exacting moral strenuousness and based (to a largely unsuspected degree) on the presumption of the Edwardsian concept of fully accountable natural ability. "What is perfection?" Finney asked, then replied in 1837: "The law itself goes no further than to require the right use of the powers you possess, so that it is a simple matter of fact that you possess natural ability, or power, to be just as perfect as God requires." This turned Oberlin perfectionism, as it had turned the New Divinity, into a kind of anti-antinomianism, a species of moral rigorism designed to force saints and sinners into a full realization of the obligations and opportunities of natural ability. "By entire sanctification, I understand the consecration of the whole being to God," wrote Finney in the *Oberlin Evangelist.* "Do nothing, be nothing, buy nothing, sell nothing, possess nothing, do not marry nor decline marriage, do not study nor refrain study, but in a spirit of entire devotion to God."[18] There was no relaxation in Finney's model of the Christian: the key words of the Oberliners were *law* and *duty,* not *grace* and certainly not *rest.* "*What is perfection in holiness?*" asked Mahan. "Perfection in holiness implies a full and perfect discharge of our entire duty, of all existing obligations in respect to God and all other beings." In the simplest terms, "*Moral perfection*" was "*simply inward & outward sincere performance* of *all duty.*"[19]

This might have been all well and good for Finney and Mahan, who were "not satisfied to *merely live* without *positive disobedience*" but who wanted to press "to the *highest* degree of *likeness* to *God,*" but it seemed to offer to more ordinary mortals no more hopeful prospect than "constant *battling* with *every opposition.*" What saved Oberlin perfection from demanding more than human flesh could normally sustain was the reminder that natural ability and moral accountability extended only to "a perfect conformity of the will to God's law, or willing right." Perfection was a rule which applied strictly to the conduct of the will—to self-conscious volitions—as the only moral faculty or attribute which humans exercised. "Sin and holiness are confined to the attitude or action of the will," according to Fairchild. "Evil tendencies or impulses, in the nature, are temptations, not sin; and good impulses are not virtue." It was possible, therefore, to have benevolent feelings or inclinations, but they counted for nothing beside the demands of the Oberliners until they were translated into action; likewise, it was possible to be tempted, in the sense that some "appetite" or "passion"—say, for sexual or material satisfaction—might stimulate a selfish or immoral urge for disobedience of the divine law. "But, in such cases," explained Finney, "the sin is not wilful, in the sense of being deliberate or intentional . . . it is rather a slip, an inadvertency, a momentary yielding under the pressure of highly excited feeling," and hence is not really counted as a sin at all.[20]

Thus, no matter how forbidding their brand of perfection seemed, the Oberliners were at pains to make clear that perfection did not mean that one could not make mistakes, nor did it mean that one could not experience temptation or even make moral misjudgments based on one's "natural" faculties of perception and reason. What it meant was that one did not *act*—that the will did not execute—on those temptations or misjudgments, since, after all, it was only on the abilities of the will that freedom and accountability could be assessed. "However excited the states of the sensibility may be," cautioned Finney, "if the will does not yield, there is strictly no sin." Finney unwittingly illustrated this distinction in the spring of 1836 when he urged Arthur Tappan not to jeopardize the antislavery cause by agitating too publicly for the social integration of the races. "I admit that the distinction on account of color & some peculiarities of physical Organization is a silly & often wicked *prejudice,*" Finney conceded. The key word was *often,* for such a prejudice would only be genuinely wicked if one was naturally able to think otherwise; whereas "a man may entirely from *constitutional taste* be unwilling to marry a colored woman or have a daughter marry a colored man & yet be a devoted friend of the colored people"—and still be entirely sanctified, too, since a "*taste,*" unlike the will, cannot help being anything other than what it is.[21]

This, as the Oberliners were eager to point out, set them off decisively from the perfectionism being practiced by come-outer communities like the Shakers and the Amana brethren, or by spiritual permissives like John Humphrey Noyes. Finney was appalled that "so many, that have embraced the doctrine of entire sanctification, have coupled it with the errors of the perfectionists," which Finney dismissed as "the most loathesome form of fanaticism that ever existed." The Oberlin doctrine of perfection and its "doctrine of *the unity or simplicity of moral action,*" insisted Fairchild, "has been maintained by Theologians of New England, and cannot be considered original here."[22] But Finney was just as eager to distance himself from the Methodists, the other major claimant, through Wesley, to perfection. Both Finney and Mahan read Wesley's *Plain Account* and had numerous direct dealings with Methodism (it is likely, for instance, that Finney copied the device of the celebrated "anxious bench" from Methodist camp meetings, although he cast his rationale for its use in terms of Edwardsian "natural ability" rather than Wesleyan free will). But the Oberliners rejected Wesley's construction of perfection as "*superficial*" and bound "almost altogether to states of the sensibility" rather than the intellect. Finney was also offended by Wesley's insistence that perfection sprang from "that aid of the Holy Spirit" in "what the Arminians call a *gracious* ability, which terms are a manifest absurdity." If ability came by grace, then without grace the entire human race was naturally unable to obey God and had a perfect excuse for its sinfulness. "If I rightly understand him," Finney wrote about Wesley, "he makes perfection to consist in just what you do with the exception of freedom from mistake." The *Oberlin Evangelist* attacked the Methodists as a "hindrance to evangelical piety" because Methodism "has no taste at all for the solid indoctrination of Puritan times—but an insatiable itching for something that will put good feeling into the heart." Thus Finney could "by no means adopt" the perfectionism of the Wesleyan writers, "& few

Calvinistic Ministers I believe have had more Collision with them than myself. . . ."[23]

Surprisingly for most modern commentators, the Methodists were inclined to agree with Finney's distinction between Wesleyan and Oberlin perfection. The American theorist of Methodist perfectionism, George Peck, insisted that "Christian perfection . . . does not imply perfect obedience to the moral law," and the Oberlin theory consequently "is understood by their opponents to differ in this respect from the Wesleyan theory." The Oberliners, in fact, "have finally taken up views essentially defective, and views which, as Wesleyans, we can have no sympathy." Daniel Denison Whedon, the editor of the influential *Methodist Quarterly Review* who had been a Finney convert but had chosen to follow Wesley instead, attacked Finney's perfectionism as mere "New Divinity . . . on every point," full of "*perplexity and contradiction.*"[24]

In fact, it was on precisely the issue of "gracious ability" that Finney and Mahan came to a dramatic falling out in the 1840s, as Mahan's personal experience of perfection became interlocked with what Mahan called "the baptism of the Holy Ghost." Mahan, whose personal connections with the Methodists were substantially more numerous than Finney's, came to see perfection as a second experience of conversion, "a *work* wrought in us by the Holy Spirit" and not a product of natural ability. By the mid-1840s, he was advising his Oberlin colleagues that "when our Methodist brethren speak of 'indwelling sin,' and pray to be delivered from it, they use language perfectly Scriptural and proper, and which, I think, Calvinists of the New School have unwisely dropped." The more Mahan spoke of perfection as "an *instantaneous* work," the more Finney and the other Oberliners suspected that Mahan was making perfection over into a matter of natural inability, which therefore offered a ground of excuse to every moral laggard to claim helplessness in obeying divine law.[25] Finney broadly suggested that Mahan had been deluded by the Methodists into thinking that "the Spirit leads the people of God by impressions on their sensibility or feelings" or other "constitutional" faculties rather than "obedience to the demands of reason or to the law of God as it lies revealed in the reason." Fairchild seconded Finney's condemnation of Mahan by disputing "the idea of a definite experience marking the instant of entire sanctification," and he too suggested that this led people into a "form of religious life which is much below holiness." James Armstrong Thome distanced the *Oberlin Evangelist* from what was already being called in 1860 "the higher life" by insisting that "there is but one sort of Christian life—that which is lived by the faith of the Son of God." As a result, beginning in 1844, the Oberlin faculty began a steady campaign to oust Mahan from the presidency of the college, and in August 1850 they succeeded. In time, Mahan converted outright to

Methodism, which only confirmed the Oberliners in their assertion that Oberlin's perfection was another thing indeed from Wesley's.[26]

Finney's most fundamental objection to Mahan's "baptism of the Holy Ghost" was the loss of the legal imperative for moral perfection, which was also what the Oberliners most feared from antinomianism. What Finney saw in Mahan was, in effect, a privatization of holiness, turned this time into a personal and ineffable experience which made demands only upon the interior life of the individual. Despite the stage-show paraphernalia of the "new measures" and the "anxious bench," Finney's rhetoric remained firmly rooted in the eighteenth century's use of rationalized public communication between autonomous individuals to create consensus. Accordingly, Finney's perfectionism conceived of holiness as a quality to be produced by a logical movement from rational propositions to action, whereas in Mahan's hands perfectionism was turning into a holiness to be consumed, a personalized commodity whose need was created by the "sensibility or feelings." What sharpened this contrast was Finney's apprehension that, against the background of the market revolution which was transforming United States society during the very decades of the 1830s and 1840s when Oberlin perfectionism was being articulated, the Finneyite version of *visible* holiness would be the one with which the society would grow increasingly uncomfortable.[27]

Finney and the Oberliners, fearing this and resenting its implications, railed unceasingly against the consumerization and privatization of piety. "How much evil is done by temporizing and keeping out of view the great and numberless points of difference between Christianity and the spirit of the world?" asked Finney. "Is it not most manifest that a want of thoroughly taking up and pressing this subject of entire consecration upon Christians in revivals of religion, is the very reason why they decline and react to the great dishonor of the Savior?" Finney was aware of the voices which "objected that Christians should leave human governments to the management of the ungodly," but he countered, "The promotion of public and private order and happiness is one of the indispensable means of saving souls." By making Christianity legally and rigorously visible, the Oberliners hoped to keep down the rising wall between public and private in a consumer-driven society—and nothing stymied them more than to know that they were failing. "Men are put in nomination for president; how few care to inquire whether they are licentious or not," complained Henry Cowles, as he watched Christianity rendered politically invisible. "Whether they are for virtue, or no virtue; for moral purity, or no moral purity, is a small affair." But Oberlin College, in the end, could not even keep Oberlin perfect. In 1855, an Episcopal parish—representing a denomination whose wealth and status were the very embodiment of commercial success in U.S.

society—was opened in Oberlin, over the college's impotent complaints. Finney came to suspect Fairchild of half-heartedness in the pursuit of holiness, and eventually came to dread the prospect of leaving the college in Fairchild's hands; and Finney even came to mistrust Edwards, turning the essays in his *Lectures on Systematic Theology* in 1846 and 1847 into criticisms of Edwards for not having given more space to the demands of natural ability.[28]

If Oberlin perfectionism was a failure, however—and as a living force, it really died with Finney, although Fairchild would have surprised him by the consistency with which he upheld the old arguments in the 1880s—it was an important failure. The demonstrable linkages between Oberlin and the eighteenth-century Edwardsians demonstrate the remarkable persistence of Edwards's potent theological formulae, especially on freedom of the will. At the same time, the Oberlin propensity to overdramatize natural ability beyond what all but its apologists would call Calvinism and to make perfection (which in the hands of the New Divinity had been little more than a logical possibility) their central theme underscores the degree to which the Oberliners found no easy method of transferring the agenda of the Edwardsians to the cultural climate of the antebellum republic. Still, Finney's demand for a holiness which would be visible and public rather than privatized and sentimental did not entirely lose its voice, even within the modern holiness movement. This raises an interesting question, not just about Finney's connections to the modern holiness movement but also about the historical diversity of the holiness movement itself. It may be a mistake to rest so much of the origins of the holiness movement on Wesley and Methodism, for as Donald Dayton and Bruce Moyer have suggested, the moral and ethical demands of the most radical strains of the holiness movement are representative of a more rigorous version of visible Christianity that runs back through Finney.[29] But, to the surprise of some of its modern proponents, this also means that the most ethically demanding variations of holiness theology may owe more, through Finney, to Edwardsianism and the New England Calvinist theological tradition than they have realized.

Oberlin perfectionism was not, in that sense, a forward-looking, democratic, or even revolutionary doctrine. Whatever the other influences on it, its most important intellectual roots lay in the eighteenth century, not the nineteenth, and it owed its distinctive architecture much more to Jonathan Edwards than Andrew Jackson. At a time when the market revolution seemed intent on privatizing and sentimentalizing piety for the purpose of consumption, Oberlin asserted the public claims of Edwardsian moralism and disinterested benevolence on the will, not the feelings. Perhaps, like the New Divinity, Oberlin perfectionism had no chance of success in the real world of the nineteenth century; perhaps it was only predicated on an arrangement of terms and signs that could only have worked in a small colony of New Englanders in rural Ohio. But to believe in a world of visible signs is, after all, the ultimate Edwardsian virtue.

NOTES

1. For the prevailing treatment of Finney as an expression of Jacksonian democracy or democratic culture, see E. Douglas Branch, *The Sentimental Years, 1836–1860: A Social History* (New York, 1934), p. 349; Whitney R. Cross, *The Burned-Over District: The Social and Intellectual History of Enthusiastic Religion in Western New York, 1800–1850* (1950; New York, 1965); Glenn A. Hewitt, *Regeneration and Morality: A Study of Charles Finney, Charles Hodge, John W. Nevin, and Horace Bushnell* (Brooklyn, N.Y., 1991), pp. 22–23, 47–51; James E. Johnson, "Charles G. Finney and Oberlin Perfectionism," in *Journal of Presbyterian History* 46 (March–June 1968), pp. 42–57, 128–138, and "Charles G. Finney and a Theology of Revivalism," in *Church History* (Spring 1969), pp. 338–58; William McLoughlin, *Revivals, Awakenings and Reform: An Essay on Religion and Social Change in America, 1607–1977* (Chicago, 1978), pp. 125, 128; Perry Miller, *The Life of the Mind in America: From the Revolution to the Civil War* (New York, 1965), pp. 3–85; Garth M. Rosell, "Charles G. Finney: His Place in the Stream of American Evangelicalism," and Carol Smith-Rosenberg, "Women and Religious Revivals: Anti-Ritualism, Liminality and the Emergence of the American Bourgeoisie," in *The Evangelical Tradition in America,* ed. Leonard Sweet (Macon, Ga., 1984), pp. 131–47, 214, 224; Timothy L. Smith, *Revivalism and Social Reform: American Protestantism on the Eve of the Civil War* (1957; Baltimore, 1980), pp. 88–89; and David L. Weddle, *The Law as Gospel: Revival and Reform in the Theology of Charles G. Finney* (Metuchen, N.J., 1985), pp. 3–30. For two dissenting views, see Leonard Sweet, "The View of Man Inherent in New Measures Revivalism," in *Church History* 45 (June 1976), pp. 211, 213, and Sydney E. Ahlstrom, *A Religious History of the American People* (New Haven, 1972), pp. 460–61.

2. James Harris Fairchild, "Oberlin Theology," in Manuscript articles, Box 29, James Harris Fairchild Papers, Oberlin College Archives; Fairchild, *Moral Philosophy; or, the Science of Obligation* (New York, 1869), p. 13; Albert Temple Swing, *James Harris Fairchild, or Sixty-Eight Years with a Christian College* (New York, 1907), pp. 79, 165, 255.

3. James Harris Fairchild, *Oberlin: The Colony and the College, 1833–1883* (Oberlin, 1883), pp. 46–47.

4. Henry D. Rack, *Reasonable Enthusiast: John Wesley and the Rise of Methodism* (London, 1989), pp. 395–402; Jaroslav Pelikan, *The Christian Tradition: Christian Doctrine and Modern Culture* (Chicago, 1989), pp. 146–62; R. Newton Flew, *The Idea of Perfection in Christian Theology: An Historical Study of the Christian Ideal for the Present Life* (London, 1934), pp. 313–41; Leo George Cox, *John Wesley's Concept of Perfection* (Kansas City, Mo., 1964), p. 74; Martin Schmidt, *John Wesley: A Theological Biography* (Nashville, 1966), vol. 2, pp. 52–58; John Leland Peters, *Christian Perfection and American Methodism* (Nashville, 1956), pp. 33–60.

5. Henry Abelove, *The Evangelist of Desire: John Wesley and the Methodists* (Stanford, 1990), p. 91; Richard E. Brantley, *Locke, Wesley, and the Method of English Romanticism* (Gainesville, 1984), p. 75; Frederick Dreyer, "Faith and Experience in the Thought of John Wesley," in *American Historical Review* 88 (February 1983), pp. 12–30.

6. Jonathan Edwards, "No. 123. Spiritual Sight," in *The Philosophy of Jonathan Edwards from His Private Notebooks,* ed. H. G. Townsend (1955; rept. Westport, Conn., 1972), pp. 246–47; *Religious Affections,* ed. John Smith (New Haven, 1959), pp. 383, 398, 406–7; "Observations on the Facts and Evidences of Christianity" and "The Propriety of a General

Judgment, and a Future State" in *The Works of Jonathan Edwards,* ed. Edward Hickman (1834; London, 1976), vol. 2, pp. 460, 471.

7. Jonathan Edwards, *Freedom of the Will,* ed. Paul Ramsey (New Haven, 1957, 1979), pp. 160–64; Clyde Holbrook, *The Ethics of Jonathan Edwards: Morality and Aesthetics* (Ann Arbor, 1973), pp. 42–43; Arthur Murphy, "Jonathan Edwards on Free Will and Moral Agency," in *Philosophical Review* 68 (1959), p. 196; and Allen C. Guelzo, *Edwards On The Will: A Century of American Theological Debate* (Middletown, Conn., 1989), pp. 47–53, 100–102.

8. Samuel Hopkins, "The Knowledge of God's Law Necessary," in *The Works of Samuel Hopkins* (Boston, 1854), vol. 3, p. 524; Joseph Bellamy, *True Religion Delineated, or, Experimental Religion as distinguished from formality and enthusiasm* (Morristown, N.J., 1804), pp. 72, 253, 268, 332, 423; Joseph Conforti, *Samuel Hopkins and the New Divinity Movement: Calvinism, the Congregational Ministry, and Reform in New England between the Great Awakenings* (Grand Rapids, 1981), pp. 164–67; Frank Hugh Foster, *A Genetic History of the New England Theology* (1907; rept. New York, 1963), p. 177.

9. Fairchild, *Oberlin: The Colony and the College,* pp. 10–27; Swing, *Fairchild,* pp. 18, 42, 52.

10. George Frederick Wright, *Charles Grandison Finney* (Boston, 1893), pp. 178–81; David L. Weddle, *The Law as Gospel: Revival and Reform in the Theology of Charles G. Finney* (Metuchen, N.J., 1985), p. 148; Asa Mahan, *Autobiography Intellectual, Moral and Spiritual* (London, 1882), pp. 115, 177; Edward H. Madden and James E. Hamilton, *Freedom and Grace: The Life of Asa Mahan* (Metuchen, N.J., 1982), pp. 13–24; Barbara Brown Zikmund, "Asa Mahan and Oberlin Perfectionism" (Ph.D. diss., Duke University, 1969), pp. 4–12; Robert Samuel Fletcher, *A History of Oberlin College: From Its Foundation through the Civil War* (Oberlin, 1943), vol. 2, p. 689.

11. Keith J. Hardman, *Charles Grandison Finney, 1792–1875* (Syracuse, 1987), pp. 28–33, 158; Foster, *Genetic History,* pp. 453–69; George Frederick Wright, *Charles Grandison Finney* (Boston, 1893), pp. 178–81; David W. Kling, *A Field of Divine Wonders: The New Divinity and Village Revivals in Northwestern Connecticut, 1792–1822* (University Park, Pa., 1993), pp. 31, 67, 120, 232, 249; Fletcher, *History of Oberlin College,* vol. 2, pp. 688–91; Mahan, *Autobiography,* pp. 115, 117.

12. Henry Cowles, "Oberlin Theology—Heresy," in *Oberlin Evangelist* (October 22, 1856), p. 172; Finney, "Thy Will Be Done," in *Oberlin Evangelist* (July 20, 1842), p. 114, "Professor Finney's Letters No. 33," in *Oberlin Evangelist* (May 26, 1841), p. 84, "Rejoicing in Boastings," in *Oberlin Evangelist* (March 26, 1845), p. 49, and "Submission to God," in *Oberlin Evangelist* (January 6, 1841), p. 2; Finney, *Lectures to Professing Christians, Delivered in the City of New York in the Years 1836 and 1837* (New York, 1837), p. 256; see also Benjamin B. Warfield, *Perfectionism,* ed. S.G. Craig (Philadelphia, 1967), p. 8.

13. Cowles, "Election and Reprobation," in *Oberlin Evangelist* (February 12, 1851), p. 26, "God A Sovereign," in *Oberlin Evangelist* (August 19, 1846), p. 134, and "Address," in *Oberlin Evangelist* (July 31, 1850), p. 122.

14. Fairchild, "Revealed Theology," Lecture Notebook No. 1, Fairchild Papers, Oberlin College Archives; Finney, *Lectures on Revivals of Religion,* ed. W.G. McLoughlin (Cambridge, Mass., 1960), pp. 107–8; Fairchild, *Elements of Theology Natural and Revealed* (Oberlin, 1892), p. 40; Cochran, "Chalmers on the Romans," in *Oberlin Quarterly Review* 1 (August 1845), pp. 129, 130.

15. Finney, *Lectures to Professing Christians,* pp. 255–56; Fairchild, "Revealed Theology," in Lecture Notebooks, Box 25; Mahan, *Doctrine of the Will* (Oberlin, 1847), pp. 155, 156; Morgan, "The Holiness Acceptable to God," in *Oberlin Quarterly Review* 1 (February 1846), pp. 321–22.

16. Fairchild, "Oberlin Theology," Manuscript articles, Box 29, Fairchild Papers; see also Finney, *Lectures on Systematic Theology* (Oberlin, 1847), vol. 2, p. 204.

17. Finney, *The Memoirs of Charles Grandison Finney: The Complete Restored Text,* ed. G. M. Rosell and Richard A. G. Dupuis (Grand Rapids, 1989), p. 409, and *Lectures on Systematic Theology* (Oberlin, 1847), vol. 2, pp. 169–71; Mahan, *Autobiography,* pp. 323–24, and

Christian Perfection (London, 1874), pp. 184–85; Finney, *Lectures to Professing Christians,* pp. 255–56.

18. Finney, *Lectures to Professing Christians* (New York, 1837), pp. 255–56; Finney, "Sanctification," in *Oberlin Evangelist* (January 1, 1840), p. 1, and "Grieving the Holy Spirit," in *Oberlin Evangelist* (December 4, 1839), p. 193.

19. Mahan, *Christian Perfection,* pp. 1–2; Fairchild, "Revealed Theology," Lecture Notebook No. 1, Box 25, Fairchild Papers; Finney, Sermon Outline, 1870, in Finney Papers. It was not clear precisely what the Oberliners meant by *law,* since the definitions varied from a strict application of biblical injunctions to Mahan's appeal to "fundamental elements of human nature itself." In general, however, the Oberliners increasingly appealed to an intuitive apprehension of moral obligation, which they owed largely to the rising influence of Scottish "common sense" philosophy in Oberlin's thinking, mixed with the Hopkinsian directive to express that obligation in the form of a universal "disinterested benevolence." See Mahan, "Certain Fundamental Principles, together with their Applications," in *Oberlin Quarterly Review* 2 (November 1846), p. 232; Finney, *Lectures on Systematic Theology* (Oberlin, 1846), vol. 1, p. 544, and "The Inner and the Outer Revelation," in *Oberlin Evangelist* (February 15, 1854), p. 25. See also James H. Fairchild, *Moral Philosophy; or, the Science of Obligation* (New York, 1869), p. 40.

20. Finney, Sermon outline, 1863, in Finney Papers; Finney, "Sanctification—No. 2," in *Oberlin Evangelist* (January 15, 1840), pp. 11, 12; Finney, *Revivals of Religion* [British version of the 1868 text of the "Lectures on Revivals of Religion"], (London, n.d.), p. 516; Fairchild, "Revealed Theology," in Fairchild Papers.

21. Finney, *Lectures to Professing Christians,* p. 256; Finney to Arthur Tappan, April 30, 1836, in Finney Papers [microfilm reel one], and Sermon outline, 1870, in Finney Papers; see also George Nye Boardman, *A History of New England Theology* (New York, 1899), pp. 277–81.

22. Finney, "Professor Finney's Letters—No. 5," in *Oberlin Evangelist* (April 24, 1839), p. 73; "Extract from Prof. Fairchild's Address on Oberlin: Its Origin, Progress and Results," in *Oberlin Evangelist* (October 10, 1860), p. 162.

23. Mahan, "Is Perfection in Holiness Attainable in This Life?" in *Oberlin Evangelist* (November 1, 1838), p. 4; Finney, "Letters on Revivals—No. 4," in *Oberlin Evangelist* (March 12, 1845), p. 44, and *Memoirs,* p. 391; R. Hatch, "The Perils of Modern Piety" [Address to the Oberlin Alumni Society], in *Oberlin Evangelist* (September 13, 1854), p. 147; Finney to J. P. Cowles, June 29, 1839, in Finney Papers, Oberlin College Archives, and, *Sermons on Important Subjects* (New York, 1836), p. 17.

24. Peck, *The Scripture Doctrine of Christian Perfection Stated and Defended* (New York, 1842), pp. 175–76, 193, 244; Whedon, "Arminian Theology," in *Statements Theological and Critical,* ed. J. S. Whedon and D. A. Whedon (New York, 1887), p. 246.

25. Mahan, *Autobiography,* pp. 204–6, 292, 295; Mahan, "A Letter from President Mahan," in *Oberlin Evangelist* (May 21, 1845), p. 84; see also James H. Fairchild, "The Doctrine of Sanctification at Oberlin," *Congregational Quarterly* 18 (April 1876), pp. 241–42, and Zikmund, "Asa Mahan and Oberlin Perfectionism," p. 123.

26. Finney, "Professor Finney's Letters to Christians, No. 1," in *Oberlin Evangelist* (December 23, 1846), p. 203, and "Letters on Revivals—No. 4," in *Oberlin Evangelist* (March 12, 1845), p. 44; Finney, *Lectures on Systematic Theology,* vol. 1, p. 213; Finney, "Danger of Delusion," in *Oberlin Evangelist* (August 17, 1842), p. 130; Fairchild, "Revealed Theology," Lecture Notebook No. 1, Box 25, Fairchild Papers; Thome, "The Higher Life—the Higher Law," in *Oberlin Evangelist* (April 25, 1860), p. 70. See also Warfield, *Perfectionism,* pp. 50–54, 120–24, 130–34, and E. H. Madden, "Asa Mahan and the Oberlin Philosophy," in *History, Religion, and Spiritual Democracy: Essays in Honor of Joseph L. Blau,* ed. M. Wohlgelernter (New York, 1980), pp. 174–80.

27. Mahan to Finney, February 26, 1832, in Finney Papers [microfilm reel one]; Cowles, "The Holiness of Christians in the Present," *Oberlin Evangelist* (January 1, 1839), p. 11; Finney, "Positive and Negative Testimony," in Finney Papers.

28. Finney, "Christians the Light of the World," in *Oberlin Evangelist* (August 12, 1840), p. 130; Cowles, "Proximate Effect of the Libertine's Code of Morals," in *Oberlin Evangelist* (February 15, 1843), p. 27; Thome, "The City Where Fashion's Seat Is," in *Oberlin Evangelist* (April 10, 1850), pp. 58–59; Finney, "Professor Finney's Letters—No. 10," in *Oberlin Evangelist* (February 26, 1840), p. 36; Rosell and Dupuis, Introduction to Finney, *Memoirs,* xxxix; Finney, *Lectures on Systematic Theology,* vol. 1, p. 430.

29. Donald Dayton, *Discovering An Evangelical Heritage* (New York, 1976), p. 17ff.; Bruce Eugene Moyer, "The Doctrine of Christian Perfection: A Comparative Study of John Wesley and the Modern American Holiness Movement" (Ph.D. diss., Marquette University, 1992), pp. 26–27, 45, 48, 52–53, 70–72.

ELEVEN

"Reason for a Hope"

EVANGELICAL WOMEN MAKING SENSE OF LATE EDWARDSIAN CALVINISM

GENEVIEVE McCOY

In the late eighteenth and early nineteenth centuries the New England ministers who claimed the mantle of Jonathan Edwards developed their theology in an arena of elaborate and abstruse debate. To the modern observer these prolix formulations can easily appear to have been irrelevant to anyone except a small group of contentious clerics. Thus it is not surprising that northern middle-class women are assumed to have had little familiarity with or interest in the conundrums of the New Divinity Calvinist theology with which so many of them were raised. Generally these evangelical Protestant women who participated in the revival meetings and benevolent societies of the Second Great Awakening are portrayed as bound by the conventions of a gender ideology that restricts them to the domestic sphere. However, their involvement in religious activities brings them into contact with a wider public realm, which while still partitioned by gender roles, affords them greater personal and social empowerment.[1] Obviously, women practiced their faith for a number of reasons. But I have discovered that, apart from the emotional and social satisfactions derived from religious practice, a number of orthodox women followed and sometimes engaged in the debates concerning fundamental tenets of the New Divinity and other forms of "moderate" Calvinist theology.[2] However, these beliefs were also understood in conjunction with secular discourses with which they seemed to intersect. Articles in Congregational and New School Presbyterian journals, intended for both a clerical and a lay audience, reveal how basic tenets of New Divinity and other variants of late-Edwardsian Calvinist dogma were interpreted within the context of the prevailing attitudes about woman's "nature" and gender-prescribed behavior. The reflections by and about women in these publications suggest that the liberalization or so-called feminization of theocentric and patriarchal Calvinism that occurred during the first half of the nineteenth century was neither as anti-intellectual nor as enabling for women as has generally been represented.[3] The inherent contradictions of orthodox Calvinist doctrine both drew women to the forefront of the evangelical crusade and frustrated their efforts there.

Scholars have considered New Divinity theology to be *the* New England theology because it became the dominant theological form of New England Congregationalism and it represented the most sustained Congregational effort to build a systematic divinity.[4] However, the second and third generations of New Divinity ministers did more than accept and, in some cases, extend the departures from Puritan covenant theology made by Edwards. For having rejected the Halfway Covenant like Edwards, the New Divinity men were committed to an "experimental" or experiential religion that centered on gracious conversion. Filling the new pulpits that opened in the backwoods of Vermont, Maine, western Massachusetts, western Connecticut, and later western New York, they became a major conduit for spreading the revival to every town and village. It was chiefly in these rural regions that the new interdenominational benevolent societies sought and found their most loyal membership and greatest financial support.

Usually the great appeal of early nineteenth-century revivalism is attributed to its Arminian nature. The so-called "hard doctrines" of late Edwardsian Calvinism are said to have been all but given up by such influential clerics as Timothy Dwight, Nathaniel William Taylor, Lyman Beecher, and Charles G. Finney. Their accommodations to Enlightenment reason and Scottish common sense realism conformed with a shift away from a corporate and hierarchic social order to an emergent entrepreneurial and increasingly democratic American society, as impatient with a paternalistic elite as with the rhetoric of an outmoded Calvinism.[5] The ability to control their own spiritual transformation was necessary, scholars argue, if men and women were to take part in this more individualistic and opportunistic culture—especially if women were to exert the great moral "influence" they were now expected to have over their families and society at large. However, if the liberalization of orthodox Calvinism was a "natural" application of Jeffersonian or Jacksonian democratic values to religion, few scholars have demonstrated the correlation.[6] Even granting that these were much less deferential times than formerly, women were still subject to the patriarchalism of the liberal political order. Classical liberalism, which assumes that maximum human potential will be achieved through freedom from economic dependence and through the cultivation and exercise of the "higher" faculties, was not developed with women, the poor, or other dependent and unenfranchised groups in mind. From my perspective, liberal free-will individualism had far from triumphed in the North by the Age of Jackson—particularly among and for women. This was due partly to their dependent and subordinate position in society and partly to the conflictual rhetoric of late Edwardsian Calvinist theology, which was perpetuated with the revival.

Even into the 1830s and 1840s the New Divinity descendants of Jonathan Edwards, who dominated the Congregational and Presbyterian pulpits in rural New England and New York, insisted that the so-called hard doctrines of God's absolute sovereignty and human depravity must be preached to ensure the descent of the Spirit's "irresistible showers." However, they knew that these doctrines could be serious theological hindrances to the conversion of new members and the recommitment of backsliders. So even while intent on sustaining the Edwardsian paradigm of conversion as a work of unmerited free grace, the self-proclaimed "Consistent Calvinists" preached a partially preparationist or Old Calvinist form of Edwardsian theology because it had to be "practical" as well as "true."[7] The fact that clerics and their church members, most of whom were women,[8] still debated the nature of conversion and to what degree they could or should participate in their spiritual transformation indicates that Calvinist theology still struck a chord in the hearts of many. If the prolific religious press of New England and New York is any indication of its readership's views, the truths of divine sovereignty, human depravity *and* moral accountability, and the reconciliation of necessity and freedom, despite their apparent contradictions, continued to agitate the orthodox faithful. The women who converted and joined missionary, maternal, and other female voluntary societies in such great numbers during the revival responded to Calvinist theology because its representation of the redeemed self was based on the same kind of ambiguous and paradoxical powers and responsibilities ascribed to women.

The Congregational and Presbyterian women who supported the causes of the benevolent empire had been instructed in the existential truth of both natural depravity and human accountability for sin. Predestination and free grace did not violate human free will and moral responsibility. Humans had the ability to choose God over sin and were obligated to use the means of grace and perform their gospel duties, even while they recognized their moral inability to succeed in them—without God's supernatural gift. To uphold both divine sovereignty and human free agency and yet defend themselves against their liberal opponents' charges of illogic and divine tyranny, orthodox preachers disconnected the relationship between election and the atonement. Contradicting Edwards, they preached that everyone was eligible for the benefits of Christ's sacrifice. However, a general atonement made the salvation of all men and women possible, not necessary. All must still strive to obey God's law and make use of the means of grace. But because their spiritual transformation was finally effected by the visitation of the Spirit, the consequences of their actions would never depend on their choices and efforts alone. Even so, they must act as if they did since they would be held responsible for them.[9] "Christians should use means, as if all depended upon them, and then all their dependence should be upon God," Calvin Colton advised in his handbook defending American revivals.[10]

Philippians 2:12–13 was often used to explain this enigma. According to Bennet Tyler, a New Divinity Hopkinsian,[11] "When God works in men to will and to do, it is not to *enable* them to do their duty; but to incline them to do what they are *able* to do, and what they ought to do, without any supernatural Divine influence."[12] The professor of didactic theology at Yale Divinity School, Nathaniel William Taylor, rejected the New Divinity position that the will was limited by a moral inability or sinful inclination that prevented it from choosing good until it was transformed by the power of saving grace. However, and a big "however" it was, Taylor argued that no one ever did repent and choose God over the world until God's grace was conferred.[13] Charles Grandison Finney, usually represented as both an exponent of Taylor's New Haven theology and a staunch anti-Hopkinsian, concurred that sinners' obligations rest "not upon the Spirit's influences, but upon the powers of moral agency which they possess; upon their ability to do their duty." But while "not one of them ever will repent without the influences of the Spirit, still they have power to do so, and are under obligation to do so, whether the Spirit strives with them or not," Finney lectured.[14] If they could show how sinners were both passive *and* active in their spiritual rebirth, Edwardsians, attempting to avoid the heretical Arminian and Antinomian extremes on the use of the means of grace, hoped to encourage sinners to come forward immediately.

In order to prove that their faith was actually a practical and benevolent system, New Divinity and other late Edwardsian divines incorporated many of the same rationalist and humanitarian assumptions of their more liberal opponents.[15] Take Timothy Dwight, the grandson of Jonathan Edwards, who is sometimes considered a transitional figure helping to turn the New Divinity's Edwardsian emphasis on the religious affections toward the more legalistic and rationalist position of the Old Calvinists.[16] Like Solomon Stoddard, Edwards's grandfather and predecessor in his Northampton pulpit, Dwight saw no contradiction between a conversion that occurred instantaneously as a gift of the Spirit to the elect and one for which all believers were expected to prepare by using the traditional means of grace. Although the prayers of the unregenerate were not virtuous, the Yale College president preached, they *might* become the objects of divine mercy. At least it was clear that all sinners under conviction prayed and "of such sinners all converts are made."[17] At any rate, there were good reasons "why most Christians should be left in some degree of uncertainty." In this way, "their fears serve to quicken them no less than their hopes" in the cultivation of spiritual pursuits throughout the lifelong process of sanctification.[18] Dwight was able to reconcile contradictory doctrines with simple assertions of "fact" and probability. The fact that God knew beforehand what individuals would do did not make them less free to do it. God could create a free agent whose actions were foreknown to him and accomplish his own ends without influencing the character of the individual's activity.[19] The hard doctrines may have appeared at first glance unjust and illogical. However, Dwight, Finney, Taylor, and even the latter's arch-opponent Bennet Tyler could all deliver the orthodox fundamentals in a package of reasonable, if confusing, possibilities.

To liberals who prided themselves on their rationality, these arguments made no sense at all. No one but the young, female, and ignorant would "subscribe to a creed that nobody can understand," the *Universalist* decried in a column on "Female Character."[20] However, reconciling apparent contradictions and opposing dualisms was nothing new for women accustomed to reading the orthodox press. Although one can never know precisely how much practice followed prescription, clearly these women had plenty of advice. Like orthodox preachers who prided themselves on their "still" and "sober" revival meetings, ministers and others writers of prescriptive literature urged Christian women to be both actors and acted upon. A woman should be "active but retired" and feel that "she has something to do, not merely to be led and influenced."[21] For liberals and evangelicals alike, the dichotomies of active and passive and head and heart were tied to powerful gender associations. Men were identified with reason, mind, and objectivity, and women stood for feeling, imagination, and subjectivity or intuition. For woman intellect must be compatible with nurturing, compassion, and "doing good."[22] Religion came naturally to her because it was based on "deep feeling and faith which 'with her is natural, the growth of her moral being; [while] in man it is usually acquired as the result of thought.'"[23] However, women, like the hopeful undergoing conversion, must not confuse mere feeling or "animal spirits" with true faith. Passion, enthusiasm, and imagination, women's peculiar weaknesses, had to be controlled, for otherwise they produced "effeminacy," irrationality, "false impressions of life," and, of course, hypocritical religion.[24] According to orthodox prescriptions, admirable Christian women subdued the "truant quality" of imagination and "curb[ed] the irregular sallies of passion" by inculcating "an habitual submission to the restraints of reason."[25] They must experience their piety as "deep feeling" but avoid indulging their female passions.

Although New Divinity theology eventually adopted a more legalistic Old Calvinist orientation, it never abandoned the Edwardsian principle that religion by its nature was centered in the heart.[26] This meant that orthodoxy's scholastic attempts to make revelation conform to the dictates of reason or "common sense," in order to explain away the contradictions, would inevitably fail. Calvinist dogma was a conceptual framework that could logically sustain itself only as long as it did not admit any other system of meaning. But when orthodoxy insisted that its fundamental doctrines and the "objective" truths of the Bible were verified in the heart, in personal experience, it had to admit, respond to, and be transformed by the meaning systems that all its believers brought to it. It could not uphold a transcendental, "rational," and masculine order of meaning outside of lived experience when it demanded that all lived experience, female and male, establish and verify the meaning of the transcendental order. It was inherently unstable. But the contradictions were necessary to maintain the truths of the gospel and the primacy of regeneration. A system that tried to bring the infinite into the realm of the finite without diminishing either God's or humanity's self-determining power was bound to preach that the will was both determined and free, that individual salvation was both always and forever predetermined by God and yet the responsibility of the sinner.

If it is true that the logic of Edwardsianism could no longer be sustained by the 1820s,[27] it was not merely because it was out of touch with the widening opportunities for social and political equality among men in the United States. It was also because it had adopted a rhetoric possessing feminine associations that contravened contemporary meanings of manhood and masculine power. For the question is not only why Calvinist clerics felt the need to defend and modify their theology, but also why orthodox female adherents so seldom asked them to. Of course, since women's voices are so often absent from publications debating theological issues, it is difficult to know from these sources what they believed. Generally their acquiescence to hierarchical and patriarchal Calvinism is explained through the association of religion and the domestic sphere.[28] In order to reconcile woman's inequality in society, she was granted an exalted position as guardian of morality not only in the home but for the entire nation and for generations to come. No doubt many evangelical Protestant women, especially mothers, had difficulty accepting the divine decrees and original sin. But if they at times believed and acted as if they could control their own and their children's salvation, they were doing no more than what they were expected to do by their Calvinist theology and by their society as women and mothers. Like hopeful saints who could never be certain of their redeemed state, they were to pray faithfully and regularly perform their Christian and parental duties, recognizing that all their exertions could come to naught. In their dependent and subordinate position in a liberal patriarchal society that had low expectations of but high praise for them, women could more easily than men accept such a perplexing theology and wield its contingent power.

During the revivals, orthodox doctrine was reduced to those "simple," "self-evident" points that had proved to be the universal and unalterable truths that procured human salvation. Among these the tenets of natural depravity, election, and limited atonement were difficult for many men to accept, particularly those who joined the northern liberal churches or no church at all.[29] Universalist, Unitarian, deist, and "unchurched" men were apt to argue that such dogma violated human free agency and God's rational and benevolent nature. Evangelical women, on the other hand, were inclined to interpret the concepts of original sin, election, and the atonement more positively, even while they expressed feelings of inherent sinfulness more frequently than men.[30] They could accept their native depravity and possible condemnation because the hard doctrines also allowed optimistic interpretations which late Edwardsian revivalists relied upon to bring sinners to Christ. These understandings afforded the faithful "reason for a hope." For instance, election and moral inability could as easily be reassuring as discouraging, since the responsibility to do all one could as if one could control one's salvation applied whether one was saved or not. And doing something could make one feel that something could be done, especially when one contemplated God's goodness and mercy.

Reason for a hope came in several doctrinal forms. To encourage men and women in the pursuit of righteousness while trying to preserve dependence on divine will, theologians and revivalists such as Samuel Hopkins, Timothy Dwight, Lyman Beecher, Nathaniel William Taylor, and Charles G. Finney preached a theology that conflated piety and moralism, or "disinterested benevolence" and Christian duty. Following Edwards, these men taught that true religion became visible only in its fruits, or holy action. Accordingly the Christian obligation to be "useful," to actively participate in the reformation of one's self, family, community, and all human society, became the chief means of proving one's saintly character. Many women from evangelical Calvinist families, raised to be unselfinterested and directed to the needs of others, readily responded to this association. By the second quarter of the nineteenth century, women constituted the bulk of reform and benevolent society supporters, and some of them wanted to do more than join local societies or female auxiliaries to raise money for missions and ministerial education. In ever greater numbers orthodox young women attended female seminaries that eschewed the traditional "ornamental" education for "useful" types of knowledge that would prepare them to become schoolteachers, wives of ministers and missionaries, or just good Christian wives and mothers.[31] After a year or two at these seminaries, many young unmarried women began teaching Sunday or summer schools, and the boldest offered their lives to the evangelization of the "heathen." The best way for a woman who hoped she was redeemed to glorify God and at the same time produce the highest good for humanity without winning personal honor was missionary service. There she could stay in the shadow of her husband (the *real* missionary, since women could be assistants only) and sacrifice herself to God's will as she demonstrated her piety and disinterested benevolence. One of the primary functions of periodicals she read, like the *Panoplist* and the *Connecticut Evangelical Magazine,* later the *Missionary Herald* and *The Religious Intelligencer,* respectively, was to demonstrate that benevolence was not only the chief fruit of conversion but the moving cause behind missions.

Another reason for a hope that attracted women to orthodox Calvinism and its benevolent causes derived from the idea of Christian nurture. Years before Horace Bushnell wrote his most famous work, *Christian Nurture,* in 1847, Timothy Dwight, Lyman Beecher, and other orthodox revivalists and preachers, concerned about the spread of infidelity and the importance of Christian example, urged their congregations to be constant in their parental duties. Many pastors were encouraged by the organization of maternal associations, which often formed during or after revivals. These societies, which flourished in New England and New York in the 1810s through 1840s, were formed by Baptist, Congregational, and Presbyterian women to aid each other in the regular performance of parental and religious obligations. Members mutually pledged to attend meetings regularly, report to each other on the literature of children's Christian education, and daily pray for and set a pious example for their family.[32] With the salvation of their children as their primary goal, they felt a kinship with their evangelical sisters stationed at foreign missions. Correspondence with their sisters abroad became a standard part of their association and issues like that of sin in children a common topic.

The question of infant depravity had always been a sticky one for New Divinity clerics. It was on this issue, as well as that of eternal reprobation, that they were most often attacked by the liberals. Even among their congregations New Divinity–, New School–, and New Haven–trained ministers alike approached the question delicately and often hedged. But orthodox religious publications did not hesitate to discuss original sin in order to remind mothers of their grave responsibility for the eternal condition of their children. Even the *New York Evangelist,* published by Finney supporters, continued to warn of the danger of parental indulgence toward children who before conversion were in "imminent peril." Probably "ninety-nine hundredths" of them were "enemies of God."[33] Both the scriptures and their children's early sinfulness gave proof that there was no period of life "before sin commences."[34] Mothers were obligated to educate their children whose final fate, they were told, was "suspended on the education, the early lessons, and habits" they received—even though it was God who would or would not save them.[35] Mothers had to have an understanding of the principles of orthodoxy so that they could teach and defend them with evidence to their children.[36] But to finally overcome a will inclined to evil, it was a mother's tears and prayers that would in the end "subdue" her child, just as the agony of the cross melted the pagan soul. By awakening her children's sympathies for the "condition of the heathen world,"[37] and through her own humble "daily, fervent, IMPORTUNATE prayer," the day would "*probably* come" when the "early counsels of a mother, pressed home by the Spirit" would bring her loved ones to repentance and salvation.[38]

The affective vocabulary that was often used by orthodox preachers and periodicals, in contrast to some of their liberal and antirevivalist opponents, drew many women who took seriously their formidable parental responsibilities. But obviously the child-raising advice they received was anything but consistent and often disquieting. Even before marriage evangelical women held themselves accountable for the virtues or vices of the young men with whom they socialized.[39] After marriage, if their offspring were not converted it was because their mothers lacked "self-denying *duty* which the gospel requires."[40] Not only were women responsible for the eternal fate of their own children, but "the regeneration of mankind" depended on maternal influence.[41] Consequently they reasoned that "if our influence is great, our responsibility is proportionately great." On the day of final retribution the vices "which our influence is not exerted to suppress, will be imputed to us, and must be answered for as our deeds."[42] As much as a mother did to instruct the minds and consciences of her children to prepare them for the coming of the Spirit, her power was always and already circumscribed not only by her culturally defined nature and prerogatives but also by an inscrutable divinity outside her control.

Such exacting accountability could be borne only because the doctrine of general atonement provided the greatest reason for hope.[43] It gave orthodox ministers and mothers the means to uphold God's sovereignty and at the same time contain it within a loving and merciful framework. Calvinist assemblies had long since discovered that the story of Christ's sacrifice was the truth most likely to influence the will. "Who does not know, that the only cure for the deep-seated disorders of mankind must be wrought in the heart," Rufus Anderson, secretary of the American Board of Commissioners for Foreign Missions (ABCFM), wrote, "and that nothing operates there like the doctrine of salvation by the cross of Christ?"[44] Incorporating the Calvinist fundamentals of native depravity and unmerited free grace, the atonement could be taught in a way that inspired love and gratitude to God, as well as distrust of the self and the self's actions. God had been under no obligation to provide a savior or the offer of salvation to the fallen human race. But in his gracious forgiveness he gave his son as a propitiation for their sins and offered pardon on terms with which all were capable of complying. The atonement provided spiritual comfort and held out the promise of salvation to sinners who did not deserve and could not win it through their own efforts. "If I am saved I am sure it will not, it cannot, be because of any intrinsic worth in me," Narcissa Whitman wrote her sister from the ABCFM mission in Oregon, "but solely and alone for His sake who gave His own life as a ransom to save a lost world."[45]

The atonement could also be a practical doctrine that allowed the clergy to press the notion that salvation required complete obedience and humble resignation to God's will. By the late eighteenth century, Edwardsian notions of true virtue had coalesced with a prescriptive canon of idealized but reputedly natural female qualities that, no doubt, most orthodox women were happy to claim.[46] Obedience, self-sacrifice, humility, and self-abasement were ways for the pious woman to demonstrate her sainthood and achieve self-mastery and self-respect.[47] Clearly these were not traits universally admired in men, and certainly not in men outside the evangelical community. To illustrate contemporary gendered definitions of morality, Kathryn Kish Sklar quotes the writings of Baptist minister and president of Brown University Francis Wayland that "typically condemned an 'angered and turbulent' woman as unnatural, but nevertheless praised righteous 'indignation' among men."[48] Men in the early national and antebellum period were creating a society based on a free market economy and liberal political institutions that involved the free expression of the traditional manly passions—ambition, competitiveness, and lust for power.[49] Reason, order, and emotional control were allied to the dominant masculine discourses of political and economic power, and emotional expression, obedience, and nurturing were clearly relegated to the dependent, the uncontrolled (which often had class and racial overtones), and the feminine. Following the revolution many men had developed the habit of resisting authority, making it all the harder to accept the disciplinary rules that came with orthodox church membership.[50] Nevertheless, the conflation of female and spiritual beauty, which was partly promoted by Edwards's works on the revival and the signs of true religion, used both female and male models. The early nineteenth-century Congregational and Presbyterian-dominated religious press helped evangelical women shape their identities as both Christians and females with its regular excerpts from Edwards's works, along with lengthy obituaries of pious ministers and missionaries and/or their wives who exhibited exemplary Christian resignation.

Self-sacrifice was the greatest virtue and also the most demanding, since it meant, in principle, subordinating all one's desires to the will of God and the concerns of others. If women were not prepared to sacrifice their own lives to promote God's kingdom, they ought to be prepared to give up their children to the evangelization of society. Mothers were often informed that God had only temporarily loaned them their "darling sons" and like the biblical Hannah they must be prepared to make the ultimate sacrifice.[51] Self-sacrifice extended to a woman's willingness to happily accept an early death (one that was generally hastened by the melancholy doctrines of orthodoxy, the Universalist press claimed). Acquiescence to Christ, his earthly ministers, and the patriarchs of the family should come easily to women raised to "yield without murmuring to the unavoidable restraints imposed upon them by the customs of society." That this did not always occur is evident in the same article, which reminds women they must defer to their husbands because the possession of power would not bring them happiness.[52] Conformity to God's providential order was not mere submission to authoritarian decrees, evangelical women and men were assured, but glad obedience, "a desire springing from the supreme love to the Saviour."[53] Self-sacrifice and obedience not only were means to achieve domestic harmony and a feeling of moral superiority and personal self-worth but also were useful strategies to get through a difficult and often unhappy life. Some women saw advantages "in their retired and subordinate station," where, compared with their husbands, they were "more at leisure to feel and contemplate the moral greatness of Jesus, the sufferer."[54] Accustomed as they were to deferring to men and often priding themselves on their loving obedience, women were more willing than their husbands to accept the hard doctrines, including even some of the more severe Hopkinsian constructions.[55]

Inspired by male models that had become feminized with their incorporation of ideal Christian attributes, devout women often felt called to the missionary vocation, the highest form of self-sacrifice. The ABCFM recommended David Brainerd's life as a standard against which all aspiring and actual ABCFM missionaries should regularly compare themselves. The "soft and tender" missionary saint, who possessed a "meek and quiet spirit, resembling the lamb-like, dove-like spirit of Jesus Christ," never forgot "his own utter insufficiency, despicableness, and odiousness," Edwards wrote in his appendix to the missionary's diary.[56] Shortly after he died and his memoirs were published, Obookiah, an Hawaiian native converted in New England who had planned to return to evangelize among his people, became a paragon of Christian virtue to the U.S. evangelical public. A man unashamed to admit that he regularly retired to his closet to weep deeply for his sins, Obookiah claimed he read the memoirs of pious women "to know how Christians feel."[57] Never was Congregational missionary society leader Samuel J. Mills "more endeared," his biographer wrote, than when he was "drowned in tears and abased with self-confusion" in attempting to explain what "God had condescended to accomplish through the instrumentalities of one so worthless as he."[58]

ABCFM board secretaries often reiterated that piety, self-sacrifice, and a profound awareness of one's sinfulness and unworthiness for the calling were the prerequisites for a successful missionary career. Chief secretary Anderson and the mission board's Prudential Committee also spoke in a female idiom when they instructed their missionaries about how to conduct their work. As soon as they arrived in the field, missionaries were directed to begin preaching the gospel, even before they understood the native language. Andover-trained Anderson was not the only Edwardsian religious leader to suggest that Calvinist dogma, especially the atonement, could create such a powerful effect on the heart and conscience that language would not stand in the way.[59] Against the orthodox tradition of extensive ministerial training requiring knowledge of dogma, exegetical techniques, and classical languages, Anderson downplayed the importance for missionaries of "elevated views of theological truth."[60] Rather, he urged would-be missionaries to rely on "the idea of love, infinite and infinitely disinterested, personified in the Lord Jesus," which as long as it came "glowing from our own experience" could not fail to get the heathen's attention.[61] In the manner that women held religious meetings centering on testimony and the "melting" scenes of confession and conviction, Anderson suggested that Christian truths could be transmitted through empathy or intuition. Missionary wives, he anticipated, through their example of pious living would "shed a softening, subduing influence" over heathen children and "impress religious truth, with the aid of the blessed Spirit, upon their hearts and consciences."[62]

This "softening, subduing influence" was, of course, what mothers were supposed to exercise with their own children; but no doubt Anderson's words must have been encouraging to women envisioning a missionary future. For male missionaries, the board's policy of favoring Christianization or conversion over "civilization" or acculturation among the western North American tribes was much less promising.[63] They found it difficult to set aside their secular concerns (such as building their houses and planting fields) and rely on God for their material needs while they concentrated on their ministerial duties. Neither were the men encouraged by the board's reminders that their effectiveness ultimately depended not on their efforts but on God and upon their relationship to him, or, in other words, their piety. Obedience, self-doubt, self-sacrifice, and forbearance grated against masculine selfhood, even of Christian missionaries. Because many male missionaries were so zealous and strong-willed, they had difficulty adjusting to the missions' communal relations and decisions and consequently developed a reputation for contentiousness and an inability to work together.[64] Even so, only ordained men would be allowed to become official missionaries.

Most evangelical women promoted God's kingdom from the sidelines only—in concerts of prayer for missions, by contributing a penny a week for their support, and through prayers that their children might one day become leaders in the evangelical crusade. The few who had sufficient confidence in their piety and spiritual capacities to apply for and be accepted by the ABCFM soon discovered that the female missionary had little time to test her Christian usefulness among the natives. Dreams of enlightening the darkened mind of the heathen could not be realized because these women believed that their principal responsibility was to care for their growing families. Moreover, separation from Christian society and its supporting institutions became one of missionary wives' greatest hardships. Removed even from each other at stations often hundreds of miles apart, it often seemed that the only way to maintain a "reason for a hope" and sense of spiritual empowerment was through the literature sent them by the board and the maternal associations with whom they corresponded. Speaking of the advantages of female social prayer, their favorite periodical, *Mother's Magazine,* ambiguously counseled that "perseverance will *perhaps always* remove" the "great discouragements in the way."[65] However, a theology that taught them they were depraved by nature but responsible for their sins and that the eternal fate of their own and pagan children depended on the constancy of their faith but was ultimately determined by God could hardly inspire sustained self-confidence in their efforts.

Nevertheless, despite their self-perceived moral inability, these women considered themselves personally responsible to save at least some portion of unredeemed humanity. The hard doctrines of late Edwardsian Calvinism, which still reverberated throughout the revival culture in the antebellum North, discouraged but at the same time challenged evangelical women to achieve a superhuman level of Christian virtue. This was largely because the "nature of womanhood" was inextricably bound to these passive-active Christian qualities. Accustomed as they were to their inferior status in the family and society, women could better than men accept with "glad obedience" the divine decrees and inherent depravity. Orthodox dogma interpreted within a framework of female and domestic associations allowed them to recognize and stress the more affective and hopeful implications of doctrine that more "reasonable" men scorned as illogical and sentimental. If within her circumscribed gender-defined range the greatest service a pious woman could perform was to "preach a lecture on her dying bed," it *might* become "the means of a revival of religion in the darkest corner of the earth, which shall be felt till the end of time!"[66] This was, indeed, a mighty power based on an even mightier hope. In less sanguine moods, orthodox women must have been frustrated by the great moral "influence," or the "almost power," that burdened them with so much responsibility and left them solely answerable for failure in a work that required God's cooperation. Even so, most would probably have agreed with Jonathan Edwards that true freedom (and power) lies in the acceptance of necessity—an acceptance that is never easy to achieve.

NOTES

1. Nancy F. Cott, *The Bonds of Womanhood: "Woman's Sphere in New England," 1780–1835* (New Haven, 1977), 126–59; Mary P. Ryan, *Cradle of the Middle Class: The Family in Oneida County, New York, 1790–1865* (Cambridge, Mass., 1981), 83–144; Dorothy C. Bass, "Their Prodigious Influence: Women, Religion, and Reform in Antebellum America," in Rosemary Ruether and Eleanor McLaughlin, eds., *Women of Spirit: Female Leadership in the Jewish and Christian Traditions* (New York, 1979), 279–300; Barbara Welter, "The Feminization of Religion in Nineteenth-Century America," in *Dimity Convictions* (Athens, Ohio, 1976), 83–102; Carroll Smith-Rosenberg, "Women and Religious Revivals: Anti-Ritualism, Liminality, and the Emergence of the American Bourgeoisie," in Leonard I. Sweet, ed., *The Evangelical Tradition in America* (Macon, Ga., 1984), 199–231; Nancy Hewitt, "The Perimeters of Women's Power in American Religion," in ibid., 233–56; Sandra S. Sizer, *Gospel Hymns and Social Religion: The Rhetoric of Nineteenth-Century Revivalism* (Philadelphia, 1978); and Joan Jacobs Brumberg, *Mission for Life* (New York, 1980), 79–106.

2. The issue of who was and who was not a true follower of Edwards became so polemical during this time that making the distinction between New Divinity and Old or Moderate Calvinist theology seems to me highly arguable. After the work of Timothy Dwight, Nathaniel W. Taylor, and Lyman Beecher and the establishment of Andover Seminary, New Divinity and Old Calvinist positions seem to blend into a form of revivalistic or Edwardsian Old Calvinism, which I will call "Edwardsianism," "Calvinism," and "orthodoxy."

3. For the anti-intellectual argument, see Richard Hofstadter, *Anti-Intellectualism in American Life* (New York, 1962), 55–106, and Ann Douglas, *The Feminization of American Culture* (New York, 1977).

4. See George N. Boardman, *A History of New England Theology* (New York, 1899), and Frank H. Foster, *A Genetic History of the New England Theology* (Chicago, 1907).

5. William G. McLoughlin, Jr., in *Modern Revivalism: Charles Grandison Finney to Billy Graham* (New York, 1959), 3–165, *Revivals, Awakenings, and Reform: An Essay on Religion and Social Change in America, 1607–1977* (Chicago, 1978), 98–129, "Charles Grandison Finney: The Revivalist as Culture Hero," *Journal of American Culture* 5 (Summer 1982), 80–90, and "Pietism and the American Character," *American Quarterly* 17 (Summer 1965), 163–186, provides the most extensive treatment of the triumph of Arminianism over Calvinism as the theological side of the sociopolitical movement toward democracy. See also Sidney Mead, *Nathaniel William Taylor, 1786–1858: A Connecticut Liberal* (Chicago, 1942); Ralph H. Gabriel, *The Course of American Democratic Thought* (New York, 1940), 31–38; Perry Miller, *The Life of the Mind in America from the Revolution to the Civil War* (New York, 1965), 3–35; Donald H. Meyer, *The Instructed Conscience: The Shaping of the American National Ethic* (Philadelphia, 1972), 77–97; Earl A. Pope, "The Rise of the New Haven Theology," *Journal of Presbyterian History* 44 (March 1966), 24–44, and (June 1966), 106–21; John Opie, "Finney's Failure of Nerve: The Untimely Demise of Evangelical Theology," *Journal of Presbyterian History* 51 (Summer 1973), 155–73; Nathan O. Hatch, *The Democratization of American Christianity* (New Haven, 1989); Joseph Haroutunian, *Piety versus Moralism: The Passing of the New England Theology* (New York, 1932); and Allen C. Guelzo, *Edwards on the Will: A Century of American Theological Debate* (Middletown, Conn., 1989), 208–71.

6. Curtis D. Johnson is the only scholar I am aware of who presents empirical evidence of the relationship between the demand for expanded suffrage and (Methodist) Arminian notions of personal freedom. See his *Islands of Holiness: Rural Religion in Upstate New York, 1790–1860* (Ithaca, 1989), 30–49. In fact, the egalitarianism of northern antebellum political culture could be a deeply consensual type of liberty. Despite its appeal to principles of Lockean liberalism, it often demanded strict conformity to majority opinion and homogeneous group norms.

7. Even while they engaged in the polemics to define the truth of orthodoxy, most Congregational and Presbyterian ministers and publications, I have found, liked to consider

themselves "practical," or above the fray, that is, primarily interested in achieving evangelical harmony and maintaining Christian "unity."

8. For a good summary of the evidence and explanations for women's predominant church membership, see Leonard Sweet, *The Minister's Wife: Her Role in Nineteenth-Century American Evangelicalism* (Philadelphia, 1983), 35–43.

9. Even Charles Grandison Finney, as rationalistic and unorthodox as he often was, argued that election was no obstacle to the salvation of the nonelect and that it was not inconsistent with free agency. Simply because God knew in advance who would obey him, it did not relieve all women and men of the duty to obey. See his "Doctrine of Election" in *Sermons on Important Subjects.* This view of legal obligation is consistent with the Puritan concept of the covenant of works which, although broken with Adam's fall, was not annulled; it remained in force as God's moral law for all human action.

10. Calvin Colton, *History and Character of American Revivals of Religion* (London, 1832), 110.

11. The term "Hopkinsian" like "New Divinity" was originally intended as an epithet disparaging the innovations made to Edwards's theology. Depending on whom they were arguing with, Hopkinsians were accused of being both "hyper-Calvinist" and so liberal as to be indistinguishable from Methodist Arminians. In fact, the New Divinity men were not a united front and often disagreed among themselves.

12. Bennet Tyler, "Human and Divine Agency United in the Salvation of the Soul," *The National Preacher,* July 1832, 24. *The National Preacher: or Original Monthly Sermons from living Ministers,* which began publication in 1826, is a good example of the ecumenical spirit of several Calvinist denominations attempting to swallow their "minor differences of opinion" to unite against the forces of "infidelity" or unorthodoxy. See a review of the journal in *Quarterly Christian Spectator,* June 1829, 235–47.

13. See Nathaniel William Taylor, "On the Means of Regeneration," *Quarterly Christian Spectator,* June 1829, 209–10, and September 1829, 496–506; "Application of the Principles of Common Sense to Certain Disputed Doctrines," ibid., September 1831, 453–465; and David T. Stoddard, unpublished lecture notebook, 47, Yale Lectures, 1837–42, Box 31, Yale University Library, Manuscripts and Archives. For Taylor's amendment of Edwards's explanation of free will, see Bruce Kuklick, *Churchmen and Philosophers: From Jonathan Edwards to John Dewey* (New Haven, 1985), 94–111, and Guelzo, *Edwards on the Will,* 240–71.

14. Charles G. Finney, *Lectures on Revivals of Religion,* ed. William G. McLoughlin (Cambridge, Mass., 1960; orig. pub. 1835), 54.

15. This is basically Joseph Haroutunian's position in his classic work on the New Divinity, *Piety versus Moralism.*

16. Stephen E. Berk, *Calvinism versus Democracy: Timothy Dwight and the Origins of American Evangelical Orthodoxy* (Hamden, Conn., 1974), 74–90; Mead, *Nathaniel William Taylor;* James Hoopes, "Calvinism and Consciousness from Edwards to Beecher," in Nathan O. Hatch and Harry Stout, eds., *Jonathan Edwards and the American Experience* (New York, 1988); Mark A. Noll, "Moses Mather (Old Calvinist) and the Evolution of Edwardsianism," *Church History* 49 (September 1980), 273–85; and Guelzo, *Edwards on the Will,* 208–29. Dwight's theology, most of which is contained in a four-year cycle of Yale revival sermons, is generally overlooked by those studying the New England theology because of its unsystematic, unoriginal, and practical nature. Dwight was important for the influence he had on his students, among them Nathaniel William Taylor and Lyman Beecher, and for the leading role he played in promoting the revival and the moral and benevolent societies.

17. Timothy Dwight, *Theology: Explained and Defended, in a Series of Sermons* (New York, 1830), 2: 449.

18. Ibid., 3: 51.

19. Ibid., 1: 259.

20. *Universalist,* 1 September 1832, 37.

21. *Mother's Magazine,* February 1838, 25–29. *Mother's Magazine* was originally commissioned by the First Presbyterian (New School) Church in Utica, New York, in 1833 as a

way to foster the growth of a maternal association. The monthly periodical later became the unofficial organ of these relatively small but widespread groups of orthodox women.

22. *Mother's Magazine,* November 1833, 166–68, and May 1839, 114–17.

23. A.B. Muzzey, *The Young Maiden* (Boston, 1840), 7–8, quoted in Welter, "Anti-Intellectualism and the American Women," in *Dimity Convictions,* 73.

24. *Mother's Magazine,* December 1834, 179–80, and June 1840, 131–35.

25. *Religious Intelligencer,* 25 March 1826, 672. Universalist papers frequently noted that the worst "offenders of emotional excess" at revivals were women.

26. The notion that the more "liberal" Calvinism of Dwight, Taylor, Finney, and Lyman Beecher was an attempt to accommodate it to the allegedly self-reliant and egalitarian spirit of Jacksonian society sometimes overlooks the fact that human freedom and choice, however ambiguously understood, were intrinsic parts of the Puritan, Old Calvinist, and Edwardsian traditions. From Jonathan Edwards to the common village preacher, the doctrine of human ability was repeated often in the sermons and writings of ministers who took seriously their pastoral responsibility. The opposing doctrines of divine decrees and human depravity were also stressed when the careful balance between Antinomian and Arminian extremes seemed in danger of being upset, which it often was.

27. Kathryn Kish Sklar, *Catharine Beecher: A Study in American Domesticity* (New Haven, 1973), 40.

28. See n. 1.

29. In his study of Courtland County in rural New York, Curtis Johnson found that Universalism had much more support among men than women. See his *Islands of Holiness,* 98–99. David W. Kling, *A Field of Wonders,* 218, also notes that "the charge of infidelity—a catchword for deism or Universalism or any departure from New Divinity Calvinism—applied nearly exclusively to males."

30. Through her study of published and unpublished conversion narratives, diaries, and letters, Barbara L. Epstein found that women often expressed their sinfulness in terms of original sin, whereas men referred to particular misdeeds. I agree with Epstein that women were more prone to condemn themselves partly because of their inferior social position, but I do not agree that their conversion experiences were an expression of anger toward and then accommodation to male dominance. See Epstein, *The Politics of Domesticity: Women, Evangelism, and Temperance in Nineteenth-Century America* (Middletown, Conn., 1981).

31. Leonard I. Sweet, "The Female Seminary Movement and Women's Mission in Antebellum America," *Church History* 54 (March 1985), 41–55. At these seminaries, according to the *Quarterly Christian Spectator,* September 1831, 493, a woman was provided with "useful knowledge, cultivated power, and fixed principles, without being metamorphosed into a literary, philosophical, moral, or intellectual Amazon."

32. According to Mary P. Ryan, *Cradle of the Middle Class,* 101, maternal associations "put in motion the forces that would lead almost inevitably" to the new affectionate child-rearing based on the belief that infants were born sinless. While I agree with most of Ryan's findings regarding maternal associations, from my reading of *Mother's Magazine* and the letters of women who eagerly read and wrote to it, at least before 1850, its readership never lost sight of the doctrine of infant depravity.

33. *New York Evangelist,* 1 January 1831, 2.

34. *Quarterly Christian Spectator,* March 1837, 2.

35. *Mother's Magazine,* March 1833, 44; *Panoplist,* August 1813, 154–58.

36. *Mother's Magazine* recommended women read William Paley's *Christian Evidences* (June 1834, 83–85). See Berk, *Calvinism versus Democracy,* on how Dwight "borrowed heavily from Paley's utilitarianism," 84.

37. *Mother's Magazine,* February 1834, 24.

38. Ibid., May 1833, 69. Author's emphasis.

39. *Religious Intelligencer,* 11 November 1826, 358; *Mother's Magazine,* March 1838, 68–69.

40. *Mother's Magazine,* February 1839, 32. Author's emphasis.

41. Ibid., April 1841, 83.

42. *Religious Intelligencer,* 25 August 1827, 201.

43. As part of his moral government theory, Joseph Bellamy, one of Edwards's closest students, revised his mentor's view of the atonement, suggesting that it would be general rather than limited to the elect. This interpretation was furthered by Samuel Hopkins and other New Divinity theologians so that by the early nineteenth century it had become standard and was sometimes even attributed to Edwards himself.

44. Rufus Anderson, "The Theory of Missions to the Heathen," in R. Pierce Beaver, ed., *To Advance the Gospel: Selections from the Writings of Rufus Anderson* (Grand Rapids, 1967), 85. The most influential of the ABCFM's executive secretaries, Anderson formulated mission policies that would direct the American foreign missionary enterprise throughout most of the nineteenth century. Some may view this use of the atonement as anti-intellectual and a practical measure of ministers employing the lowest common denominator to win new members. However, as watered down as it became in revivalistic preaching, the doctrine was still discussed at a high level of discourse, not only among competing clerics and institutions, but also in the popular religious press.

45. Narcissa Whitman to Jane Prentiss, July 11, 1843, in *The Letters of Narcissa Whitman* (Fairfield, Wash., 1986), 163. In published deathbed accounts, usually written by their ministers or minister husbands, pious women almost inevitably express their final and exemplary struggle to overcome their sinfulness in terms of Christ's loving sacrifice.

46. The feminization of the virtuous Christian self derived from other nonconformist and evangelical sources such as the writings of Hannah More, Andrew Fuller, Philip Doddridge, and Richard Baxter, who were popular among women because they appealed to alleged feminine sensibilities. See *Quarterly Christian Spectator,* March 1835, 127–51, for a favorable assessment of the "Character and Writings of Hannah More" and a review of the memoirs of Andrew Fuller, a British disciple of Edwards and New Divinity exponent (December 1830, 577–98). See also Geoffrey R. Nuttall, *Richard Baxter and Philip Doddridge* (London, 1951), a book about English dissenters whom Nuttall claims represented a "middle way" between Calvinism and Arminianism (3).

47. In one of its "Hints to Young Ladies" columns, *Mother's Magazine* encouraged its readers to be independent, think for themselves, and do what they think is right, regardless of what anyone else thought. At the same time they should "cultivate a conciliatory disposition," for "true humility" ennobled its possessor. Humility was the "only passport to self-respect," which also demanded self-censure (August 1838, 172–75).

48. Sklar, *Catharine Beecher,* 83–84. See also *Quarterly Christian Spectator,* March 1831, 14–15, where the association of strength among men's ruling passions is made in reference to a notable and pious minister.

49. E. Anthony Rotundo, *American Manhood: Transformations in Masculinity from the Revolution to the Modern Era* (New York, 1993), 16. Rotundo claims that by the late nineteenth century "the tender, reflective male . . . not only bore the social stigma of male femininity in a society that elevated gender separation to the highest level of principle, but he was also a threat to his nation and even to the progress of human civilization" (270).

50. See Johnson, *Islands of Holiness,* 55–58, on men's preference for religious societies over church membership.

51. *Mother's Magazine,* June 1833, 93–95; January 1836, 14–16; December 1836, 177–80; and March 1837, 53–55.

52. *Religious Intelligencer,* May 1826, 785.

53. Rufus Anderson, "Ought I to Become a Missionary to the Heathen?" in Beaver, ed., *To Advance the Gospel,* 178.

54. *Religious Intelligencer,* 3 March 1827, 679.

55. Samuel Hopkins's doctrine that the saved must be willing to be damned for the greater glory of God and the common good was the most extreme New Divinity version of disinterested benevolence and often misrepresented and ridiculed by opponents. However,

it was arguably not that different from the conviction stage of conversion where potential converts recognized God's justice in condemning them. See, for instance, "Narratives by a Young Lady," *Massachusetts Missionary Magazine,* July 1804, 60–64, and *Hopkinsian Magazine,* November 1824, 251, 259.

56. Jonathan Edwards, *The Life of David Brainerd,* ed. Norman Pettit (New Haven, 1985), 506–7.

57. Edwin Dwight, ed., *Memoirs of Henry Obookiah* (1818; reprint, Honolulu, 1968), 53–54. Obookiah's letters and diary immediately became a bestseller, going through 50,000 copies and twelve editions.

58. Gardiner Spring, *Memoirs of the Rev. Samuel J. Mills* (New York, 1820), 43. Such pious rhetoric was often dismissed by liberals as hypocritical religiosity and the maudlin and manipulative sentimentality of "priests" and women. See Universalist papers such as the *Gospel Advocate* and the *Religious Inquirer.*

59. Anderson, "The Theory of Missions to the Heathen," in Beaver, ed., *To Advance the Gospel,* 85; *Panoplist,* December 1814, 544–45.

60. Anderson, "The Theory of Missions to the Heathen," in Beaver, ed., *To Advance the Gospel,* 83.

61. Ibid., 85.

62. Rufus Anderson, "The Marriage of Missionaries," in Beaver, ed., *To Advance the Gospel,* 212.

63. Most of my conclusions in this and the next paragraph are based on my study of the Oregon mission and its correspondence with other ABCFM North American and Hawaiian stations. See my Ph.D. dissertation, "Sanctifying the Self and Saving the Savage: The Failure of the ABCFM Oregon Mission and the Conflicted Language of Calvinism" (University of Washington, 1991). See also Robert F. Berkhofer, Jr., *Salvation and the Savage: An Analysis of Protestant Missions and American Indian Response, 1787–1862* (New York, 1976). For the civilization versus Christianization dilemma, see William R. Hutchison, *Errand to the World: American Protestant Thought and Foreign Missions* (Chicago, 1987), 62–90.

64. The ABCFM mission board and articles directed to those considering the missionary vocation often stressed the necessity for missionaries to yield their opinions to others—a concession that, based on the board's correspondence with male missionaries, was not often achieved. Evangelical men also had to be reassured that their "melting" religious feelings would not be mistaken for weakness but were, in fact, a sign of manliness and vigor. See the review of Robert Philip, *Manly Piety in Its Principles* (New York, 1833) in *Quarterly Christian Spectator,* June 1834, 267–91.

65. *Mother's Magazine,* September 1835, 132. Author's emphasis.

66. Ibid., January 1836, 16.

TWELVE

Edwards A. Park and the Creation of the New England Theology, 1840–1870

JOSEPH CONFORTI

Andover Seminary's Edwards A. Park emerged in the middle of the nineteenth century as the most knowledgeable authority and most prolific interpreter of Edwardsian theological tradition. Park served Andover from 1836 to 1881, first as professor of sacred rhetoric and then for thirty-four years as the prestigious Abbot professor of theology; he also edited the seminary's journal, *Bibliotheca Sacra,* for thirty years. By family background and education Park was a Hopkinsian, a disciple of Samuel Hopkins (1721–1803), and a partisan of the "exercise" theological scheme which derived from Edwardsian doctrinal positions in *Freedom of the Will* and which held that there was no "taste" or spiritual substance behind the will; sin and virtue consisted of exercises of the will. Park's unrivaled knowledge of New England theological history and his position as Abbot professor at the oldest and largest postgraduate seminary in the United States secured his cultural authority and influence as an interpreter and guardian of Edwardsian theological tradition.[1] Park made major contributions to the mid-nineteenth-century consolidation and perpetuation of Edwardsian tradition. First, Park not only helped create and popularize the now familiar historical designation "the New England theology"; through his journal essays, lectures and books, he also composed the first "genetic" history of Edwardsian theological tradition. Second, Park found in an Edwardsian line of exercise thought a theology that reconciled divine sovereignty and human accountability, provided a narrative thread for his genetic history of

New England theology, and offered a "Consistent" Calvinism appropriate for the revivalistic and activist evangelical culture of the nineteenth century. Third, in addition to Edwards and Hopkins, a key figure in Park's historical narrative of Edwardsian tradition was the great exerciser, the now neglected and misunderstood Bartleby of New England theology—Nathanael Emmons (1745–1840). As a creator of tradition, rather than as an original thinker, Park was not only the last major Edwardsian Consistent Calvinist; he was the first to imbue the term New England theology with historical meaning.

I

The phrase "New England theology" originated in the doctrinal compromise between New Divinity men and Old Calvinists that led to the founding of Andover in 1808 and was embodied in the seminary's Associate Creed. How to sum up the theological orientation of the seminary with a descriptive name or doctrinal shorthand proved problematic. The available terms—Old Calvinism, New Divinity, Hopkinsianism—threatened to reopen the factional disagreements that had only been resolved by the diligent negotiation of the creed's language. "New England theology" emerged as a useful compromise, simultaneously historical and imprecise, evoking tradition but not weighed down with the doctrinal freight of the past. But like the Associate Creed itself, "New England theology" seemed unsatisfactory to both Old Calvinists and Hopkinsians, and the label was not used extensively within or beyond Andover during the early nineteenth century. In fact, the seminary's creed was usually referred to as "Andover Calvinism."[2]

Park revived the term "New England theology" in the 1830s, when he joined the Andover faculty.[3] By 1852, when Park published a lengthy and learned historical exposition in the *Bibliotheca Sacra* titled "New England Theology," the metonymic transformation of the label was far advanced; it had become widely recognized as denominating the hundred-year-old New Divinity movement—the doctrinal interpretation and "improvement" of Edwards initiated by his closest disciples in the decades after the colonial awakening. Moreover, the New England theology now had an historical narrative that legitimized its claim as the exclusive school of Edwards. Of course such a claim did not go unchallenged. Park's narrative marginalized Old Calvinist supporters of Andover, some of whom heaped scorn on the Abbot professor.[4] More important, Park's genetic history was challenged by seminary journals, whose contributors launched a paper war at midcentury over Edwards's theological legacy.

At that time, Park was not a solitary academic voice fashioning a history of the New England theology and using the *Bibliotheca Sacra* as a kind of personal platform for his views. Former students and ministerial associates contributed to the journal and to the creation of a genetic history of the New England theology.[5] Above all, Park relied on a steadfast theological confederate at Bangor Seminary. Enoch Pond, another student of Nathanael Emmons and now an obscure figure, followed a course into the ministry that paralleled Park's. Like Park, Pond was a Hopkinsian shaped by Emmons's exercise doctrines. In 1832, Pond joined Bangor Seminary, a small New Divinity institution and outpost of Andover founded in 1814, as professor of theology. He also served as professor of church history and president of the seminary. In nearly forty years on the faculty, Pond instructed hundreds of students and came to be called "the second founder" of the seminary. Pond also contributed dozens of articles, perhaps two hundred in all, to seminary journals and religious periodicals.[6] Many of these pieces reinforced and appear to have been coordinated with Park's publications on the history of New England theology. In the 1850s, for example, Pond published a series of articles in the *Congregationalist* that offered a general evangelical audience a narrative history of the New England theology that was consistent with but more accessible than Park's scholarly version in the *Bibliotheca Sacra.* Pond's essays were subsequently published as *Sketches of the Theological History of New England.*

Park and Pond appropriated the term "New England theology," constructed a genetic doctrinal history under its rubric, and removed "the obloquy of the name which it has worn for more than fifty years, the name of 'new divinity.'"[7] Edwards, of course, was the "father of New England theology," but from the perspective of one hundred years of theological history, "he had only laid the foundation of the tradition." In the aftermath of Edwards's premature death, new patriarchs—from Hopkins to Edwards the Younger to Emmons—continued his work. Edwards and these "fathers," Park observed, conferred on New England "a theological character, not faultless indeed but one that we love to eulogize."[8]

But far more than eulogy was at stake in the creation of an Edwardsian narrative of New England theological history. Grounded as Park and Pond were in the writings and thought of the progenitors of New England divinity, Andover and Bangor held an historical advantage in the mid-nineteenth-century, seminary-based paper war over Edwards's theological legacy. As Mark Noll has pointed out, Old School Presbyterians "did not possess the same intimacy with Edwards," let alone with his New Divinity disciples, as New England Congregationalists.[9] Even closer to home, the dogmatic history of Park and Pond disrupted claims to Edwardsian tradition. By appropriating the term "New England theology," Park and Pond not only attempted to neutralize the "obloquy" of the past; they also endeavored to distinguish their school from the "New Divinity" of the present, the doctrines of Nathaniel Taylor (1786–1858) of Yale, whose journal—the *New Englander*—claimed to continue Edwards's "spirit" and "bold" "new method" of theological inquiry. While Park presented the New England theology as a developing tradition, his historical narrative drew on Hopkins and Emmons to impose boundaries on Edwardsianism. For Park, Edwardsian tradition was not so expansive that it embraced Taylor's New Haven theology.[10]

II

Park used the designation "New England theology" to "traditionalize" a hundred years of doctrinal development that originated with Edwards. Under this rubric, Park constructed the first Edwardsian dogmatic canon, the first genetic history of Edwardsian theological development.[11] He focused on an exercise line of Edwardsian rhetoric and theological discussion that balanced an emphasis on human accountability with a recognition of divine sovereignty. In the process he extended the theological influence of Edwards and his New Divinity disciples into the middle of the nineteenth century.

Neither Park's work nor the exercise line of thought in New England theology is sufficiently understood. The term "exercise," though it referred primarily to interior movements of the heart or will rather than to external action, nevertheless resonated with the discourse of activism, voluntarism, and moral energy that pervaded nineteenth-century evangelical culture. It would be easy to dismiss Park as a liberal or Arminian Calvinist, as Joseph Haroutunian did when he relegated the Andover professor to a footnote in *Piety versus Moralism: The Passing of the New England Theology*.[12] But, in fact, Park's exercise theology was rooted in Edwards and remained consistently Calvinist.

The exercise-taste controversy in New England theology derived from Edwards's reconciliation of divine sovereignty and human moral accountability in *Freedom of the Will* and from the text's famous distinction between natural and moral necessity.[13] For Edwards natural necessity referred to physical and intellectual capacities, to the "necessity as men are under through the force of natural causes." Individuals suffered under a necessary natural inability if they faced "some impeding defect or obstacle that is extrinsic to their will, either in the faculty of the understanding, constitution of body or external objects."[14] A man cannot lift a thousand-pound boulder; an infant cannot solve complex mathematical problems. Such "cannots" of the natural world differed, however, from the "will not" of the moral realm. Moral necessity referred to the certainty between the "inclination," "disposition," or "motive" of the will and "volitions and actions." Moral necessity meant that individuals acted voluntarily, according to the disposition of their hearts or wills. Human beings were free as long as they could do as they willed, that is, as long as they could act according to the inclination of their wills. Sinners were naturally able to repent; their moral inability was only "the want of an inclination, or the prevalence of a contrary inclination"; their cannot was merely a will not.[15]

Edwards's distinction between natural and moral necessity was critical to Park and to the preaching and doctrinal improvements of his New Divinity predecessors. In the *Bibliotheca Sacra* Park summarized the historic "consistent" Calvinist framework that originated with *Freedom of the Will.* The New England theology offered a comprehensive "Edwardean scheme" that

> unites a high but not an ultra Calvinism, on the decrees and agency of God, with a philosophical, but not an Arminian theory, on the freedom and worth of the human soul. Its new element is seen in its harmonizing two great classes of truth; one relating to the untrammelled will of man, another relating to the supremacy of God. Because it has secured human liberty, it exalts divine sovereignty; and its advocates have preached more than others on predestination, because they have prepared the way for it by showing that man's freedom has been predestined. They insisted on an eternally decreed liberty, and on a free submission to the eternal decrees.[16]

From Hopkins's rejection of a gradual approach to conversion dependent on the means of grace to Park's position that "an entirely depraved man has a natural power to do all which is required of him," natural ability became the "far-famed" doctrine of New England theology.[17] *Freedom of the Will* bequeathed to the New Divinity both a Calvinist definition of liberty and an evocative, manipulable vocabulary that supported the evangelical work of the pulpit. By teaching that "sinners *can* do what they certainly *will* not do,"[18] the New Divinity developed a theology that reconciled determinism and accountability, promoted conversions and revivalistic religion, and remained vital through the middle of the nineteenth century.

Yet *Freedom of the Will* also generated dogmatic camps of "tasters" and "exercisers" among New England theologians who claimed to be loyal nineteenth-century Edwardsians. Tasters held that a spiritual substance, "taste," "relish," or "disposition," lay behind the will and governed choice; such a depraved taste, which was sinful itself, also led sinners certainly to choose sin. Exercisers denied knowledge of a spiritual substance in back of the will; choice was the immediate exercise of the heart or will without an antecedent passive principle or taste. "All sin consists in sinning," Nathanael Emmons, the most controversial exerciser, asserted.[19] From the *Religious Affections* to *Freedom of the Will* and *True Virtue,* Edwards used language—"taste," "relish," "exercises of the heart," "sensible exercises of the will"— that was invoked to endorse both positions.

The debate between Edwardsians who identified themselves as "exercisers" or "tasters" has not fared well in the hands of most historians of the New England theology. The dispute can be easily interpreted as a kind of New England doctrinal glossolalia of a cultish movement devolving into obfuscation. But how, then, does one explain Park's historical and apologetic engagement in the particulars of the exercise-taste controversy? The *Bibliotheca Sacra* continued to discuss the history of the exercise-taste debate into the 1860s; and Park devoted two lengthy memoirs to Hopkins and Emmons, who represented the exercise genealogy from Edwards. In fact, the exercise theology reconciled divine sovereignty and human moral accountability in a way that extended Edwards's doctrinal influence into the middle of the nineteenth century. Through his teaching of hundreds of ministers and through his books, essays, and republication efforts Park became the major interpreter and custodian of Edwardsian theological tradition in the mid-nineteenth-century United States.[20]

Drawing on Edwards's distinction between natural and moral ability, Park adopted the Edwardsian view that free will, and therefore moral accountability, resided in choice or the exercise of the will, not in the cause, inclination, or taste behind choice. For Park and for exercisers from Hopkins to Emmons whom he admired, acceptance of the notion of a corrupt involuntary taste undermined the Edwardsian idea that all sin resulted from a voluntary choice, or exercise, of the will. At issue for Park in the exercise-taste controversy was the very marrow of the New England theology: the balance or "harmony" between divine sovereignty and human accountability and the interpretation of sin, virtue, and regeneration that flowed from this dual emphasis and promoted practical Edwardsian divinity.[21]

To answer the tasters, Park drew on constitutional and occasionalist explanations of causality in New England theology that derived from Edwards. Taste was used in New England theology, Park insisted, primarily to describe the law of nature or the "foundation" or "occasion" of choice, not a passive sinful principle or faculty behind choice. Taste, disposition, relish referred to a divine constitution, a "neutral occasion," that furnished the foundation for sinful exercises of the will. Moral agency remained in the will, not in a new faculty behind the will. When pressed, the most Park would concede was that "there is lying back of our sinful choices and occasioning them" a divinely constituted taste that "our emotions often prompt us to stigmatize . . . as itself sin." But our intellects tell us differently; "antecedent to choice," we cannot be "guilty for the very make of our souls" or for the "natural existence" of constitutional principles like taste.[22]

Moreover, not only sin but virtue resided in voluntary exercises of the will rather than in a passive taste or disposition distinct from or behind the will. "Where there is no exercise of heart, nothing of the moral inclination, will or choice," Park asserted, "there can be neither sin nor holiness."[23] Edwards and Hopkins had defined true virtue as disinterested benevolence toward Being in general. This Edwardsian or New England theory did not locate virtue "in something prior to benevolent choice, viz. in a taste or relish for holiness, or . . . holy things on account of their moral beauty or excellence . . . ," though Edwards's works, Park and other writers in the *Bibliotheca Sacra* acknowledged, sometimes suggested such an interpretation. But taste in itself was neither virtuous nor sinful; it furnished the foundation or occasion for holy, or sinful, exercises. Edwards repeatedly described virtuous affections, Park correctly pointed out, as "modes of exercise of the will" and as "*vigorous* and *sensible* exercises of the inclination and will." True holiness consisted in benevolent, voluntary exercises of the will—in a "free choice of the general above the private good."[24]

Regeneration, then, involved a change of the will from sinful and selfish exercises to benevolent ones. Here again Edwards could be read in support of the taste scheme. For Edwards did say, a writer noted in the *Bibliotheca Sacra,* that "regeneration consists in imparting to the soul a new spiritual taste, relish, or principle which is prior to, and which lays a foundation for, holy exercises." But this involuntary change of taste was not in itself moral or virtuous; for taste only described the law of nature through which God worked. Thus the change in taste that took place in regeneration simply supplied the occasion or foundation for virtuous voluntary exercises of the will. As Park described the new taste imparted by regeneration, "Unless it be *exercised,* the man who has it as a passive quality, will not be saved."[25] Park and other Andoverian exercisers appealed to no less an authority on Edwards than Samuel Hopkins to clarify the "New England" theory of regeneration. For Hopkins had distinguished between "regeneration," in which an individual passively receives God's grace, and "active conversion," in which an individual achieves salvation by holy exercises and actions. Following Edwards and Hopkins, nineteenth-century exercisers preached that the sinner not only possessed the natural ability to repent but could "actually . . . renew his own heart under the operations of the Spirit" in active conversion.[26]

Several points seem to be clear concerning Park's interpretive efforts to establish the Edwardsian origins of the exercise scheme in New England theology. Park interpreted Edwards through Samuel Hopkins, not through Nathaniel Taylor as some students of nineteenth-century theology have suggested. At critical points in his exposition of the exercise doctrines of Edwardsianism—in examining New England doctrines of virtue and regeneration, for instance—Park invoked Hopkins. No wonder the Abbot professor wrote to the historian George Bancroft in 1859, "I am more convinced that Hopkins was a great man, that he had great influence over Edwards, and that in many respects he is of more *historical* importance than any other American divine, unless Pres. Edwards himself be excepted." No wonder erstwhile Calvinist Harriet Beecher Stowe, whose husband, Calvin, was Park's colleague at Andover, accused the Abbot professor of constructing a "dry, shingle palace of Hopkinsian theology."[27] Park, Pond, and their supporters in and outside Andover and Bangor were identified by their critics as "Hopkinsians." The exercise scheme was central to their efforts to define Edwardsianism and the distinctiveness of the New England theology. Park's genetic history of that theology preserved and developed the exercise emphasis on natural ability, active conversion and the personal, voluntary nature of all sin and virtue—Edwardsian doctrines suitable for the reformist evangelical culture of the nineteenth century.

III

Park's work in constructing a genetic history of exercise doctrines in New England theology stimulated renewed interest in Edwards's New Divinity disciples—interest that suggests the persistence of influential Calvinist and Edwardsian perspectives in the middle of the nineteenth century. Between 1842 and 1861, memoirs and collected works of all the major New Divinity disciples of Edwards were published: Jonathan Edwards, Jr. (1842), Joseph Bellamy (1850), Samuel Hopkins (1852), and Nathanael Emmons (1842 and 1861). Because he lived until 1840, trained 100 ministers, and became the most outspoken advocate of the exercise theology, Emmons emerged as the central nineteenth-century figure in Park's genetic history. And yet, like the exercise theology he championed, Emmons has been dismissed and ignored by scholars as an eccentric corrupter of Edwards's thought. How, then, did he attract 100 students? Why, on the eve of the Civil War, did Park toil on a voluminous memoir of such a seemingly singular thinker? Why did Enoch Pond dedicate his *Lectures on Christian Theology*, published in 1867, to Emmons?[28]

The exercise notions and vocabulary that Emmons derived from Edwards and Hopkins came to permeate New England theology in the nineteenth century; "all sin consists in sinning" became something of a doctrinal motto at Andover. In a fifty-page critical essay on Park's *Memoir of Emmons* (1861), which appeared in *The American Theological Review* in 1862, Union Seminary's Henry Boynton Smith, who had studied at Andover and Bangor but who was no partisan of the exercise school, perceptively observed that "isolated and peculiar as he [Emmons] seems to be, his scheme is vitally interwoven with antecedent theories and it has affected subsequent speculations." Smith characterized Park's nearly 500-page *Memoir* of his mentor and family friend as "the most entertaining, ingenious and finished piece of ecclesiastical biography which New England has as yet sent forth in honor of her religious patriarchs."[29] This classic but neglected memoir illuminates Park's role in fashioning the first genetic history of New England theology, in codifying exercise doctrines, and thereby in perpetuating Edwards's theological influence through the middle of the nineteenth century.

Emmons came to be seen as the father of the exercise scheme because he was so bold in advancing its positions. Emmons sometimes stopped short of denying the existence of a taste behind the will, claiming that we could only know with certainty the exercises of the heart, the choices of the will. At other times Emmons incorporated taste into exercise; he suggested that taste or disposition was not distinct from the will but simply, as Edwards often indicated, the activities or operations of the will. This line of reasoning, however, led Emmons to make God the "efficient" cause of moral exercises; that is, God acted directly on the will. "God," Emmons argued, "exerts his agency in producing all the moral and voluntary exercises of every moral agent. . . ." Even Adam's volitions resulted from a "divine energy [which] took hold of his heart and led him to sin."[30] While Emmons never described the soul as a "chain of exercises" sustained by divine efficiency, as his critics often claimed, such an interpretation was a legitimate conclusion from his most radical statements that no spiritual substance, principle, or taste lay behind the will.

Emmons's exercise scheme incorporated Edwardsian notions of human accountability and divine sovereignty. Rejecting the position of the tasters, Emmons adopted the Edwardsian view that free will, and therefore moral accountability, resided in choice, not in the cause or inclination behind choice. Emmons's exercise notions also drew on Edwards's idea of "continual creation," the view that God sustains the universe and every person and thing in it through continual new exertions of the divine will.[31] But Emmons's exaltation of divine sovereignty often ignored Edwards's views of the laws of nature and the constitutional arrangements through which God exercised sovereignty over his creatures and creation. Thus Emmons sometimes described moral exercises—sin and virtue—as the consequences of God's *direct efficient* power.

Among the interpretive challenges that Park faced in composing the *Memoir of Emmons* was to show how the great exerciser achieved an appropriate Edwardsian balance between divine sovereignty and human accountability. Thus Park drew on all of his seminary-acquired exegetical abilities to moderate Emmons's statements on divine efficiency and to amplify his seeming acknowledgments of Edwardsian occasionalism. When Emmons used language that suggested divine efficiency, Park argued, he was merely "expressing his religious emotions," his disinterested love of a sovereign God. Divine "efficiency" simply meant divine "independence." Good Edwardsian that he was, Emmons denied the self-determining power of the will: "Man does not begin his moral action by choosing to choose." For Park, Emmons's interpretation of divine efficiency boiled down to the fact "that all other choices are put forth by the intervention of powers which absolutely depend on the first external choice of the First Cause."[32]

Having tempered Emmons's doctrine of divine efficiency, Park went on to reaffirm his Edwardsian recognition of the secondary causes and laws of nature through which God operated. Park admitted that Emmons, in his desire to assert divine sovereignty, had not given adequate notice "to the mode in which God executes" his decrees. But Park was still able to assemble passages from Emmons's works that invoked the laws of nature and secondary causes. One crucial passage confirmed for Park why Emmons tended to ignore the "modes" of divine operation: "God employs so many secondary causes in bestowing blessings upon mankind, that they are extremely apt to overlook the *primary* and *supreme Cause* from which they flow."[33] Similarly, Emmons spoke and wrote as if there was nothing behind exercises of the will because he did not want sinners to plead that an involuntary, corrupt nature or taste presented, as he put it, "an *insurmountable* obstacle or natural inability, in the way of their loving God, repenting of sin, or doing anything in a holy manner." Emmons followed Hopkins in arguing that "it is impossible to conceive of a corrupt and sinful nature, *prior to,* and *distinct from,* corrupt and sinful *exercises.*"[34] But such a perspective, Park proposed, did not preclude the existence of taste as a morally neutral constitutional foundation of choice—an inclination of the will that did not acquire moral character until it was "freely" exercised.

Park's incorporation of taste into the exercise scheme involved far more than a semantic sleight of hand; it derived from his reaffirmation of Edwardsian occasionalism and constitutionalism. Still, Park's *Memoir of Emmons* discloses how he "improved" the improvers of Edwards to construct his genetic history of New England theology. Through an interpretive process that involved tugging and tucking Emmons's thought and snipping and pasting from his works, Park restored a balance between divine sovereignty and human accountability in the theology of the most famous exerciser. He also reasserted Emmons's Edwardsianism, underscored the Franklin divine's Hopkinsian line of descent, and assimilated him to the mediating exercise theology of Andover and Bangor. In *The American Theological Review* Enoch Pond lauded the memoir of his teacher and endorsed Park's explanation of Emmons's exercise theology. "Prof. Park," Pond enthused, "has erected a monument . . . to the memory of his friend, and his father's friend—a monument that will stand and be studied and admired, in years to come."[35]

Yet, as Henry Boynton Smith's fifty-page critique in the same journal suggests, Park's *Memoir of Emmons,* like his earlier historical reconstructions of the New England theology, incited yet another skirmish in the midcentury seminary war of words over Edwardsian tradition. One tack of Park's most voluble critics at Princeton was to strip *Freedom of the Will* of any novelty. Edwards's distinction between natural and moral ability, Princeton's Lyman Atwater and Charles Hodge maintained, was mistakenly held up as "the invention and glory of American theology." But Edwards was not "the inventor of this distinction"; it had been "familiar to theologians, not only before the time of Edwards, but from the time when the heresies of Pelagius first occasioned thorough discussion of the subject of sin and grace." *Freedom of the Will,* Atwater insisted, discussed natural and moral ability as "terms already established" and well known "among divines of the Augustinian school."[36] Through such arguments Princetonians sought to de–New Englandize Edwards—to rescue him from Park's historical narrative and exposition of exercise theology.

IV

Park resigned as president of Andover's faculty in 1868, seven years after the publication of his memoir of Emmons. Park's resignation announced both the demise of Edwards's doctrinal influence at Andover and the actual passing of the New England theology. Park became increasingly strident in his protests against changes at Andover that signaled the beginnings of "Progressive Orthodoxy" and dislodged the New England theology from its powerful institutional base. Park was hardly reassured by the pronouncements of new faculty members such as Egbert C. Smyth, the liberal professor of ecclesiastical history, who was fond of saying of Edwards, "We shall not go back to him, nor yet go forward without him."[37]

Park never finished the labor of his life—a memoir of Edwards that would have completed the biographical trilogy of the exercise genealogy in New England theological history. Yet major elements of Park's historical and apologetic perspective persisted into the post-Edwardsian era through the work of his students. *A History of New England Theology,* the first post-Calvinist overview of the subject, was published in 1899 by George Boardman, a former Park student who acknowledged the influence of his mentor's historical perspective.[38] A more significant work was Frank H. Foster's *Genetic History of New England Theology,* published in 1907. Foster was to Park as Samuel Hopkins had been to Edwards—his closest disciple. Park even tried to have Foster succeed him as Abbot professor of theology. In his *Genetic History* Foster acknowledged Park "for much help of a historical character, both personal and through his historical writings, as well as for the dogmatic view of the whole period."[39]

Foster's volume remained the standard work on the New England theology for a generation—until the publication of Joseph Haroutunian's *Piety versus Moralism,* an enormously influential neo-orthodox dirge on the degradation of Edwards's thought. Haroutunian responded directly to Foster and shifted lines of interpretation away from the nineteenth-century preoccupation with *Freedom of the Will.* "The chief aim of the Edwardsian theology was not to formulate a theory of the will," Haroutunian confidently asserted; "it was inspired by a piety which sought to glorify God and His sovereignty over men."[40] Not surprisingly, Haroutunian consigned Park to one footnote, completely dismissed the exercise school of thought, and flogged Edwards's New Divinity disciples for moralizing their mentor's Calvinism. Haroutunian's narrative diverted scholars from a balanced assessment of Edwards's theological legacy. Such an assessment should reserve a prominent place for Park and the Edwardsian tradition that he codified and extended into the middle of the nineteenth century. Park's efforts to create a genetic history of New England theology reveal the complexity and vitality of Edwardsianism and suggest how doctrinal traditions rooted in Edwards's thought were constructed and contested through the middle of the nineteenth century.

NOTES

1. The most recent biographical study of Park is Anthony C. Cecil, Jr., *The Theological Development of Edwards Amasa Park: Last of the "Consistent Calvinists"* (Missoula, Mont., 1974). Cecil's interpretation of Park's theological development is marred by his seeming unfamiliarity with New Divinity theology after Edwards. Kenneth Rowe's analysis of Park is overly dependent on the piety to moralism thesis of Joseph Haroutunian; see Rowe, "Nestor of Orthodoxy, New England Style: A Study in the Theology of Edwards Amasa Park" (Ph.D. diss., Drew University, 1969). Helpful biographical material on Park is also found in Frank H. Foster, *The Life of Edwards Amasa Park* (New York, 1936); R. S. Storrs, *Professor Park and His Pupils . . .* (Boston, 1899); Storrs, *Edwards A. Park, A Memorial Address* (Boston, 1900); and Alexander McKenzie, *Memoir of Professor Edwards Amasa Park* (Cambridge, Mass., 1901). For a fuller discussion of the issues raised in this essay as well as for other Edwardsian traditions constructed in the nineteenth century, see Joseph A. Conforti, *Jonathan Edwards, Religious Tradition, and American Culture* (Chapel Hill, N.C., 1995).

2. The most suggestive discussion of the history of the term "New England theology" is found in Enoch Pond, *Sketches of the Theological History of New England* (Boston, 1880), esp. p. 58. Compare his account of theological developments behind the founding of Andover with Leonard Woods's *History of the Andover Theological Seminary* (Boston, 1885), chap. 2. See also Park, "New England Theology," *Bibliotheca Sacra* 9 (January 1852): 174–76. This work was republished in the 1850s as a separate text.

3. See, for example, Park, "The Duties of a Theologian," *American Biblical Repository* 2 (October 1839): 374, 380.

4. See, for example, Nathan Lord, *A Letter to the Rev. Daniel Dana on Professor Park's Theology of New England* (Boston, 1852).

5. See, for example, Edward Beecher, "The Works of Samuel Hopkins," *Bibliotheca Sacra* 10 (January 1853): 63–82; Daniel Fiske, "New England Theology," ibid. 22 (July 1865): 467–512, and (October 1865): 568–88.

6. The best introduction to Pond's activities and to the history of Bangor Seminary is in *The Autobiography of Enoch Pond, D.D. . . .* (Boston, 1883), esp. p. 73.

7. Park, "The Duties of a Theologian," p. 354.

8. Ibid., p. 380; Fiske, "New England Theology," p. 469.

9. Mark Noll, "Jonathan Edwards and Nineteenth-Century Theology," in Nathan O. Hatch and Harry S. Stout, eds., *Jonathan Edwards and the American Experience* (New York, 1988), p. 263.

10. Noah Porter, "The Princeton Review on Dr. Taylor and the Edwardean Theology," *New Englander* 18 (August 1860): 739. George Park Fisher became Yale's most perceptive critic of both Park and Princeton. Several of his major essays on the New England theology that appeared in the *New Englander* were reprinted in *Discussions in History and Theology* (New York, 1880). For a more expansive view of Edwardsian tradition than Park would have acknowledged, see Douglas Sweeney's essay on Taylor in this book (chap. 9).

11. In addition to his essay "New England Theology," another of Park's major historical works is *The Atonement: Discourses and Treatises by Edwards, Smalley, Maxcy, Emmons, Griffin, Burge and Weeks, with an Introductory Essay* (Boston, 1859).

12. Joseph Haroutunian, *Piety versus Moralism: The Passing of the New England Theology* (1932; rpt. 1970), pp. xxxi, 305n.

13. Helpful recent discussions of the exercise-taste controversy are James Hoopes, "Calvinism and Consciousness from Edwards to Beecher," in Hatch and Stout, eds., *Jonathan Edwards and the American Experience,* pp. 216–18; Allen C. Guelzo, *Edwards on the Will: A Century of Theological Debate* (Middletown, Conn., 1989), pp. 109–10, 214–15; and Bruce Kuklick, *Churchmen and Philosophers: From Edwards to Dewey* (New Haven, Conn., 1985), pp. 55–59. For excellent analyses of the way New Divinity theology balanced divine sovereignty and human accountability, see William Breitenbach, "The Consistent Calvinism of the New Divinity Movement," *William and Mary Quarterly* 41 (April 1984): 479–502, and "Piety and Moralism: Edwards and the New Divinity," in Hatch and Stout, eds., *Edwards and the American Experience,* pp. 177–204. For the most recent contribution to the reassessment of the New Divinity followers of Edwards, see Mark Valeri, *Law and Providence in Joseph Bellamy's New England* (New York, 1994).

14. Jonathan Edwards, *Freedom of the Will,* ed. Paul Ramsey, *Works of Jonathan Edwards, 12* (New Haven, Conn., 1957), 1:156–57, 159.

15. Ibid., pp. 156, 159.

16. Park, "New England Theology," p. 212. For similar statements about the balance of divine sovereignty and moral accountability in the New England theology, see Pond, *Sketches of the Theological History of New England,* pp. 60–62, and Fiske, "New England Theology," pp. 472–95, 584.

17. Park, "New England Theology," pp. 177, 178, and "Unity amid Diversities of Belief, Even on Imputed and Involuntary Sin," *Bibliotheca Sacra* 8 (July 1851): 604–5; Enoch Pond, "Review of Edwards on the Will," *Literary and Theological Review* 1 (December 1834): 523–39, and "Natural and Moral Ability and Inability," *New Englander* 13 (May 1855): 387–96. The best discussions of the impact of *Freedom of the Will* on the New Divinity men are Guelzo, *Edwards on the Will,* p. 122, and Breitenbach, "The Consistent Calvinism of the New Divinity Movement," pp. 256–64.

18. Fiske, "New England Theology," p. 506.

19. Quoted in Edwards A. Park, *Memoir of Nathanael Emmons with Sketches of His Friends and Pupils* (Boston, 1861), p. 365; Fiske, "New England Theology," p. 492; see also Park's careful discussion of the epigram in "New England Theology," pp. 192–95, where he attempted to counter what he saw as Princeton's interpretation of "moral exercises" as "moral acts."

20. Seminary enrollment in 1840 was as follows: Andover, 153; Bangor, 44; East Windsor, 29; Harvard, 20; Princeton, 110; Union (N.Y.), 90; Yale, 72. Park's students assumed diverse professional roles—parish ministers, revivalists, college instructors, seminary professors, journal editors, missionaries and agency reformers—reflecting a transformed ministry. For seminary enrollment, see Glenn T. Miller, *Piety and Intellect: The Aims and Purposes of Ante-Bellum Theological Education* (Atlanta, 1901), p. 201. On ministerial changes in the nineteenth century, see Donald Scott, *From Office to Profession: The New*

England Ministry, 1750–1850 (Philadelphia, 1978). For Andover, see *General Catalogue of the Theological Seminary, Andover, Massachusetts, 1808–1908* (Boston, 1909), pp. 241–302 for students of the 1850s.

21. See Park, "New England Theology," p. 212, and "Unity amid Diversities," p. 605.

22. Park, "New England Theology," pp. 203–5, "Unity amid Diversities," p. 627, and *Memoir of Nathanael Emmons,* pp. 412–13.

23. Park, "New England Theology," p. 197.

24. Fiske, "New England Theology," p. 484; Park, "New England Theology," pp. 196, 200; [Park et al.], "President Edwards's Dissertation on the Nature of True Virtue," *Bibliotheca Sacra* 10 (October 1853): 717.

25. Fiske, "New England Theology," p. 569; Park, "New England Theology," p. 202, and *Memoirs of Emmons,* pp. 405–6.

26. Hopkins, *An Inquiry concerning the Promises of the Gospel: Whether Any of Them Are Made to the Exercises and Doings of Persons in an Unregenerate State* (Boston, 1765), pp. 54, 78–79; Fiske, "New England Theology," p. 574.

27. Park to Bancroft, quoted in Donald Weber, "The Image of Jonathan Edwards in American Culture" (Ph.D. diss., Columbia University, 1978), p. 156n. Stowe, quoted in Joan Hedrick, *Harriet Beecher Stowe: A Life* (New York, 1994), p. 184. For a different reading of Park, which claims that he was essentially a Taylorite, see Kuklick, *Churchmen and Philosophers,* pp. 59n, 212–15.

28. Pond, *Lectures on Christian Theology* (Boston, 1867). Park worked through the Congregational Board of Publication in Boston to promote republication of the works of Edwards's New Divinity disciples.

29. Henry Boynton Smith, "The Theological System of Emmons," *The American Theological Review* 13 (January 1862): 13. The only extended study of Emmons is John Terrence Dahlquist, "Nathanael Emmons: His Life and Work" (Ph.D. diss., Boston University, 1963).

30. See Emmons, "Man's Activity and Dependence Illustrated" and "God Sovereign in Man's Formation," *Works,* ed. Jacob Ide (Boston, 1842), 4: 355–56, 366, 373, 387, 397. See also E. Smalley, "The Theology of Emmons," *Bibliotheca Sacra* 7 (April 1850): 253–80, and (July 1850): 479–501.

31. Edwards offered the idea of continual creation in *Original Sin,* where he argued that God creates all things "out of nothing at each moment of their existence." See Edwards, *The Great Doctrine of Original Sin,* ed. Clyde Holbrook, *Works of Edwards, 3:* 401.

32. Park, *Memoir of Emmons,* pp. 387, 402.

33. Ibid., pp. 386, 417.

34. Ibid., pp. 379, 412.

35. Pond, "The Life and Character of Emmons," *The American Theological Review* 3 (October 1861): 633.

36. Lyman Atwater, "Modern Explanations of the Doctrine of Ability," *Biblical Repertory and Princeton Review* 26 (April 1854): 236; Charles Hodge, "Professor Park and the Princeton Review," ibid. 23 (October 1851): 693. See also Atwater, "Jonathan Edwards and the Successive Forms of the New Divinity," ibid. 30 (October 1858): 589, 614, 619. For a full discussion of the counternarrative of New England theological history that Park's work provoked, see Conforti, *Jonathan Edwards, Religious Tradition, and American Culture,* chap. 5.

37. Intellectual changes at Andover are discussed in Cecil, *The Theological Development of Park,* chap. 6, and Foster, *Life of Park,* chap. 14. Smyth is quoted in Daniel B. Shea, "Jonathan Edwards: The First Two Hundred Years," *Journal of American Studies* 14 (August 1980): 197.

38. Boardman, *A History of New England Theology* (New York, 1899); Storrs, *Professor Park and His Pupils,* p. 74.

39. Foster, *A Genetic History of New England Theology* (Chicago, 1907), pp. v–vi. It is important to keep in mind that both Foster and Boardman were writing from a post-

Calvinist perspective after the collapse of the New England theology. Their doctrinal sympathies were with Taylor, who emerges as the theological liberator in both books. Foster had difficulty dealing with Park, who remained heavily Edwardsian and came after Taylor. Foster concluded (p. 504) that "a new thought, new for Calvinism, was struggling in Park's mind, as yet not quite able to come to the birth. It was the idea of freedom."

40. Haroutunian, *Piety versus Moralism,* p. xxxi.

CONTRIBUTORS

AVA CHAMBERLAIN is Assistant Professor of American Religious History at Wright State University. She has published in *Church History.* She is at work on an edition of Jonathan Edwards's "Miscellanies," entry nos. 501–832.

JOSEPH CONFORTI is Director of the American and New England Studies Program at the University of Southern Maine. He is the author of *Samuel Hopkins and the New Divinity Movement: Calvinism, the Congregational Ministry and Reform in New England between the Great Awakenings* and *Jonathan Edwards, Religious Tradition and American Culture.*

CHRISTOPHER GRASSO is Assistant Professor of History at St. Olaf College, Northfield, Minnesota. He has published essays in the *William and Mary Quarterly* and *Early American Literature.* He is at work on a study of the transformation of public discourse in eighteenth-century Connecticut.

ALLEN C. GUELZO is Grace F. Kea Associate Professor of American History at Eastern College, St. David's, Pennsylvania. He is the author of *Edwards on the Will: A Century of American Philosophical Debate, 1750–1850* and *For the Union of Evangelical Christendom: The Irony of the Reformed Episcopalians.*

RICHARD A. S. HALL is Visiting Assistant Professor of Philosophy at Fayetteville State University. He is the author of *The Neglected Northampton Texts of Jonathan Edwards: Edwards' Social and Political Philosophy.*

PAUL R. LUCAS is Professor of History at Indiana University, Bloomington. He is the author of *Valley of Discord: Church and Society along the Connecticut River, 1636–1725* and *American Odyssey, 1607–1789.* He is at work on a study of Solomon Stoddard and his legacy.

GENEVIEVE MCCOY is Adjunct Assistant Professor of History at Seattle University and the University of Washington. Her essay "Post-Edwardsean Calvinism and the Women of the ABCFM Oregon Mission," published in *Church History,* was awarded the Jane Dempsey Douglass Prize.

GERALD R. MCDERMOTT is Assistant Professor of Religion and Philosophy at Roanoke College, Salem, Virginia. He is the author of *One Holy and Happy Society: The Public Theology of Jonathan Edwards.* He is at work on a study of Edwards's typological hermeneutic.

KENNETH P. MINKEMA is Executive Editor of *The Works of Jonathan Edwards* at Yale University. He is co-editor of *The Sermon Notebook of Samuel Parris, 1689–1694* and *A Jonathan Edwards Reader.* He is at work on an edition of Jonathan Edwards's sermons from 1723 to 1729.

WAYNE PROUDFOOT is Professor of Religion at Columbia University. He is the author of *Religious Experience* and co-editor of *Faithful Imagining: Essays in Honor of Richard R. Niebuhr.*

STEPHEN J. STEIN is Chancellors' Professor of Religious Studies and Department Chair at Indiana University, Bloomington. He is the editor of *Apocalyptic Writings,* volume 5 in *The Works of Jonathan Edwards.* He is at work on an edition of Edwards's "Notes on Scripture."

WILLIAM K. B. STOEVER is Professor and Chair, Department of Liberal Studies, Western Washington University. He is the author of "*A Faire and Easie Way to Heaven*"*: Covenant Theology and Antinomianism in Early Massachusetts.*

DOUGLAS A. SWEENEY is Assistant Editor of *The Works of Jonathan Edwards* at Yale University. He has published essays in *Church History* and *Fides et Historia.*

INDEX

Accountability, moral, xvi, 151, 164–67, 177, 193, 196–98, 201–2. *See also* Responsibility, moral
Admission controversy. *See* Church membership; Communion controversy
Aesthetics, 105–6, 108–12, 116, 120n.39
Affections, religious, 9, 12, 90, 98n. 22, 136n.9; genuine/true, 21, 85–86, 122–23, 124–32, 135
Alciphron, or the Minute Philosopher (Berkeley), xiv, 100, 101, 103–17, 117nn.4,5, 120n.43
Aldridge, Alfred Owen, 120n.43, 121n.67
Alexander, Archibald, 142
Allegory, use in exegesis, 54, 57, 60
American Board of Commissioners for Foreign Missions (ABCFM), 143, 183–84, 185–87, 191n.44, 192n.64
American Tract Society, 143, 153n.6
Ames, William, 86–87, 98n.27
Anderson, Rufus, 183, 185–86, 191n.44
Andover Seminary, xvi–xvii, 188n.2, 193, 203, 205n.20; *Bibliotheca Sacra,* 177, 193, 194–95, 198, 199; founding, 143, 144, 194
Anglicanism, 72, 116
Antichrist, the, 33, 42–43, 72, 74
Antinomianism, xiv, 12, 78, 85, 97n.4, 169, 190n.26; condemned by New Divinity, 162, 166
Apologetics, 41–43, 46, 57, 103–5, 105, 118n.26
Appleton, Nathaniel, 37n.82
Architecture, 108, 110, 120n.39
Arminianism, xvi, 79, 147, 149, 151, 190n.26, 191n.46; attributed to Park, 196; attributed to Taylor, 140, 151; embraced by Wesley, 161; linked with democracy, 188n.6; in 19th-century revivalism, 176, 188n.5; in Oberlin perfectionism, 160
Ashley, Jonathan, 27, 36n.52
Assurance, 4, 12, 14–15, 27, 87, 93; for Shepard, 93, 98n.22; treatment in Matthew 25:1–12 sermons, 4, 8–11, 12
Atonement, 44, 177–78, 181, 186; general, 183–84, 191nn.43,44
Atwater, Lyman, 202–3
Augustine, 54, 56, 60, 135, 150, 203
Authentic religion. *See* True religion
Awakening, the. *See* Great Awakening; Second Great Awakening
Axiology. *See* Value(s)
Ayers, M. R., 103

Backus, Azel, 145
Bacon, Leonard, 144, 146–47
Bangor Seminary, 195, 200, 205n.20
Baptism, 19, 23, 73, 133, 146
Baxter, Richard, 43, 191n.46
Beauty, 47, 101, 105–15, 117, 119n.33, 120n.39; moral, 105, 106–7, 109–14, 121n.49, 129, 161
Beecher, Lyman, 140, 146, 151, 181–82, 188n.2, 189n.16; and Edwardsianism, 147, 155n.15, 176; on original sin, 148, 150
Behavior, 25, 91; moral appraisal of, 10–11, 126–28, 130–32. *See also* Holy practice
Belief, language of, xv, 126–27, 130
Bellamy, Joseph, 28–29, 32, 38n.84, 143, 145, 161–62, 200; on the atonement, 191n.43; pastoral apprentices, 141
Benefit of the doubt, 24, 25–26
Benevolence, 104–5, 119n.30, 125
—disinterested, 34, 109–10, 181, 198–99; for Hopkins, 185, 191n.55, 198; Oberlin perfectionism predicated on, 160, 165, 170, 173n.19
Benevolent societies, xvi, 175, 176, 177, 181–82, 189n.16
Bentley, William, 142, 144
Berkeley, George, xiv, xviii, 55, 100–102, 119n.28, 120n.39, 121n.57; *Verses by the Author. . . ,* 102, 118n.12. *See also Alciphron*
Berman, David, 103, 119n.33
Bible, the, xiii, 52–53, 56–59, 62, 86–89. *See also* Exegesis; New Testament; Old Testament; Revelation; *individual books by title*
Bibliotheca Sacra (periodical), 177, 193, 194–95, 198, 199
Blake, Mortimer, 142
Boardman, George, 203, 206n.39
Brainerd, David, 142, 185
Breitenbach, William, 147
Butler, Joseph, 55, 103–4, 117

Calvin, John, 43, 54–55, 135
Calvinism, 79, 116, 139–44, 154n.7, 176–77, 190n.26, 191n.46; doctrine of depravity, 148, 164, 190n.26; on inner relationship of the Bible, 54; in Oberlin Theology, 160; Park's theology consistent with, 196–97; preached by 19th-century missionaries, 186; Scottish thought used to support, 158n. 28; women's acceptance of, 179–84, 187. *See also individual schools of thought by name*
"Catalog" (bibliographical register), xvii, xixn.13, 16n.6, 58–59, 64nn.16,23; *Alciphron* in, 117n.5; anti-Muslim works, 48n.10; items on rabbinic

"Catalog" (*cont.*)
learning and cabal, 65n.30; works by Shepard, 97n.4

Catholicism, 42, 46, 51n.52, 72–76, 78, 102; Edwards's attitude toward, 33, 43, 48n.19

Cause(s): primary, 202; secondary, 150, 157n.25, 158n.27, 202

Cecil, Anthony C., Jr., 204n.1

Chamberlain, Ava, xi–xii, 97n.14

Chandler, Edward, 59

Charity. *See* Benevolence, disinterested

Charity and Its Fruits (Edwards), xiv, 3, 86, 89. *See also* I Corinthians 13

Charles I (king of England), 73, 76

Charles II (king of England), 77, 83n.35

Children, salvation of, 180, 182–83

Chinese, the, 40, 46, 50n.41

Christ, xi–xii, 5–8, 54, 62, 87–88; laws of, 88, 90, 97n.10; as the Messiah, 53, 55, 58, 59; in the Qur'an, 39–40, 46, 47n.3

Christian practice. *See* Holy practice

Christianity, propagation of, 44–45, 50n. 35

II Chronicles 23:16, sermon on, 22–24, 35nn.13,18

Chubb, Thomas, 43–44

Church(es), 9, 58, 73–74, 89, 141; Christ's union with, 6–7, 8; communion of saints as, 20, 77–78; "instituted," xiii, 69, 72, 74–75, 76–77, 81n.4; visible, 94, 96

Church courts, 73, 74, 76

Church covenant, 30, 37n.70. *See also* Covenant(s)

Church membership, 78, 83n.37, 142, 146, 155n.13, 177; Edwards's position on, 21–22, 24, 30, 96, 99n.35, 132–33

Church of England, 72, 116

Civil War, English (1642–51), 72

Clarke, Samuel, 55, 59, 64n.26

Class distinctions, 78, 83n.37

Collins, Anthony, 57, 58, 59, 64n.26

Common Sense (Scottish) Philosophy, 150–51, 158n.28, 173n.19, 176

Communion, 24, 30, 73; open, xiii, 69, 72, 74, 79–80

Communion controversy, 19–21, 24–25, 52, 79, 92

—Edwards's position in, xii, 19–21, 22, 24, 27–28, 32–33; bearing on view of religious experience, xv, 36n.5, 132–33

Communion of saints. *See* Church(es); Saints

Complacence, moral goodness as, 104, 119n.30

Concerts of prayer, 28, 29–30, 142, 186

Conforti, Joseph, xvi-xvii, 193–207

Congregationalism, xvi, 77–79, 83n.37, 153n.4, 175–76, 182, 195; Calvinism, 116, 143; on covenants, 30, 37n.70; New Divinity theology, 176, 177, 188n. 7

Connecticut, 71, 77, 142–43, 153n.4

Connecticut Valley, 70–71, 75, 77, 78, 80. *See also* New England; Northampton

Connecticut Valley revival (1734–35), xi, 3, 7, 30, 78; Edwards's attitude toward effects, 14–15, 22–23, 91–92

Conscience, 21, 86–87, 92–93, 114

Consent: to covenant of grace, 24; place in aesthetics, 105–6, 108–10

Constitutionalism, 198, 202

Conversion (Regeneration), 26–27, 86–93, 161, 191n.55; Edwards on, 9, 12, 14, 17n.28, 89–96, 97n.4; in 19th-century theology, 165, 168, 176–80, 199

Conversion to Islam, 41, 46, 51n.50

Conversion narratives, 12, 26–27, 78, 83n.37, 123–26, 133, 136n.7

Conversions, 76, 168–69, 180, 183, 186; of Indians, Stoddard on, 75–76, 78, 83n.29; during revivals, 8, 22–23

Converting ordinances, 69, 72, 74, 76, 79–80, 82n.24

I Corinthians 13, sermons on, xiv, 3, 85–86, 89–91, 93–94, 97n.14

II Corinthians 13:5, sermons on, 13, 17n.33

Corporate identity, language of, 20–21, 29, 33–34, 34n.6. *See also* National covenant

Covenant(s), xii, 28–33, 37n.70, 43, 141; of grace, 5–6, 21, 23–24, 30–32, 37nn.70–72; Half-Way Covenant of 1662, 80, 141, 145–46; owning the, 19, 22, 24–25, 28; in Puritan theology, 28, 36n.52, 176; of 1742, 23, 35n.21, 94, 98n.20; Stoddard on, xii, 24–26, 29, 30, 37n.70; Williams on, 24, 25–26, 27, 30–31, 33–34, 37n.72. *See also* National covenant

Covenant people. *See* God's (Covenant) People

Cowles, Henry, 160, 163, 164, 169

Cowles, John P., 160, 163

Creation, 45, 55, 201, 206n.31

Decalogue, 88, 90, 91

Deism, 39, 43–46, 49n.34, 50n.40, 51n. 49, 54, 115; Berkeley on, 102, 104, 115–16, 117; challenges to orthodox Christianity, xiii, 39, 53–56; Edwards on, xiii, xviii, 39, 50n.39, 53, 64n. 23, 115–16, 117; on sufficiency of reason, xii–xiii, 44–45; support for among men, 181, 190n.29

Delattre, Roland, x, xixn.5

Denny, Frederick, 51n.50

Dependence, divine, 151, 181

Depravity, doctrine of, xvi, 147–48, 160, 177, 181, 187, 190n.26; applied to infants, 182–83, 190n.32; Oberliners' denial of, 164–65

Depression (Melancholy), among Connecticut Valley people, 77, 79

Desire, language of, xv, 126–27, 130

Devil, the, 14, 42, 77

Dickinson, Jonathan, 51n.49

Discourse, 19–28, 34

Dissenters (Nonconformists), 54, 59, 60, 191n.46. *See also* Separatists

Distinguishing Marks (Edwards), 11–12, 13, 17nn.28,35, 125, 127
Divine efficiency, 148, 201–2
Divine operations, true religious affections arising from, 128–29, 131
Divine right bishops, English, 72–73
Divorce, in Islam, 41, 46
Domestic order/sphere, 4–5, 7–8, 16n.19, 180; marriage metaphors in context of, xii, 4–5, 7–8, 15; 19th-century, 175, 180, 182–83, 187
Duties/duty, 128, 166, 181–82, 189n.9; women's, 16n.19, 180, 182–83, 187
Dutton, Samuel W. S., 153n.4
Dwight, Sereno, 17n.38, 59, 64n.24, 99n.35
Dwight, Timothy, 96, 104, 146, 176, 181–82, 188n.2; on conversion and election, 178–79; differences with Edwards, 140, 143; influence on Taylor and Beecher, 145, 189n.16; *Travels in New England and New York,* 84n.45, 145

Ecclesiastes 5:4–6, sermon on, 23, 35n. 23
Ecumenism, xiii, 189n.12
Edwards, Jonathan
—critical studies of, ix–xviii, xixnn.3–6,9, 17n.27, 203
—influences on, 100; Shepard, 85–87, 89, 91, 93, 97n.4, 98n.22; Stoddard, xiii, 69, 78–80, 84n.42, 98n.23
—in Northampton (1729–50), 4, 5–11, 21–23, 29, 78–79, 85, 132–33; dismissal from pulpit, xii, 19–20, 52, 78, 132. *See also* Communion controversy
—at Stockbridge (1751–57), 28, 32–34, 47n. 7, 52, 118n.6; 1757 letter to trustees of the College of New Jersey, xiii, 52, 53, 59
—*published works,* xixnn.5,7,15, 59, 64n.24; bibliography, ix, xixn.3; *Concerning the End...,* 104; "Divine and Supernatural Light," 17n.29; *Farewell Sermon,* 19; *Humble Attempt...,* 29; *Life of Brainerd,* 142, 185; "Mahometanism," 39–41; "The Mind," 62, 65n.37; *Misrepresentations Corrected,* 29; *Original Sin,* 116, 206n.31; *Some Thoughts Concerning the Revival,* 11–12, 125–26. *See also individual works by title*
—*unpublished works. See* Manuscripts, unpublished; Miscellanies; Notebooks; Sermon series
Edwards, Jonathan, Jr., 143, 145, 146, 195, 200
Edwardsianism, xv–xvii, 139–45, 147, 155n.15, 170, 188n.2; compromise with Old Calvinism, 143, 144, 188n.2; divisions among, 148–51, 157n.24; effect on women during Second Great Awakening, 175–81, 184, 187; in Oberlin perfectionism, 159–60, 162–66, 170; Park's interpretation of, xvi–xvii, 193–94, 196–200; Taylor's place in, 139–40, 145–51. *See also* New Divinity
Election, 77, 93, 177–78, 181, 189n.9, 197
Eliot, John, 78, 83n.29
Elsbree, Oliver Wendell, 154n.7
Emmons, Nathanael, xvii, 38n.84, 141, 143–44, 153n.4, 195–98, 200–202; covenant defined by, 32; occasionalism of followers, 158n.27; sin debate position, 148, 197
Emotions, gender ideology on, 179, 184, 190n.25, 191nn.48,49
Empowerment of women, 175, 187
England. *See* Great Britain
Enlightenment, the, xiii, xiv, 55, 102, 104, 160, 176; Edwards's planned response to, xvii–xviii; Scottish Philosophy's emergence, 158n.28. *See also* Deism; Free thought
Enthusiasm, religious, 12, 26, 57
Episcopal parish, in Oberlin, 169–70
Epistemology, 20, 25, 135
Epstein, Barbara, 190n.30
Eschatology, xii–xiii, 8, 42–43
Ethics, 36n.63, 97n.14, 105–6, 116. *See also* Morality
Evangelicalism, xviii, 29, 70, 79–80, 123, 188n.7
Evangelism, 101–2
Exegesis and hermeneutics, xiii, 52–57, 61; in "Harmony of the Old and New Testament," 54, 57–65
Exercise/taste controversy, xvii, 196–201, 204
"Exercisers," 148, 150, 193–94, 196–201, 205n.19
Exodus 33:19, sermon on, 38n.87
Experiential religion, 11, 94–95, 122
Ezekiel 44:9, sermon on, 22, 25, 30, 36n. 38, 37n.71

Fairchild, James Harris, 159–60, 162, 164–68, 170
Faith, 4, 32, 62, 97n.4, 117n.4; justification by, 4, 116; light about given to Muslims, 39–40, 45; nature explored in Matthew 25:1–12 sermons, 4, 8–10. *See also* Profession of faith; Trials of faith
Faithful Narrative (Edwards), 23, 125–26, 128, 136n.7
Fast days, 29, 142
Fear, among Connecticut Valley people, 70–71, 75, 79, 80
Female seminaries, 181, 190n.31
Feminization of religion, 19th-century, xvi, 176, 184–85, 191n.46
Fiering, Norman, 36n.63, 101
Finney, Charles Grandison, xvi, xvii, 163, 176, 178–79, 181, 189n.9; role in Oberlin Theology, 159–60, 163–70
Fisher, George Park, 147, 205 n.10
Fitch, Eleazar, 146, 148, 150, 155n.14
Foster, Frank H., 203, 206n.39
Foxe, John, 73, 74
Free thought, 41, 54–55, 104; criticisms of, 53, 102, 117, 118n.26. *See also* Deism; Moral sense theory
Free will, 163–64, 177, 180; Edwardsian idea of, 117n.4, 197–99, 201

Freedom of the Will (Edwards), 147, 148, 193, 196–200, 202–4; on natural ability/moral inability dichotomy, 160, 161–62, 164, 165
Frei, Hans, 54, 62
French, Stanley Goodwin, Jr., 158n.28
French, the, 70–71, 75–76, 78, 102
French and Indian Wars, 70–71, 75, 77
Frothingham, Ebenezer, 20, 25–26, 34n.5

Gaustad, Edwin S., xiv, 100–103, 116, 119n.33
Gender ideology, 19th-century, 175–76, 179, 180, 184, 186–87
God, xii–xiii, 40, 45, 55–56, 201–2; for Berkeley, 107, 112, 115–16; for Edwards, 19, 90, 91, 104, 107, 115–16, 129; fear of, 131; moral government, 32, 112, 121n.50, 139; in moral sense theory, 114–15; transcendence, 161, 163–64; will of, 86–91, 93, 116, 184. *See also* Love for God; Sovereignty
Godliness, 9, 25–27, 61, 73, 85–86, 92–93, 98n.27
—true, xiv, 21, 91–96, 98nn.21,22, 99n. 36; distinguished from counterfeit, 85, 89–91, 93–94; for Shepard, 87–89, 93, 97n.10
God's (Covenant) People (God's New Israel), xii, 20–25, 28–34, 35n.21
Goodrich, Chauncey A., 146, 148, 150, 155n.14, 157n.20
Grace, 14, 62, 91–92, 94–95, 151, 153n. 4, 167; common, 27, 114; covenant of, 5–6, 21, 23–24, 30–32, 37nn.70–72; means of, 35n.13, 177–78; sacraments as a means for receiving, 73–74, 86; saving, 17n.28, 25, 27, 90, 93, 115, 178; for Shepard, 87–88, 97n.10, 133; signs of, xii, 4, 8–15, 17n.28
Grasso, Christopher, xii, 19–38
Great Awakening (1720–1750), 5, 11–13, 30, 52, 78, 85–86, 194. *See also* Connecticut Valley revival; Second Great Awakening
Great Britain, 22, 29, 70–72, 102; religious struggles, 71–77, 81n.4, 83n.35, 191n.46
Griffin, Edward Dorr, 143–44
Guelzo, Allen C., xvi, 141, 144, 156n. 18, 159–74
Guyse, John, 136n.7

Half-Way Covenant of 1662, 80, 141, 145–46, 176
Hall, Richard A. S., xiv, xviii, 100–121
Hall, Robert, 104
Harmony, in aesthetics, 106, 108
Haroutunian, Joseph, xv, 140, 152n.1, 189n.15, 196, 203–4
Hart, William, 104
Hedenius, Ingemar, 118n.26
Heimert, Alan, 29, 32, 37n.67
Hermeneutics. *See* Exegesis and hermeneutics
Hierarchical relations, in domestic order, 5, 7–8, 16n.10
A History of the Work of Redemption (Edwards), 3, 15n.4, 49n.33, 53, 63n. 4. *See also* Matthew 25:1–12
Holifield, E. Brooks, 81n.11
Holiness, 129, 136n.14, 165–66, 169–70, 199; indwelling, 86, 89–91. *See also* Saints
Holiness movement, xvi, 160, 170
Holy love. *See* True religion
Holy (Christian; Religious) practice, xi, 14, 89–91, 98n.20, 131–32, 161; identity as God's people made manifest by, 23, 35n.18; true religion visible in, 124–26, 181; as the 12th sign, 12, 14, 18n.39, 92–93, 131–32
Holy Spirit, 46, 50n.41, 115, 167; baptism of the, 168–69; role in true religious affections, 128–29, 131; at work in revivals, 11, 123–25
Hopkins, Samuel, 28–29, 143, 161–62, 181, 195, 199–200; differences with Edwards, 140; on disinterested benevolence, 185, 191n.55; on general atonement, 191n. 43; influence on Emmons, 202; *Life and Character of . . . Jonathan Edwards,* 63nn. 2,4; Park as disciple of, 193, 196, 198, 199–200
Hopkinsianism, 142–43, 145, 178, 189n. 11, 195, 199–200; at Andover, 144, 154n.9, 194; in Oberlin perfectionism, 159, 165, 173n.19
Human nature, 14, 45, 113, 115–16, 148; genuine changes in, 130, 131
An Humble Inquiry (Edwards), 19, 24, 26, 34n.2, 132–33
Humility, 127, 130–32, 184, 191n.47
Hutcheson, Francis, 105–7, 113, 115, 119n.33, 120n.39; concepts compared with Berkeley's and Edwards's, 105, 108–10, 112, 120nn.41,43; influence on Edwards, 36n.63, 116–17, 121n.67
Hypocrisy, 4, 8, 95–96, 127, 130; contrast with true godliness, xii, 8–11, 13–15, 85, 88–91, 93–94

Immaterialism, 116, 161
Imperialism, 70, 71, 74, 78, 80
Independents (Separatists), 20, 24–26, 71, 73, 77
Indians, American, 44–45, 47n.7, 70–71, 74–75, 118n.6; missionary efforts aimed at, 33, 78, 79, 83n.29, 102, 118n.6, 186; Stoddard on conversion of, 75–76, 78, 83n.29
Infidelity, theological, 182, 189n.12, 190n.29
"Instituted church," xiii, 69, 72, 74–75, 76–77, 81n.4
Intention, 90–92
Intuition, 90, 122, 134
Intuitionism, 110–12
Islam, 40–46, 48nn.16,18, 50n.35, 51n. 50; Edwards's judgments on, xii–xiii, 39–41, 42–47, 47n.3

Jacksonian Democracy, 159–60, 170, 176–77, 190n.26
James, William, xiv–xv, 122–25, 133–35
Jeremiah 51:5, sermon on, 38n.87
Jessop, T. E., 103–4, 118n.26, 119n.33
Jesus Christ. *See* Christ
Jews, 30–31, 37n.71, 44
John 10:37, sermon on, 63n.13

I John 4:1, discourse on, 17n.35
Johnson, Curtis D., 188n.6, 190n.29
Joshua 7:12, sermon on, 30, 32, 38nn.74,86
Joshua 24:15–27, sermon on, 35n.21
Joshua 24:21–22, lecture on, 23, 35nn.24,25
Joy, 124–25, 126
Justice, 104, 106, 109–10
Justification, 4, 88, 97n.10, 116

Kant, Immanuel, 113, 120n.43, 121n.50
Kimnach, Wilson H., x, xixn.5
King Philip's War (1675–76), 70, 71
I Kings 8:44–45, sermon on, 38n.87
Knox, John, xiii, 70, 71, 74, 76

Lamont, William, 72–73
Language, 186; of Christian community, 20, 21–28, 34; of corporate identity, 20–21, 29, 33–34, 34n.6; Edwardsian, xv, 29, 126–27, 130, 156n.17; linguistic analysis, 156n.17; Lockean, 27–28, 122; of public profession of faith, 19, 34n.2
Law: fundamental, 73; natural, 56, 111, 202; for Oberlin Theology, 166, 168–69, 173n.19
Lee, Sang Hyun, 150, 157n.25
Leviticus 26:3–13, sermon on, 30, 37n.74
Locke, John, 27–28, 55–56, 122, 160, 188n.6
Love, 26, 90, 106, 124–29, 135, 160; of self, 127, 130, 132. *See also* Affections, religious; Benevolence, disinterested; True religion
Love for God, 89–90, 91, 98n.22, 104, 119n.30, 130; distinguishing between self-love and, 127
Lucas, Paul R., xiii–xiv, 69–84
Luke 16:19, sermon on, 32
Luminousness, sense of, 133–34
Luther, Martin, 43, 54

McConnell, F. J., 118n.26
McCoy, Genevieve, xvi, 175–92
McDermott, Gerald R., xii–xiii, xixn.5, 29, 32, 39–51
Mahan, Asa, 160, 165–66, 168–69
Malebranche, Nicolas de, 101, 158n.27
Manton, Thomas, xviii, 4, 16n.6
Manuscripts (unpublished) by Edwards, xi–xiii, xvii, 52, 54, 63n.2, 141; "Blank (or Interleaved) Bible," 54, 64n.20; "Christ's Example," 65n.37; "Harmony of the Old and New Testament," xiii, 52–54, 55, 57–62, 63n.4; "Places of the Old Testament that Intimate a Future State," 64n.16. *See also* Miscellanies; Notebooks; Sermon series
Mark 10:17–27, sermons on, 15n.3
Market economy, 7, 169, 170, 176, 194
Marriage, 5, 6–7, 7, 46; as metaphor, xii, 4, 5, 7–8, 15
Massachusetts, 71, 77, 83n.30, 142–43. *See also* Connecticut Valley; Northampton
Mastricht, Peter van, 86
Maternal associations, xvi, 177, 182, 189n.21, 190n.32
Mather, Increase, 72, 77, 82n.24, 83n. 34
Mather, Moses, 37n.71, 47n.71
Matthew 7:15, sermons on, 13–14, 17n.38
Matthew 13:3–8, sermons on, 15n.3
Matthew 13:47–50, sermons on, 15n.3
Matthew 15:26, sermons on, 12–13
Matthew 25:1–12, sermons on, xi–xii, 3–5, 15n.2, 85, 89, 91–93; arguments in compared with *Religious Affections,* 11–13; pastoral purpose, 6–11, 15; published as *The History of the Work of Redemption,* 3, 15n.4, 63n.4; Shepard's influence, xiv, 97n.4; speculative purpose, 11–12, 13–15
Matthew 25:1–12, treatment by others, 4, 16n.6; Shepard's *Parable,* xiv, 4, 15, 16n.5, 87–89, 95, 96, 97n.4
Mead, Sidney, 144–45, 152n.1
Meaning: for Locke, 28; in religious discourse, 20, 21–22, 24
Melancholy (Depression), among Connecticut Valley people, 77, 79
Messiah. *See* Christ
Messiah (Handel), 58
Metaphor, marriage as, xii, 4, 5, 7–8, 15
Metaphysics, xiv, 101, 104–5, 112, 150–51, 157n.25
Methodism, xvi, 80, 147, 160–61, 167–69, 170; Arminianism, 188n.6, 189n.12
Mill, John Stuart, 103, 118n.26
Millennialism, ix, 29, 43, 77, 143; in English nationalism, 73, 74
Miller, Perry, xviii, 17nn.27,29, 20, 69, 72, 83n.28; on covenant theology, 36n.52; on Edwards as Lockean, 122; on knowledge of Berkeley, 101; on *True Virtue,* 105
Miller, Samuel, 142
Mills, Samuel J., 185, 192n.58
Mind, philosophy of, 62, 122, 124, 134
Ministerial associations, 141–42, 146, 153n.4
Minkema, Kenneth P., x, xiii, xixn.5, 52–65
Miracles, 41, 56, 63n.13, 64n.23
Miscellanies (Edwards), xii–xiii, 18n. 39, 52, 63n.2, 97n.4; "Prophecies of the Messiah," 58; "Reason and Revelation," 64n.15; "Sense of the Heart," 17n.29; "Signs of Godliness," 17n.30; "Types of the Messiah," 59–61, 64n.24. *See also* Manuscripts, unpublished; Notebooks
Missionary service, 76, 83n.29, 183–87, 191n.44, 192n.64; among American Indians, 33, 78, 79, 83n.29, 102, 118n.6, 186; training for, 101–2, 162; women's role in, 181–82, 185–87
Missionary societies, xvi, 142–43, 177
Moral ability, 163, 190n.26; distinction between natural ability and, 147, 148–51, 155n.15, 156n.18, 202–3. *See also* Moral inability
Moral accountability. *See* Accountability, moral
Moral action, 9, 12, 113, 148, 165
Moral agency, 148–49, 163, 178–79

Moral appraisal, 110–12, 115, 123, 126–32, 135. *See also* Self-examination
Moral beauty, 105, 106–7, 109–14, 121n. 49, 129, 161
Moral inability, 178, 181, 197. *See also* Moral ability; Natural ability/moral inability dichotomy
Moral law, 9, 12, 88, 97n.4, 168; and covenant terminology, 24, 28–29, 31, 32
Moral necessity, 196–97. *See also* Moral ability; Moral inability
Moral order, 110, 112, 121nn.50,51, 189n.16; under God's governance, 32, 112, 121n.49, 139
Moral perfection. *See* Perfectionism
Moral reform, xiii, 73–74, 76–77
Moral sense theory, xiv, 100, 105–17, 119n.33
Moralism, 12, 181
Morality, 27, 50n.38, 86, 104–5, 119n. 30; as component of religious experience, 123–25, 133–35; decline in, 75, 102; gendered definitions of, 184, 191n.48; women as guardians of, 176, 180, 182–83. *See also* Accountability; Ethics; Virtue
Morgan, Edmund S., 36n.59, 99n.36
Morgan, John, 160, 163, 165
Morse, Jedidiah, 143
Mother's Magazine, 187, 189n.21, 190n. 32, 191 n.47
Motive, 90–91, 105, 112–14, 162
Music, 111, 120n.39
Muslims. *See* Islam

National (Public) covenant, xii, xiii, 20–22, 28–34, 37n.70, 73–74, 76
Nationalism, Christian, 70, 71
Nationalism, English, 73, 78
Natural ability, 197; distinction between moral ability and, 147, 148–49, 155n. 15, 156n.18, 202–3
Natural ability/moral inability dichotomy, xvii, 161–62, 196–98; Oberlin perfectionism predicated on, xvi, 160, 163–66, 167–68, 170. *See also* Moral inability
Natural inability, 196
Natural necessity, 196–97. *See also* Natural ability
Natural religion, 44–45, 55–56, 61
Nature, laws of, 56, 111, 202
The Nature of True Virtue (Edwards), xiv, xvii, 100, 101, 104–21, 197
Neill, Stephen, 115
Neoplatonism, 47, 109, 150
New Divinity, xvi, 20, 139, 140–45, 177, 189n.11, 204n.1; blend with Old Calvinism, 179, 188n.2, 194; effect on evangelical Protestant women, 175–80, 182; on general atonement doctrine, 191n.43; influence on Oberlin perfectionism, 160, 162–64, 166, 168, 170; on moral and natural ability, 147, 156n.18, 162; national covenant as concern, 28–29, 33; New England theology used to designate, 194–95; and Park's work on exercise doctrines, 200–201, 206n.28. *See also* Edwardsianism
New England, 69; corporate identity, 20–22, 28–34, 34n.6; Edwardsian enculturation of, xv–xvi, 140–44; Oberlin area settlers from, 162. *See also* Connecticut Valley; Northampton
New England theology, 140–44, 148–49, 160, 170, 176, 196–204, 206n.39; history of the term, 104n.2, 193–96
New English Israel. *See* God's (Covenant) People; National covenant
New Haven Theology, 139–44, 146–49, 152n. 1, 157n.20, 167, 196
New Israel: England seen as, 73. *See also* God's (Covenant) People
New Lights, 5, 11–12, 15, 29, 46, 96. *See also* Great Awakening; Revivalism
New Testament, 59–61, 63n.2. *See also* Bible, the; *individual books by title*
Newton, Isaac, 52, 55–56, 101
Noesis. *See* Mind, philosophy of
Noll, Mark A., 34n.6, 195
Nonconformists (Dissenters), 54, 59, 60, 91n.46. *See also* Separatists
Northampton community (Massachusetts), xii–xiii, 15, 20, 23, 35n.18, 78; late 18th-century conditions, 4, 5–11, 70–71; 1734–35 revival, xi, 7, 22–23, 30, 91–92. *See also* Communion controversy; Edwards, Jonathan: in Northampton
Notebooks, of Edwards, xii–xiii, xvii–xviii, 32, 52, 63nn.2,13, 150; "Controversies," 64n.15; "Images of Divine Things," 60–61; judgments on Islam, xii–xiii, 39–41, 42–47, 47n.3; "Notes on the Scripture," 48n.11, 54, 63n.13; "On the Christian Religion," 63n.13; "Signs of Godliness," 17n.31, 98n.21; "Subjects of Inquiry," 63n.2. *See also* "Catalog"; Miscellanies
Nurture, Christian, 182–83
Nuttall, Geoffrey R., 191n.46

Obedience, 90, 91, 168, 184–85; Shepard on, 88–89, 93, 97n.10; universal, 89, 91–93, 98nn.22,23
Oberlin College (Oberlin Collegiate Institute), 162–63; Oberlin Theology, xvi, 159–60, 163–71
Obligation, 23, 173n.19, 178, 189n.9
Obookiah, 185, 192n.57
Occasionalism, 150, 157n.25, 158n.27, 198, 201, 202
Old Calvinism, 140–47, 149, 154n.7, 194, 288 n.2; attribution to Taylor, 140, 151, 178; blend of positions with New Divinity, 179, 188n.2, 194
Old Lights, 12
Old School Presbyterians, 139, 195

Old Testament, 30, 59–61, 63n.2. *See also* Bible, the; Pentateuch
Order, in aesthetics, 106, 108
Original sin, doctrine of, xvi, 147–51, 156n.19, 157n.20, 164; gender differences in interpretation, 180–83, 190n.30

Paley, William, 50n.35, 104, 117
Papacy. *See* Catholicism
Parable of the Ten Virgins Unfolded (Shepard), xiv, 4, 15, 16n.5, 87–89, 95–96, 97n.4
Parables, sermons on, 15n.3. *See also* Matthew 25:1–12
Park, Edwards Amasa, 140–41, 196, 204, 204n.1, 205n.10, 206n.39; at Andover, 144, 193, 203; Edwardsianism, xvi–xvii, 193–94; *Memoir of Emmons,* 200, 201–2. *See also Bibliotheca Sacra*
Patriarchalism, 176, 180
Pearson, Eliphalet, 144
Pelagianism, 160, 203
Pentateuch, 56, 63n.13, 64n.16
Perception: in faith, 160–61; religious experience described in terms of, 122–25, 128–30, 133–34, 135
Perfectionism, xvi, 159–61, 164–70
Perseverance, 11, 18n.39
Philosophy, xi, xiii–xv, 45, 103, 104, 105; ancient, Edwards on, 40, 44, 50n. 41; modern, assumptions of in James's approach, xiv–xv, 123–24, 135. *See also* Metaphysics
Piety, xvi, 8, 16n.19, 118n.26, 133, 135n.6; conflation with moralism, 181; consumerization and privatization of, 169–70; decline in, 7–8, 102; defined in *Religious Affections,* 104; paradox of experiential, in Puritanism, 94–95; importance of in missionaries, 186
Piety versus Moralism (Haroutunian), 152n.1, 196, 203–4
Plato and Platonism, 40, 44, 46, 50n.41, 101, 104
Polemics, 53, 95–96, 105, 123
Politics, 74, 76–77, 176–77, 188n.6
Pond, Enoch, 143, 195, 199–200, 202, 204nn.2,6
Porter, Noah, 147, 149
Porterfield, Amanda, xii, 4, 5–6, 15, 16n.12
Power, 21–22, 73–74, 76
Practice. *See* Holy practice
Predestination. *See* Election
Presbyterianism, xvi, 73, 175–76; English, 71, 73–74, 77; 19th-century, 80, 142, 177, 182, 188n.7; Scottish, 74, 82n.24; of Stoddard, xiii, 76, 77, 79
Princetonians, 105, 139, 142, 202–3
Profession of faith, 9, 19–28, 35n.14, 92, 132–33, 146
Prophecies, biblical, xiii, 53–55, 58–62, 63n.2, 64n.26. *See also* Exegesis
Proportion, in aesthetics, 105–11, 120n. 43
Protestantism, 29, 33, 39, 54, 69, 102. *See also* Reformed Christianity; *individual denominations by name*
Proudfoot, Wayne, xiv–xv, 122–36
Prynne, William, xiii, 70, 71–74, 76–77, 80, 83n.34
Psalms 111:5: sermon on, 23, 35n.25
Psychology, xiv–xv, 97n.4, 104, 117n.4, 123–24, 150–51
Public covenant. *See* National covenant
Public worship, 21, 26, 29, 30
Puritanism, xii, xiv, 15, 20, 69, 72–73, 85; covenant preaching, 29; historical approach to Scripture, 57; introspection, 135n.6; paradox of experiential piety, 94–95; signs of genuine religion for, 128
Purpose, 105, 107, 110, 112, 120n.39

Qur'an, 39–40, 43–44, 46, 48n.18

Rabbis, way of the, 60, 65n.30
Rationalism, 54, 123, 150, 158n.28
Reason, 44, 54–56, 124, 180; in aesthetic and moral evaluation, 105, 110–12, 115–16; sufficiency of, xii–xiii, 44–47
Redemption, 43, 62, 86, 93, 115
Reformed Christianity, 39, 46, 60, 86–87, 93, 135n.6. *See also* Protestantism
Regeneration. *See* Conversion
Religion, true. *See* True religion
Religious Affections (Edwards). *See Treatise concerning Religious Affections*
Religious declension, 4–5, 7–8, 140
Religious experience, xv, 11, 26, 85–86, 122; James on, xiv–xv, 122–25, 133–35; public examination of, 78, 83n.37. *See also* Affections, religious; Experiential religion; *Treatise concerning Religious Affections*
Repentance, 114, 146, 164, 178, 183
Responsibility, moral: of 19th-century women, 177–78, 180, 182–83, 187. *See also* Accountability, moral
Revelation, 44, 50n.40, 54–57, 62, 180; Edwards's defense of, xii–xiii, 41, 44–45, 50n.41, 52, 56
Revisionism, xv–xvii, 58–59, 62
Revivalism, 5, 11–12, 15n.4, 123, 125–26. *See also* Affections, religious
—18th-century, 13–14, 28, 29, 30. *See also* Connecticut Valley revival; Great Awakening; New Lights; Second Great Awakening
—19th-century, xvi, 69, 80, 146, 155n.14, 176; effect on women, 175, 181; New Divinity role in, 141–42. *See also* Second Great Awakening
Reward and punishment, as motive for virtue, 113–14
Rhetorical strategies, 20, 32–33
Robertson, William, 50n.35
Rotundo, E. Anthony, 191n.49

Rutherford, Samuel, xiii, 70–72, 74, 76, 82n.24
Ryan, Mary P., 190n.32

Sacraments, 71, 73–74, 76. *See also* Baptism; Communion
Saints, 5, 17n.38, 35n.10, 128–31, 184, 191n.47
—James's picture of, 133–35
—true, 11–13, 61, 133; contrast with hypocrites, xii, 4, 8–11, 13–15, 88–89, 93
—visible, 20, 22, 25–27, 28; churches of, xiii, 73, 79
—*See also* Holiness
Sale, George, 48n.18
Salvation, 44, 177–78, 180–81, 183–84, 189n.9, 191n.45; mothers' responsibility for, of children, 180, 182–83, 187; of non-Christians, 43, 49n.33
Sanctification, xiv, 86–87, 89, 93–96, 97n.4, 179; entire, 160, 167, 168
Saving grace. *See* Grace, saving
Saybrook Platform, 78
Schafer, Thomas A., x, xixn.5, 17n.29, 47n.7, 117n.5
Scientific method, 55–56, 125
Scotland, 77, 83n.35
Scottish (Common Sense) philosophy, 150–51, 158n.28, 173n.19, 176
Scottish Presbyterianism, 74, 82n.24
Scripture. *See* Bible, the
Scrupulosity argument, 75, 77, 79–80
Second Great Awakening (1795–1835), xvi, 141, 142–43, 146, 172–92. *See also* Revivalism, 19th-century
Selby-Bigge, L. A., 119n.33
Self-deception, 12, 96, 123, 130, 135
Self-examination, 13–14, 95, 123, 130–32, 135; Charity sermons on uses of, 89–91; moral appraisal, 127
Selfishness, 104, 127, 132
Self-knowledge, in moral appraisal, 130, 135
Self-love, 127, 130, 132
Self-sacrifice, 184–87
Seminaries, 101–2, 205n.20. *See also* Andover; Bangor; Yale
Sensationalism, language of, 160–61
Separatists (Independents), 20, 24–26, 71, 73, 77
Sermon series (by Edwards)
—*published.* See *Charity and Its Fruits; A History of the Work of Redemption*
—*unpublished,* xi, xii, xvii, 12–14, 17n.33, 22; place of national covenant in, 28–29, 30, 32–34; during the 1740s, 13–14, 15n.3, 17n.38, 32
Sermon series, use by Puritan theologians, 4
Seven Years' War (1756–63), xii, 20, 32–34. *See also* French and Indian Wars
Shaftesbury, Anthony Ashley Cooper, 3rd earl of, 101, 105, 112–13, 115–16, 119n.33, 121n.57
Shepard, Thomas, xviii, 4, 15, 87–89, 95, 97n.4; influence on Edwards, 85–87, 89, 91, 93, 97n.4, 98n.22; *Parable of the Ten Virgins Unfolded,* xiv, 16n.5, 87–89, 95, 96, 97n.4
Sherlock, Thomas, xviii, 59, 64n.23
Sign(s), 21, 26, 31, 34n.2, 136n.10; Edwards's attempt to control meaning of, 19–20, 34; Edwards's theory of, xv, 28; of godliness, 98n.22, 127–32, 136n.12; of grace, xii, 4, 8–15, 17n. 28. *See also* Twelfth sign
Simon, Richard, 57, 59
Sin, 9, 47n.3, 114, 181, 190n.30; New England theology on, 148, 200; Oberlin Theology on, 164, 165–66; place in exercise/taste debate, 193, 197–99, 201. *See also* Original sin
Skelton, Philip, 50n.46, 64n.23
Smalley, John, 38n.84, 143
Smith, Henry Boynton, 200, 202
Social conditions, in early 18th-century New England, 4, 5–11, 75
Socrates, 46, 50n.41, 104, 113
Soul, 62, 86–90, 134
Sovereignty, divine, 163–64, 177, 183, 193, 196–98, 201–2
Spiritual awakening, 74, 77, 81n.4, 87–88. *See also* Revivalism
Spiritual principle, 10, 14, 17n.29, 62, 88–89, 93–94
Spirituality, xii, 76, 128–29, 131
Spring, Samuel, 143, 148
Stackhouse, Thomas, 50n.35
Stapfer, Johann Friedrich, 40, 47n.8, 48 n.9
Stein, Stephen J., 52, 62
Stiles, Ezra, 50n.38, 139
Stoddard, Solomon, xii, 69–70, 71–80, 81n.4, 84n.45, 178; *An Appeal to the Learned,* 37n.70; on covenants, 30, 37n.72; *Doctrine of Instituted Churches,* 71, 74, 77, 83n.34; influence on Edwards, xiii, 78–80, 84n. 42, 98n.23; on visible and real sainthood, 25–26
Stoddardean churches, 29, 99n.36
Stoddardeanism, 24–26, 78–79, 84n.42; Edwards's break from, 22, 24, 25, 132–33; Williams as representative of, 20, 25–26, 34
Stoever, William K. B., xiv, xviii, 85–99
Stout, Harry S., 28, 32, 36n.58
Stuart, Moses, 144, 146
Sweeney, Douglas, xv–xvi, 139–58
Syllogisms, practical: Shepard's use of, 87, 89, 90

Tappan, Arthur, 162–63, 167
Tappan, Lewis, 162–63
Taste of honey, analogy of, 122, 124, 128–29
"Tasters," 148, 150, 197–98. *See also* Exercise/taste controversy
Taylor, Nathaniel William, 139–41, 144–52, 178–79, 188n.2, 195–96, 199, 206n. 39; conflation of piety and moralism, 181; Dwight's influence on, 189n.16; and Edwardsianism, xv–xvi, xvii, 139–40, 145–50, 176
Taylorites, 146, 148–51, 157n.24, 158n. 28

Teleology, 105, 107, 110, 112, 120n.39
Theological Miscellanies. *See* Miscellanies
Theology, xii, 3–4, 86, 105, 114–15, 141; Edwardsian culture of, xi, xv-xvi, 139–44, 141. *See also individual issues and schools*
Thomas Aquinas, 41
Thome, James Armstrong, 160, 168
Tillotson, John, xviii, 16n.6
Tindal, Matthew, 44, 56, 59, 64n.15
Toland, John, 44, 56
Tracy, Patricia, 7, 8
Transcendence, 112, 121n.49, 161, 163–64
Treatise concerning Religious Affections (Edwards), xvii, 85, 91–96, 104, 124–27, 133; analysis of religious experience compared with James's, xiv–xv, 122–25, 133–35; on assurance, 12, 93, 98n.2; common features with sermon series on Matthew 25:1–12, xii, 4–5, 11–13, 15; on distinguishing marks of a true saint, 11, 17n.28; intended audience, 96, 99n.35; on moral goodness, 104, 119n.30; Sereno Dwight on, 17n.38, 99n.35; Shepard's influence on, xiv, 16n.5, 87, 97n.4; on signs of true godliness, 89, 98nn.21,22, 127–32, 161; textual similarities with sermons on Matthew 7:15, 17n.38; use of "taste" and "exercise" language, 197
Trials of faith, 125, 127; behavior during, 10–11, 13–14, 131–32
True religion (Holy love), 181
—Edwards's treatment of, xii, xv, xvii, 45, 104, 127; in sermons on Matthew 25:1–12, 4, 8–10
True Virtue (Edwards). See *The Nature of True Virtue*
Turner, James, 49n.34
Turretin, Francis, 87
Twelfth sign, 12, 14, 17n.30, 18n.39, 91–93, 131–32, 161; Shepard's influence on, 98n.22. *See also* Grace, signs of
Tyler, Bennet, 142, 148, 156n.19, 163, 178, 179
Tylerites, 139, 157n.24
Typology, 54, 64n.26; in Edwardsean exegesis, xiii, 53, 59–61, 117n.4

Understanding, xv; role in religious affection, 126–27, 130
Uniformity, in aesthetics, 108, 116, 120nn.41,43
Unitarianism, 147, 154n.7, 156n.19, 181
Universalism, 181, 190n.25, 190n.29
Unworthiness, sense of, xvi, 75, 77, 80, 150
Urmson, J. O., 103, 119n.33, 120n.39
Utilitarianism, 134–35
Utility, in aesthetics, 105–12, 116–17, 120nn.39,43

Valeri, Mark, 28–29, 32, 36nn.59,63
Value(s), 104–6, 110–12, 134
Varieties of Religious Experience (James), xiv–xv, 122–25, 133–35
Virtue, 101, 105, 112–14, 123–25, 129–32
—in exercise/taste debate, 193, 198–99
true, 104, 114, 127, 129–32, 136n.14; and canon of idealized female qualities, 184–85, 191n.46; as disinterested benevolence, 109–10, 198–99; relationship to true beauty, 101, 109, 112
Visibility of Christianity, 160–61, 169
Visible church, 94, 96
Visible saints. *See* Saints, visible

War(s): in the Connecticut Valley, 70–71, 75, 77; English Civil War, 72; role in interest in Islam, 41; Seven Years' War, xii, 20, 32–34
Warburton, William, xviii, 64n.16
Ware, Henry, 147, 156n.19
Warnock, G. J., 103
Watts, Isaac, 136n.7
Wesley, John, 48n.18, 160–61, 167–69, 170
Whiston, William, 58
Whitefield, George, 5, 51n.49
Whitman, Narcissa, 184
Will, the, xv, 109, 134, 178, 180, 183; "exercise/taste" controversy over, xvii, 193, 196–201; Oberlin perfectionism applied to, 166–67, 170; transformed by conversion, 86, 87–89. *See also* Free will
Will of God, 86–91, 93, 116, 184
Williams, Solomon, 20, 34n.5, 79, 84 n.42; on covenants, 24–27, 30–31, 33–34, 37n.72
Wilson, John F., 15n.4, 52
Women, evangelical Protestant: during Second Great Awakening, xvi, 175–92
Woods, Leonard, 144, 147, 156n.19, 204n. 2
Woolston, Thomas, 58, 59
Worcester, Samuel, 142, 143
Worship, public, 21, 26, 29, 30

Yale Divinity School, 141, 145, 146–47, 155n.14, 205n.20; Taylor at, xv, 139, 146, 195–96